THE LANGUAGE OF
RENAISSANCE POETRY

THE LANGUAGE LIBRARY

EDITED BY ERIC PARTRIDGE AND SIMEON POTTER

ALREADY PUBLISHED

A. C. PARTRIDGE

THE LANGUAGE OF RENAISSANCE POETRY

Spenser, Shakespeare
Donne, Milton

ANDRE DEUTSCH

FIRST PUBLISHED 1971 BY
ANDRE DEUTSCH LIMITED
105 GREAT RUSSELL STREET
LONDON WC1

COPYRIGHT © 1971 BY A. C. PARTRIDGE
ALL RIGHTS RESERVED

PRINTED IN GREAT BRITAIN BY
TONBRIDGE PRINTERS LTD
TONBRIDGE KENT

ISBN 0 233 96284 0

CONTENTS

1158471

CONTENTS

To the memory of
J. Dover Wilson, F. P. Wilson and Sir Walter Greg,
great exemplars of Shakespearian Scholarship

PREFACE

This study of one century of Renaissance Poetry (1575–1675) may be regarded as a sequel to my earlier volume in The Language Library on *Tudor to Augustan English*. Although it is concerned at every point with the exegesis and elucidation of texts, its purpose is primarily analytic, and that analysis is tripartite: rhetorical, literary and linguistic.

I am convinced that a healthy revival of the old terms used in the classical schools of rhetoric will lead to a fuller and deeper understanding of our four great Renaissance poets – Spenser, Shakespeare, Donne and Milton – who were themselves influenced immeasurably, directly or indirectly, by those same rhetorical schools. The principal aim of rhetoric was diversity of external effects; it was regarded as 'a delight in verbal patterning for its own sake'.

My endeavour has been to ascertain why the diction of poetry from Chaucer to Milton has a distinct character, and one unlikely to be revived. What seemed equally important was the light language analysis was able to throw on literary appreciation. It was to this end that T. S. Eliot constantly encouraged further investigation into the language of poetry, as it evolved in the sixteenth and seventeenth centuries. The pity is that he had not the leisure to undertake the task himself.

Acknowledgement is gratefully made to the following authors and their publishers for the use of quotations from the works consulted:

The late Professor Philip Wheelwright and the *Kenyon Review*, for some lines from the article 'On the Semantics of Poetry' in *Essays on the Language of Poetry*, Houghton Mifflin, 1967. Professor W. L. Renwick and Edward Arnold Ltd, for material from *Edmund Spenser*, 1925. Mr William E. Baker and the Regents of the University of

California Press, for a passage originally published (1967) in their book *Syntax in English Poetry 1870–1930*.

The late Professor H. Darbishire and the Clarendon Press for a citation from the 1952 edition of the *Poetical Works of John Milton*.

Mr F. E. Halliday and Gerald Duckworth Ltd. for material from *The Poetry of Shakespeare's Plays*, 1954.

Professor R. D. Emma and Mouton and Co, for lines from *Milton's Grammar*, 1964.

Mr F. E. Berry and Routledge, Kegan Paul Ltd, the Humanities Press Inc, New York, and the Oxford University Press, New York, for material from 'Prose Rhythm and Metre' in *Essays on Style and Language* (ed. R. Fowler, 1966) from *Poets' Grammar* (1958), and from *Poetry and the Physical Voice* (1962).

I am indebted to the Senate and Council of the University of the Witwatersrand for a Senior Research Fellowship which provided the means for this study. The University Librarian, Mr John Perry, and his staff were most helpful. My greatest debts are, however, to Professor Simeon Potter for his inestimable advice, and to my wife, who typed the manuscript, and helped with the index and correction of proofs.

University of the Witwatersrand,
Johannesburg.   A. C. PARTRIDGE
March 1970

I

INTRODUCTORY NOTES ON METHOD

The Jesuit's *Ratio Studiorum*, 1599 (translated by A. R. Ball, 1933) contains advice on three aspects of literary analysis (pp. 212–13), which resemble the French *explication de texte:*

(1) Explanation of a difficult speech or poem should begin with its meaning, after different interpretations have been studied.

(2) Workmanship follows, implying originality, arrangement and presentation. The technique to be examined includes ability to select, to improve topics by ornament, to convince through schemes of thought and word, to arouse feelings and to observe proprieties.

(3) Finally, comparison with the work of other writers. The examples produced should be alike in subject, treatment and expression; in the case of speeches, the analogous passage should use similar arguments.

An adaptation of this exposition will be used in studying the language of Spenser, Shakespeare, Donne and Milton, at different stages of development. Whatever classification is adopted, the elements of a poetic style will be found to interact and coalesce. There are senses in which Buffon's dictum 'style is the man himself' is a limitation. Characteristics come to be regarded as idiosyncrasies to the neglect of general principles, on the one hand, and subtleties and variations, on the other.

The meaningful aspects of poetic language seem to me the following (I give the linguistic terms in parenthesis):

1. *Word choice* (Lexis). This includes borrowings, coinages, poeticisms, colloquialisms, compounding, epithets both decorative and functional, and the relative use of different parts of speech.

2. *Movement* (Metrics). Prosodic patterns and their modulations by means such as enjambement and rhyme; rhythm and the distribution of stresses; accent and sound-texture (phonemics), including the sequence of vowels and consonants.

3. *Grammatical Structure* (Morphemics, Phrasis, Syntagmata and Transformational Grammar). Phrasal and clausal syntax, including word order, subordination and the use of connectives. The means of dislocation, fragmentation and elaboration.

4. *Meaning* (Semantics). Levels of understanding and their relation to context; the force of metaphor, simile, personification and metonymy; the use of symbols and iconography; the currency of poetic ideas.

5. *Rhetorical Devices* (Stylistics). Gnomic utterance, epigram, parallelism, repetition, climax, antithesis, contrast, hyperbole, oxymoron.

Each of the above heads calls for amplification, and for comment in relation to the English Renaissance.

(a) *Word Choice:* In the theory of Greek thinkers, language had its origin in the naming process, beginning with the objects of nature; Plato was not alone in holding that names were ideal. In the earliest poetry (and as late as the seventeenth century) words were not scientific in connotation; their meaning was less important than emotional suggestion. The associations that words in time acquire with states of feeling are sources of poetic ideas, abstract and concrete. The special significance names achieve through poetry depends on relations with other words, such as verbs and adjectives. Adjectives are among the most revealing elements of a poet's vocabulary, tell-tale pointers to his fertility, propriety and discipline. Verbs activate ideas, and provide the sinews of poetic utterances.

Every period, tradition and kind of poetry develops deviations from the norm of spoken language. The study of these by structural linguists has the disadvantage of focusing attention on the byways of diction. Deviations are less numerous than the orthodox uses of words, and should not be regarded as poetic licences. One form is the use of archaic, exotic and dialectal words and phrases, which linger in the poetry of subsequent ages. There may be several stratifications in a long Renaissance poem. Spenser, whose uses include technical terms and grammatical forms, is not an isolated example of layers of poeticism. Spitzer believes that deviations of this kind 'reveal a shift of the soul of an epoch, which the writer . . . would translate into a necessarily new linguistic form' (*Linguistics and Literary History*, Princeton, 1948, Chap. 3).

(b) *Movement*: This term incorporates a wide range of prosodic effects (sound, pause, tempo, rhythm and accent), not peculiar to poetry.

Feet or units of measurement are groups of syllables ordered to express meanings simultaneously with a controlled stream of sounds; one function of sound is to stimulate emotional response in the reader. Four basic feet in English poetry are the Iamb, Anapaest, Trochee and Dactyl. To these should be added the Spondee and Pyrrhic, two feet in which length is a determining factor in English. The six foot-types cover all emergencies of English scansion.

Metre, the external form of poetry, is a pattern of auditory effects. From the contrast of metre and rhythm the pulse of movement in verse arises. No two lines or stanzas of a poem are identical in rhythm; but it is the theme that properly determines the metre and its rhythmic variations. Robert Graves says: 'One of the most difficult problems is how to use natural speech rhythms as variations on a metrical norm.' (*The Crowning Privilege*, Cassell, 1955, Lecture 4).

Accent is the habitual emphasis given to a syllable of a word in pronunciation; stress or *ictus* is acquired specially in the verse, and may be logical or rhetorical. For this reason the stress of verse syllables cannot be validated until the reader knows the semantic associations. Metre becomes mechanical only if divorced from meaning. The correct distribution of stresses in a line often becomes debatable when two monosyllables of similar import occur in one foot.

Rhythm depends on variation in the incidence of stress, intonation on variation of pitch, the extent to which the voice is raised or lowered. Raising the pitch of the voice on a syllable invariably has the effect of stressing it also. Music, with its determined pitches and intervals, can hardly be compared with the changes of intonation practised by the speaker of prose or verse sentences. Nor can the syllables composing English feet be constant in time; the intervals a sensitive reader perceives are largely subjective.

For the phonetician, secondary stress is classed as indeterminate. A subdivision has been created in linguistics for tertiary stress, earning its status because it is followed by a syllable still weaker in emphasis than itself. The four-level system of stress has proved useful in the prosody of blank-verse drama, the first conscious use of it being attributed to Marlowe. He and Spenser were fortunate in showing that the English language is rich in polysyllables 'with full vowels disposed in alternate syllables' (S. Chatman, *Theory of Meter*, Mouton, The Hague, 1965, p. 126). The Renaissance dramatists exploited tension between the metrical pattern of the verse, and the natural rhythm of spoken English. The variety of tensions possible makes metre an important factor in analysing the peculiarities of an individual poet's style.

Chatman maintains that the English methods of elision and syllable transformation impose greater regularity of rhythm on the poet than on the prose writer; in prose there is less syllable adjustment, other than is requisite for colloquial contractions.

Conventions in language become 'conventional' mainly because they are devices tried repeatedly and proved to be successful. In the poetry of the English Renaissance, metre is such a convention. It establishes a phonetic correlation between sound and meaning, which critics have been quick to observe; and they use this correlation as the basis of some aesthetic judgements, which Chatman calls 'the folk-lore of literary criticism' (p. 197). Coleridge perceived the organic function of metre, which is to fulfil a variety of expectations, as well as to spring occasional surprises. Through metre a poet communicates some of his craftsmanship and control.

In accentual verse the aim is to preserve the natural stress of the language as normally spoken; complete regularity in the incidence and force of stresses is, however, skilfully avoided. It is the relative strength of contiguous stresses that is paramount. Stresses may have the effect of lengthening the vowels on which they fall; long vowels retard the tempo and so affect the rhythm of verse. The duration of syllables was known in Latin poetry;

metrically, the syllables were independent of the poet's ideas or feeling. For this reason the quantitative measures of classical verse eventually lost touch with the emotional rhythm of words, became artificial and fell into disuse.

Rhyme has the effect of emphasizing the end of a line and inducing a slight pause; this result is more pronounced if an unstressed end-syllable is incorporated in the rhyme. A principal effect of rhyme is to remind the ear of the metrical pattern, which is sustained by the normal accents of the words, as spoken. For this reason rhyme has a significant function in stanzaic verse. In songs and ballads, however, rhyme may have the opposite effect of relaxing the metrical pattern.

Poets since Wyatt and Surrey have tried to suggest the right nuance of meaning by means of their vowel sounds. But the art of adjusting consonant sequences to the distribution of long open vowels and diphthongs, is a more significant contribution to the rhythmic effect. Robert Graves has suggested that the technique of a poet may be assessed by his handling of the sibilant *s*. Modulation, called by Leigh Hunt 'the principle of variety in uniformity', operates without undermining the basic pattern. Lascelles Abercrombie thought of metre as 'the modulated repetition of a rhythmic pattern' (*Poetry: Its Music and Meaning*, p. 21); the metrical framework has come to be regarded as the constant, the natural rhythm of speech as the variable. The poet proposes the nature, number and arrangement of his metrical units and then proceeds to modify them according to conventional principles:

(1) By varying the relative force of the stresses themselves, syllables being weighed according to a four-fold scale; primary, secondary (semi-strong), tertiary (semi-weak), and weak. Secondary and tertiary are often difficult to distinguish.

(2) By varying the positions of the pauses. Sense pauses assist the meaning, and generally correspond with grammatical stops. Metrical pauses (originally breathing-spaces) help the reader in performance, being caesural (within the line) or final. After both types of pause inversion of stress (e.g. the substitution of a trochaic for an iambic foot) may take place.

(3) By the omission or addition of a syllable or foot. In the case of omissions, the length of the accompanying pause should be compensatory.

(4) By varying the speed and therefore the animation of the line. Speed is usually accelerated in proportion as the unstressed syllables outnumber the stressed ones. The device oftenest used is to vary iambics with trisyllabic feet. The traditional time-equality of trisyllabic and disyllabic feet is not real, but used as a metrical convenience. Pope noticed two phonetic principles that affect the movement of verse: clusters of consonants between syllables tend to make the verse move more slowly, because of the difficulties of articulation; and the excessive use of open vowels can be wearisome, for if juxtaposed, they create an hiatus that is also retarding.

(5) By smoothening. This is best secured by the use of semi-vowels *w* and *y*, and liquid and nasal consonants *l*, *m* and *n*.

Sound texture and its effects produce only scepticism in I. A. Richards. In Chapter XVII of *Principles of Literary Criticism* (1924) he writes:

> The sound gets its character by compromise with what is going on already. . . . There are no gloomy and no gay vowels or syllables, and the army of critics who have attempted to analyse the effects of passages into vowel and consonantal collocations have, in fact, been merely amusing themselves. The way in which the sound of a word is taken varies with the emotion already in being. But, further, it varies with the sense. For the anticipation of the sound due to habit, to the routine of sensation, is merely a part of the general expectancy. . . . And the sound of words comes to its full power only through rhythm.

Richards's underestimation of the aesthetic effects of vowels and consonants may be due to his greater interest in the emotive and psychological effects of words than in phonemics.

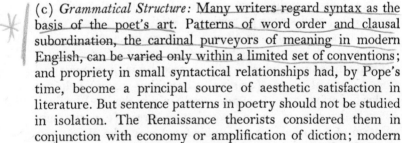

(c) *Grammatical Structure:* Many writers regard syntax as the basis of the poet's art. Patterns of word order and clausal subordination, the cardinal purveyors of meaning in modern English, can be varied only within a limited set of conventions; and propriety in small syntactical relationships had, by Pope's time, become a principal source of aesthetic satisfaction in literature. But sentence patterns in poetry should not be studied in isolation. The Renaissance theorists considered them in conjunction with economy or amplification of diction; modern critics connect them also with layers of meaning. Satirical and witty poets often play sentence structure against rhetorical or emotive uses of words.

Poetry has characteristic modes of progression in employing connectives and clauses; and these have enabled investigators to assign unknown poems to particular periods; but it would be naïve to attempt chronology solely on the evidence of grammar. In original editions, spelling and punctuation, word-compounding and rhetorical figures, are more reliable pointers. Josephine Miles found that certain eras are distinguishable by their preference for phrasal or for clausal groupings (see *PMLA*, LXX, Sept. 1955, pp. 853–75). The English generation of 1570–1600 was remarkable for the cultivation of balanced structures; this and the use of Latin participial phrases mark the age as the precursor of a classical era, which followed in Jonson and the Augustan poets. The principle of balance in poetry is accompanied by increasing metrical regularity.

Miles maintained that poems which favour clausal development tend to be stanzaic in structure, narrative and formal in style. Poems with a phrasal development concentrate on the perfection of the single line, either in blank verse or couplets; they are mainly descriptive and fond of participial modification. Dryden ingenuously described the true classical line as containing 'an adjective, two nouns and a verb'. Movements in poetry seem to Miles to exhaust themselves by excessive self-discipline, which invariably leads to a classical reaction.

A different view of sentence structure is that of William E. Baker in his dissertation *Syntax in English Poetry 1870–1930* (California UP, 1967). The deviations from common speech, which he considers, are also found in earlier centuries. The first is *dislocation*. Parentheses, inversions and elliptical phrases, are seldom arbitrary manipulations, he argues; they are restrained by poetic tradition as much as by the grammatical nature of the language. Baker does not mean by dislocation the disruptions of rhythm of Robert Browning, using dashes and other marks of punctuation.

Syntactical completeness is not essential to meaning; Baker therefore characterizes the poet's omission of articles, conjunctions and stops by the name of *fragmentation*. He includes the repetition of key nouns, which produces phrase-structures to replace grammatical sentences, as in the *Cantos* of Ezra Pound. Fragmentation, so described, is a form of impressionism, extended by Whitman, Lawrence and Wallace Stevens; but it is not unknown in poets like Shakespeare and Donne. Baker accounts for the phenomenon, broadly, as follows:

> A poet may go a step beyond monologue to interior monologue and reverie – with a corresponding decay of formal syntax. . . . The structure of a language is, after all, neither the rational imposition of presumptive theoreticians nor a heap of raw words. Language is thought itself. It is born, bent and broken by the mind of all but according to the whim of each. One would expect, then, some sentences – thought on the verge of utterance – some parts of sentences to represent those half-formed or abandoned thoughts of which writers speak, and the verbal equivalents of sense impressions, which are, one assumes, the stuff out of which thought is by some mysterious process created. (p. 75)

Much commoner in the poetry from Spenser to Milton is the poet's use of *elaboration*. This is one of the principal arts of baroque writing, and Baker traces its origin to the sustained epic simile. The elaboration often takes the form of a digression tangential to the theme, introduced by a verbal echo, an analogy or a comparison. Grammatical means may involve a proliferation of subordinate clauses.

(d) *Meaning:* Culture and tradition impose unconscious effects upon the language used for poetry in any cycle. The important poet has the intuition and skill, not only to break through the rules, but to escape the obsessions and limitations of taste of his period. Freshness of the style, rather than originality, give him his unique position. But the meaning of anything a poem says rests ultimately in the aesthetic ambience in which it has been conceived.

In the English Renaissance, alliteration, assonance and rhyme all contributed to a poem's significance; sound-symbolism made palpable for the reader the interdependence of music and meaning. G. M. Hopkins in his *Journals* (ed. H. House, 1959) referred to the structure of poetry as a 'continuous parallelism'. Likeness is brought out by metaphor and simile, unlikeness by antithesis and contrast.

Two aspects of meaning may be simultaneous in a poetic style. In rhetorical, dialectical or witty verse, for instance, dictionary meanings may be moulded or stretched to accommodate a message or slant of the poet. The two levels of meaning usually implied in duality of language are the indicative and the expressionistic. The one enables the literal reader to arrive at the plain prose sense of the words; the other conveys the ulterior suggestive purpose of the poet, as artist. The case for two aspects of meaning is illustrated in Philip Wheelwright's essay 'On the Semantics of Poetry' (*Essays on the Language of Literature*, 1967):

> In poetic language, which keeps as close as possible to the experiential flow, the meaning of a word is in each instance determined partly by the specific context of words, rhythms, images, mythological allusions, etc., in which it occurs. . . . Shakespeare is a gold mine of examples: his ability to control meanings contextually is unsurpassed. . . .
>
> The recognition of an evocative quality as co-present everywhere in genuine poetry along with whatever specific denotations the poem may carry suggests a further distinction between the literal and poetic uses of language, i.e., between monosign and plurisign. It may be stated thus: *the monosign is purely referential , the plurisign is to some degree reflexive and evocative.* The monosign is referential in the sense that what it means, what it refers to, its referend, is something distinct from itself. This is proved and illustrated by the familiar fact that a monosign is exactly translatable. . . . The plurisign, on the other hand, while never entirely lacking in referential function, is at the same time semantically reflexive in the sense that it *is* a part of what it means. That is to say, the plurisign, the poetic symbol, is not merely employed but enjoyed; its value is not entirely instrumental but largely aesthetic, intrinsic. . . .
>
> A poetic statement differs from a literal statement not, as Dr Richards thinks, in that the one has a merely subjective, the other an objective reference, – at least this is an unnecessary and generally irrelevant difference – but in their manner of asserting. There are differences of what may be called *assertive weight*. A literal statement asserts heavily: it can do so because its terms are solid. A poetic statement, on the other hand, consisting as it does in a conjunction or association of plurisigns, has no such solid foundation, and affirms with varying degrees of lightness. . . .
>
> The total statement of *Measure for Measure* is asserted more lightly, though I suspect with a more deadly seriousness, than the total statement of *Richard II*. (pp. 252–63)

Figurative language is a cover-term for a variety of poetic phenomena, conveniently divided into metaphors, symbols and associated ideas, such as the figures of thought, metonymy and synecdoche. The function of symbols seems to be to connect the conscious with the unconscious mind. F. W. Bateson has likened them to 'shorthand transcriptions', and says they are transferable from poet to poet, whereas metaphor is peculiar to the individual poet. The power of communication of symbols is universal; they do not depend on the nuances of a particular language. Symbols belong to a primitive age of mysterious relationships between man and his environment; their roots are anthropologically and psychologically deep, and the emotions they evoke are often unaccountable.

In the sixteenth century many of the images were emblematic in origin, the emblem being an icon of allegorical or religious meaning, appearing as a wood-cut in printed books. Textbooks used the word 'colours' for figurative language. Metaphor was regarded as a new verbal colour, more expressive in the sense that it changed the meaning of a word to suit a context. Metaphor has now a more relevant function, to convey a complex idea in a single effective word or phrase. The poet arouses feelings by the apt perception of relationships in the objects he associates. Structural linguists find metaphor an embarrassment, in that the dictionary or scientific meanings of metaphorical words are of small importance. Cicero remarked that the pleasure derived from metaphor is in 'jumping over the obvious'. Simile involves comparison of the same essence; but the likeness is explicit, whereas in metaphor it is implied. This is how Christine Brooke-Rose explains the phenomenon:

> Metaphor consists of two terms, the metaphoric term and the proper term which it replaces. But the result is a new entity, more or less successfully fused according to how it is expressed, and there is no need to emphasise its separateness. . . .
> In metaphor, it is possible to equate one whole phrase with another, or with a single noun, or to point back to a whole action-complex and summarise it with one metaphoric noun.
> (*Grammar of Metaphor*, Secker & Warburg, 1958, pp. 9 and 17)

Figures based upon the association of ideas invite the reader to interpret in terms of personal experience. If he has lived in Arcadian illiteracy or through an era unshaken by war, he is unlikely to understand the force of 'The *pen* is mightier than the *sword*'. *Metonymy* and *synecdoche* are made possible by sentiments and mental habit-patterns. The 'name' implied in metonymy is foreign to the thing it symbolizes; in synecdoche there is a relationship, apart from the word's use as a figure of thought. Association of ideas also explains the *transferred epithet.* In the sentence 'and entertain the *harmless* day/ With a Religious Book or Friend', the adjective *harmless* is strictly an attribute of 'religious book' or 'friend', not of *day*, with which it is *poetically* linked. There is no logical reason why this transference should be more appropriate in poetry than mixed metaphor. The latter is ludicrous only when no passionate intensity fuses the elements; Shakespeare mixed metaphors successfully in the great speeches of *Macbeth*.

There are double-purpose figures, having a foot also in the camp of rhetorical devices; they undoubtedly contribute to poetry's different levels of meaning. These are personification, hyperbole and oxymoron. *Personification* (prosopopoeia) is the giving of human attributes and powers to inanimate objects or abstract ideas. *Hyperbole* is the licence of poetic heightening, employed effectively to describe unusual mental states, which arise from the stress of emotion (e.g. in the storm scene of *King Lear*). Susenbrotus, the Renaissance scholar of rhetoric, said that 'we use an incredible saying, to show that the thing we affirm is almost incredible'. *Oxymoron*, a poetical paradox, contains an inherent contradiction, but reflects ambivalent emotion. Occasionally Shakespeare combines these two figures poetically, as in *Romeo and Juliet*, I.1.181–8:

> Heres much to do with hate, but more with love:
> Why then O brawling love, O loving hate,
> O anything of nothing first created:
> O heavie lightnesse, serious vanitie,
> Mishapen Chaos or wellseeing formes,
> Feather of lead, bright smoke, cold fier, sicke health,
> Still waking sleepe that is not what it is.
> This love feele I, that feel no love in this.

The word *trope* is difficult to describe and define; for it once included aspects of discourse, such as allegory and irony. The meaning of *trope* (turn) is 'the use of a word or phrase in a sense other than that which is proper to it' (OED). Among the reforms of language advocated in the cause of science in the seventeenth century was the abolition of tropes, as an instrument of falsification. Thus Bacon spoke of them in *The Advancement of Learning* (1605) as 'deceiving expectation' (II.V.3). Thomas Sprat in his *History of the Royal Society* (1667) wrote: 'Who can behold without indignation how many mists and uncertainties these specious tropes and figures have brought to our knowledge?' And Dryden in his *Juvenal* (p. 53) says 'Where the Trope is far fetch'd, and hard, 'tis fit for nothing but to puzzle the Understanding'.

G. N. Leech regards tropes as 'unorthodox or deviant forms of language' (*Essays on Style and Language*, p. 136). He may be right in asserting that the interest in metaphor lies outside of language, because such figures are concerned with 'appropriate analogies', which are the province of psychological, emotional and perceptual relations (p. 154).

(e) *Rhetorical Devices:* Rhetorical schemes were to stimulate attention by various subtleties of word play. The aim was a sustained attack on the reader's or listener's capacity for distinctions, through the elements of surprise.

Aristotle's *Rhetoric*, as de Quincey explained in his four essays on 'Style' in *Blackwood's Magazine* (July 1840 to February 1841), was a practical course for extempore speakers and speech-teachers, rather than an analysis of commendable writing. The Greeks of the century from Pericles to Alexander did not instruct in what de Quincey was the first to call 'composition'. Aristotle taught rhetoric as an art of persuasion, of presenting a theme in an acceptable moral light; hence the connection of rhetoric with logic and ethics.

Latin rhetoric, contained in Cicero's *Rhetorica ad Herennium* and Quintilian's *Institutio Oratoria*, involved the study of three categories, *inventio*, *dispositio* and *elocutio*, the discovery of material, its arrangement, and its manner of presentation, or style. This chapter is concerned principally with the last.

According to de Quincey, Aquinas and the scholastic monks of the Middle Ages were responsible for extending the principles of rhetoric to subjective reasoning; they even applied it to metaphysics and theology. The manner of thought now became inextricably woven with the matter; and thus a theory of style, in the modern sense, was born. The manner consisted predominantly of subtleties, refinements, abstractions and distinctions. The scholastic rhetoricians began to teach that language and thought, in what is written, are ideally inseparable.

The intellectual revolution described by de Quincey is, perhaps, over-simplified. It is true, however, that in Athens the arts of the orator and the actor had been the only means of reaching the public. In practice, the styles known to a writer were limited, and much less individual than those of the Renaissance; for then the publication and distribution of printed books became a reality. The circulation of printed books in the sixteenth century was sufficient to promote the growth of a small but select reading public. Treatises of all kinds were produced for the silent reader rather than the public speaker. The concept of rhetoric as an educational tool was thus radically transformed. This cultural revolution was attended by disadvantages; the stage, as Shakespeare proved, was a more lively, vivid and sympathetic medium of publication.

In the western languages of Renaissance Europe, rhetoric, founded upon the teaching of Quintilian and Erasmus, produced a certain mannerism of diction. Quintilian encouraged the art of amplification, Erasmus showed the methods of combining figures intelligently in writing. Amplification did not imply wordiness, rather deliberate choice of words to stimulate visual impressions. Words, by association, were believed to be the source of new ideas.

Rhetoric is not bad when declamatory or persuasive, but when it is too monotonous to adapt itself to variations of emotional tone. The entrenched position of rhetoric in Elizabethan education was due entirely to its prominence in classical literature, where it promoted a different patterning of words in prose from that thought proper to poetic rhythm.

The books commonly used in England in the sixteenth century were Joannes Susenbrotus's *Epitome Troporum ac Schematum* (1540) and Richard Sherry's *Treatise of Schemes and Tropes* (1550). In both may be found the academic, but rather vague, division of figures into tropes, schemes of words and schemes of thought (conceptions). This classification is now largely neglected as irrelevant to the purposes of poetry. But the teaching of rhetoric at an impressionable time in a youth's mental development was influential in forming the style of creative writers. In the Elizabethan period it provided the only practical lessons in English composition. At Cambridge Gabriel Harvey advised his students, in *Ciceronianus* (1577), against useless classifying of figures observed in reading, and urged the study of structural functions. Peter Ramus, in Paris, taught dialectic with illustrations from Vergil, and appropriated from rhetoric the two divisions of *inventio* and *dispositio*, as proper to logic.

Quintilian's rhetoric was better suited to the humanistic aims of Renaissance idealism than Aristotle's or Cicero's; but no Greek or Roman instructor attempted to extend his principles to poetry and creative writing generally. Julius Scaliger, in the *Poetics* (1561), anticipated Ramus in this departure, and included in his treatise a section on metre and rhythm.

The treatise of Susenbrotus contains about one hundred and thirty-five figures. Henry Peacham's *Garden of Eloquence* (1577) included as many as one hundred and ninety-six. The first writer to substitute English names for Latin and Greek rhetorical terms was Puttenham in the *Arte of English Poesie* (1589); he illustrated over a hundred figures.

From this numerical discrepancy it is concluded that the classification of figures of rhetoric in the English Renaissance was personal rather than systematic. The schematization of utterances was to end in near chaos.

Rhetorical terms that have survived in the vocabulary of critics are plentiful; for example, allegory, ambiguity, antithesis, barbarism, climax, emblem, emphasis, enigma, epithet, eulogy, fable, hyperbole, irony, litotes, metaphor, metaplasm, metonymy, onomatopoeia, oxymoron, paradigm, parenthesis, parody, periphrasis, pleonasm, solecism, synecdoche, synonym, urbanity. These are no longer considered as ornaments superadded to the diction of the poet. But the Elizabethans, accepting Quintilian, thought that tropes were verbal substitutions; that literary art was actually a means of translating reality into words.

Schemes of words are stylistic, and need not subvert traditional order; schemes of thought were held to transmute words, through feeling, as they passed through the mind. The distinction is confusing and difficult to defend when examining instances. But the rhetoricians were nothing if not abstract; and the poets, often for diplomatic or security reasons, became masters in the art of ambiguity.

Except in the Scottish academies, the study of rhetoric fell into disuse towards the end of the eighteenth century. It can hardly be coincidence that a special diction for poetry began only then to be discredited. Chaucer had no need of a science of metrics; but he could hardly have dispensed with the arts of rhetoric. The interdependence of poetic and rhetoric persisted until the time of Gray and Dr Johnson.

In this study tropes are considered in their relation to meaning; the rhetorical schemes of words and sentences (arrangement, gradation and amplification), are classed as *devices.* Several of the devices are concerned with formulae of repetition or logical progression; for example, *anaphora*, *climax* and *anticlimax*.

Anaphora is the repetition of a word at the beginning of each of a group of parallel clauses or phrases, e.g. Spenser's '*Some* laught for sport, *some* did for wonder shout.'

Climax leads the mind, by a mounting pattern, to the most significant statement, which is placed last, e.g. Shakespeare's 'There is Teares for his Love; Joy for his Fortune; Honor for his Valour; and Death for his Ambition.'

Anticlimax offers the reverse or descending pattern, familiar in satirical verse. Usually it lets the reader down with abrupt discomfiture.

Metaplasms (transformations) are standard devices of word contraction and elision, the commonest examples being *aphæresis*, *syncope*, *apocope* and *synalœpha*.

Sententiae (pithily expressed thoughts) include proverbs, aphorisms and other gnomic expressions of ideas.

Antithesis is structural contrast, one notion being set against another, with a pause as the fulcrum. In Renaissance and Augustan poetry the contrast had to be incisively expressed, because the best effect was achieved in a balanced line, e.g. Spenser's 'Att once he wards and strikes, he takes and payes.'

Euphuism usually employed a mechanical form of antithesis; alliteration might be invoked to balance the phrases neatly.

Epigram is allied to antithesis and paradox; it makes a point often unexpected or incongruous, e.g. Wordsworth's 'The child is father to the man.' In Renaissance and Augustan poetry it was skilfully handled in a rhymed couplet.

A question of some importance to critics has been the analogy drawn between poetry and music or painting. In his W. P. Ker

Memorial Lecture of 1942, T. S. Eliot doubted whether, phonetically, one word could be more musical than another; the music of a word 'arises from its relation . . . to the words immediately preceding and following it'. He argued that a musical pattern of sound goes along with a musical pattern of the secondary meaning of the words, and that 'the sound of a poem is as much an abstraction from the poem as the sense'.

The use of sounds to support the rhythm, if carried too far, as in the poems of Swinburne, may lead to a mindless incantation. In a musical poem pace and animation are as important as sound. Hopkins's Sprung Rhythm was a calculated attempt to imitate musical counterpoint in poetry (the 'mounting of a new rhythm on the old'); but G. Whalley in *Poetic Process* (Routledge and Kegan Paul, 1953) maintains that, 'in poetry there can be no strict analogy to musical polyphony' (p. 205). Poetry is musical because it springs from the same primal roots in man, not because it shares the special resources of music.

In Northrop Frye's *Anatomy of Criticism* (1957) phrasal analogies of poetry with music are said to be sentimental, rather than technical. A sensuous flow of sound, produced by balancing vowels and consonants, (he says) paradoxically reflects an unmusical poet, of whom Keats and Tennyson are examples, though the term 'unmusical' is not used in a pejorative sense.

Melic poetry, that of the later Shakespeare, Cowley, Crashaw and Browning, with a crabbed language and numerous poly-syllables, bears a closer resemblance to the technique of music. For Frye, the characteristic of such poetry is 'gnarled intellec-tualism' (p. 174). Milton was one of the few poets who used the word *musical* technically. What most critics mean by musical is 'the physical pulsation of the dance' (p. 175) usually with a slow and resonant rhythm. Frye concludes that Spenser was unique in his ability 'to catch visualization through sound' (p. 177). But effects of colour and picturesqueness are probably best re-created by the use of colloquial speech.

Diction is a word that has virtually disappeared from the critical vocabulary. But there existed in the Renaissance an idealized language of poetry typified by Spenser, which aroused a number of notable rebels, such as Donne and Wordsworth. Gray, Coleridge and Eliot were convinced that the language of poetry will always differ, in important particulars, from that of everyday speech; otherwise it would never be read. But the main currents of poetry suggest that the extent of this divergence has varied considerably in the history of English.

II

CHAUCER AND HIS SUCCESSORS

Chaucer was the first English poet with a style recognizably his own. The excellence of his achievement clinched the dominance of syllabic verse, already flourishing in France and Italy. Both in syntax and vocabulary, there was less to distinguish the language of late medieval poetry and of prose than there was in Anglo-Saxon times. The Old English poet was a craftsman in parallelism, rather than an inventor, a humanist or a wit, as Chaucer appears now.

The transition from quantitative to syllabic measures was gradual, and aided by the necessity of fitting words to music. The new measures are said to have begun with post-classical Latin verses, written to be sung in Church services; in St Ambrose's four great hymns, for instance, the rights of both accent and quantity are preserved. From Latin free verse arose most of the accentual rhythms of the Romance and Teutonic languages; and they were facilitated by the adoption of rhyme in South Western Europe in the fourth century A.D.

Provençal poets, using the accented vernacular, were the first to exploit stanza forms in lyrical and didactic verse of the twelfth and thirteenth centuries. The metres were iambic more often than trochaic, and their common ten-syllable line admitted of feminine endings. Rhyme schemes and stanzas were infinitely varied, yet the structure of the verse remained fundamentally simple. One function of rhyme in this poetry was to assert the metrical form of the stanza. For the audience, verse was thus clearly distinguished from prose. In England before Chaucer the vernacular poets and ballad-writers found rhyme indispensable to bolster a general want of metrical skill; and this function it has never lost.

The instability of English accent and the dissolution of inflexions gave Chaucer the linguistic freedom he needed; but it led to formlessness in less gifted successors. When he began,

there was no naturalized accentual verse in English. He experi-
mented with French stanza forms, and independently evolved
types used by Boccaccio, before he could read Italian. He
perfected the decasyllabic line, which came to be known as
heroic verse, using it in the Chaucerian stanza, an adaptation of
French rhyme-royal. This stanza of *Troilus and Criseyde*
terminates in two decasyllabic couplets.

Chaucer frequently began the decasyllabic line with a mono-
syllabic foot. The caesural pauses, unlike those of the French,
are movable; the innovation, borrowed from Italian poets, gave
his line flexibility and ease. Some scholars think that the
caesural pause inhibits elision, and that the decasyllabic line of
Chaucer may therefore have a redundant internal syllable,
usually a light one, such as unstressed *-e*. This vowel often
represents a weakened form of an Old English inflexion. But it
was also a scribal addition to monosyllabic words indicating a
preceding long vowel, e.g. *stone* (for *stoon*); as such it was not
intended to be pronounced. Often the final *-e*, as in *Aprille*, was a
caprice of the copyist, for which the poet was not responsible;
for most manuscripts of Chaucer belong to the fifteenth century.

Saintsbury in his *History of English Prosody* makes more than
he should of the scansion underlying the prosody, and less of the
natural rhythms of speech, which Chaucer undoubtedly appre-
ciated. The poet could not have written without knowledge of
the alliterative revival that was popular in the western and
northern regions of England. Many of Chaucer's rhythms
echoed the movements of these anonymous poets; the less
skilful he parodied. He knew that a poet could avoid dulness by
using the rhythms of common speech; there is realism, for
instance, in the style with which he portrayed the Wife of Bath.
Chaucer's alliteration confirms the use he made of traditional
Old English verse.

Chaucer's departures from the natural rhythms were due to
conflict with his metrical pattern; the opposition was not as
violent, however, as it became in Lydgate. Both poets call for a
knowledge of Middle English word stress, which critics
frequently do not possess. A modern reader feels that he has to
make too many concessions to the exigencies of metre; he
finds, in scanning Chaucer, that the beginning of a line permits
of more variation of word stress than the end of it. In words of

romance origin, such as *argument*, Chaucer, under the influence of French, commonly reversed the normal order of primary stress in Germanic words, and placed it last, giving only a secondary stress to the initial syllable. This anomaly occurs frequently at the end of a line.

Chaucer's redundant syllable at the caesura is said to have been a relic of French practice in decasyllabic verse, in which the medial pause was fixed after the fourth syllable. An unstressed syllable in this position would, however, have been inconsistent with the Chaucerian and Italian movable caesura.

The will-o'-the-wisp caesura may be said to determine the rhythmical nature of Chaucer's heroic verse, its variety and singular freedom of movement. Chaucer's line did not often risk the liberty of a late, or even an early, pause. The metrical break, furthermore, does not have to coincide with the sense-pause of syntax, as the use of virgules in the best manuscripts reveals.

Chaucer gave the heroic line a firm iambic character by not imposing romance metrics upon a language whose syntax was essentially Germanic. His use of run-on lines in rhymed couplets was exemplary in tact and restraint. Enjambement is never sustained beyond the listener's capacity for grasping the sense as a whole. Chaucer demonstrated that the run-on line in heroic verse could and should be associated with the adjustment of pause and discreet use of inversion, e.g.

> Prol. *CT* 133-5 Hir over-lippe wyped she so clene
> That in hir coppe ther was no ferthing sene
> Of grece/ whan she dronken hadde hir draughte

In rhyme, Chaucer's pairing matches phonetically, both in quality and quantity of the vowels; he shows equal skill in the management of masculine and feminine rhymes.

J. G. Southworth in *Verses of Cadence* (Oxford, 1954) cites the following lines from *The House of Fame* to refute the prosodic theories of Tyrwhitt, Child, Ellis, Ten Brink, Skeat, and many others:

> Although that in thy hed ful lyte is
> To make bookys, songes, dytees,
> In ryme, or elles in *cadence*
> As thou best canst   (lines 621-4)

Cadence, here, must surely mean 'unrhymed verse', with which listeners or readers were familiar in the form of alliterative poetry. Southworth takes it to imply Chaucer's ignorance of foot division in heroic verse (see p. 53), and consequent neglect of a regular number of stresses in the line; he suggests that the line stresses were determined by the requirements of rhetoric, to which the use of virgules was the obvious guide.

According to Southworth, the eighteenth and nineteenth century editors of Chaucer showed their misunderstanding of the internal structure of his line by insisting on his intricate recourse to the final -e; the theory was urged to make his lines scan correctly, by Augustan principles.

Wyatt, who stood at the end of one tradition, and on the threshold of a new, still used the virgule to mark rhetorical units rather than metrical ones, as his manuscript poems show. He did not conceive verses in the unit of the single line, but used virgules to mark the cadence, for the assistance of the reader; e.g.

Oh dyverse er the chastysinges off syn
in mete/ in drink/ in breth that man doth blow
In slepe/ in wach/ in fretyng still within
(Poem 174, p. 398, Richard Harrier edition)

Southworth maintains that the late sixteenth century humanist poets, including Gascoigne and Spenser, 'continued to have an essentially correct understanding of what Chaucer did' (p. 89). Learned poetry became metrical, while popular verse remained rhythmical.

G. J. Tamson shows in *Word Strees in English* (Halle, 1898) that the metrical stress in Chaucer, Spenser, Marlowe, Shakespeare and Jonson is on the first syllable of certain pre-fixed polysyllables such as *uncouth;* he produces an example from as late as Browning's *Sordello.* Similarly, the pronunciation of *archbishop, archdeacon, portray, profess* and *pursuit,* with the primary stress on the first syllable, was the commonest in use from *Piers the Plowman* to Spenser and Shakespeare; for instance Shakespeare in *Sonnet* CXLIII.4 has

In *pursuit* of the thing she would have stay

following the accentuation of Chaucer in *Troilus and Criseyde* II.959. This movable accent is sometimes called 'hovering stress', because the pronunciation cannot, from the verse, be determined with any certainty. Throughout the New English period, dissyllabic compound relation-words, such as *before*, *therefore* and *without*, retained their metrical ambivalence.

French influence on the phenomenon of stress shifting seems improbable, since borrowings were adapted to the English stress system. In alliterative poetry, however, word stress agreed with the metrical stress asserted by the staves. After exhaustive analysis of alliterative examples, Tamson came to the following conclusions:

1. Dissyllabic romance nouns, the first element of which is a prefix, have the stress on the first syllable in the alliterative poems contemporary with Chaucer, e.g. *compas, prologe, relikes, surcotte*. Exceptions are *defaute, defence, dispite, redresse*, because in such cases the prefix had actually become meaningless. Chaucer's education in Latin and French seems, however, to have induced him to stress the root syllable, especially where the prefix is *a-* or *de-*. But the alliterative poets tend to stress the prefix. Spenser in his poetry usually followed the stress-practice of Chaucer.

2. Dissyllabic romance nouns, without prefix, also have the stress on the first syllable. One general exception is *uságe*; but Chaucer, and earlier *King Horn*, also preserve the French end-stress on many other words, such as *folýe, honoúr, manére, pitée, vertú*. Sometimes this retention of the French practice was due to the requirement of rhyme; Spenser, indeed, often retained end-accentuation as a conscious archaism.

3. Polysyllabic romance nouns, with prefix, have the stress usually on the prefix, e.g. *áventure, cóndycyone, cónfusion, délyverans, díscrecioun, répentance*, all of which are found in the *Troy Book* and *Morte Arthure*. *Absólucion* and *injúrie*, with stress on the second syllable, are exceptions; and there are others where the modern practice is anticipated, e.g. *acórdaunce, allówance, assémbly, atténdant, enchaúntement, discóverour*; here the stress follows the accentuation of the corresponding verb. The practice in identically-derived words of different speech function is very inconsistent. Chaucer usually favours an accentuation based on the Latin originals, which is now that of modern English, in most cases. Where he elects to follow the Germanic practice of stressing the first syllable, he usually compromises with French inclinations by placing a secondary stress on the final syllable of the word. Tamson has no doubt

that he adapted his practice of word stress to the requirements of the metre, and that Shakespeare did the same. He does, however, assume a basic metrical pattern in Chaucer.

4. Polysyllabic romance nouns, uncompounded, were mostly derived from French, the accent being on the final syllable or on the penultimate, if the word ended in unaccented -*e*. Here the practice varied, according to the number of syllables:

(i) The primary stress in Chaucer and Middle English (as usually in modern English) was on the first element in tri-syllables, e.g. *cúratour, aúditour, élement, máryner, órisoun, únite*.

(ii) In four-syllable words, the alliterative poets tended to place the primary stress on the first syllable and the secondary accent on the last, e.g. *ábilitỳ, dívinitè, fílosophèr, grámmarièn, sálvaciòn*. Chaucer usually placed the primary stress on the second syllable, however, his reasons seeming to be (a) the Latin practice, and (b) greater convenience for his metrical pattern. Chaucer's choice has invariably prevailed in modern English.

(iii) In five-syllable words the primary stress was again on the first syllable in alliterative poets as well as Chaucer. Only in the case of -*aunce* and -*ion* endings was the secondary accent on the last syllable. There were a number of five syllable words ending in -*e*, -*ie* or -*ye*, however, whose secondary accent was on the penultimate, assuming that final -*e* was pronounced; e.g. *ástronomỳe, déseueraùnce, évangelistè, ýpocrisìe*.

In the case of verbs, Chaucer's general practice was to accent the root syllable, whether the verb was compounded with a particle or not. He was arbitrary in accenting the same proper name in different ways, according to metrical requirements, especially when the names were not of Latin or French origin. The majority of proper names in Middle English show a general preference for Germanic stress on the first syllable, unless the word is trisyllabic and begins with a vowel (which was not frequently an alliterating letter). Proper names have especial interest as criteria of comparison between the alliterative poets and Chaucer, because the two schools seldom agreed on accentuation. Where the names provide the staves of alliterative poetry, the accentuation is often arbitrary; lack of learning can only explain the mutilated forms in which names appear, such as *Aufrike* (Africa), *Bedleem* (Bethlehem), *Bedwar*

B

(Bedevere), *Florent* (Florence), *Lettowe* (Lithuania), *Philon* (Pylos), *Ysay* (Isaiah). The *Troy Book*, being in alliterative verse, accentuates *Achilles, Cassandra, Diana, Medea* and *Pendragon* all on the first syllable; modern English has confirmed the original classical stress on the second. *Morte Arthur* has the alliterative preference for *Gólias* (Goliath), and *Piers the Plowman* for *Ýpocras* (Hippocrates).

Chaucer attempted a compromise between French and Germanic accentuation, in the interests both of his Latin scholarship and his avowed preference for syllabic verse. His poetic practice had an immense influence on the pronunciation and future metrical use of borrowed words of more than one syllable.

C. S. Lewis in 'The Fifteenth Century Heroic Line' (*Essays and Studies* XXIV, 1938) regarded the line as two separate rhythmic units, on the ground that this is the effect of true caesura. He argued that the heroic line, as we have known it since Surrey and Marlowe, has no true caesura or pivot, but only a pause, which is mythical. For such a pause need not appear at all; but when it does, can do so at virtually any point within the line. The function of this pause is rhetorical and syntactical; probably emotional, too, in the delight it excites. The caesura is an adjunct of metrical science, the pause only a subtle means to musical effects.

In consequence of the abandonment of the caesura in sixteenth century decasyllabic verse, modulation of stress assumed greater importance in blank verse than it enjoyed in the medieval heroic line; it had, moreover, to be achieved within the limits of natural pronunciation. Blank verse, since Marlowe, demands a leverage against the hypothetical pattern so that works of large scale can become tolerable to the reader. No poetic of this kind was in existence in English before the grand style of the Renaissance; and Lewis suggests that this verse requires to be read with 'double audition'.

That Chaucer intended what Marlowe achieved is extremely unlikely; for if this kind of modulation was part of his design, his audience would not have had the capacity to understand him. Even a scholar could not have been expected to read Chaucer's heroic verse as we now do. Lewis maintains that Chaucer *did* write many lines with the old caesural pauses and extra-metrical syllables; that he commonly admitted the monosyllabic first foot, thereby throwing the iambic rhythm out of gear for modern readers, while innocently echoing types of hemistich that the native alliterative poets had inculcated; 'the one metre slips easily into the other'. Chaucer's less gifted successors were content with the shallow knowledge that the count of syllables is not really significant in the English heroic line. Only Skelton can be excepted from the general insensitivity to rhythm before the coming of Wyatt and Surrey.

That the Chaucerian tradition of spoken verse lapsed into chaos within a century of his death is shown by the texts of his poems presented in the early printed editions of Caxton, Pynson and Wynkyn de Worde. In Caxton's *Canterbury Tales*, the lines appear as a mixture of octosyllabic and decasyllabic verse, in which few can muster more than four stresses. These editions lie at the root of the metrical spinelessness and unruly rhymes of Barclay, Hawes and Lydgate. Poets seemed unaware that the number and disposition of stresses bears some relation to the number of syllables in a line.

On the testimony of William of Salisbury, final -*e* had completely disappeared from English pronunciation by the middle of the sixteenth century; but in poetry *e* was still optionally pronounced in inflexions, such as the possessive and plural ending -*es*, often written as pronounced, -*is*, or -*ys*. The -*ed* inflexion of weak verbs (in the preterite and past participle) was archaic as an extra syllable, except after dental stem-finals; it was invoked, however, to meet the rhythmical needs of poetry. When not pronounced, and especially after stems ending in liquid and nasal consonants, the *e* was placed after the *d*.

Twenty-five lines from Skelton's *Phyllyp Sparowe* will illustrate these practices, and the Tudor critical attitude to Chaucer and Lydgate:

In Chaucer I am sped,
His tale*s* I have red:
His mater is *delectable*
Solacious, and *commendable;*
His Englysh well alowed
So as it is *emprowed*, [= improved]
For as it is enployed,
There is no English *voyd*. [= lacking or useless]
At those dayes moch commend*ed*,

5

And now men wold have amended   10
His Englysh, whereat they barke;
And mar all they warke:
Chaucer, that famus clerke,
His term*es* were not darke,
But pleasunt, easy, and playne   15
No worde he wrote in vayne:
Also Johnn *Lydgate*
Wryteth after an hyer rate;
It is *dyffuse* to fynde
The sentence of his mynde,   20
Yet wryteth he in his kynd,
No man that can amend
Those maters that he hath pen*de*;
Yet some men fynde a faute,
And say he wryteth to haute.   25

(Lines 788–812, A. Dyce's edition, 1843)

These are dominantly three-stress lines, cunningly varied in rhythm by the number of syllables to the line. The precise accentuation of the words *delectable*, *commendable* and *Lydgate* in context is debatable; and the meaning of *dyffuse* in line 19 is unusual.

So far from Chaucer being 'a well of English undefyled', the custom of attempting to improve him was becoming an established malpractice. Changes in English pronunciation and word stress were so inexplicable during the period 1450 to 1550 that poets had to make shift with unstable rhythms of speech. The difficulties of orthography and orthoepy are such that modern metrical scholarship is unlikely to find a way out of the labyrinth.

Skelton, though he coincides with the advent of the Tudor monarchy, had not divested himself of the alliterative tradition of prosaic rhythms; he belonged to the Plantagenet era of Chaucer, Hoccleve and Lydgate, who were no longer regarded as viable models for Renaissance poets. Though he was an individualist and a bold experimenter, the honours conferred on him by three universities (Oxford, Cambridge and Louvain) were for skill in writing Latin verse. No one was more conscious of his deficiencies in Skeltonic verse than Skelton himself, as the following apologies show:

Go, litill quaire,
Demene you faire;

Take no dispare,
Though I you wrate
After this rate
In Englysshe letter;
So moche the better
Welcome shall ye
To sum men be:
For Latin warkis
Be good for clerkis . . .

(*Garlande of Laurell* lines 1533–43)

For though my ryme be ragged,
Tattered and iagged,
Rudely rayne beaten,
Rusty and moughte eaten,
If ye take well therwith,
It hath in it some pyth.

(*Colyn Cloute* lines 53–8)

A humanist poet is distinguished by a more scientific approach to versification than Skelton's.

In dramatic dialogue, the most representative of the Tudor writers of folk plays, who were not professional poets, was John Heywood. The language of the interlude-writers appeared in a variety of metrical forms; until George Gascoigne, however, the versification was as irregular as anything in Skelton. Any attempt at pattern was limited to the number of stresses in the line, the preference being for rhyme, sometimes in couplets, sometimes in stanzas; the commonest stanza form was the romance-six, with rhyme-scheme a b a b c c. Difficulties for the modern reader are multiplied by the inadequate printing, only three of the interludes having survived in manuscript, namely, *King John*, *Respublica* and *Witty and Witless*. The lines abound with proverbial wisdom, and are generally thought to have been spoken by child actors. The entertainers who wrote the interludes were more attentive to eye-rhyme and assonance than to identical stress in rhyming.

It is no accident that the Great Vowel Shift, which began in fourteenth century English, was in full spate when printing was introduced by Caxton. Although books were bought by a limited moneyed class, literature was perused by many more *readers* than had hitherto been possible. Reading stimulated the visual memory of many words whose pronunciation could not be verified. Polysyllables gave rise to phonetic confusion, not only in the vowel sounds, but in the location of accents; there was disagreement whether or not consonants were silent, for instance the initial aspirate in words of French origin.

The raising of long vowels in the Great Sound Shift was unluckily concealed by the retention of the old habits of spelling. At the close of the Middle English period, vowels still had their Continental value, acquired with the romic alphabet of Celtic and Old English. English spelling between 700 and 1100 A.D. came near to being phonetic, and had the merit of indicating etymology. But the attempt of fifteenth century scholars to preserve the spelling of words of Latin and Greek origin was inconsistent with phonological changes in the language during the four centuries after the Norman conquest.

Caxton found well established the habit of spelling to please the eye rather than the ear, particularly in rhyme words. No attempt at spelling reform was practicable, because Caxton had not the competence to devise a logical system. When Smith, Hart, Bullokar and Gill advocated feasible reforms, they were silently ignored by writers, printers and readers, who naturally resisted proposals for re-education.

The lack of a standard of spelling was partly responsible for the variant pronunciation of words, which confused poets committed to the adoption of accentual measures. Another difficulty was the different usage of regional dialects, especially when mingled with London English. By 1500 poets were able to draft their writings without the aid of scriveners, who previously exercised a moderating effect on casual spellings.

Schoolmasters began the debasement of Latin pronunciation in England, accelerated by the Great Vowel Shift; this resulted in such curiosities as the English versions of *viva voce* and *vice versa*. The pronunciations differed so from Continental practice that they were noticed by Coryat in 1609 (*Crudities*, II.59). English pronunciation has had to be retained in the reading of Latin phrases from Skelton to Bridges, or borrowings would appear incongruous with the language and versification in which they are embedded. If this is relevant to foreign phrases, how much more pertinent is it to the older locutions of the mother tongue, which were once the current verbal coin of the poets.

III

CRITICAL TERMS AND THEIR
RELEVANCE TO POETRY
FROM WYATT TO SIDNEY

The instability of English pronunciation and spelling remarked upon in the preceding chapter was noticed by a generation of verse theorists between 1575 and 1605. The grammarians of this period gave much attention to *orthoepy* (right speaking) and *orthography* (systematic spelling). In his correspondence with Spenser in 1580, Gabriel Harvey advocated agreement about standards upon which poets might depend; verse-writing should be 'in all points conformable and proportionate to our common prosodye' (Harvey meant by the latter word 'natural accent'). He contended that the eye misled many poets, who would not or could not trust their ears. He disliked, in particular, Spenser's forcing of metrical stress on to unusual syllables.

George Gascoigne, in *Certayne Notes of Instruction* (1575). had already maintained that the key to acceptable pronunciation of English words was the location of the principal stress, not the quantity of syllables. Gascoigne and Harvey had the advantage of sensitive English poetry on which to draw in *Tottel's Miscellany*, and the work of Sackville and Sidney.

The terminology of English Renaissance theorists can seldom be taken at its face value. For instance, at the end of his Preface to *Ane Short Treatise* (1584), as well as in Chapter II, James VI confused the word *foot* with *syllable*. *Verse* and *foot* were used by Harvey, Spenser and most early critics for quantitative measures only, and refer to temporal relations between syllables, which are not strictly measurable in English poetry. This is borne out by what Gascoigne writes in *Certayne Notes of Instruction*, § 4:

> We are fallen into suche a playne and simple manner of wryting, that there is none other foote used but one; wherby our Poemes may iustly be called Rithmes, and cannot by any right challenge the name of a Verse.
>
> (Gregory Smith, *Elizabethan Critical Essays*, Vol. I, p. 50)

Gascoigne, James VI and Harvey all spoke of *long* syllables without offering any but arbitrary means of determining length; Puttenham, most comprehensive of the theorists, was vague on quantity, and its suitability for English verse, for he wrote at the beginning of Book II, chapter III of the *Arte of English Poesie* (1589):

> Meeter and measure is all one, for what the Greekes called *Metron*, the Latines call *Mensura*, and is but the quantitie of a verse, either long or short. This quantitie with them consisteth in the number of their feete: and with us in the number of sillables.

Whenever a metrist used the term 'number' in such a context, the meaning was seldom arithmetical number, especially when the word was plural. Campion in his *Observations in the Art of English Poesie* (1602) defined the word clearly in the opening chapter:

> Number is *discreta quantitas* . . . When we speake of a Poeme written in number, we consider, not only the distinct number of sillables but also their value, which is contained in the length and shortnes of their sound . . . In a verse the numeration of the sillables is not so much to be observed as their waite and due proportion.

Most metrists were guilty of confounding terms such as *pause* and *caesura*. Campion's word for 'pause' in his *Observations in the Art of English Poesie* was *breathing*; and *caesura* usually meant, not a metrical division within the line, but a sense-pause marked by punctuation. What is now called *stress*, the metrists referred to as *accent*; and they carelessly spoke of long and short English accents, when they referred to stressed and unstressed syllables.

Gascoigne was not the only critic of the Renaissance to fail in perceiving a structural relationship between rhyme and alliteration, or in distinguishing *rhyme* from *rhythm* (§ 4 of *Notes of Instruction*). An interesting observation in William Webbe's *Discourse of English Poetrie* (1586) explains the derivation of *rhyme*:

> The falling out of verses together in one like sounde is commonly called, in English, Ryme, taken from the Greeke worde *Rhythmos*, which surely in my iudgement is verye abusivelye applyed to such a sence: and by thys the unworthinesse of the thing may well appeare, in that wanting a proper name wherby to be called, it borroweth a word farre exceeding the dignitye of it . . .
>
> (Gregory Smith, *Elizabethan Critical Essays* Vol. I, p. 267)

Gascoigne and other metrists counted the syllables in feet without appreciating the movement of verse within the line, and from one line to the next, which constitutes the true nature of rhythm. James VI in *Ane Short Treatise* (chap. II) commendably chose the word *flow* for 'rhythm', suggesting that it was halted by an excessive use of monosyllables. Strong stresses coming in immediate succession have the effect of retarding the tempo of a line. The first theorist who seemed to grasp the significance of verse rhythm, which he called 'numerosity', was Puttenham, in Book II of the *Arte of English Poesie; he* associated it with the musical effect of speech, and defined it as

> a certaine flowing utterance by slipper words and sillables, such as the toung easily utters, and the eare with pleasure receiveth. (Chap. VI)

The 'slipper sillables' were obviously ones that ran smoothly, not being overburdened with consonants, or which favoured the liquid and nasal consonants l, m, n. FLOW is, in fact, an admirable mnemonic for rhythm, whose components are Feeling, Lilt and Order of Words. English poetry before the seventeenth century was mainly of the fluid type. In the best poetry of the late sixteenth century, it had become clear that rhythm was an harmonious relationship between quantity, stress, and the meaning of the words.

Diction, as the effect of words, had been analysed by Aristotle, Longinus, Cicero, Horace, Dante, du Bellay and Ronsard; but in both Udall and Sidney the term is used as a synonym for 'word' (cf. *dictionary* 'an assemblage of words'); in English it came to mean 'word choice' or 'verbal style' only in 1700, when Dryden so defined it in the Preface to *The Fables*. Puttenham dealt with diction under the two heads 'Language' and 'Stile' in Chapters IV and V of his third Book (on 'Ornament'); he there defined style, admirably, as

> a constant and continual phrase or tenour of speaking or writing, extending to the whole . . . processe of a poeme . . . and not properly to any peece or member . . . a certaine contrived forme and qualitie, many times naturall to the writer, many times his peculiar by election and arte.

In Chapter XVII of the same Book, Puttenham deplores the seduction of epithets, even when apt, and adds:

> sometimes wordes suffered to go single do give greater sence and grace than words quallified by attributions.

Following Dante in *De Vulgari Eloquentia*, the Pléiade in France gave to poetic diction a special meaning of 'select, elegant language', the hall-mark of decorum in a vernacular poet, who sought for himself a niche in the classical tradition. This idea was present in Webbe's *Discourse of English Poetrie*:

> It is not onely a poynt of wysedome to use many and choyse elegant wordes, but to understand also and to set foorth thinges which pertaine to the happy ende of mans life. . . . a good and allowable Poet must be adorned with wordes, plentious in sentences, and, if not equall to an Orator, yet very neere him, and a special lover of learned men.
>
> (Gregory Smith, *Elizabethan Critical Essays*, Vol. I, p. 301)

On the subject of figurative language, the only Elizabethan to speak competently, though not particularly, was Puttenham in Book III, Chapter X:

> Figurative speech is a noveltie of language evidently (and yet not absurdly) estranged from the ordinarie habite and manner of our dayly talke and writing, and figure it selfe is a certaine lively or good grace set upon wordes, speaches, and sentences to some purpose and not in vaine, giving them ornament or efficacie by many maner of alterations in shape, in sounde, and also in sence . . .
>
> (Gregory Smith, *Elizabethan Critical Essays* Vol. II, p. 165)

Puttenham sees figures as being of three kinds: those that appeal to the senses (principally the ear and the eye), those that appeal to the mind (conceits), and those which are a combination of both in effect. He perceives an aesthetic function for figurative language, which is more than ornament, and recognizes the immediacy by which metaphor reaches the reader before meaning has done its work. It makes sensuous impressions real to the consciousness.

The qualities of poetic style that engaged the Ancients were perceptively treated by Sidney in the *Apology for Poetry* (1595), as in the following:

> If *Oratio* next to *Ratio*, Speech next to Reason, bee the greatest gyft bestowed upon mortalitie, that can not be praiselesse which dooth most pollish that blessing of speech, which considers each word, not only (as a man may say) by his forcible qualitie but by his best measured quantitie, carrying even in themselves a Harmonie.
>
> (Gregory Smith, *Elizabethan Critical Essays*, Vol. I, p. 182)

Gascoigne, Webbe and Puttenham thought that the innovations in English versification, for which Wyatt and Surrey were responsible, came largely from Italian poets and prosodists. Wyatt visited Italy in 1527, and the poets he studied were probably Serafino, Petrarch, Alamanni, Ariosto and Dante, in that order of importance. His tastes and capacities were not for narrative poetry, but for songs, sonnets, complaints and satires; what he wrote best was monologue based on personal experience. He had read Chaucer in Pynson's edition of 1526, and knew well the minor poems and *Troilus and Criseyde*. Chaucerian language he loved; but he found it necessary to break with many of Chaucer's verse traditions; he left the rhymed couplets of the *Canterbury Tales* to his disciple Surrey.

What attracted Wyatt to Chaucer, Italian and French poets was their diversity of stanza forms. He experimented with the rondeau and the sonnet, and may have been the originator of the Shakespearian or English form; he also introduced *terza rima* to England, chiefly from Alamanni, and used it with effect in his satires and expostulations. Wyatt is credited with no less than seventy different stanza forms; but the prestige he gave to versification was due mainly to his adaptation of English diction to popular pronunciation. Words in poetry he regarded as an exciting means to Renaissance wit. The metrical and stylistic reformation, of which he and Surrey were exponents, was established on the dominance of iambic measures in English poetry, and the recognition of rhyme, not as accessory ornament, but as the controlling medium in stanzaic verse. This reformation was appreciated by critics as diverse in time and method as Puttenham and Samuel Daniel:

> *Henry* Earle of Surrey and Sir *Thomas Wyat*, betweene whom I finde very litle difference, I repute them (as before) for the two chief lanternes of light to all others that have since employed their pennes upon English Poesie: their conceits were loftie, their stiles stately, their conveyance cleanly, their termes proper, their meetre sweete and well proportioned, in all imitating very naturally and studiously their Maister *Francis Petrarca*.
>
> (*Arte of English Poesie*, Gregory Smith, Vol. II, p. 65)

> All verse is but a frame of wordes confined within certaine measure, differing from the ordinarie speach, and introduced, the better to expresse mens conceipts, both for delight and memorie. Which frame of words consisting of *Rithmus* or *Metrum*, Number or measure, are disposed into divers fashions, according to the humour of the Composer and the set of the time. . . . As Greeke and Latine verse consists of the

number and quantitie of sillables, so doth the English verse of measure and accent. And though it doth not strictly observe long and short sillables, yet it most religiously respects the accent; and as the short and the long make number, so the acute and grave accent yeelde harmonie. And harmonie is likewise number; so that the English verse then hath number, measure, and harmonie in the best proportion of Musicke. Which, being more certain and more resounding, works that effect of motion with as happy successe as either the Greek or Latin. . . .

In an eminent spirit, whome Nature hath fitted for that mysterie, Ryme is no impediment to his conceit, but rather gives him wings to mount, and carries him, not out of his course, but as it were beyond his power to a farre happier flight. . . . Ryme, being farre more laborious than loose measures (whatsoever is obiected), must needs, meeting with wit and industry, breed greater and worthier effects in our language.

(*A Defence of Ryme* (1603), Gregory Smith, Vol. II, pp. 359–65)

Wyatt's strength was his good ear, lyrical brevity and avoidance of monotonous foot-patterns. At a time when poetry was diffuse and shapeless, self-discipline gave it a sense of form and symmetry. His metrical skill is not as derivative as some critics have believed. The use of cross-rhymes and refrains may be medieval; but Wyatt's practice is adapted to Tudor musical customs. Some lyrics surpass those of his Italian and French masters, even if insecure in the location of stresses and careless in rhythm. Rhythmical roughness seems to result from mischance, rather than method. The poems used in *Tottel's Miscellany* were often freely edited, by normalizing either the stresses or number of syllables, in order to accommodate them to late reforms in prosody; but the smoothing was seldom to their advantage. Part of the difficulty in scanning the verses of Wyatt is his borrowing from Romance languages, in which he assumes foreign pronunciation. Here is an example:

> And if the harme that I *suffre*
> Be runne to farr owte of *mesur*
> To seke for helpe any further
>   What may it availl me?
>   . . . .
> Ye, tho the want of my relief
> Displease the causer of my greife,
> Syns I remain still in *myschiefe*
>   What may it availl me?

> (Poem 58, K. Muir, *Thomas Wyatt* 1949, p. 44–5)

The words *suffre*, *mesur*, and *myschiefe* clearly require a French pronunciation; but the third rhyme-word in the first stanza, *further* is of Old English origin, and had to be tortured to bring the stress onto the final syllable.

A diction for English poetry, distinct from that of prose, begins with Wyatt; there is a fondness for archaic words, for participial adjectives, for rhetorical figures and cumulative effects (many cited by Puttenham), as well as for syntactical inversion. Vices of Augustan diction, such as periphrasis and excessive antithetical structures, were incipient in Wyatt. The artificial, rather extravagant conceits of Spenser were in profusion in Italian poetry, especially Serafino, and became the most overworked figures in the Elizabethan sonnet sequences. Wyatt's language was not without faults of ornamentation, which only the control of Shakespeare and resistance of Donne were able to moderate. Italian artificiality was observably different from the aureate disharmony of Hawes and Lydgate, which bespoke a polysyllabic fervour derived from medieval poetics.

The graceful court humanist, Surrey, was a neo-classicist, more correct, but not a better poet than Wyatt; the bulk of his archaic vocabulary (for instance, words like *clepinge* and *egal*) he owed to reading Chaucer in Thynne's edition of 1532. The adjectival suffix *-en* in words like *golden*, the prefix *y-* before past participles, later cultivated by Spenser, and the use of *for* with prepositional infinitives, to express purpose, were characteristics of his language. In his translation of some early books of Vergil's *Aeneid* (made about 1541, published 1554), he experimented in blank verse of a stiff and formal kind, the diction being indebted to Gavin Douglas's rhymed version, then in manuscript.

Surrey's celebrated smoothness, in the lyric poems before the *Aeneid*, was due partly to his skilful use of alliteration and antithesis, partly to the comparative regularity of his verse. As he was first made available in print in *Tottel's Miscellany*, some credit for this should go to the editors, who improved his manuscripts. But that Surrey himself had a sensitive ear for rhythmical balance and sound modulation is demonstrated in sonnets translated from Petrarch, in which he adapted the Italian form to the English one. The major part of his work consisted of translation or adaptation. His metrical experiments with biblical paraphrase (in unrhymed alexandrines) were full of promise.

Surrey, like Wyatt, studied Italian poets alongside of Latin, because they were the first to cultivate the vernacular Tuscan as a fit medium for poetry. In the sixteenth century the enthusiasm for the Italian vernacular, initiated by Cavalcanti and Dante, had been stimulated by Bembo, who stressed the influence of Latin Augustan poetry. Neither Wyatt nor Surrey understood the Italian linguistic background well enough to be able to use it in English as fruitfully as Milton.

Having spent a year at the French court (1532–1533), Surrey was well acquainted with the writings of the Pléiade. He, Sackville and Spenser, who have affinities with each other, improved the syntax and movement of English poetry. Surrey's service was the good taste with which he combated the diffuse and prolix in poetic language, to give his style meaningful lucidity. For the existing state of the language, this was more valuable than gifts of imagination. He became the undidactic Horace of Tudor poetry, as poem 40 (a translation from Latin) shows:

> Marshall, the thinges *for to* attayne
> The happy life be thes, I finde:
> The riches left, not got with payne;
> The frutfull grownd; the quyet mynde;
> The *equall* frend; no grudge nor stryf;   5
> No charge of rule nor governance;
> Without disease the helthfull life;
> The howshold of contynuance;
> The meane *dyet*, no *delicate* fare;
> *Wisdom* joyned with simplicitye;   10
> The night dischargéd of all care,
> Where wyne may beare no soverainty;
> The *chast wife wyse*, without debate;
> Such sleapes as may begyle the night;
> Contented with thyne owne estate,   15
> *Neyther wisshe death* nor fear his might.

(Jones's edition, p. 34)

These iambic tetrameters are modulated by trochaic substitutions in the first foot of lines 1, 10, 16. The variations of tempo in lines 9 and 16 are notable: *dyet* has the stress (as in French) on the last syllable; animation of the line is secured by the extra unstressed syllable in *delicate*. In line 16, the movement is retarded by the introduction of a spondee (*wisshe death*) in the second foot, thereby bringing the poem to a satisfying close. Note the archaic employment of the preposition *for* in the first line, the Chaucerian use of *equall* (meaning 'constant' or 'unchanging') in line 5, and the poetical placing of the noun *wife*, in line 13, between its attributes.

A virtue of Surrey's style is its relative freedom from artificial conceits. His vocabulary, generally, is in common use; the sporadic archaism is a nuance of the polite scholar, along with an occasional inversion. He avoids two-syllable rhymes, in favour of monosyllables or stressed final syllables. By combining periodic sentence-structures with syntactical enjambement, he secures a line to line rhythm. These arts produced the mellifluousness of movement which Surrey handed on to Sackville, Sidney and Spenser. Whether he writes heroic, elegiac or love poetry, his style is dignified, and often tender; he has a better sense than Wyatt of the organic unity of mood and idea in lyric poetry. The following stanzas from poem No. 27 depict life in a sixteenth-century country house at Windsor:

> The *s*tatelye *s*ales; the ladyes bright of hewe;
> The *daunces short*, long tales of great *d*elight,
> With wordes and lookes that tygers could but rewe,
> Where eche of us did plead the others right.
>
> With *s*ylver dropps the meades yet *s*predd for rewthe,
> In active games of nymbleness and strengthe
> Where we dyd *s*trayne, trayléd by *s*warmes of youthe,
> Our tender *l*ymes, that yet shott upp in *l*engthe.
>
> The secret groves, which ofte we made resound
> Of *p*leasant *p*laynt and of our ladyes *p*rayes,
> Recording soft what grace eche one had found,
> What hope of spede, what *d*red of long *d*elayes.
>
> The wyld *forést* the clothéd holtes with grene,
> With raynes avald and swift *ybrethed* horse,
> With crye of houndes and mery blastes bitwen,
> Where we did chase the fearfull hart a force.
>
> The secret thoughtes impasted with such trust,
> The wanton talke, the dyvers chaung of playe,
> The frendshipp sworne, eche promyse kept so just,
> *W*herwith *w*e past the *w*inter nightes a*w*aye.

Eache *s*tone, alas, that dothe my *s*orowe rewe,
Retournes therto a hollowe sound of playnt.
Thus I alone, where all my fredome grew,
In *p*ryson *p*yne with bondage and restraynt.

(Jones's edition, pp. 25–6)

The unobtrusive use of alliteration, the sense of vowel values, the selection of consonants is pleasing. The first stanza (second line) illustrates Surrey's restrained use of inversion; while the second stanza has syntactical enjambement in the last two lines. The last stanza employs, quite naturally, a periodic structure of sentence, inhibited in the preceding ones, because the poem had been a catalogue of Surrey's youthful recollections.

Word compounding was popularized in poetic diction by Nicholas Grimald, whose generous allocation of space in *Tottel's Miscellany* is not without significance. Phrases such as *peeplepesterd London*, *dartthirling death* and *Swanfeeder Themms* (echoes of *Beowulf*) were harmful to the language of Renaissance poetry. Grimald was a purist who admitted French borrowings only if they were vogue words. The archaisms come from the same medieval sources as Wyatt's and Surrey's. Though his diction favours a native vocabulary, its art is obtrusive. He suggested many poetical words to Spenser, such as *bewray*, *pight*, *tene*, *drent*, *stound*. Grimald illustrated a growing tendency in poetry to dislocate word order (the rhetoricians called it *hysteron proteron*) and to indulge in eccentric figures for the sake of embellishment. The following extract from a Funeral Song to his late mother shows this clearly:

You mee embraced, in bosom soft you mee
Cherished, as I your onely chylde had bee.
Of yssue fayr with noombers were you blest:
Yet I, the *bestbeloved* of all the rest.
Good luck, *certayn forereadyng* moothers have,   5
And you of mee a speciall iudgement gave.
Then, when firm pase I fixéd on the ground:
When toung *gan* cease to break the lispyng sound:
You mee *streightway* did too the Muses send,
Ne suffered long a loyteryng lyfe to spend   10

(Poem 162, H. E. Rollins's ed. of *Tottel's Miscellany*, Harvard, 1928)

The lines are end-stopped, except in the first couplet, where the enjambement is unnatural in word order. Unnecessary departures from normal syntax became a vice in Grimald and his associates in Tottel's anthology. So did the figure *cacosyntheton*, 'awkward transposition of words', such as noun preceding adjective. That this was unnatural in prose by Caxton's time is shown by his corrections in printing Trevisa's *Polychronicon*, though there were exceptions in traditional phrases, such as *heir apparent*.

In Grimald's lines the examples of word compounding and Chaucerian archaism are commonplace. The latter are the periphrastic use of *gan* to form the preterite (line 8), and the negative *ne* immediately before the verb. *Certayn* (5) has the stress on the final syllable, as in French.

The advice of du Bellay, Ronsard and the Pléiade concerning the vernacular in poetry did not prevent corruption of the English language by insensitive rhetoricians. Examples were frequent in the borrowings that came from industrious translators. Poets indulged freely in *enallage*, the rhetoricians' appropriation of one part of speech to serve as another. Shakespeare was to employ both licences with effect; but lesser poets were not so successful. Here there are instances in Grimald's use of the past participle *agilted* and Wyatt's *vapord*. The Tudor period abounded in adjectives and adverbs formed by the addition of suffixes that did not always match the etymology of the root-words. Wyatt used *consumingly, returnable* and *waky*, and *Tottel's Miscellany* has many new adjectives ending in *-ish* and *-like*. Du Bellay had advocated the growth of a poet's vocabulary by invention, but did not state the methods to be used. The Pléiade would scarcely have encouraged forms like *waky*, or compounds such as *people-pestered*; nor would du Bellay, in advising the revival of old words, have tolerated epithets such as *swan-feeder Thames*. Innovation implies taste, and the minor poets of *Tottel's Miscellany* were not writers of real sensibility.

The variety poetry required was not always served by native archaisms and foreign borrowings. Gascoigne exhorted poets to do fundamental brain-work, instead of pandering to the rhetorical fashions. In *Certayne Notes of Instruction* he condemned far-fetched conceits, unsubtle use of alliteration, and adjectives placed after the noun, except for the purpose of rhyme. Any licence that offended against natural syntax was to be discouraged.

In 1563 Thomas Sackville, a narrative and descriptive poet, prepared the way for Spenser in the Induction to *The Mirror for Magistrates* (1559); he also composed the additional *Complaint of Henry Duke of Buckingham*. The *Mirror* was a work of didactic and moral purpose, depicting episodes in the lives of some leading figures of history. It was planned as a sequel to Lydgate's translation of Boccaccio, *The Fall of Princes*, though in technical accomplishment some parts of the *Mirror* are superior to Lydgate's. Spenser wrote in *The Faerie Queene* of its 'golden verse, worthy immortal fame'. The praise that was universal among Elizabethan and Jacobean poets was largely due to the purity of Sackville's diction, the vigour of his imagination, and the dignity with which he depicted human emotions.

The mannerisms, conceits and word compounding, were all in the taste of the Tudor Renaissance, and not inconsistent with real merits. Sackville's style was entirely loyal to the precepts of the Pléiade. In sentence structure and vocabulary, he leaned heavily upon Chaucer, Wyatt and Surrey; and he acknowledged his debt in the stanzas that appear in the St John's College manuscript of the *Complaint of Buckingham*. The facts of Sackville's life point to his being the complete humanist. He employed unusual words sparingly, and aimed at ideals of humanist 'elocution' expressed by Ascham, Wilson and Cheke.

In spite of the orthographical differences of the manuscripts, Sackville was the first poet to spare the modern reader uncertainties about the incidence of stress, the pronunciation of vowels in weak inflexional syllables, and the sounding of final -*e* for metrical purposes; for example, in the following lines from the *Complaint of Buckingham*:

O trustles world I can accus*en* none
But fals*e* fayth of commontie alone

The difficulty that remains is occasional stress variation in polysyllabic words of Romance origin. Sackville used almost as many French words as Chaucer; and he accepted the current belief that poetry, as artifice, had the right to a special diction.

Sackville was more skilful than the earlier generation of poets in modulating rhythms by bringing together monosyllabic adjectives and nouns, in phrases such as *the hard colde ground*

(*Buckingham*, 265). His elevated and erudite style was not a natural language, but its impact on heroical poetry of the last quarter of the sixteenth century can be seen in that of Spenser and Marlowe. He was a zealous improver of his Chaucerian stanzas, to make them less laboured and smoother in rhythm. In revision, he removed archaisms, replacing such words as *meads* with *fields* and *sparhaak* with *falcon*.

Sackville's Vergilian strain, enriched by his study of the Latin *Aeneid*, as well as the versions of Gavin Douglas and the Earl of Surrey, can be observed in the following passage, which illustrates his metrical sureness, epic similes and tragic pathos; to these elements the Elizabethan dramatists turned for inspiration in their history plays. The text is from the poet's manuscript, *The Complaint of Henry Duke of Buckingham*, in St John's College, Cambridge, reprinted in Marguerite Hearsey's edition of 1936. Shakespeare's *Venus and Adonis* is rich in similes of the chase, such as this of the 'stricken deer', one of the commonest allegorical images of the late Middle Ages:

> Lyke to the dere that striken with the dart
> withdrawes him self in to some secret place
> and feling grene the wound about his hart
> startles wyth panges till he fall on the grasse
> and in gret feare lies gasping ther a space   5
> furth braieng sighes as though ech pang had brought
> the present dethe which he dothe drede so oft
>
> So we depe wounded with the blooddie thought
> and gnawing worme that greved our conscience so
> never toke ese but as our hart furthbrought   10
> the strained sighes in witnes of our wo
> such restles cares our fault did well beknowe
> wherwith of our deserved fall the feares
> in everie place rang deth within our eares. (p. 69)

The lines are end-stopped, but discreetly modulated by variation of vowels, which contrasts with the repeated consonants l, d, t, th, g, b and s. Interpreting the verse, one needs no more than four primary stresses in each line; their position is subtly changed to avoid monotony of rhythm. The stress is invariably located on semantically significant words. *Furth braieng* (6) (the adverb preceding the predicate) is a favourite poetical order in Sackville. For *present* (7) one should understand *ever-present*. The rhyme *brought/ oft* in lines 6 and 7 is worth noting.

In rhyme royal, Sackville wisely favoured masculine rhymes. The movement is determined by the roving stresses, the alliteration of initial, medial and final consonants, the Sackville ear for vowel play, and the syntactical linking of each stanza with the next. The syntax follows the sense, so that little punctuation is necessary. Metrical pauses are so disposed that they are never far from the centre of the line, usually after the second foot. The music of the verse is designed to suggest the nuances of effective reading.

Sackville was not an original poet, but a polished amateur in the Chaucerian tradition, both French and Italian. His language was thoroughly in accord with the diction approved by the consensus of practising poets. He thus became the best exemplar of the school of court poets who, conscious of their own limitations, wisely forsook poetry for politics. In this school he was, for a time, the most talented versifier, using rhetorical figures of thought to stylize the written language of poetry. The diction of poetry in the reign of Elizabeth was never the language of spoken English; and this was true even of drama, whether romantic or classic. Both the court comedies of Lyly and *The Alchemist* of Ben Jonson demonstrate the tendency to artificiality. A writer of talent sought 'to utter the mynde aptly, distinctly and *ornately*'. (Richard Sherry)

Similar tastes in poetry actuated the work of Sir Philip Sidney. He affected to reject Petrarch's far-fetched conceits in *Astrophil and Stella* (sonnet XV), but was unable to shed the handicap of a poetic dominated by rhetoric. Equally he repudiated 'table talke' as a suitable language for poetry. Sidney had discussed the development of English poetry with Fulke Greville and Dyer, in a society they founded, called the Areopagus. In the romance *Arcadia*, he experimented with verse and stanza forms, and included some poems in quantitative measures. A more concise, logical and orthodox syntax, with less archaism, was Sidney's contribution to the language of poetry. This sonnet from *Arcadia* is in a style that became deservedly popular among metaphysical love poets of the seventeenth century:

My true love hath my hart, and I have his,
By just exchange, one for the other giv'ne.
I holde his deare, and myne he cannot misse:
There never was a better bargaine driv'ne.
His hart in me, keepes me and him in one,
My hart in him, his thoughtes and senses guides:
He loves my hart, for once it was his owne:
I cherish his, because in me it bides.
His hart his wound receavéd from my sight:
My hart was wounded, with his wounded hart,
For as from me, on him his hurt did light,
So still me thought in me his hurt did smart:
  Both equall hurt, in this change sought our blisse:
  My true love hath my hart and I have his.
      (Poem 45, p. 75, Clarendon Press, edit. W. A. Ringler, 1962)

The French influence upon Sidney's language is found in the refined word choice recommended by the Pléiade; the neo-Platonic matter and Petrarchan form of poetry he owed to the Italian poets. The liberal culture is that of Castiglione's *The Courtier*. The mixture of styles in Sidney's poetry is characteristic of the chameleon-like humanist, who stabilized his art through classical scholarship.

The Areopagus met at the Countess of Pembroke's country house at Wilton, or at Sidney's home, Penshurst, and discussions were informal. Sidney's personal aims in reforming English poetic diction were clear: poise and control of style were its fundamentals; form and content were to be ideally matched. In his *Defence of Poesie* (1595), also known as his *Apologie*, he complained of the lack of 'poetical sinews' in all but a few sixteenth-century writers; the test, he said, was to transpose their content into prose to extract the meaning; 'it will be found', he wrote, 'that one verse did but beget another'. Without rhyme, most of the poems would be 'a confused mass of words'. (*Elizabethan Critical Essays*, ed. Gregory Smith, Vol. I, p. 196)

A more detailed account of the defects of contemporary poetry was given in *Astrophil and Stella*:

You that do search for everie purling spring
  Which from the ribs of old Parnassus flowes,
   And everie floure, not sweet perhaps, which growes
Neare thereabout, into your Poesie wring;
You that do Dictionarie's methode bring

Into your rimes, running in rattling rowes:
  You that poore Petrarch's long deceased woes,
With new-borne sighes and denisend wit do sing;
  You take wrong waies, those far-fet helpes be such,
  As do bewray a want of inward tuch:
And sure at length stolne goods do come to light
  But if (both for your love and skill) your name
  You seeke to nurse at fullest breasts of Fame,
Stella behold, and then begin to endite.

                (Sonnet XV, Clarendon edition, p. 172)

Sidney, though he possessed the 'inward tuch', was sometimes guilty of the 'denisend wit' and 'far-fet helpes' he decried. He tried too many forms and techniques to attain the *energeia* of true imagination; he thus became the delighted amateur of letters that most aristocrats were content to be.

What Sidney did accomplish was a simpler vocabulary and a normal order of words. To practise this simplicity he began by composing metrical versions of the *Psalms* in English. Experiments in quantitative measures were largely to satisfy himself that they were not adaptable to the natural music of accentual speech. English stanzaic verse, like Italian, encouraged a different, but equally satisfying, rhythm for the ear; there were infinite possibilities of counterpoint. Sidney's principles of modulation were not quite as mechanical as Sackville's; he placed a-symmetrical feet in strategic positions, and set up a tension between the rhythm and the metrical pattern. He used spondees more freely than any of his predecessors, e.g. *Astrophil and Stella*, Sonnet XXXIX:

Cóme sléepe, ô sléepe, the certaine knot of peace,
Take thou of me smoóth píllowes, sweetest bed

Trochaic inversion in mid-line is seen in

With shíeld/ of proófe/ shiéld mĕ/ from oŭt/ thĕ preáse/

No less than half of Sidney's poems were written in the Petrarchan sonnet form, in which he freely adapted the sestet to his own rhyme schemes. He tried his hand at many combinations of multiple rhyme; and as his style matured, he found in feminine rhymes another useful means of varying the rhythm of sonnets. The limits of his art in this form are those of the sentiments, and of the conventions within which he wrote.

Sidney is a paradox of insincere emotions and honest technique; form and matter are often in accord, but feeling and expression ring false. His poems are redolent of the suppressed emotions he hints at in the following lines:

> For vertue hath this better lesson taught,
> Within my selfe to seeke my onelie hire:
> Desiring nought but how to kill desire.

> (Poem 31, Clarendon edition, p. 161)

The pastoral and introspective elegiac tone was, perhaps, a convention ill-chosen by the poet. *Astrophil and Stella* contains his best work, because here he rejects the paraphernalia of complaints, and preserves the convention of the Italian sonnet's form.

Polysyllables and inversions of syntax are not frequent in Sidney's poetry; but there are exceptions, for instance in this trochaic experiment:

> *Him* great harmes had taught much care,
> Her faire neck *a foule yoke* bare.

again:

> *Wept* they had, alas the while,
> But now teares themselves did smile,
> While their eyes by love *directed*,
> *Enterchangeably reflected*.

> (Eighth song, Clarendon edition, p. 218)

Sidney was fond of using adjectives with personal pronouns, e.g. *poor me;* of forming verbs from nouns and adjectives, by means of the prefix *be-*, e.g. *becloud* and *bedim*. In figurative word compounding he imitated French and Italian models. Such phrases as *sun-stayning excellencie* are wit-conceits, rather artificial in their effect; but they are less common in the poetry than in the elaborate prose of *Arcadia*. He repressed the taste for Chaucerian archaisms, created by Wyatt, Surrey and Sackville, except in retaining the medieval adverb *eke;* he gave to the word *affectation* the meaning it now possesses.

Sir John Harington's translation of Ariosto's *Orlando Furioso,* consisting of no less than 4100 stanzas, was published in 1591. The form, *ottava rima* (stanzas of eight iambic pentameters rhymed a b a b a b c c) was used by Keats in *Isabella* and Byron in *Beppo;* it lends itself to witty narrative, when masculine rhymes give way to feminine. Here is an example:

> Why did not nature rather so provide,
>   Without your help, that man of man might come
> And one be grafted on anothers side,
>   As are the Apples with the Peare and Plome?
> But Nature can no meane, nor rule abide,
>   But still she must exceed in all or some:
> Easie it is, the cause thereof to render,
> Nature her selfe, is of the womans gender.
>
> (Book XXVII, stanza 97)

Harington, a godson of Queen Elizabeth, was regarded as one of the most versatile and talented wits at Court. Ariosto was the leading European narrative poet of the sixteenth century, the counterpart of the lyrical Petrarch. The translation was said to be a task imposed by the Queen when, for some misdemeanour, Harington was rusticated to his country estate in Somerset. On the title-page Harington classified the poem as 'heroicall verse'; and in the 'Briefe Apologie of Poetrie', which serves as a Preface, he described the verse as a stately, uplifting measure that allures the reader to 'swallow and digest the holsome precepts of Philosophie'. Poetry must not, however, deliver its matter *as* philosophy:

> The truth well saw'st with pleasant verse hath wonne
> Most squeamish stomakes with the sugred stile
>
> (Tasso, *Jerusalem Delivered*)

Word order, vigour of phrase and harmony were, for Harington, the requisites of good poetry. Translators were not, for him, mean versifiers, but among the best refiners of the English language. His distinction between prose and verse was typical of the man:

> Prose is like a faire greene way, wherein a man may travell a great iourney and not be wearie; but verse is a mirie lane, in which a mans horse pulls out one leg after another with much adoe, and often drives his master to (a)light to helpe him out.
>
> (*Orlando Furioso*, 1591, p. 266)

Although *Orlando Furioso* deals with feats of arms and love, Harington's translation is not in the grand style, but the familar, which provided his wit with finer opportunities. The devices used, among them proverbial wisdom and contemporary slang, puns and extended similes, were thoroughly Elizabethan. He employed marginal notes before they came to the academic hands of Ben Jonson. He was the first poet-critic to reveal a knowledge of Aristotle's *Poetics*, especially its views on epic poetry. He claimed that Ariosto's work was superior to Vergil's *Aeneid* in moral influence, because of its Christian background.

The diction Harington evolved for his translation was far from being the epic language of classical models; it had closer affinities to the style of Lyly:

> But as the Palme, the more the top is prest,
> The thicker do the under braunches grow,
> Ev'n so the more his vertue was opprest,
> By hard attempts, the brighter it did show.
>
> (Book XXXIV, 41)

Harington's facility of movement was superior in artifice to Lyly's; he was equally resourceful in the use of alliteration and assonance. He anticipated Butler of *Hudibras*, Swift and Byron in the cleverness of his polysyllabic and internal rhymes. The complexity of his patterns shows that he had leisure, and took pains in preserving the graceful ease of his Italian original, as this stanza shows:

> The *p*recious time that fools mispend in *p*lay,
> The vaine *a*ttempts that never take *e*ffect,
> The vows that sinners make, and never pay,
> The *c*ounsells wise that *c*arelesse men neglect,
> The fond desires that lead us *o*ft *a*stray,
> The *p*rayses that with *p*ride the heart infect,
> And all we loose with follie and mispending,
> May there be found unto this place ascending.
>
> (Book XXXIV, 74)

Much criticism of Harington's verse turns on the nature of satirical epic, for which Ariosto was responsible. The *Epigrams* reveal a loyal courtier disillusioned with contemporary politics. In *Orlando Furioso* he did justice to the Italian poet's irony, allegorizing the age of chivalry. The dignified sweep of the narrative had no small influence on the writing of Spenser's *Faerie Queene*.

* * *

Most sixteenth-century English poets were conscious of the need for a proper language for poetry, while remaining faithful to the compromise between rhetoric and poetic initiated by Chaucer. They acknowledged the authority of the Ancients, but looked for antecedents in English to justify their artistic principles. Many ideas of the Pléiade had been anticipated by Chaucer, who perpetuated a taste for archaisms. Pastoral poetry was partly an attempt to simplify language after the aureate diction of Hawes. There was no immediate reformation of diction with the advent of Wyatt and Surrey; a continuity exists in the language of poetry similar to that found by R. W. Chambers for prose.

Among English poets of the Renaissance the need was felt to embellish diction by means of figurative language and sentence-structure. Puttenham was not deterred by the profusion of classifications, but sought to codify figures under less complex headings. The Elizabethans saw the writer as a self-conscious artist, whose task was to avoid the language of the common man, and transform speech for literature. Ben Jonson wrote in *Discoveries* that 'the Poet is the neerest Borderer upon the Orator'.

The Mirror for Magistrates is now looked upon as a museum piece; but it made a contribution to the accentual patterns of English verse. Some of the earlier poems were transitional; alliteration still marked the staves sporadically, and the line was divided by its caesura. But the poems by Baldwin, Churchyard and Dolman, were very different in rhythm from Sackville's; there was, for instance, frequent use of clashing primary stresses. Dolman accommodated his metre to the dramatic demands of the thought.

The 'sugared' diction began with Surrey and Sackville, and culminated in Sidney, Spenser and Shakespeare's *Venus and Adonis*, *Lucrece* and the *Sonnets*. These poets invented a technique of harmony that kept its place for more than three hundred years. The taste could not have prevailed so long, but for progressive improvements in the modulation of the line, and the sequence of lines, both in stanzaic and blank verse.

An important principle of modulation is that the metrical pattern should not become absolute. Prosodists, such as Gascoigne, said that verse was *rough*, if the expression distorted the metre and gave primacy to the meaning. The play of opposing forces was seen by Elizabethan poets to provide infinite variety of movement within the line. Once the reader appreciated that part of the 'maker's' art was to pass off the irregular as regular, he no longer perceived a line as 'rough', nor even as licentious. For no offence to the ear is given, as long as the modulation accords with the natural emphasis of the phrasing.

Another advance was made by the dramatists, who saw the merit of making variations from the pattern coincide with the line's significant words, particularly if these conveyed an emotional change. The tone of poetry is partly conditioned by the rhythmical structure that re-inforces the sense; this feeling is probably in the mind of the poet before he comes to the actual words.

Pope believed that rhyme was not only an important factor in rhythm, but an instigator of ideas; 'words have no character as rhymes, until they become points in a syntactic succession'. A word at the end of a verse line, whether in rhyme or not, has rhetorical importance; the extra unstressed syllable of feminine endings spells a loss of power, as the pitch of the voice is lowered. The rising pitch of English iambic measures for some reason gives dignity to the language as spoken.

Important to the tempo of a verse line is the disposition of the vowels and consonants. Rapid transition in articulation from back to front vowels, or sequences of consonants of widely different organic production, retard the motion with which rhythm should flow. More than two clashing stresses in succession have a similar effect.

The later Elizabethan poets give no critical indication whether their technique was consciously or unconsciously achieved. But the theorists of the next two centuries based prosodic conclusions on the practice of poets such as Spenser, Marlowe, Shakespeare and Jonson, who considered the problems of speaking the vernacular in the theatre or before scholarly audiences. The heart of their discoveries may be summed up thus: What is commonly called accent in poetry is, in reality, a combination of stress and pitch. Pattern is the perception of a constant or abstract ideal in verse; rhythm is the variable of natural speech that modulates it. Modulation is secured in three principal ways, by changing the number of syllables in the line, the number of stresses in the line, or the order of the stresses in particular feet that form the staple of the line pattern. These changes are accompanied by variation in the position of pauses within the line.

There is another way of modulation relevant to complex stanza forms, such as the sonnet, and to blank verse – the continuation of sense or syntax into the next line. This was to become a significant structural element in the Miltonic epical paragraph. In Pindaric odes, with lines of variable length, the rhythm is better modulated by the expansion or contraction of syllables in the line; or by the introduction of trisyllabic feet into a dominantly dissyllabic pattern.

There were no defections from the above principles of English poetry, until the metrical experiments of Browning, Bridges and Hopkins in the latter half of the nineteenth century.

IV

SPENSER

Sidney and Spenser had poetical affinities; they were fruitful experimenters in *Arcadia* (first version completed about 1581) and *The Shepheardes Calender*, published in 1579. It is difficult to determine the chronology and precedence of many of their important poems. Spenser's language is in the courtly tradition of Surrey and Sackville; it was different in style from the naturalistic school of poetry, foreshadowed in Wyatt and Raleigh.

Spenser, like Chaucer, wrote best in narrative or descriptive verse. A licence he could not perpetuate was Chaucer's sounded final *-e*; except as a deliberate archaism, this was suppressed in Spenser's poetry after *The Shepheardes Calender*. The language of the early eclogues gave promise of the craftsmanship fulfilled in *Epithalamion* and *The Faerie Queene*.

Throughout his career, Spenser coined words, and borrowed from Chaucer, Lydgate and Skelton. He used figures freely for sententious or decorative effect. From Chaucer he learnt the art of linking stanzas by rhetorical methods. Occasionally, as in the first of the *Four Hymns*, where the language is expository, Spenser's diction ceases to be stylized; the unmistakable sign of this is the use of fewer conceits.

Critics who have written that Spenser is most vulnerable in his style, have not analysed its logical and simple structure, especially in complex stanza forms. Epithet-hunting, for which Spenser was indebted to Sidney, is often an attempt at condensed conceit. The decorous style Spenser evolved before 1594 showed an especial gift for modulating the tonality of words; it abounds in descriptive adjectives, compound epithets, archaisms and syntactical inversions.

Spenser read Ovid and Vergil, but learnt more from French and Italian poetry than from the classical tradition. His mellifluousness was stimulated by the Pléiade poets who encouraged melancholy reflections on the mutability of life. Edward Kirk, Spenser's friend and commentator on *The Shepheardes Calender*, remarked upon the poet's 'pithiness of expression'. Spenser can be expansive in matter, but he is seldom diffuse. His meaning is perspicuous because he is usually free from tortuous subordinate constructions.

The gentle onward movement of his verse would have been impossible without long preparation for his art. It is untrue of Spenser's diction as of Chaucer's that 'he writ no language'; for he fabricated a language that was studied by poets for several hundred years. Like Chaucer, he aspired to be both a learned and a popular poet.

The Shepheardes Calender
(*November Eclogue, omitting stanzas 2, 7, 13 and 15*)

Spenser divided the eclogues into three groups, Plaintive, Recreative and Moral (including Satirical). The ten-line stanzas selected, from Colin Clout's elegy 'November', belong to the first group. The eclogue was considered by Kirk to be the finest, and the passage (from *Minor Poems*, Variorum edition, Vol. I) illustrates Spenser's impact on the language of *Lycidas* and elegiac writing for three centuries:

Up then Melpomene thou mournefulst Muse of nyne,
Such cause of mourning never hadst afore:
Up grieslie ghostes and up my rufull ryme,
Matter of myrth now shalt thou have no more.
For dead shee is, that myrth thee made of yore.   5
   Dido my deare alas is dead,
   Dead and lyeth wrapt in lead:
     O heavie herse,
Let streaming teares be pouréd out in store:
     O carefull verse.   10

Why doe we longer live, (ah why live we so long)
Whose better dayes death hath shut vp in woe?
The fayrest floure our gyrlond all emong,
Is faded quite and into dust ygoe.
Sing now ye sheapheards daughters, sing no moe   15
   The songs that Colin made in her prayse,
   But into weeping turne your wanton layes,
     O heavie herse,

Now is time to dye. Nay time was long ygoe,
  O carefull verse.   20

Whence is it, that the flouret of the field doth fade,
And lyeth buryed long in Winters bale:
Yet soone as spring his mantle hath displayd,
It floureth fresh, as it should never fayle?
But thing on earth that is of most availe,   25
 As vertues braunch and beauties budde,
  Reliven not for any good.
   O heavie herse,
The braunch once dead, the budde eke needes must quaile,
  O carefull verse.   30

She while she was, (that was, a woful word to sayne)
For beauties prayse and plesaunce had no pere:
So well she couth the shepherds entertayne,
With cakes and cracknells and such country chere.
Ne would she scorne the simple shepheards swaine 35
 For she would cal hem often heame
  And give hem curds and clouted Creame.
   O heavie herse,
Als Colin cloute she would not once disdayne.
  O carefull verse.   40

But nowe sike happy cheere is turnd to heavie chaunce,
Such pleasaunce now displast by dolors dint:
All Musick sleepes, where death doth leade the daunce,
And shepherds wonted solace is extinct.
The blew in black, the greene in gray is tinct,   45
 The gaudie girlonds deck her grave,
  The faded flowres her corse embrave.
   O heavie herse,
Morne nowe my Muse, now morne with teares besprint.
  O carefull verse.   50

Ay me that dreerie death should strike so mortal stroke,
That can undoe Dame natures kindly course:
The faded lockes fall from the loftie oke,
The flouds do gaspe, for dryéd is theyr sourse,
And flouds of teares flowe in theyr stead perforse. 55
 The mantled medowes mourne,
  Theyr sondry colours tourne.
   O heavie herse,
The heavens doe melt in teares without remorse.
  O carefull verse.   60

The feeble flocks in field refuse their former foode,
And hang theyr heads, as they would learne to weepe:

The beastes in forest wayle as they were woode,
Except the Wolves, that chase the wandring sheepe:
Now she is gon that safely did hem keepe.   65
    The Turtle on the baréd braunch,
    Laments the wound, that death did launch.
        O heavie herse,
And Philomele her song with teares doth steepe.
        O carefull verse.   70

The water Nymphs, that wont with her to sing and daunce,
And for her girlond Olive braunches beare,
Now balefull boughes of Cypres doen advaunce:
The Muses, that were wont greene bayes to weare,
Now bringen bitter Eldre braunches seare: 75
    The fatall sisters eke repent,
    Her vitall threde so soone was spent.
        O heavie herse,
Morne now my Muse, now morne with heavie cheare.
        O carefull verse.   80

O trustlesse state of earthly things, and slipper hope
Of mortal men, that swincke and sweate for nought,
And shooting wide, doe misse the markéd scope:
Now have I learnd (a lesson derely bought)
That nys on earth assuraunce to be sought: 85
    For what might be in earthlie mould
    That did her buried body hould,
        O heavie herse,
Yet saw I on the beare when it was brought,
        O carefull verse.   90

But maugre death, and dreaded sisters deadly spight,
And gates of hel, and fyrie furies forse:
She hath the bonds broke of eternall night,
Her soule unbodied of the burdenous corpse.
Why then weepes Lobbin so without remorse?   95
    O Lobb, thy losse no longer lament,
    Dido nis dead, but into heaven hent.
        O happye herse,
Cease now my Muse, now cease thy sorrowes sourse,
        O ioyfull verse.   100

Unwise and wretched men to weete whats good or ill,
We deeme of Death as doome of ill desert:
But knewe we fooles, what it us bringes until,
Dye would we dayly, once it to expert.
No daunger there the shepheard can astert: 105
    Fayre fieldes and pleasaunt layes there bene,

The fieldes ay fresh, the grasse ay greene:
   O happy herse,
Make hast ye shepheards, thether to revert,
   O ioyfull verse.   110

Word Choice: The diction has an air of unreality, for nothing like this had yet appeared in English. *Grieslie ghostes* and *rufull ryme* (3) might be described as poeticisms, even alliterative clichés; there are many of this kind: *fayrest floure* (13), *clouted Creame* (37), *dolors dint* (42), *kindly course* (52), *mantled medowes* (56), *feeble flocks* (61), *balefull boughes* (73), *fyrie furies* (92). Spenser announced in his Argument that he wrote within the Theocritan convention, which explains why the epithets are decorative rather than functional. By functional epithets is meant adjectives that clarify or refine the meaning; substantive and adjective enrich each other, as in lines 81–2:

   O trustless state of earthly things, and *slipper* hope
   Of mortal men (The adjective is found in the eleventh century;
   slippery was used by Coverdale in the Bible of 1535).

Spenser's diction unhappily tends to be assessed by his choice of epithets. The conventional linking of adjective and noun became a habit of style in his successors and imitators, as late as Thomson. The mass of epithet-couplings therefore deserves scrutiny. The remainder are: *mournefulst Muse, heavie herse, streaming teares, carefull verse, better dayes, wanton layes, woful word, simple shepheards, happy chere, heavie chaunce, gaudie girlonds, faded flowers, dreerie death, mortall stroke, faded lockes, lofty oke, sondry colours, former foode, wandring sheepe, baréd branch, water Nymphs, greene bayes, bittre Eldre, braunches seare, fatall sisters, vitall threde, heavie cheare, trustless state, earthly things, mortal men, markéd scope, earthlie mould, buried body, dreaded sisters, deadly spight, eternall night, burdenous corpse, happy herse, ioyfull verse, ill desert, fayre fieldes, pleasaunt layes, fieldes ay fresh, grasse ay greene.* These are mainly trisyllabic combinations, whose metrical pattern is / x /.

Excluding the epithets in the repetitive refrains, there are thus 54 nouns qualified by descriptive adjectives in 110 lines. This proportion is high, and the epithets, in all but half-a-dozen cases, seem handy and unimaginative; 22 were chosen for their

C

alliterative effect. In general, the adjectives lack evocative power.

In Spenser's eclogue the primitive goatherd is the putative author of the elegy. But more important is the iconography. Kirk noted that the poem was an imitation of Clément Marot's *Complaint* of 1531 'upon the death of Loys the frenche Queene'. Marot's emblem (a thumb-nail engraving) bore the punning motto *La mort ny mord* ('Death biteth not'). Archaisms are skilfully woven into the description in order to secure the effect of verbal tapestry.

Two key words occur in the double refrain. The figurative use of *herse* for 'a solemn obsequy' (Kirk's gloss) is peculiar to this eclogue, and may imply a misconception of the meaning of the fourteenth-century word, according to the OED 'the frame to carry the coffin of a noble person, and its decorations'. The other word *carefull* means 'full of care', not 'painstaking'; Spenser's is the earlier significance.

Alliteration is a device practised by young poets who are learning the rudiments of technique. Spenser associates alliteration with smoothness, as in lines 56–7: 'The mantled medowes mourne,/ Theyr sondry colours tourne.' The couplet illustrates Spenser's partiality for eye-rhyme (spellings that satisfy visually as well as phonetically). The past participle *mantled* has little effective meaning; the verb was rarely used before Spenser, and Shakespeare employed it later with considerably more imagination.

The conceits in this couplet and the next two stanzas are worth considering. Spenser says that Death has undone the course of Nature; that Autumn is the 'dying' season of the year; the pasturage has lost its appeal for the flocks, hence their feebleness and the danger of attack from beasts of prey. With mythological licence, the Fates are likened to avenging Furies, *fyrie* because they are from infernal regions. At the end of the poem, *heavie herse* becomes 'happy herse', and *carefull verse*, 'ioyfull verse'; this symbolizes the belief that Death, rightly understood, is not a tragedy, but a fulfilment.

The largest class of words that calls for study is the archaic. Uncertainty about Elizabethan dialect forms makes it difficult to distinguish poeticisms from dialect words, which Spenser introduces to give *The Shepheardes Calender* a pastoral tone.

Heame (36) is a sixteenth-century variant of *hame* (home); *sike* (41) seems to be a pseudo-dialectal word adopted by Spenser to represent the genuine forms *silk* or *sich* (such). *Swincke* (82) was from the OE strong verb *swincan*, and in good literary use until the sixteenth century, when it became archaic and dialectal. That this verb is still found in Shelley and R. L. Stevenson confirms its perpetuation in the language of poetry. In the verbs *reliven* (27), *sayne* (31), *doen* (73), *bringen* (75) and *bene* (106), the interest lies in the *-en* or *-ne* inflexion. It marks the infinitive in the rhyme-word *sayne*, which was archaic by the sixteenth century, and survived into the seventeenth only as a poetic licence; in the other verbs the inflexion indicates the present indicative plural. These endings can only be explained as dialectal archaisms which Spenser cultivated for their supposed poetic value in the eclogues. *Woode* (63), meaning 'mad', was in current literary use until the early seventeenth century, but was confined to dialects after that date.

The poeticisms are themselves difficult to classify etymologically: there are neologisms as well as archaisms. For instance, Spenser seems to have coined the past-participle *tinct* (used by Keats), and the verb *embrave* ('adorn'), in lines 45 and 47; while *burdenous*, according to the OED, was the invention of Sir Thomas More, and was supplanted by *burdensome* in the seventeenth century, as in the King James Bible (1611).

The apparent archaisms are so numerous that they are here listed with appropriate comment. Some words, such as *dint*, *dolor*, *wonted*, *launch* and *revert*, appear to be archaisms when used by Spenser, but they are not so historically:

Grieslie (3) 'horrifying, repulsive'. In poetic use since the twelfth century, and found in Chaucer.

Rufull (3) 'sad', thirteenth century word favoured by Chaucer and Malory.

Yore (5) 'long ago', derivative of OE *gear*.

Store (9) 'plenty', from O.Fr. *estor*, used since Caxton and now obsolete. Poets from the fifteenth to the eighteenth centuries found it useful as a rhyme-word.

Moe (15) 'more'; already archaic in Spenser's time, but retained for the sake of rhyme.

Ygoe (19) 'ago', a spelling variant and rhyme-word cultivated by Spenser.

Flouret (21), diminutive of *flour* (flower), first cited in OED from the *Romaunt of the Rose*.

Bale (22) OE *bealu*, dates from the eleventh century, and was in literary and poetic use until the nineteenth century.

Pleasaunce (32 and 42) 'pleasure-giving quality', was borrowed by Chaucer from Old French in *Troilus and Criseyde*. According to the OED it has always been archaic; it sounded more poetical than 'pleasantness', and was used later by Byron and Tennyson.

Couth (33). This OE past tense of *can* was still in literary use in the earlier sixteenth century, alongside of *coud*, since the fourteenth century. The modern spelling with *l* was erroneously introduced in the first quarter of the sixteenth century, by analogy with *would* and *should*. Archaic uses occurred sporadically in the seventeenth century.

Dolor (42) 'pain', from O.Fr., came into English in the fourteenth century, and was not essentially poetic until Spenser used it.

Dint (42) 'blow', has the same origin as *dent*, an OE word. The *i*- spelling is now archaic, except in the weakened sense of the phrase *by dint of* ('means'). *Dint* does not seem to have become a poetical word until the eighteenth century.

Wonted (45). This new past participle of *wont* began to appear in English in the middle of the fifteenth century, and was used in verse and prose until the nineteenth century (by Tennyson and Carlyle). It was at no time a genuine poeticism.

Besprint (49) 'besprinkled'. The past participle derived from OE *besprengan* was usually *besprent*. The latter form was in common use in ME literature, but became a poeticism in the hands of Chaucer, Spenser, Milton, Wordsworth, Browning and Morris.

Launch (67) 'pierce or cut', from the beginning of the fifteenth century (French borrowing). The modern form is *lance*. The word was in common use in verse and prose, until the seventeenth century, when it became dialectal, in this sense.

Eke (76) 'also', OE *eac*. The word, in Spenser's spelling, dates from the thirteenth century, and was archaic by the late sixteenth century, after which it fell into disuse.

Maugre (91) 'in spite of'. As a preposition, the word was commonly used from the thirteenth century, but apparently became archaic in the sixteenth, surviving until the nineteenth century.

Hent (97) 'carried off', of OE origin. The word was in general use in the Middle Ages, but already archaic by Spenser's time.

Weete (101) 'know'; used by Surrey in 1547, and according to the OED archaic from its inception, though still used poetically by Patmore and Swinburne in the nineteenth century.

Expert (104) 'to experience', a rare fifteenth century Latin borrowing, used by Hakluyt and Spenser; but the verb did not survive the sixteenth century.

Astert (105). The meaning of this pseudo-transitive verb is 'befall', not 'startle'; (*shepheard* is the relic of an old dative). Spenser's spelling in *F.Q.* III.2.29 is *astart*, used intransitively, and signifying 'start up'. The word, dating from the thirteenth century, was already obsolete when Spenser used it, apparently for the last time.

Ay (107) 'always, ever'. This was a Northern dialect word which came into general poetic use in the thirteenth century. It was used by both Chaucer and Langland, and survived as a literary poeticism until the nineteenth century.

Revert (109) 'go back'. This fifteenth century Latin borrowing, in Spenser's sense, did not survive the eighteenth century.

The list demonstrates that, although Spenser cultivated poetic archaism, he was not prodigal as compared with many of his contemporaries, and could not have been aware that many words were already becoming, or would become, obsolete. Shakespeare's power over language was such that his exotic borrowings excite little comment, even although they are not always understood. Spenser's are often obtrusive, because, in his phrasing and syntax, he strove to be a poet of plain statement; his borrowings remind us of Chaucer or Malory. He believed that a liking for antiquity in words was in good taste, that there was no necessary connection between archaism and artificiality.

Movement: The 'emotional colouring' of Spenser's verse goes deeper than word choice; it is sensed at the level of metrical and rhythmical resources. The melodic subtlety is conveyed through the collocations of sound and the modulations. Milton emulated Spenser's painstaking symbolization of poetic ideas through their movement and dress; in both poets the cult became an aesthetic religion resembling the art of ballet. The smoothness and decorousness of the verse are due, in part, to the leisurely progression, in part, to the phonetic sensibility with which Spenser weaves the verbal threads of allegory.

A study of Spenser may have been at the root of Graves's assertion that a poet's skill is to be seen in his mastery of sibilants. Spenser's patterns of intonation, stress and rhythm, and his pleasing junctures (transitions between adjacent linguistic units) is a study for the phonetician. Within the framework of predominantly iambic measures, Spenser is a symmetrical poet, solicitous for internal harmonies of vowel and consonant; he is tasteful, if ornamental, in verbal modification, and particularly adept at linking whole rhythmical groups. He prefers, for this reason, to confine the sense to the individual line, as do all poets skilled in rhetoric. In the November elegy, modulation of the line hardly ever disturbs the metrical regularity. Spenser obviously preferred the final pause to the tentative rest within the line.

The stanza form in the November elegy is original and designed for its simple scheme of modulation:

Line	Metrical feet	Rhyme pattern
1	six	a
2	five	b
3	five	a
4	five	b
5	five	b
6	four	c
7	four	c
8	two	d
9	five	b
10	two	d

In structure, the verse is reminiscent of Old English, the *staves* or principal stresses being marked by alliteration. Occasionally this sounds contrived, as in line 61:

The feeble flocks in field refuse their former foode

The vowels of the rhyme-words and stressed syllables are invariably long in long lines. For relief, the rhyme-vowels of the short lines are often short. The dominant consonants are the liquids (l, m, n, r), the sibilant s, and the rounded bilabial w.

The punctuation is generally an aid to the reading; colons demarcate rhythmical units, and are more significant than the grammatical periods. The elocutionary pauses occur most persistently at the end of the second and fourth lines, less frequently at the end of the seventh; nearly all the other lines are end-stopped by lesser pauses, such as the comma. The comma, unless it marks off a relative clause or an appositional phrase, is not necessarily indicative of a medial pause. Enjambement occurs only twice, namely at lines 15 to 16, and 81 to 82. The regularity of the metre is emphasized by the position of medial pauses, usually after the second foot, e.g. in lines, 1, 3, 5, 14, 19, 24, 29, 31, 43, 45, 49, 54, 62, 64, 71, 79, 82, 84, 91, 92, 97, 99, and 107. Thus, one fifth of the lines have the medial pause in precisely the same place. The variations are in:

7 Dead/ and lyeth wrapt in lead (pause in middle of first foot)

11 Why doe we longer live (ah why live we so long) (A pause is not uncommon in the middle of the six-foot line; but Spenser skilfully varies the position of the caesura in other stanzas, to avoid monotony).

15 Sing now ye shepheards daughters sing no moe (pause in middle of fourth of foot)

81 O trustlesse state of earthly things/ and slipper hope (pause after fourth foot)

89 Yet saw I on the beare/ when it was brought (pause at the end of third foot)

96 O lobb/ thy losse no longer lament (pause at the end of first foot)

104 Dye would we dayly/ once it to expert (pause in middle of third foot)

109 Make hast ye shepheards/ thether to revert (pause in middle of third foot)

Spenser's trochaic substitutions (inversions of stress) are after pauses, and usually in the first or third foot, e.g.

Initial inversion: lines 1, 4, 6, 7, 11, 15, 21, 31, 49, 79, 84, 95, 97, 99, 104

Medial inversion (third foot): 53, 55, 93, 103

Thus initial inversion of stress is five times as frequent as medial inversion, which is constantly in the third foot. Line 7 looks like a thorough-going trochaic inversion. My reading, however, is:

Déad/ anᵡd lý/eᵗʰ wrápt/ iñ leád

If the line is a four-footer, the better reading is with the monosyllabic foot at the beginning and not at the end of the line; the reason is that *dead* in line 7 immediately repeats the final word of the preceding line (*anadiplosis*) and is thrown into desirable prominence by a long pause immediately after it, to compensate for the absence of a short syllable.

Modulation by defection or increase of syllables is rare in Spenser; extra syllables can usually be normalized by elision (but this is a matter of abstract metrics, not of locution):

> 16 The songs that *Colin* made in her prayse (where Colin is monosyllabic by elision of unstressed *i*)
> 19 *Now is* time to dye. Nay time was long ygoe (Elision of unstressed *i* produces the reading *Now's*)

The word *heavens* is traditionally monosyllabic or disyllabic in Elizabethan poetry:

> 59 The *heavens* doe melt in tears without remorse (a disyllabic use occurs in line 97)

There are only two instances of an excessive foot (five feet instead of four):

> 17 But into weeping turne your wanton layes
> 97 Dido nis dead, but unto heaven hent

There is a single instance of a defective syllable:

> 96 O Lobb thy losse no longer ∧ lament (this may be a scribal error)

but two lines lack a whole foot:

> 56-7 The mantled medowes mourne,
> Theyr sondry colours tourne.

Spenser makes occasional use of the unstressed extra syllable *-ed* of past participles, e.g. *pouréd* (9), *dryéd* (54), *baréd* (66), *markéd* (83). His greatest licence is to eke out the syllables of a line by the use of the periphrastic auxiliary verb *do, did*. This occurs in lines 21, 43, 54, 59, 65, 67, 69, 73, 83, 87 (10 times in 110 lines).

That assonance of the vowels is the most significant factor in rhymes is shown in lines 1/3 *nyne/ryme*; 42/44/45 *dint/extinct*, *tinct*; 92/94 *forse/corpse* (in sixteenth century English, the *p* was sometimes pronounced, but usually mute, *corse* being an alternative spelling). *Warke* (12) was a Northern and Scots dialect form of *work*, cultivated by Spenser for the sake of rhyme; so was the spelling *heame* to rhyme *Creame* (36). In lines 26/27 *budde/good*, 56/57 *mourne/tourne*, 61/63 *foode/woode/* and 66/67 *braunch/launch*, the rhymes were good in Spenser's time. There are no feminine rhymes in the elegy; perhaps this contributes to the dignified tone.

In Spenser's expansive network of sound combinations, the metrical form sets up a tension at significant points in the stanza. It is usually between the musical effect and the lexical meaning of the words; and this some prosodists have regarded as counterpoint. Word choice in composition turned on careful adjustment of the sense to the stanza pattern, involving many resources of rhetoric. Spenser gained a reputation as the most skilful rhetorician before Pope.

English theories of metre were the product of the Renaissance verse tradition. Roger Fowler in 'Prose Rhythm and Metre' (*Essays on Style and Language*), describes the Spenserian concept of counterpoint as follows:

> The grammar of a poem may reinforce or subtly resist the division into lines which is implied by other features – number of syllables, end-rhyme, arrangement on the printed page. . . . There are degrees of enjambement, degrees of tension between the metre, wanting to make a break, and the grammar, wanting to be continuous.
>
> We can hardly talk about 'counterpoint' unless there is an extensive and *regular* relation between grammatical and metrical patterns. . . . We find our best examples of this in the blank verse of Shakespeare's later plays. Kermode speaks of 'straddled lines', sentences or clauses which start in the middle of one line and end half-way through the next, forming a pentameter within two pentameters.
>
> A number of English constructions fit the iambic pattern: for example, prepositional phrases (*for me*); monosyllabic subject plus monosyllabic verb (*ye fight*); auxiliary plus verb (*does give*); certain two-syllable words (*alarmes*). Lines which utilize these grammatical patterns exclusively have their iambic metrical patterns reinforced: there is coalescence of the prose rhythm and the metre. They are used either to establish the metre against which the prose rhythm is later to play to produce syncopation (so Spenser often puts them at the beginnings of stanzas) or for special effects: *I burne, I burne, I burne, then loud he cryde*. (Ibid, pp. 85–96)

The relevance of this to Spenser's poetic development may be seen in the November elegy. Lines 29, 45, 89, and 107 are examples in which *diæresis* occurs (monosyllabic words coinciding with metrical syllables). Isochronism (the regular spacing of stresses) is, however, common in this poem, and syncopation is of a non-disruptive kind, as in lines 9, 12, 14, 21, 24, 25, 34, 44, 65, 66, 74, 84, 85, 89, 94, 97, 103, 109. Spenser's most effective way of changing the beat is by stress inversion. But he is just as partial to an initial spondee, in which the relative weight of stresses is undetermined, e.g. *Up then* (1), *sing now* (15). Other examples are to be found in the first foot of lines 3, 23, 33, 41, 43, 49, 50, 73, 79, 89, 95, 99, 106, 109. The device is effective in slowing the tempo to suggest the tone of a funeral dirge.

Grammatical Structure: Though mannerisms of Chaucer and Lydgate do occur, and the effect is important in Spenser, the stylistic force of archaism has been overstated. Archaisms are more significant for accidence than for syntax. Syntax is modified in Spenser to suit the theory of diction and the needs of stanza forms. In relation to the practice of his time, Spenser's grammar is orthodox, less latinized than that of most contemporaries, and contains fewer anacoluthic constructions.

Placing the object or complement before the verb is the commonest deviation from normal syntax in the November elegy; there are 13 examples in the passage. E.g.

   1 (rhyme) Thou mournefulst Muse *of nyne* (normal order 'of nyne Muses')

   2 (rhyme) *Such cause of mourning* never hadst afore (object before main verb)

   4 (rhyme) *Matter of myrth* now shalt thou have no more (object before main verb)

   5 (rhyme) For *dead* she is, that *myrth thee* made of yore (double inversion)

Inversions of the subject are not so frequent:

  54   The flouds do gaspe, for dryed is *their source*
  89   Yet saw *I* on on the beare
  103   But knewe *we* fooles, what it us brings until (conditional clause inversion)
  104   Dye would *we* dayly

Other inversions worthy of note are

45 The blew in black, the green in gray, *is tinct* (the final words would normally come after *blew*)

106 *Fayre fieldes and pleasaunt layes* there bene (inversion of complement)

Inversion was considered by Puttenham in Book III ('Of Ornament') in *The Arte of English Poesie*. He devoted Chapter XIII to 'figures of disorder' and Chapter XXII to 'intolerable vices'. He did not approve of excessive *hysteron proteron* ('the preposterous') to which category the order of line 5 belongs, as well as 'our gyrlond *all emong*' in line 13. The placing of adverbs and adverbial phrases was more flexible, and subject to the exigencies of rhyme and metre; e.g. *buryed long* (22), *for her girlond* (72), and *thether to revert* (109).

Puttenham equally disliked *cacosyntheton* ('the misplacer', unusual transposition of words or phrases) among which he included the placing of adjectives after nouns, e.g. *braunches seare* (75). The two epithets *bitter* and *seare* were separated by Spenser to bring the latter at the end of the line, for rhyme and symmetry. The Spenserian practice was lasting, and found as late as Keats and Tennyson.

Spenser's syntax is usually uncomplicated in its employment of subordinate clauses; they are used mainly to qualify nouns or to modify verbs. The sixth stanza begins with the conventional expletive of regret *Ay me* (= It is a sad reflection); the remainder of line 51 may be regarded as a makeshift noun clause. In eleven relative clauses, Spenser prefers the defining link-word *that* (5, 16, 25, 52, 64, 65, 67, 71, 74, 87); but in these adjectival clauses the relatives are apparently non-defining in 52, 64, 71, 74. *Whose* (12) is used because the relative is possessive.

Stanzas four, five and nine are truly Spenserian in structure. Line 31, with an interpolated principal clause, begins with an anticipatory *She*, whose predicate is *had no fere* (32). Five words are morphologically archaic, *sayne* (infinitive), *couth* (preterite), *Ne* (negative particle used immediately before the verb), *hem* (dative plural, third personal pronoun) and *Als* (conjunction.) The passive construction in lines 41–2 is a syntactical variation, dictated by the desired rhyme-words. Spenser's deft use of linking conjunctions to join verse-line clauses is one of the sources of his smooth versification; *For* and *Yet* (86 and 89) are good instances. He does not often use present participial constructions, such as *shooting wide* in line 83. *Nys* (85 = there is no) is a typically archaic negative compound.

The omission of unemphatic parts of speech is characteristic of Spenser's style, as of Milton's. E.g.

2   Pronominal subject *thou* omitted (carried over from previous line)
19   Pronominal subject *it* omitted before *is*
23   Comparative adverb *as* omitted before *soon*
51   Indefinite article *a* omitted before *stroke*
19, 25, 61, 63, 102   Definite article *the* omitted.

Spenser's morphological and syntactical taste is thus antique, deliberately indulged to give the diction a Chaucerian tone. Yet the structure of the verse is predominantly that of plain statement, linked by the versification as much as by conjunctions. The rhythm is modulated not a little by the placing of adverbial modifiers and inversion, sometimes of subject and verb, but more frequently of object and verb. Like most Renaissance poets he omits articles and personal pronouns to secure regularity of metre; and he makes use of syllable expansion or contraction for the same purpose. His versatility in grammatical modulation exceeds that of predecessors; but the resources are consonant with the simplicity of the versification, which is his greatest contribution to poetry.

Meaning: Elegiac poetry, preserving the conventions of Greek pantheism and pastoralism, was destined from the beginning to sound artificial. First came an invocation to one of the Muses; then questionings about the justice of Fate; and finally the consolations of philosophy or (in the Renaissance) those of the Christian religion. The classical formula required the mourning figures to masquerade as shepherds in rustic settings, and this was not in keeping with genuine springs of grief. The Greek conception of natural beauty, moreover, was inconsistent with the romantic aura current in the Elizabethan period. Pantheism presumed a sympathetic association of nature with the dead; the dying year symbolized universal decay. Spenser's Platonic idealism unconvincingly accepts the immortality of the soul;

the poet (when lamented) is no longer dead, but translated to a more enduring supernatural world.

Spenser's poetry conflates allegory (fabulous disguise) with pastoral; but he also withdraws from the world to the Puritan resources of his imagination. Throughout *The Shepheardes Calender* the poems are imitative, eclectic in matter and manner; they are too experimental to have arrived at a personal style. C. H. Herford, in the introduction to his edition of *The Shepheardes Calender* (1895), spoke of 'beautiful redundancies', and said that Spenser 'lingers luxuriously over the sweetness of his own music'.

What Spenser sought, beyond this melody, was a dignified antiquity, such as the painter Giotto created; what Malory achieved in prose. Because pastoral poetry was ancient, he admitted more archaisms than in his other poems. His language in *The Shepheardes Calender* became a word craft, created in defiance of critical and rhetorical dicta at Cambridge. Spenser agreed with the Pléiade that the poet, without giving offence, should be free to modify the genius of a language, as his own talent dictated.

Spenser's intention and meaning in the November eclogue may be seen in some effects of the figurative language. The Alexandrine in the first line of each stanza sets the pace, feeling and tone; line 9 sums up the stanza's significance.

In the first stanza, the invocation is not only to Melpomene, the Muse of tragic poetry, but to the Furies of the tragedians, and to the spirits of the dead.

The second stanza expresses doubts about the value of life. The image in line 11

Whose better dayes death hath shut up in woe

recalls the rape of Persephone by Pluto; hence the reference to garlanding flowers in the following line. The invocation to shepherds' daughters (15–17) explains Colin's (Spenser's) *lament* for Dido, to whom he had previously offered songs of praise. *Wanton layes* means 'undisciplined' lyrical verse of anapaestic type. The ninth line is significant in having no relation to the invocation. 'Now is time to dye' refers to the passing of the year, November being the month that marks the advent of Winter.

In the third stanza questions on the meaning of death continue; lines 21-4 describe the pagan cycle of fertility. The figure in line 22, with its cross-alliteration,

And lyeth buryed long in Winters bale

suggests, through the Old English word *bale* (torment, evil, death) that Winter is also a time of suffering. In 'spring his mantle hath displayed' (23), the word *mantle* is a conventional image denoting the advent of a new season. Spenser in lines 25-9 does not accept death as a good. In the sustained Platonic metaphor, virtue is the branch, beauty the bud of the tree of life (Dido's). The poet suggests that virtue and beauty are one; if the former goes, the latter must follow.

Stanza four is biographical; *was* (31) means 'lived, existed'. The choice of words, with the repetition in parenthesis, is designed for cross-alliteration between *s* and *w*, as well as vowel variation. The sequence of the vowels or diphthongs in this line reveals eight different qualities in twelve syllables; the sibilant *s* is continued in the three semantically important words of the next line. *Cracknells* (35), a fifteenth century French borrowing meaning 'crisp biscuits', is used with onomatopoetic effect. Lines 36 and 39 introduce an English note: the allegorical aristocratic lady had no antisocial prejudices towards the rustic class. This being a factual stanza, there is no live metaphor.

The fifth stanza returns to the symbolism of mourning. *Chaunce*, the emphatic word in the first line, has the original meaning of 'accident' or 'misfortune'. The phrase *dolors dint* ('sad blow') in line 42 carries euphemistic overtones; elegant periphrasis had poetic value for Spenser. More effective, however, is the personification in line 43:

All Musick *sleeps*, where death doth leade the daunce.

The figure of the 'dance of death' introduces personal metaphor. The pastoral lament of the shepherds seems out of place in the songless underworld of death (44). The liturgical colours *blew* and *greene* in 45 (blue for celestial things, green for hope) suggest brightness of life transformed to drabness of death (black and grey). The gay flowers that Dido garlanded for joy fade in sympathy, and adorn her grave (46-7). Spenser, the Platonist, was partial to the pathetic fallacy.

Images of personification continue in the first five lines of stanza six (51–5), the most pleasing being in lines 53–4:

The *faded lockes* falls from the loftie oke,
The *flouds do gaspe*, for dryéd is their source.

The 'faded locks' are autumn leaves; 'flouds do gaspe' is a Spenserian conceit. Imagination has to concede too much to the comparison, especially in lines 55, 56 and 57. The last reads

The heavens do melt in teares *without remorse*.

This must refer to unabating November showers. The entire stanza, and the next two, are extended conceits to depict sympathetic nature partaking in the universal woe.

Elizabethan readers must have delighted in far-fetched personifications, such as flocks that 'hang theyr heads' and 'learne to weepe' (62); for modern tastes these conceits are quaint fancies, of pictorial interest only. There is a comic note in line 63:

The beastes in *forest* wayle as they were *woode*

This may be an intentional pun, known to the rhetoricians as *antanaclasis*. Line 67 suggests that the lady 'snatched away in beauty's prime' did not die a natural death. The language at this point is romantically vague, possibly insincere. Philomele (the nightingale) 'steeping' her song in sympathetic tears does not sound a natural note.

The Nymphs, the Muses and the Fates, with their mythological offices, are introduced in stanza eight to preserve the conventions of Greek and Latin elegiac traditons.

Stanza nine returns to a philosophic strain, in which Spenser is happier. Kirk speaks of these ten lines with admiration for their moral wisdom and passionate feeling. In line 83,

And shooting wide, doe misse the markéd scope

the image is drawn from archery, 'marked scope' being the target. But the metaphors do not reveal the philosophic concept of death. Lines 86, 87 and 89 present the only difficulties of textual interpretation; the awkward word is the past participle *buried*. The meaning seems to be: 'the body of Dido, being buried, contained all virtues earthly mould bestowed; I still could see her on the bier, when it was carried to the grave.'

What happens to the virtuous soul after death is disclosed by Spenser in the tenth stanza. Life has been a battle to avoid the Fates, the Furies (instruments of evil) and the gates of Hell (91–7); but the meritorious soul escapes from the grossness of the flesh, and ascends to heaven. Why, then, should mortals, like Lobb, who loved Dido, lament? The song of despair should be a song of joy.

The poet concludes that man is unwise to attempt to know the difference between good and evil. He looks upon death as a punishment for sins; but if, despite his folly, he could foresee his ultimate destiny, man (in the words of Plato's *Phaedo*) would face death daily, in order to taste its benefits, such as the absence of fear. Death is a kind of canonization, a return to Elysian fields. The thought underlying the poem shows it to be a curious blend of paganism, Platonism and Christian belief in the sanctity of the soul. The words embody liturgical rather than philosophical truths.

The double refrain of the November elegy, separated by an intervening pentameter, is lyrically effective, but often inconvenient to the syntactical development of the thought. The intrusion is most noticeable where the language is philosophical, not pictorial.

Rhetorical Devices: The elegy abounds in rhetorical figures, such as formulae of repetition (which Spenser called 'turns'), amplifications and metaplasms (word transformations).

Figures of Repetition:
Anaphora, a sequence of clauses or phrases beginning with the same word, was a favourite with Spenser. Puttenham called it the figure of 'report'. E.g.

> 1 and 3   *Up* then Melpomene . . ./ . . ./ *Up* grieslie ghostes and *up* my
> rufull ryme

Anadiplosis, in which the first word of a new clause or line repeats the last word of the preceding clause or line, Puttenham called the 'redouble'. E.g.

> 6 and 7   Dido my deare alas is *dead,*/ *Dead* and lyeth wrapt in lead

Ploce is the recurrence of the same or a derived word, in one or more verse lines, with other words intervening. The meaning is 'plaiting', and the intention emphasis. E.g.

> 15 and 16 *Sing* now ye shepheardes daughters, *sing* no moe/ the *songs* that Colin made
> 31 *She* while *she was*, (that *was* a woful word . . .)

Repeated *was* carries also a suggestion of *paronomasia* (play upon words), and has the double function of noun and verb.

Chiasmus contains the same words in parallel clauses, but in inverted order. E.g.

> 11 Why do *we* longer *live*, (ah why *live we* so long)
> 49 *Mourne nowe* my Muse, *now mourne* with teares besprint

Asyndeton is a scheme of phrases, short clauses or sentences in parallel construction, employing no conjunctions. E.g.

> 71–5 *The water Nymphs, that wont* with her to sing and daunce,
> And for her girlond Olive braunches beare,
> *Now* balefull boughes of Cypres doen advaunce;
> *The Muses, that* were *wont* greene bayes to weare,
> *Now* bringen bitter Eldre braunches seare:

Note the balanced structure of definite article, adverb *now*, relative *that* and verb *wont*.

Schemes of thought and amplification:
Epanorthosis creates the illusion of conversation by simple statement or question, which is then repeated in stronger or more precise terms. Often, but not always, the modification is in parentheses. E.g.

> 11 Why doe we longer live, (ah why live we so long)

Three figures are actually used in this line, *chiasmus*, *epanorthosis* and *erotema* (see below).

> 19 Now is time to dye. Nay time was long ygoe

Ecphonesis (Latin *exclamatio*) arouses attention by simulating a cry of emotion, especially wonder or admiration. E.g.

> 51 Ay me that dreerie death should strike so mortall stroke
> 81 O trustless state of earthly things

Erotema (Latin *interrogatio*) is now called 'rhetorical question', because an answer is not expected. Vehemence of feeling was thought to be added to the idea. E.g.

21   Whence is it, that the flouret of the field doth fade?
95   Why then weepes Lobbin so without remorse?

Apostrophe implies 'turning away' from the language of discourse to address a particular person or deity. Spenser invokes the Muse in this fashion. E.g.

49   Morne nowe my Muse, now morne with teares besprint

(cf lines 79, 99, 101 and 109. Spenser in this elegy favoured apostrophe in the ninth line of the stanza.)

Epiphonema (Latin *acclamatio*) sums up in a pithy dictum the final conclusion of the poet's questioning. E.g.

102–4   We deeme of Death as doome of ill desert:/ But knewe we fooles, what it us bringes untill,/ *Dye would we dayly,* once it to expert.

Comparatio. Rhetoricians distinguished between the comparison of things like or unlike, and simile, in which a poet discovers a nonce similitude, appropriate to his thought or feeling; except for the purpose of the simile, the things compared are quite dissimilar. The following is an example of *comparatio*:

23–7   Yet soone as spring his mantle hath displayed,/ It [the blossom] floureth fresh, *as it should never fayle?*/ But thing on earth that is of most availe,/ *As vertues braunch and beauties budde,*/ Reliven not for any good

Metaplasms: Among the word transformations (by addition or loss of a syllable), only three need here be considered. Metaplasms were poetic licences phonetically justified by contemporary habits of speech.

Aphæresis, the sacrificing of a letter or syllable, may be actual or implied:

19   Now *is* time to dye. Nay time was long ygoe (the metre requiring 's)
101   Unwise and wretched men to weete what*s* good or ill

Syncope is the loss of a letter or syllable in the middle of a word. E.g.

1   Up then Melpomene thou mournefulst Muse of nyne
          ^

Synalœpha is the coincidence of two vowels, the first being elided. E.g.

85 That *nys* on earth assurance to be sought (coalescence of *ne* and *is*. Cf *nis*, 97)

Rhetoric covered all aspects of language, because, as becomes clear from the above analysis, they cannot be separated. Its merit was to make the study of language a means to practical criticism. Its demerit was the pseudo-scientific exhaustiveness with which it sought to classify and define every phenomenon, however mean its influence on the art of writing.

Rhetoric could be a disservice to Spenser in cantos that contained much dialogue, and in Sonnets, Complaints and Elegies, such as *Daphnaida*, where the form is patterned and intricate. To recognize Spenser as a dedicated rhetorician is fundamental to understanding the method he adopted. He believed in the sustained figurative power of allegory, as a way of conveying truths to readers who could penetrate the disguise of appearance; allegory began with the names of figures that people his best poems. Lobbin stands for the Earl of Leicester in the November elegy; and there is some unfathomed purpose in calling the lady elegized Dido.

Prosopopoeia (Mother Hubberd's Tale), lines 1033–63

The style is 'meane, yet carrieth some delight', wrote Spenser in his Dedication to Lady Compton. *Meane* describes the middle, familiar style of the rhetoricians, in which proverbial wisdom was popularly approved. The irony calls for rhetoric *in extenso;* but it is found mainly in the set speeches, the intention being to expose the morality of leading politicians. The mingling of allegory with caricature is in Chaucer's vein; hence the sub-title *Mother Hubberd's Tale;* but the satire lacks his subtlety of humour.

Probably written in 1579–80, the work was re-touched ten years later for publication by William Ponsonbie in 1591. An addition of about one hundred lines, from 643, apparently accompanied this revision. *Prosopopoeia* implied 'slanted personification'; in the fable human qualities are attributed to the Lion, the Ape and the Fox, whose characteristics are boldness, greed and cunning.

Quoting from Chaucer's *Troilus and Criseyde*, *Prologue* and *The Clerk's Tale*, Spenser also drew upon two Italian works,

Castiglione's *The Courtier* and Machiavelli's *The Prince*. The language is that of the ecclesiastical eclogues in *The Shepheardes Calender*, and resembles in its tone parts of *Piers Plowman* and Lyndsay's *Satyre of the Threi Estatis*.

> Nay (said the Foxe) Sir Ape you are astray:
> For though to steale the Diademe away
> Were the worke of your nimble hand, yet I
> Did first devise the plot by pollicie;
> So that it wholly springeth from my wit: 5
> For which also I claime my selfe more fit
> Than you, to rule: for government of state
> Will without wisedome soone be ruinate.
> And where ye claime your selfe for outward shape
> Most like a man, Man is not like an Ape   10
> In his chiefe parts, that is, in wit and spirite;
> But I therein most like to him doo merite
> For my slie wyles and subtill craftinesse,
> The title of the Kingdome to possesse.
> Nath'les (my brother) since we passéd are   15
> Unto this point, we will appease our iarre,
> And I with reason meete will rest content,
> That ye shall have both crowne and government,
> Upon condition, that ye ruléd bee
> In all affaires, and counselléd by mee;   20
> And that ye let none other ever drawe
> Your minde from me, but keepe this as a lawe:
> And hereupon an oath unto me plight.
> The Ape was glad to end the strife so light,
> And thereto swore: for who would not oft sweare,   25
> And oft unsweare a Diademe to beare?
> Then freely up those royall spoyles he tooke,
> Yet at the Lyons skin he inly quooke;
> But it dissembled, and upon his head
> The Crowne, and on his backe the skin he did,   30
> And the false Foxe him helpéd to array.
>   (*Minor Poems*, Variorum Edition, Vol. II)

These rhymed couplets gave more than a hint to Dryden for *Absalom and Achitophel*; there is epigrammatic force and occasional mastery of antithesis, as in line 10. Adroit versification, realism and terseness characterize the passage. *Ruinate* (8), *plight* (= pledge, 23) and *quooke* (28) were not archaic to an Elizabethan reader. The strong past tense of *quake* was a dialect form, in general use from the fourteenth to the sixteenth century.

Spenser's innovation is an attempt at prosaic rhythms for satirical muscularity. A few lines are deficient in syllables; but the distribution of primary stresses is freer than in the eclogues and more varied. Many lines (e.g. 27) have only four principal stresses; and nine (2, 5, 6, 14, 16, 18, 19, 23 and 29) have only three. No less than ten verses are run-on, which is an unusual proportion for Spenser. Trisyllables are used as rhyme-words in lines 4, 8, 13 and 18, (*pollicie, ruinate, craftinesse* and *government*), with the result that the echo falls on syllables with only secondary metrical stress. Feminine rhyme occurs in 11/12 (*spirite/ merite*), a good rhyme in Spenser's day, as *head/ did* (29/30) may have been in some quarters.

Stress-inversion is here a Spenserian device to simulate conversation, as in the first foot of lines 1, 3, 5, 8, 10, 15, 28 and 29. Line 3, between two normal iambic pentameters, contains the most daring of the stress modulations:

Wére thĕ/ wórke ŏf/ yoŭr nímblĕ hańd, yĕt Í

There is a further inversion in the second foot of line 6. Sometimes, when the first foot is pyrrhic, the second is a spondee, as in lines 11, 13 and 31. Ease and naturalness result also from variations of internal pause. Spenser's medial break in the pentameter is normally after the second foot, as in 1 and 7; but in line 4 the pause is after the fourth foot, in 15 and 29 in the middle of the third foot, and in 30 after the first foot. Spenser's skill in modulating the tempo is evident in lines 1, 3, 8, 10 and 11. In the remainder of the passage the sense is confined to the couplet, occasionally with individual verses end-stopped. The relation of syntax to the couplets could hardly have been bettered by Dryden and Pope.

In grammatical structure the passage would be unremarkable, but for disturbances of word order to which Spenser was prone, e.g. in lines 12, 14, 15, 17, 19, 23, 25, 26, 27, 28, 29, 30, 31. In the last seven lines the syntax seems strained to accommodate the versification. The only uses of the periphrastic auxiliary *do* are in lines 4 and 12; but the colloquial weakening *ye* for *you* occurs throughout the poem, here four times (9, 18 19, 21). The comparative degree *more fit* (6) was a frequent licence of rhyme in Elizabethan poetry; so, too, was the adverbial use of adjectives, such as *light* (24).

The meaning of Spenser's lines is seldom in doubt; difficulties that arise are due largely to the allegory and untraced topical allusions. Figurative language would have disturbed the closely-knit argument; *springeth* (5), and *iarre* ('disagreement') in 16, were already dead metaphors.

Of the repetitive figures, *Chiasmus* is found in line 10, and *Ploce* in 25 and 26. *Prosopopoeia* abounds in rhetorical questions, e.g. lines 25 and 26. Metaplasms are minimal, for instance *Nath'les* in 15, and the sounded inflexions of past participles, *passéd* (15), *ruléd* (19), *counselléd* (20) and *helpéd* (31).

This satire is economic in its use of alliteration, the function being metrical. It is the least elaborate of Spenser's longer poems.

Epithalamion, lines 56–91

Written to celebrate Spenser's marriage to Elizabeth Boyle in 1594, *Epithalamion* is a nuptial song, with a complex stanza pattern, derived from the Provençal and Italian *canzone*, which Spenser introduced to England. The Romance form consisted of two symmetrical *pedes* and a *cauda* (comparable to the *coda* in music); but Spenser's stanzas are anisometrical; most have eighteen or nineteen lines, but one only seventeen. Despite their formal conventions, canzoni are notable for rhythmical freedom, using lines of different length and irregular rhyming pattern. The selected fourth and fifth stanzas of *Epithalamion* happen to be of the same structure (18 lines). Iambic penta-meters dominate the leisurely movement; but lines 6, 11 and 16 are trimeters, and the coda is a neatly modulated Alexandrine. The rhyme scheme of the stanza is a b a b c c (trimeter) d c d e e (trimeter) f g g f f (trimeter) h h (Alexandrine):

Ye Nymphes of Mulla which with carefull heed,
The silver scaly trouts doe tend full well,
And greedy pikes which use therein to feed,
(Those trouts and pikes all others doo excell)
And ye likewise which keepe the rushy lake,   5
Where none doo fishes take,
Bynd up the locks the which hang scatterd light,
And in his waters which your mirror make,
Behold your faces as the christall bright,
That when you come wheras my love doth lie,   10
No blemish she may spie

And eke ye lightfoot mayds which keepe the deere,
That on the hoary mountayne use to towre,
And the wylde wolves which seeke them to devoure,
With your steele darts doo chace from comming neer,   15
Be also present heere,
To helpe to decke her and to help to sing,
That all the woods may answer and your echo ring.

Wake, now my love, awake; for it is time,
The Rosy Morne long since left Tithones bed,   20
All ready to her silver coche to clyme,
And Phoebus gins to shew his glorious hed.
Hark how the cheerefull birds do chaunt theyr laies
And carroll of loves praise.
The merry Larke hir mattins sings aloft,   25
The thrush replyes, the Mavis descant playes,
The Ouzell shrills, the Ruddock warbles soft,
So goodly all agree with sweet consent,
To this dayes merriment.
Ah my deere love why doe ye sleepe thus long,   30
When meeter were that ye should now awake,
T'awayt the comming of your ioyous make,
And hearken to the birds lovelearnéd song,
The deawy leaves among.
For they of ioy and pleasance to you sing,   35
That all the woods them answer and theyr eccho ring.

Epithalamion has been praised for its pantheistic natural tone
and Platonic sensuousness; it contains all the elements of
Spenser's dignified lyrical style, diversified in an inconspicuous
way. The extract opens with a lengthy invocation to the Muses,
to Hymen and to the Nymphs of Mulla, the river near Cork
where the marriage was solemnized.

The mature diction is remarkable more for its choice of
epithets than for its archaisms. Among the latter may, however,
be noted the use of connectives *the which* (7) and *whereas* (10).
Descant in line 26 (originally a technical term), *make* in 32
(for 'mate') and *pleasance* (35) are examples of Spenserian
poeticism. Spenser's fondness for descriptive adjectives ending
in -*y*, e.g. *scaly* trouts (2), *greedy* pikes (3), *rushy* lake (5),
hoary mountayne (13), *Rosy* Morne (20), *merry* Larke (25),
deawy leaves (34), is discreet enough to avoid mannerism; but
the pictorial compounds are more pleasing: *silver scaly trouts*
(2), *lightfoot mayds* (12), *love-learnéd song* (33). Some epithets,
notably christall *bright* (9), *wylde* wolves (14), *silver* coche

(21), *glorious* hed (22), *cheerefull* birds (23), *sweet* consent (28), *ioyous* make (32), are part of the conventional machinery of nuptial poetry; but Spenser's touch is colourful, quaint and lively.

He is always happy in the choice of poetic names, for instance, the Larke, the Mavis, the Ouzell and the Ruddock, the 'cheerefull birds' of lines 25–7. They are the occasion for Spenser's musical imagery; they *caroll, sing, reply, descant, shrill, warble* and *agree with sweet consent*, the terms being taken from partsong, madrigal and psalmody, in which the educated Elizabethan gentry excelled. Spenser's word painting is better than his use of Greek mythology (Tithon and Phoebus), which is not here very original; *Rosy Morne* (20) is more becoming than Aurora in the pastoral setting; the figure is known as *antonomasia*.

The movement of the verse depends, as usual, on the interplay of vowel and consonant sounds. When alliteration blends with vowel modulation and the use of liquids, nasals and sibilants, the harmony is most pleasing, as in lines 25 and 28:

> The *m*erry *L*arke hir *m*atti*n*s *s*ings a*l*oft
> *S*o good*l*y a*l*l agree with *s*weet con*s*ent

There are few metrical substitutions; trochees for iambs occur four times in the first foot (7, 19, 23 and 30), and once (possibly) in the second foot (*likewise*, 5). A favourite device of Spenserian modulation is the spondee in the second foot of lines 14 and 15 (*wylde wolves* and *steele darts*), which follows a pyrrhic first foot.

The hortatory language of the two stanzas enables Spenser to confine the sense to the verse line. There is not an enjambement in the 36 lines though there are 24 in the whole poem (433 lines). The medial pause is not prominent as a means of modulating the rhythm; in each stanza there are only four conventional pauses, after the second foot. In the first there are three pauses in the middle of the third foot (1, 9 and 17), and one *after* the third foot (13). The most unusual pause is that in the coda of each stanza, after *answer* (middle of the fourth, pyrrhic foot); it suggests an additional short line, beginning with an anapaest.

The grammatical structure illustrates Spenser's partiality for inversion of word order, e.g. in lines 2, 4, 6, 8, 11, 14, 18, 21,

25, 26, 34, 35, 36. Many of the numerous inversions are for the sake of rhyme, for instance christall *bright* (9). Spenser liked to get the verb in the emphatic end-position (rhyme-word), and so to make the object precede it, e.g. the Mavis *descant playes* (26). The object may also precede the preposition, as in 'The deawy leaves *among*' (34). These devices became poetical licences for centuries, comparable to verse-syllable expansion through the periphrastic auxiliary *do*, which occurs 6 times in these two stanzas (2, 4, 6, 10, 15, 23). Retrenchment of a syllable is secured by the omission of the pronoun *it* after *meeter* in line 31.

Which as a relative pronoun for persons (1 and 12) was still grammatically approved in Elizabethan English, though falling out of favour. *Ye*, the nominative plural of the second personal pronoun (1, 5, 12), was the literary form proper to invocation, not the colloquial weakening found in *Mother Hubberd's Tale*. The use of *ye* in the singular (30 and 31) is deferential and respectful.

Expansiveness characteristic of Spenser's method is shown in the gratuitous detail of lines 4 and 6. By *prosopopoeia* Mulla is of masculine gender, e.g. '*his* waters' (8). *Towre* (13) is an effete metaphor. The second stanza teems with personification, beginning with lines 20–2:

> The Rosy Morne long since left Tithones bed,
> All ready to her silver coche to clyme,
> And Phoebus gins to shew his glorious hed.

Then follows the *prosopopoeia* of singing birds, pictured as choristers (23–9), who are 'answered' by echoing woods in 36. Both stanzas are hyperbolic in fancy.

The rhetorical device *parenthesis* (4) with its beginning and end pauses, has an important effect upon the rhythm. The collocation of four monosyllabic infinitives of purpose in line 17 illustrates the figure known as *synathroismus* (parallel phrases of different meaning, all contributing to a single idea):

> To helpe to decke her and to help to sing

Lines 25–7 exemplify *asyndeton*:

> The merry Larke hir mattins sings aloft,
> The thrush replyes, the Mavis descant playes,
> The Ouzell shrills, the Ruddock warbles soft

Line 30 begins with *ecphonesis* ('ah my deere love') and ends
with *erotema* ('why doe ye sleepe thus long'); while *lovelearnéd*
(33) is an instance of transferred epithet. Among the meta-
plasms, *gins* (22) is a case of *aphæresis*, and *T'awayt* (32) *of
synalœpha*.

Miss C. Ing writes of Spenser's technical accomplishment:
'He makes words sing, partly because he is apparently little
interested in playing tricks with rhythm' (*Elizabethan Lyrics*,
Chatto and Windus, 1951, p. 218). *Epithalamion* was the first
of the great irregular odes of English poetry; they owed much
more to Italian canzoni than to the odes of Pindar.

The Faerie Queene Book II, Canto VI, stanzas 12–15

The principal advance in the nine-line stanza of *The Faerie
Queene* was greater flexibility. The descriptions of Nature (a
Supreme Being in the allegory) are varied in rhythm and stress.
Rhythmic control enabled Spenser to do almost anything with
the stanza, whose origin is uncertain. It was probably a
modification of the eight-line stanza of Chaucer's *The Monk's
Tale*, by the addition of a final Alexandrine, the pattern being
a b a b b c b c c.

It was a chosen plot of fertile land,
    Emongst wide waves set, like a litle nest,
    As if it had by Natures cunning hand
    Bene choisely pickéd out from all the rest,
    And laid forth for ensample of the best: 5
    No daintie flowre or herbe, that growes on ground,
    No arboret with painted blossomes drest,
    And smelling sweet, but there it might be found
To bud out faire, and her sweet smels throw all around.

No tree, whose braunches did not bravely spring;   10
    No braunch, whereon a fine bird did not sit:
    No bird, but did her shrill notes sweetly sing;
    No song but did containe a lovely dit:
    Trees, braunches, birds, and songs were frameéd fit,
    For to allure fraile mind to carelesse ease.   15
    Carelesse the man soone woxe, and his weake wit
    Was overcome of thing, that did him please;
So pleaséd, did his wrathfull purpose faire appease.

Thus when she had his eyes and senses fed
    With false delights, and fild with pleasures vaine,   20

Into a shadie dale she soft him led,
And laid him downe upon a grassie plaine;
And her sweet selfe without dread, or disdaine,
She set beside, laying his head disarm'd
In her loose lap, it softly to sustaine, 25
Where soone he slumbred, fearing not be harm'd,
The whiles with a loud lay she thus him sweetly charm'd.

Behold, O man, that toilesome paines doest take,
The flowres, the fields, and all that pleasant growes,
How they themselves doe thine ensample make, 30
Whiles nothing envious nature them forth throwes
Out of her fruitfull lap; how, no man knowes,
They spring, they bud, they blossome fresh and faire,
And deck the world with their rich pompous showes;
Yet no man for them taketh paines or care, 35
Yet no man to them can his carefull paines compare.

Ensample (lines 5 and 30), from Anglo-French *asaumple*, was not archaic to Spenser. The word came into the language in the fourteenth century, as did *example*, a refashioning of the word after Latin. Uses of *ensample* survived until the nineteenth century, owing to the influence of the New Testament in the King James Bible. The prepositional phrase *For to* (15) and the conjunctival combination *The whiles* (27) were already conscious archaisms; but the preposition *to*, meaning 'by' (17) and the strong past tense *woxe* (16) became archaic only after the seventeenth century.

Sweet or *sweetly* is used five times, on three occasions adverbially. The epithet suggests the dalliance of blissful life on the island, where Phaedria is the symbol of effeminacy. Milton's partiality for the adjective *sweet* must have been influenced by Spenser's; by the eighteenth century the word had become a ready-to-hand, lazy and meaningless cliché. The other epithets (except *loose* in line 25) now appear trite, but were not so in Spenser's conventional scheme: *fertile* land, Nature's *cunning* hand, *daintie* flowre, *painted* blossomes (in the sixteenth century sense of 'adorned with bright colours', 'variegated'), *fine* bird, *shrill* notes, *lovely* dit, *fraile* mind, *careless* ease, *weake* wit, *wrathfull* purpose, *false* delights, pleasures *vaine*, *shadie* dale, *grassie* plaine, *loose* lap (perhaps a reference, with moral overtones, to the garment worn by Phaedria), *loud* lay, *toilesome* paines, *envious* nature, *fruitful* lap, *rich pompous* showes, *carefull* paines (where the expression is tautological). The mechanical frequency of epithet-use is most open to modern criticism; Tennyson in the descriptive passages of *The Lotus Eaters* was more discriminating.

Except in the final Alexandrines, few lines have the five stresses of the ideal form suggested in line 6:

No daintie flowre or herbe, that growes on ground.

Other verses have four or even three primary stresses, as in 2 and 3. Line 2 is an interesting example of stress modulation:

Emongst/ wide waves/ sét, like/ a lit/le nest (Initial pyrrhic spondee and trochee, with internal pause in middle of third foot)

Inversion of stress is more frequent than in the earlier poetry, and the position of the internal pauses more diversified. In the first four lines of the second stanza, pauses are found after the first foot. Spenser's syntax is preponderantly a verse-line syntax, making for metrical and semantic lucidity; enjambement occurs only four times, at the end of lines 3, 16, 19 and 31.

There are twenty inversions of word order in 36 lines; they are in 2, 3, 7–9, 12, 16–21, 23, 25, 27–31, 35 and 36. Six uses of the periphrastic auxiliary *do/did* occur in lines 12, 13, 17, 18, 28, 30; examples in negative statements (10 and 11) are not included. There are two omissions of parts of speech for the sake of metre: the definite article before *fraile mind* (15), and the preposition *to* before *be harm'd* in 26. The rhetorical structure of the second stanza is emphasized by omission of the verb *to be* in the first foot of lines 10 to 13, and by the use of *but* as a negative relative conjunction (meaning *that . . . not*) in lines 12 and 13:

No bird, *but* did her shrill notes sweetly sing;
No song *but* did containe a lovely dit:

Spenser's defining and non-defining relative clauses are an interesting study. H. W. Sugden wrote in *The Grammar of Spenser's Faerie Queene* (Linguistic Society of America, No. 22, April–June, 1936):

On the evidence of syntax alone, it is quite clear that Spenser's fondness for descriptive clauses, for picturesque details, additions, and elaborations, is much greater than his desire for the purely defining or restrictive clause. His style is revealed as loose, discursive, diffuse, highly-colored and emotional. (p. 55)

Such an estimate, if based on the use of relative clauses, would apply to most Elizabethan poets, including Shakespeare.

The predominant image of the selected stanzas is personification, for instance, in lines 3 to 5. The verbs *fed* and *charm'd* in 19 and 27 are personal metaphors. Nature seems a beneficent goddess that seduces unthinking man from predestined toil; but Nature's very fecundity is evidence of life's arduous rhythm (stanza IV).

Rhetoric is potent in producing the sense of unreality in these stanzas. The second has been considered a model of deliberate patterning. The images of lines 10 to 13 are neatly assembled in 14 by the device of *gradatio*. Scaliger in *Poetics* (185) described such arrangements as poetic correlatives, 'determined not by metrical feet or rhythm, but rather by the words themselves'. The name given to this figure was *synathroismus*. The repetition of the word *carelesse* (15 and 16) is an example of *ploce*. Another device of repetition is *epanaphora* (parallel clauses beginning with the same word), as in line 33:

> *They* spring, *they* bud, *they* blossome fresh and faire

Both *anaphora* (consecutive verses beginning with the same words), and *antimetabole* (adjacent use of the same words in inverse order, for contrast) occur in lines 35 and 36:

> *Yet no man* for them taketh *paines* or *care*,
> *Yet no man* to them can his *carefull paines* compare.

Metaplasms are confined to the addition and loss of a syllable in *pickéd* (4), *framéd* (14), *pleaséd* (18) and *dit* for 'ditty' (13). The last is a licence of rhyme.

The Faerie Queene, Book VII, Canto VI, stanzas 48-50

Like as an huswife, that with busie care
　　Thinks of her Dairie to make wondrous gaine,
　　Finding where-as some wicked beast unware
　　That breakes into her Dayr'house, there doth draine
　　Her creaming pannes, and frustrate all her paine;　　　5
　　Hath in some snare or gin set close behind,
　　Entrappéd him, and caught into her traine,
　　Then thinkes what punishment were best assign'd,
And thousand deathes deviseth in her vengefull mind:

So did Diana and her maydens all
   Use silly Faunus, now within their baile:
   They mocke and scorne him, and him foule miscall;
   Some by the nose him pluckt, some by the taile,
   And by his goatish beard some did him haile:
   Yet he (poore soule) with patience all did beare;   15
   For, nought against their wils might countervaile:
   Ne ought he said what ever he did heare;
But hanging downe his head, did like a Mome appeare.

At length, when they had flouted him their fill,
   They gan to cast what penaunce him to give.   20
   Some would have gelt him, but that same would spill
   The Wood-gods breed, which must for ever live:
   Others would through the river him have drive,
   And duckéd deepe: but that seem'd penaunce light;
   But most agreed and did this sentence give,   25
   Him in Deares skin to clad; and in that plight,
To hunt him with their hounds, him selfe save how hee might.

This extract shows how the language of narrative differs from that of description. The style is closer to the method Chaucer used in *The Nun's Priest's Tale*. Lines 1–11 emulate the complex epic similes of Vergil, who often kept the principal clause to the end. Preserving Spenser's scheme of subordination, it is difficult to convey the sense in plain statement. The following attempts to transmute, rather than paraphrase, the first eleven lines:

Diana and her maidens treated silly Faunus like a revengeful housewife, who plans to make a handsome profit from her dairy. Picture this woman as finding, to her chagrin, that a secret thief has visited her cooling-room and drained her creaming pans. She sets a trap for him, takes him captive, and is planning a thousand deaths as punishment.

Despite the involution of relative and noun clauses, Spenser's language manages to convey the meaning with lucidity. Logical orderliness was not the only way of Elizabethan poets, such as Spenser.

Epithets are less numerous in Spenser's narrative. *Busie* care, *wondrous* gaine, *vengefull* mind, *goatish* beard and penaunce *light*, confirm the belief that conventional epithets were the deliberate tools of formalized fable.

The Romance vocabulary in this passage has interesting aspects. *Wondrous* dates from the sixteenth century, and was favoured by Dunbar, Hawes and Coverdale; the OED suggests that it was formed from the plural *wonders*, by analogy with *marvellous*. *Baile* (custody) was borrowed for legal use from Anglo-French in the thirteenth century, but appropriated for literature in the Coventry Mysteries of the fifteenth century. *Haile* (haul), derived from Old Frankish *halon* (Dutch *halen*), appeared in Middle English romances of the thirteenth century, and became archaic before the Restoration. *Countervaile* (prevail against), from Anglo-French, seems first to have been borrowed by Wyclif in the late fourteenth century; it, too, became archaic in the seventeenth century.

The archaic tone of the narrative owes more, however, to words and phrases of Old English origin, for instance, the double connectives *Like as* and *where-as* in lines 1 and 3; the negative particle *Ne* in 17; the Chaucerian preterite *gan*, used as a periphrastic auxiliary, in 20. *Unware* (3) was in common use from Alfred the Great to Milton; but the form was gradually superseded by *unawares*, which Coverdale employed in 1535. The past participle *drive* for *driven* (23) was probably a licence of rhyme; but the form was used by Chaucer in *The Franklin's Tale* and occasionally found until the sixteenth century. The present infinitive *clad* (for *clothe*) in 26 was a rare usage from the fourteenth to the seventeenth century; it was revived archaically by William Morris in *The Earthly Paradise*.

There is one enjambement in these three stanzas, at the end of 10. The sense-rhythm overruns the first stanza, taking in lines 10 and 11 of the second. The rhythm is, therefore, syntactical, and suggested by the pauses, which coincide with subordinate phrases and clauses. The internal breaks in lines 1–11 are as follows:

1   Líke as an húswife/ that with búsie care (middle of pyrrhic third foot)
3   Fínding where-as some wícked beast/ unwáre (after fourth foot)
4   That bréakes intò her Dáyr-house,/ there dóth dráine (middle of fourth foot)
5   Her créaming pánnes,/ and frustráte all her páine; (after second foot)
7   Entrápped hím,/ and caúght intò her tráine, (after second foot)
11 Use síllý Faúnus,/ now within her baíle: (middle of third foot)

The incidence of pause for sense is thus skilfully varied;

modulations of stress and pause occur principally in verses that are not normal iambic pentameters. Spenser pays careful attention to pause variation in his narrative scenes; he does not disconcert the line-to-line development by feminine rhymes. He makes play with the stress ambivalence of disyllabic conjunctions and prepositions, such as *where-as, into, within*. In his time the word *frustrate* had its principal stress on the first syllable.

Regarding the inflexion of verbs in the third person singular present indicative, Spenser uses the *-s* or *-es* ending predominantly in verse, but *-th* or *-eth* in his prose work *The Present State of Ireland*. He never gives the *-es* spelling a syllabic value. One reason for the *-s* preference in poetry is the frequency of verbs in this form as rhyme-words, which are conveniently matched with plurals of nouns. The exceptions are *hath* and *doth*, which he uses considerably more often than the *-s* alternatives in *The Faerie Queene*, as in lines 4 and 6 of this extract. The Elizabethan poets before 1600 generally preferred to retain the *-th* ending for notional verbs whose stems ended in a sibilant, e.g. *deviseth* (9); one reason for this is that the inflected form has precisely the same number of syllables, whatever inflexion is used.

In lines 8 and 9, Spenser uses the *th* digraph, voiced or unvoiced, five times (*Then, thinkes, thousand, deathes* and *deviseth*); and he alternates this with the sibilant, voiced or unvoiced, in the words think*es*, puni*s*hment, be*s*t, a*s*sign'd, thou*s*and, deathe*s*, and devi*s*eth. These lines are good examples of consonantal and vowel modulation. There are six different qualities of vowel in line 8, and eight differences in 9.

Two lines contain uses of the old subjunctive:

8   Then thinkes what punishment *were* best assigned (= would be)
27   To hunt him with their hounds, him selfe *save* how he might (= and let him save himself as best he could)

In 27 the economy of words is considerable.

There are fourteen inversions of word order in twenty-seven lines, and six uses of the periphrastic auxiliary *do*. An instance of the historic-present tense, interposed among preterites, occurs in line 12:

They mocke and scorne him, and him foule miscall

The common Elizabethan omission of the indefinite article

before *thousand* (9) and of the pronoun *he* before *himselfe* (27) deserve notice.

The rhetorical devices are minimal. *Epanaphora* and *parenthesis* occur in lines 13–15:

> *Some by the* nose him pluckt, *some by the* taile,
> And by his goatish beard *some* did him haile
> Yet he (*poore soule*) with patience all did beare

There is an unusual licence of *syncope* (rejection of a letter or syllable in the middle of a word) in *Dayr'house* (4).

The Faerie Queene established Spenser as a poet, not of the particular metaphor, but of personification, alliteration and *allegoria*, or 'extended metaphor'. Vowel-music pervades his poetry, in whatever metre it is written; the rhymes are especially functional in the Spenserian stanza. As George Saintsbury observed in his *History of English Prosody* (Russell and Russell, N.Y., 1961), 'Rhythm and rhyme are so thoroughly married in *The Faerie Queene* that the marriage is indissoluble – the rhythm seems to be wholly prepared for the rhyme, the rhyme to carry out exactly, and add exactly what is wanted by, the rhythm' (p. 417).

The conclusions derived from linguistic analysis point to unmistakable elements in Spenser's style:

1. Deliberate borrowing of words known to be archaic from Chaucer, Langland, Lydgate, Malory, Skelton and other writers of the two preceding centuries.
2. Preference for conventional, rather than imaginative, epithets.
3. Taste for Sidney-like word compounds.
4. Skill in the modulating of vowel sounds and the patterning of liquid, nasal and sibilant consonants.
5. Fondness for alliterating doublets, such as *do or die, sweat and swinke, watch and ward, wayle and weepe*.
6. Old-fashioned spelling for the sake of visual rhyme.
7. Frequent inversion of the normal order of words.
8. Plentiful use of schematic figures of rhetoric, and of metaplasms, as a means to metrical regularity.
9. Simplicity of syntactical structure, especially in subordination.

D

10. Partiality in iambic pentameter verse for an internal pause after the second foot.

Archaisms are not as numerous as is generally suggested. B. R. McElderry in 'Archaism and Innovation in Spenser's Poetic Diction' (*PMLA* 47 (1932) pp. 144–70) finds that only 320 words in the works are deliberate archaisms, more than half of which appear in *The Shepheardes Calender*. The criterion for archaism is a word not quoted at least ten times in the OED for the period 1500–1650. On the other hand, Spenser has nearly 600 innovations (deviations from the standard English of his time), half of which are nonce words employed for special purposes; 59 are importations and about 20 appear to be coinages. Kirk glossed nearly 300 words from *The Shepheardes Calender*, but 46 proved not to be archaic, and 37 were dialect words. McElderry adds:

> No one person can 'create' a poetic diction. The most he can do is to embellish incidentally a relatively standard idiom. The main poetic effort is latent in that standard idiom, and it is the poet's business to bring it out. This is what Spenser did.

Spenser's tastes in literature were medieval romances, satires, bestiaries, fables and allegories. The nature of his subject-matter called for less modern words, and a large proportion of his vocabulary thus consists of monosyllables. Roger Sale suggests in 'Spenser's Undramatic Poetry' (*Elizabethan Poetry*, ed. P. J. Alpers, OUP, 1967) that adjectives are often used as 'metrical and stanzaic fillers' (p. 434); that most groups of epithets are constellations of mechanical association, strokes accumulated to produce a moral or pictorial effect.

Several critics have commented on Spenser's disregard for stress in some rhymes, of which the following are examples:

Shepheardes Calender, April 140–5
Strowe me the ground with Daffadowndíllies,
And Cowslips, and Kingcups, and lovĕd Líllies.
The pretie Pawnce,
And the Chevisaunce,
Shall match with the fayre floure Dĕlíce.

Faerie Queene, II.5.31 (8–9)
    And made emongst them selves a sweet cŏnsórt
    That quicknd the dull spright with musicall cŏmfórt

Ibid, II.10.23 (6-9)

He with his victour sword first ópéned
The bowels of wide Fraunce, a forlorne Dáme
And taught her first hów tŏ bĕ cónquerèd
Since which, with sundrie spoiles shĕe hăth bĕene ransăckèd.

Ibid, II.12.32 (8-9)

This is the Port of rest from troúbloŭs toýle,
The worlds sweet In, from paine and wearisome turmoýle.

Thomas Warton wrote in *Observations on the Fairy Queen of Spenser* (1762):

> There cannot be in a maker a fowler fault than to falsifie his accent to serve his cadence; or by untrue orthography to wrench his words to help his rhyme; for it is a sign that such a maker is not copious in his own language.
>
> (*Spenser's Critics,* ed. W. R. Mueller, Syracuse U.P., 1959, p. 55)

But what these apparent irregularities illustrate is the fluidity of accent in polysyllabic borrowings, especially from French sources. Spenser took the same liberties with stress in rhyming as did Gower and Lydgate.

Spenser's periphrases in *The Faerie Queene* are metaphors of a rhetorical kind, designed to avoid the commonplace locution; for instance, *watrie wildernesse* (I.3.32); *heavens fruitful ray* (III.6.6); *his finny drove* (III.8.29); *fraile mansion of mortality* (VI.3.28). Lines like the following belong to the same hyperbolic turn of expression as *The Song of Solomon:*

> And let the ground, whereas her foot shall tread,
> For feare the stones her tender foot should wrong,
> Be strewed with fragrant flowers all along,
> And *diapred* lyke the *discolored* mead.
>
> (*Epithalamion,* 48–51)

The final line means 'patterned like the many-coloured meadow'; but Spenser preferred an elegant image. The alliterating words reveal interesting changes of meaning. *Diapred* (from Greek *dia* 'through' and *aspros* 'white') signified 'white throughout'. The name *diaper* was later given to a white linen fabric, with a small diamond pattern; and thence, to a diamond-patterned design for walls, panels etc. The past-participle, *diapred* came finally to mean 'variegated in colour'. *Discolored* does not mean 'faded'; the prefix *dis* has here the sense of 'different'.

The vices of style to which Puttenham drew attention in

Book III of *The Arte of English Poesie* were mainly of French origin, such as *ambage* (periphrasis), *enallage* (the figure of exchange, e.g. *dit* for *ditty*), *rabbate* (shortening of words by apocope, aphæresis, syncope) and *surpluse* (lengthening of words by prothesis, epenthesis and paragoge). The commonest words could be morphologically varied in ways not permissible to modern poets. The fanciful employment of word patterns lost its audience when rhetoric, as the educational basis of writing, went out of fashion in the latter half of the eighteenth century. Conventional epithets wilted under the analytical criticisms of Dr Johnson, and the dissection of Gray. About the same time the use of the auxiliary *do* to augment the syllables of a line, was deprecated; and modulation by means of metaplasms was out of place by the mid-nineteenth century.

The evidence of language supports many twentieth-century literary estimates of Spenser's style, the most valuable of which are those of W. L. Renwick, W. B. C. Watkins and C. S. Lewis. Renwick writes with understanding of the musical aspect of Spenser's poetry:

> Spenser, with a certain training in music and considerable practice in the weighing and measuring of syllables, learned from the musician that the ear is able to contain the whole sum of a rhythm, and to compare and contrast it with others both in sequence and together. Music thus assisted in forming the conception of verse as a sequence of variable rhythms. . . . Elizabethan music was largely for the voice, and based thus on speech. The musical rhythms conformed normally to the natural rhythms of English – that is, to the rhythms imposed by English syntax and vocabulary. . . . When poet and musician worked in such close co-operation each was bound to have regard to the other's medium – the poet to 'keep a good cadence' and a pleasant variety, and the musician to bring out the meaning of the words.
>
> (*Edmund Spenser*, Arnold, 1925, pp. 112–13)

W. B. C. Watkins, in his comparative study *Shakespeare and Spenser* (Princeton U.P., 1950), described Spenser's technical faults as excessive use of particles, auxiliaries and epithets. Because he composed for the ear, he relied too slavishly on the adjective. His mastery of dialogue, both colloquial and courtly, shows that he could dramatize emotion. But Watkins disliked Spenser's similes, because they led him to elaborate rather than condense expression. Poetry, at its best, uses the metaphorical associations of words, because they encourage different levels of interpretation; but Spenser prefers to be explanatory, and thus seldom suggests a meaning beyond the compass of words (pp. 264–91).

According to C. S. Lewis, Spenser's style shows no real development; at all periods it was, spasmodically, either good or indifferent. 'He does not know the rhetoric of the passions and substitutes that of the schools.' There is a lack of ambiguity or tension in the mind, because Spenser was the poet of tranquillity, not of discord. While realizing the true historical situation, he contrived to inhabit a world of 'total illusion'.

It is difficult to escape the conclusion that Spenser's genius was of the passive kind, which relies more upon rhythm than imagery, more on the sounds and pliancy of words than their emotive power. His ideal of expression was that of a song-writer, and the virtues of his diligence were orderliness, clarity and ease. The perspicuity of his syntax passed into narrative prose of the seventeenth century, and was perpetuated in the *King James Bible* and Bunyan's *Pilgrim's Progress*. The tradition of poetic allegory lasted much longer, through Thomson and Keats to the neo-Romantics of the later nineteenth century.

V

NON-DRAMATIC POETRY:
MARLOWE AND SHAKESPEARE

Ovid, the preceptor of love, and master of limpid, narrative verse, was the most popular Latin poet in England from the thirteenth century, especially admired for the *Metamorphoses*, *Heroides* and *Ars Amatoria*. Different adaptations of Ovidian mythology and style may be used to distinguish the characteristics of Spenser, Marlowe and Shakespeare, who were the honoured poets in the last two decades of the sixteenth century.

That Marlowe had a finer classical scholarship than Spenser or Shakespeare is shown in his better understanding of paganism in early Greek poetry. Spenser's attitude in the *Four Hymns* and *The Faerie Queene* had been filtered through humanism, and held that the destiny of man was largely in his own hands. Though Spenser knew Ovid and Vergil well, he apparently read little Greek. H. G. Lotspeich, in *Classical Mythology in the Poetry of Edmund Spenser* (Princeton Studies 9, 1965), has shown that he relied for his mythological narrative on quotations from the *Genealogica Deorum* of Boccaccio (Basle 1532) and the *Mythologiae* of Natalis Comes (Venice, 1551). Both writers attached a mystical moral value to the writings of Ovid and Apuleius; the literary tradition of mythology was, for them, a 'great cosmic principle of generation and growth and fertility'. Spenser in *The Faerie Queene* may even have accepted Boccaccio's belief in the fable of the *Aeneid* as historical truth. Spenser's Venus is a Platonist ('the divine idea of Beauty'), Shakespeare's a 'bold-faced' sensualist. But mythology suggests pagan naturalism to Marlowe; neither he nor Shakespeare used myth as a philosophical mystique indispensable to the interpretation of the fable.

Italianate erotic fables, such as Thomas Lodge's *Scillaes Metamorphosis* (1589), became a literary fashion, which, during the temporary closing of the theatres, was taken up by Marlowe in *Hero and Leander* (entered in the Stationer's Register, 1593),

102

and by Shakespeare in *Venus and Adonis*, published in the same
year. It is generally assumed (for instance by W. B. C. Watkins
in *Shakespeare and Spenser*) that the former was the earlier work,
to which Shakespeare had access; but the only extant text of
Marlowe's poem is that of 1598. The genus to which these
Ovidian minor epics belong is now called 'epyllion', the name
devised by M. M. Crump in 1931 for the title of his book *The
Epyllion from Theocritus to Ovid*.

Hero and Leander, lines 209–50

Marlowe, the translator of Ovid's *Amores*, cannot be over-
looked in any account of the development of English poetry in
this period. *Hero and Leander* was probably left unfinished
because it was among the last things Marlowe wrote. It was
suggested by a poem on the same theme by the Alexandrian
Musaeus; also by Books XVIII and XIX of Ovid's *Heroides*;
both sources resembled each other in style. Marlowe re-captured
the spirit of detachment, and preserved the fanciful artificiality
of their expression. Artifice can be discerned in Marlowe's
hyperbolic language; he is never troubled by the knowledge
that what he expresses exceeds the bounds of nature. 'Vaulting
ambition' in words is Marlowe's principal characteristic; and it
continued through the plays from *Tamburlaine* to *Dr Faustus*.

The difference in style between writers of epyllia and Spenser
is their greater ingenuity in decorative effect and rhetorical
figure. Ornament was more coveted than lively narrative;
elaborate sophistry dominated the fashionable love contentions.
In this phase, Marlowe and Shakespeare were unashamedly
voluble in pleas for sensual indulgence; biological needs were
disguised in learned neo-Platonic philosophy. The naturalism
of the myths was pliant material for this kind of thinking; in the
burden of luxuriousness, the wit and the humour can easily be
overlooked. These were derived from Lucian, whose irony at
the expense of the gods appealed to the occasional decadence of
the Elizabethan aristocracy. Marlowe's rebellious attitude to
love is the mocking antithesis to the reasoning in Spenser's
Four Hymns and *Epithalamion*. The splendour of his language
and the naiveté of his arguments are signs of intellectual
immaturity; there is want of sophistication in his handling of

love situations, compared with those of Chaucer and Shakespeare in the Troilus and Cressida theme.

C. S. Lewis says 'Marlowe's hyperboles are so towering that they become mythopoeic'; but they have 'their own wild consistency' (British Academy Lecture XXVIII, 1952). Some of the elements discussed are conspicuous in the following passage:

> A Diamond set in lead his worth retaines,
> A heavenly Nimph, belov'd of humane swaines,
> Receives no blemish, but oft-times more grace;
> Which makes me hope, although I am but base,
> Base in respect of thee, divine and pure,   5
> Dutiful service may thy love procure,
> And I in dutie will excell all other,
> As thou in beautie doest exceed Loves mother.
> Nor heaven, nor thou, were made to gaze upon:
> As heaven preserves all things, so save thou one.   10
> A stately builded ship, well rig'd and tall,
> The Ocean maketh more majesticall:
> Why vowest thou then to live in Sestos here,
> Who on Loves seas more glorious wouldst appear?
> Like untun'd golden strings all women are,   15
> Which long time lie untoucht, will harshly jarre.
> Vessels of Brasse oft handled, brightly shine,
> What difference betwixt the richest mine
> And basest mold, but use? for both not us'de,
> Are of like worth. Then treasure is abus'de,   20
> When misers keepe it; being put to lone,
> In time it will returne us two for one.
> Rich robes, themselves and others do adorne,
> Neither themselves nor others, if not worne.
> Who builds a palace and rams up the gate,   25
> Shall see it ruinous and desolate.
> Ah simple Hero, learne thy selfe to cherish,
> Lone women like to emptie houses perish.
> Lesse sinnes the poore rich man that starves himselfe,
> In heaping up a masse of drossie pelfe,   30
> Than such as you: his golden earth remains,
> Which after his disceasse, some other gains,
> But this faire jem, sweet, in the losse alone,
> When you fleet hence, can be bequeath'd to none.
> Or if it could, downe from th'enameld skie,   35
> All heaven would come to claime this legacie,
> And with intestine broiles the world destroy,
> And quite confound natures sweet harmony.
> Well therefore by the gods decreed it is,

We humane creatures should enjoy that blisse.   40
One is no number, mayds are nothing then,
Without the sweet societie of men.

The greater part of this speech is oracular, and rich in gnomic
utterances, the sense of which is confined, either to the single
line, or to the couplet. There are consequently only two run-on
lines (18 and 35), two uses of the periphrastic auxiliary *do* (8
and 23) and one metaplasm (*th'* in 35). The syntax, with eight
unobtrusive inversions of word order (1, 10, 11, 14, 15, 27,
29 and 39), is more modern than Spenser's.

The vocabulary, too, is current; the poetic archaism *swaines*
(2) is a rhyme-word. *Pelfe* (30), of Norman origin, originally
meant 'stolen goods' (cf pilfer); later it became a pejorative
term for 'money', and was then used in the sense of 'rubbish'.
The epithets are less numerous than Spenser's, and the choice
of them less conventional, exceptions being *heavenly* Nimph (2),
Dutifull service (6), *richest* mine (18), *basest* mold (19), *Rich*
robes (23), *Lone* women and *emptie* houses (28), *faire* jem
(33), *sweet* harmony (38), *sweet* societie (41). Marlovian
splendour is present in the compounds, *stately builded* ship (11),
untun'd golden strings (15), and the oxymoron *poore rich* man
(29); also in *drossie* pelfe (30), *golden* earth (31) and *intestine*
broiles (37). *Enameld* skie (35) is one of few signs of artifice
in this passage; the epithet is a figurative use of what was
originally a technical French word, dating from the fourteenth
century. The past participle was employed poetically from
Marlowe to Milton in the sense of 'ornamented, decorated,
variegated in colour', probably by analogy with the heraldic
paintings on metal shields and armour.

The movement of Marlowe's pentameter verse in rhymed
couplets is different from Spenser's. It relies less upon the
linking device of alliteration, and the smoothening effect of the
interplay between long open vowels and liquid and nasal
consonants. The internal pauses are more varied, too; though
Marlowe follows Spenser in his preference for a pause after the
second or third foot, as well as in the middle of the third, as in
lines 2, 3 and 5. His fondness for mid-foot pauses after a weak
syllable gives his line great flexibility of rhythm. In the majority
of his verses the primary stresses are four or three in number,
and he does not hesitate to employ feminine rhymes for

modulation, as in lines 7/8 and 27/28. The only seemingly forced rhyme is *destroy/ harmony* (lines 37/38); but in the conjectured Elizabethan pronunciation of the final syllables [aI], the assonance was not a licence.

Marlowe rivals Spenser in the clarity of his meaning through syntax. His ellipses, as in lines 16 (*if they* omitted), 17 (*is there* omitted), and 24 (*but do adorn* understood), do not harm the progression of his logic; and he is happier in the employment of participial phrases instead of clauses, as in lines 16 (conditional) and 21 (temporal). Long similes do not perplex the train of thought in Marlowe; lines 15 and 16 are exemplary in their condensation. Typical use of Marlovian metaphor and hyperbole is contained in lines 33–40. The switch from *thou*, in lines 5 to 27, to *you* in lines 31 and 34, has no semantic significance. Hero is addressed throughout as a goddess 'divine and pure'; *you* in the latter lines is plural, referring to *women* (as a class) in line 28.

There are several uses of the repetitive and schematic effects of rhetoric, e.g.

4–8   Which makes me hope, although I am not *base*,
       Base in respect of thee, divine and pure,
       *Duti*full service may thy *love* procure,
       And I in *dutie* will excell all other,
       As thou in *beautie* doest exceed *Loves* mother.

There are four figures here. The repetition of *base* at the beginning of line 5 is *anadiplosis*. The play upon *dutie* and *love* in lines 6–8 is *ploce;* and the similar play upon *dutie* and *beautie* in lines 7 and 8 is *prosonomasia* (the use of words similar in sound but not homonyms). In line 8 the periphrasis *Loves mother*, for Venus, is an instance of *antonomasia*. *Hyperbole* (35–40) and *oxymoron* (29) have already been mentioned; *ecphonesis* (27), *apocope* (35), and *hysteron proteron* (passim) should be added. Nine examples of rhetorical device in 42 lines demonstrate the attention to this art paid by Marlowe. The *poor rich* oxymoron (29) is repeated by Shakespeare in *Lucrece:*

140   That they prove banckrout in this poore rich gain.

Venus and Adonis
Lines 1–24, 127–50, 163–74, 211–16, 253–8, 343–8, 355–60

In the dedication to the Earl of Southampton, Shakespeare speaks of this poem as 'the first heire of my invention'; but *Venus and Adonis* (Quarto 1593) can hardly have been prentice work, unless written considerably earlier than the date of publication suggests. Opinion among scholars favours a date of composition between 1588 and 1592, preferring the latter year.

The humility of the dedication implies the author's fear that the poem might seem a light-weight piece, not to be compared with his 'graver' compositions. Shakespeare used the Puritan, Arthur Golding's version of the *Metamorphoses* (1567), and took the fable less seriously than the translator. The sportive and witty intention of *Venus and Adonis* is easily lost, if the reader ignores the humour of some situations. Shakespeare added a subtler quality to the fantasy; he made the figure of Venus larger than life to satisfy a vein of Lucianic caricature. Venus becomes an amorous aggressor, who, throughout the poem, protests too much. A tone in the dedication suggests that the poet may even have titillated the taste of the Earl of Southampton. If Shakespeare believed that his invention was 'deformed', aristocratic readers did not think so; the poem ran through seven more editions in the next nine years.

In the treatment of mythology, Shakespeare had a courtly model before him in Lyly's *Endimion* (1591). The skill of his work was bound to be compared with the craftsmanship of Lyly, Spenser and Marlowe; the reference to 'Rose-cheekt Adonis' in line 3 recalls Marlowe's *Hero and Leander* (93), which he may have read in manuscript. Shakespeare, as usual, borrowed, but remained himself. The most original contribution in his poem is personal observation of, and feeling for, nature. In the mating of horses, the love of hounds and the vivid description of hunting a hare, he forgets artifice and convention and becomes a sensitive and enthusiastic countryman. Marlowe's *Hero and Leander* uses words with a tendency to Latin generalization; the pictorial vision of Shakespeare is remarkable for minute particularity.

A large proportion of the 1194 lines of *Venus and Adonis* is devoted to dialogue, which is useful for comparison with Marlowe's language. The selection of fourteen stanzas contains examples of the persuasive speech of Venus. The difference in movement of the two passages is due, partly, to the pattern of development. Marlowe's arguments are marshalled in animated, rhetorically balanced couplets; Shakespeare's medium is a leisurely six-line stanza, rhyming a b a b c c, which is related in rhythm to the last six lines of the Shakespearian sonnet. In the Sonnets there is a similar use of figurative language, of visual simile and metaphor. The images in *Venus and Adonis* are largely drawn from the hunted or predator animals Shakespeare knew from his experience of the chase.

> Even as the sunne with purple-colourd face,
> Had tane his last leave of the weeping morne,
> Rose-cheekt Adonis hied him to the chace,
> Hunting he lov'd, but love he laught to scorne:
>> Sick-thoughted Venus makes amaine unto him,   5
>> And like a bold fac'd suter ginnes to woo him.
>
> Thrise fairer than my selfe, (thus she began)
> The fields chiefe flower, sweet above compare,
> Staine to all Nimphs, more lovely then a man,
> More white, and red, then doves, or roses are: 10
>> Nature that made thee with her selfe at strife,
>> Saith that the world hath ending with thy life.
>
> Vouchsafe thou wonder to alight thy steed,
> And raine his proud head to the saddle bow,
> If thou wilt daine this favor, for thy meed   15
> A thousand honie secrets shalt thou know:
>> Here come and sit, where never serpent hisses,
>> And being set, Ile smother thee with kisses.
>
> And yet not cloy thy lips with loth'd sacietie,
> But rather famish them amid their plentie,   20
> Making them red, and pale, with fresh varietie:
> Ten kisses short as one, one long as twentie:
>> A sommers day will seeme an houre but short,
>> Being wasted in such time-beguiling sport.
>
> The tender spring upon thy tempting lip,   25
> Shewes thee unripe; yet maist thou well be tasted,
> Make use of time, let not advantage slip,
> Beautie within it selfe should not be wasted,
>> Faire flowers that are not gathred in their prime,
>> Rot, and consume them selves in little time.   30
>
> Were I hard-favoured, foule, or wrinckled old,
> Il-nurtur'd, crooked, churlish, harsh in voice,
> Ore-worne, despiséd, reumatique, and cold,
> Thick-sighted, barren, leane, and lacking iuyce;

Then mightst thou pause, for then I were not for thee,   35
But having no defects, why doest abhor me?

Thou canst not see one wrinckle in my brow,
Mine eyes are grey, and bright, and quicke in turning:
My beautie as the spring doth yearelie grow,
My flesh is soft, and plumpe, my marrow burning,   40
My smooth moist hand, were it with thy hand felt,
    Would in thy palme dissolve, or seeme to melt.

Bid me discourse, I will inchaunt thine eare,
Or like a Fairie, trip upon the greene,
Or like a Nimph, with long disheveled heare,   45
Daunce on the sands, and yet no footing seene.
    Love is a spirit all compact of fire,
    Not grosse to sinke, but light, and will aspire.

Torches are made to light, iewels to weare,
Dainties to tast, fresh beautie for the use,   50
Herbes for their smell, and sappie plants to beare.
Things growing to them selves, are growths abuse,
    Seeds spring from seeds, and beauty breedeth beauty,
    Thou wast begot, to get it is thy duty.

Upon the earths increase why shouldst thou feed,   55
Unlesse the earth with thy increase be fed?
By law of nature thou art bound to breed,
That thine may live, when thou thy selfe art dead:
    And so in spite of death thou doest survive,
    In that thy likenesse still is left alive.   60

Fie, livelesse picture, cold, and sencelesse stone,
Well painted idoll, image dull, and dead,
Statue contenting but the eye alone,
Thing like a man, but of no woman bred:
    Thou art no man, though of a mans complexion,   65
    For men will kisse even by their owne direction.

Now which way shall she turne? what shall she say?
Her words are done, her woes the more increasing,
The time is spent, her obiect will away,
And from her twining armes doth urge releasing: 70
    Pitie she cries, some favour, some remorse,
    Away he springs, and hasteth to his horse.

O what a sight it was wistly to view,
How she came stealing to the wayward boy,
To note the fighting conflict of her hew,   75
How white and red, ech other did destroy:
    But now her cheeke was pale, and by and by
    It flasht forth fire, as lightning from the skie.

> Oh what a war of lookes was then betweene them,
> Her eyes petitioners to his eyes suing,   80
> His eyes saw her eyes, as they had not seene them,
> Her eyes wooed still, his eyes disdaind the wooing;
>   And all this dumbe play had his acts made plain,
>   With tears which Chorus-like her eyes did rain.

The speech of Venus, glowing with imagery and colour, is preoccupied with the instinctive life of the senses. Rather than goddess, she is a lustful huntress bent on self-indulgence; and Adonis, in his effeminate beauty, is her prey. Inversion of the customary roles of wooing is like the un-Petrarchan love of the adulated youth of the sonnets; but the speech of Venus is more down-to-earth. The tone of the language suggests young Shakespeare of *Two Gentlemen of Verona*, especially the rapid transition from realism to romance.

To squeamish critics, the brash naturalism of Venus's overtures seems crude and indelicate; it oversteps the suave sophistry of Marlowe and Ovid. C. S. Lewis said of *Venus and Adonis* 'I have never read it through without feeling that I am being suffocated' (British Academy Lecture XXVIII, 1952). 'Smother thee with kisses' (18) must have induced this feeling of oppression. The poem is in the Alexandrian lyrical tradition of Musaeus (fifth century A.D.); it also anticipates the Caroline decadence of Carew, Suckling and Lovelace.

Shakespeare rivals Spenser as a resourceful compounder of epithets, such as *time-beguiling* sport (24). Although the arguments of Venus are conventional, the adjectives, single or double, are rarely so. There are four compound epithets in the first stanza: *purple-colourd* face (Latin *purpureus* meant bright red; the epithet is taken from Ovid), *Rose-cheekt* Adonis, *Sickthoughted* Venus (melancholy), *bold-fac'd* suter. In line 31–4 occur several descriptive compounds for Venus: *wrinckled old*, *hard-favourd*, *Il-nurtur'd*, *harsh in voice*, *Ore-worne*, *Thicksighted* (i.e. short-sighted), *lacking iuyce*. These polysyllabic combinations are often used at the beginning of a line; they animate the rhythm by an early inversion of stress. Other compounds are: spirit *all compact of fire* (47), *Well painted* idol (62) and *Chorus-like* (84), used adverbially. Only three compounds might be regarded as decorative; *purple-colourd*, *Rose-cheekt* and *Well painted*.

The double epithets arise mainly from the needs of the context, and have separate semantic function, e.g. flesh *soft, and plumpe* (40), *Smooth moist* hand (41), *long disheveled* heare (45), *cold, and sencelesse* stone (61), image *dull, and dead* (62). Single epithets are not as frequent or stereotyped as Spenser's: *weeping* morne (2), flower, *sweet* (7), *proud* head (14), *honie* secrets (16) (this substantive use is a happy variation from *sweet*), *loth'd* sacietie (19), *fresh* varietie (21), *tender* spring and *tempting* lips (25), *Faire* flowers (29), *foule, crooked, churlish, despised, reúmatique* (stress on first syllable), *cold, barren, leane* (31–4), pejorative adjectives used against herself by Venus, marrow *burning* (40), spirit *grosse/ light* (47–8), *sappie* plants (51), *liveless* picture (61), *twining* armes (70), *wayward* boy (74), *dumbe* play (83). The only syllable-fillers are *sweet* and *faire*, in descriptions of flowers. *Weeping morne* and *sappie plants* are mutual enrichments.

Despite the artifice of the language, the poeticisms are not many. *Tane* (2) is a conventional metaplasm for *taken; amaine* ('with all one's might'), though of OE origin (*on mægn*), is a literary coinage not found in poetry before the sixteenth century. The hyperbolic use of *Staine* (9), in the sense of 'injury', is a good example of Shakespeare's gift for modifying the sense of words by metaphor; figuratively, he implies that Adonis was 'superior in looks' to all the nymphs and thrice as fair as Venus herself. *Vouchsafe* (13) is taken directly from Golding's Ovid. *Daine* (deign) in line 15 has the same meaning; it was a commonplace Old French borrowing from the thirteenth century. *Meed*, in the same line, of OE origin, became archaic and poetical after the seventeenth century only. The past participle *set* for *seated* was in regular employment until the same century; *seated* was often found in attributive uses, however, e.g. Shakespeare *Macbeth* I.3.136 And make my *seated* Heart knock at my Ribbes. The spelling *sacietie* (19) is an interesting indication of Shakespeare's pronunciation. *Wistly* (73), which came into English at the beginning of the sixteenth century, meaning 'intently, silently', was in earlier use than *wistfully*, but did not survive the eighteenth century.

Of *Venus and Adonis* Coleridge said in *Biographia Literaria*:

The first and most obvious excellence is the perfect sweetness of the versification; its adaptation to the subject; and the power displayed in

varying the march of the words . . . The sense of musical delight, with
the power of producing it, is a gift of imagination.

The poem reveals as delicate an ear as Spenser's; the same
respect for metrical regularity, and a flowing eloquence that
seldom pretends to high seriousness. Shakespearian dialogue
rarely makes so much use of antithesis; an internal pause points
the opposed ideas and balances the syntax. Ovid exploited the
same device in *Metamorphoses* (though it was missed by
Golding) and Lyly in the Euphuistic comedies. Here are some
examples:

> 8–10   The fields chiefe flower,/ sweet above compare,
> Staine to all Nimphs,/ more lovely than a man,
> More white, and red,/ then doves, or roses are:
>
> 40–42   My flesh is soft, and plumpe,/ my marrow burning,
> My smooth moist hand,/ were it with thy hand felt,
> Would in thy palme dissolve,/ or seeme to melt.
>
> 49–51   Torches are made to light,/ iewels to weare,
> Dainties to tast,/ fresh beautie for the use,
> Herbes for their smell,/ and sappie plants to beare.

The poem has all Spenser's rhythmical subtlety, indicating that
Shakespeare was already grappling with the complex internal
harmonies of the sonnet. He had developed an intuitive sense
for modulating by pause position; vowel and consonant variation
is less obvious than Spenser's, but omnipresent; alliteration is
unobtrusive. E.g.

> 61–4   Fie, *liveless* pic*t*ure, co*l*d, and *senceless st*one,
> We*ll* pain*t*ed *idoll, im*age *d*ull, an*d dead*
> *St*a*t*ue con*t*en*t*ing bu*t* the eye a*l*one,
> Thing *l*ike a *m*an, *b*ut of *n*o *w*oman *b*red

Shakespeare favours 'structural' alliteration, rather than orna-
mental plenitude; alliteration is the servant of what Saintsbury
calls 'rhythm-groups within the line'. Thus lines 61 and 62 are
repetitive in metrical structure and antithetical phrasing; 'cold
and *senceless s*tone' is neatly balanced against 'image *d*ull and
dead'. Alliteration is confined to consonants in accentual verse;
idoll and *image*, *eye* and *alone* (62 and 63) would have been
alliterating staves in Old English poetry.

Shakespeare follows Spenser in confining the sense to the
line in stanzaic verse; the only enjambements are at lines 15/16
and 77/78; in the poem, as a whole, all but 17 lines are end-

stopped. He admits more feminine rhymes (e.g. 35/36, 38/40)
than either Spenser or Marlowe. They play their part in the
modulation of the rhythm, and are most effective in the final
couplet. The defect of these couplets is that they are seldom
happily combined with the preceding quatrain; at least half of
them are self-contained. In the last stanza selected (79–84) all
the rhymes of the quatrain are feminine; the final couplet has
masculine rhyme, for variation. The following lines are
metrically noteworthy:

80–83 Hér eýes/ pèti/tiŏnérs/ tŏ hís/ eýes súiňg,
         Hís eýes/ sǎw hér/ eýes, aš/ théy hàd/ nǒt séen thĕm,
         Hér eýes/ woóed stíll,/ hís eyés/ dišdaínd/ the woóiňg:
         Aňd àll/ thĭs dumb/ pláy hǎd/ hĭs acts/ mǎde pláin

The passage illustrates the extent of Shakespeare's modulations
of tempo and stress through substitutions of spondees and
trochees. In line 81 the medial pause is in the middle of the third
foot, a trochee. Spondees are deliberately emphatic and retarding
in tempo. One of Shakespeare's masculine virtues is that he
seems to use less ambiguously stressed feet at the beginning of
a verse line than Spenser. Feet, it has already been suggested,
are most likely to be ambiguous in stress when they contain
two monosyllabic words; but it is not unreasonable to urge six
primary stresses in the first three feet of line 82.

The determination of ictus in iambic verse is vital for
appreciation of Shakespeare's movement; he aimed at a little
more than the 'sophisticated smoothness' of Spenser's poetry.
He was before Milton and Pope in practising the modulation of
level and reversed feet. Syntax becomes doubly meaningful
through indicating the precise accent and juncture the scansional
ear demands. Thus, in the opening stanza, the first foot is a
reversed one, and, theoretically, *Even* is expected to be taken
as a monosyllable. *Rose-cheekt* (3) is a putative spondee or level
foot, as is *Sick-Thought/ed* (5). In line 6, however, the compound
bold fac'd, technically split by foot division, is a unity in reading;
metrical exigency alone requires that the second element should
be less weighted. The tension of metrical stress against the
natural emphasis of speech is well illustrated.

But a better example of so-called counterpoint occurs in line 5

Sićk-thóught/ĕd Vé/nŭs mǎkes/ amǎine/ ŭntò him

The distribution of primary, secondary and neutral stresses is instructive. The second syllable of *unto* has a metrical stress for the purpose, partly, of the rhyme (cf the rhymes *for thee/ abhor thee* in 35/36). One of the significant effects of verse modulation is the stress-ambivalence of most disyllabic prepositions; in other situations the stress may become *úntŏ*. Because the terminal syllables are here syntactically unemphatic, it is necessary, metrically, to assert a primary stress on the second syllable of the adverb *amaine*. An equally important syntactical change is the graphic use of the historic present in the final couplet.

The role of grammatical form is important in Shakespearian verse; for instance, the inflexion of the 3rd person singular present indicative of verbs. Endings in *-th* are normal with the notional verbs *saith, hath* (12) and *Doth* (70); but *breedeth* (53) and *hasteth* (73) are metrical uses; *hastens* would have served for the latter. In the whole poem metre accounts for 44 of the *-th* inflexions, 28 of them within the line, 16 at the end; 8 uses are explained by the stem-final of the verb being a sibilant or affricative sound (a tradition in Elizabethan grammar). *Hisses*, however, appears for *hisseth* (18), in order to rhyme with *kisses*. *Hath* is used 23 times in the whole poem, and *doth* no less than 45 times; *saith* 5 times, and *sayes* or *saies* precisely the same number. *Venus and Adonis* contains 69 uses of the periphrastic auxiliary verb *do/did*.

Mine and *thine* (not *my* and *thy*) are the approved possessives before nouns beginning with a vowel sound, as lines 38 to 43 show. The metrically curtailed forms *tane* (2) and *begot* (54) are typical of the ambivalent terminations of strong past participles in all Elizabethan poetry. *Set* (18) is an assimilated form of *seated*. Elsewhere in the poem, *wert* is used twice and *wast* once in the 2nd person singular present indicative. *Bin* (which is not a colloquialism, but a literary weakening) occurs twice for *been*. *Sometime* is more frequently used adverbially than the *-s* form. The relative *who* is commonly employed for things, as contemporary usage permitted. The plural of the indefinite pronoun *other* is normally *others;* but the OE uninflected plural is once employed to rhyme with *mother*. The morphological licences of Elizabethan poets were numerous, and reflect the fluidity of grammatical practice.

Syntactical features present few difficulties. It is worth noting that Shakespeare, like Spenser, did not distinguish the relatives *that* and *which* for defining and non-defining functions (see line 11). The present participial phrase *being set* (18), instead of an adverbial clause of time, was not as yet a common usage of poetic syntax. There is an improperly related participle *having* in 36 – a lapse of clarity widespread among poets of the time. The old past subjunctive in 31, 35, 41 and 56 was regarded as dignified and poetical. The employment of the definite article in the phrase *for the use* (50) is a metrical licence. The idiomatic use of the preposition in *to themselves* (52) has the significance of 'personal advantage'. There are only 10 inversions of word-order in the 84 lines selected, a much smaller proportion than is usual in Spenser. These inversions are of two poetically licensed kinds: the governing verb is preceded either by its object, or by a modifying adverb or adverbial phrase.

Except in a few passages, the surface meaning of *Venus and Adonis* is seldom in doubt. Shakespeare's economy of words is surprising in view of the *copia rerum ac verborum* of contemporary taste. In line 13 the preposition *from* is omitted after *alight* for metrical reasons, converting the latter into a pseudo-transitive verb. The infinitive of the verb *to be* is omitted before *seene* (46). The pronoun *it* (54) is a utility word for 'progeny', as is *thine* for 'thy offspring' (58). The phrase *by their own direction* (66), meaning 'instinctively', or 'self-instructed', is dictated by the exigency of feminine rhyme. *Fighting conflict* (75) is one of the occasional redundancies.

Shakespeare modified Ovidian mythology in a way significant to the secondary meaning of the poem; the conflict of nature and art is superseded by that of natural growth and death. Animal, plant and earth lore are the sources of nearly all the imagery. Nature has made Adonis the perfect specimen of physical man, and is content to let the world perish with him. This is the meaning of lines 11–12:

> Nature that made thee with her selfe at strife,
> Saith that the world hath ending with thy life.

In Venus's argument, Chaos is a dark world where love and beauty have no power. Thus Venus, apprehensive of Adonis's death, says in 1015–20:

> . . . how much a foole was I,
> To be of such a weak and silly mind,
> To waile his death who lives, and must not die,
> Till mutual overthrow of mortall kind?
> For he being dead, with him is beauty slaine,
> And beautie dead, blacke Chaos comes againe.

This sentiment is echoed in *Othello*.

Venus and Adonis is a paean, not only of physical love, but of life in the open air. It begins with the goddess of dawn, Aurora (Eos), weeping at the departure of the sun-god Apollo. The lover of the air-goddess in classical mythology was Tithonus, brother of Priam, who besought her to make him immortal, then pined for death as he became decrepit. Shakespeare substituted Apollo, the giver of light and life, presumably after Spenser had done so in *The Faerie Queene* I.5.2. He repeated this new version of mythology in *3 Henry VI*, II.1.21–2 and, more elaborately, in Sonnet *33*. Shakespeare believed with Ficino that 'Love has the enjoyment of beauty as its end'; the words and images of the poem are chosen to that end. E.g.

53   Seeds spring from seeds, and *beauty breedeth beauty*.

In 8–9 Adonis is characterized in two metaphors: 'The fields chiefe *flower*' and '*Staine* (i.e. rival) to all Nimphs'. Lines 25 and 26 contain sensual images, *tender spring* ('down on the lip'), *tempting* (personification), and *unripe* fruit, that may be *tasted*. The last is sustained in *34*, Venus protesting that she does not lack *iuyce*. Metaphor is not readily recognized in *Ore-worne* (*33*), marrow *burning* (*40*), *inchaunted* (*43*), *aspire* (*48*), *fed* (*56*), *likenesse* (*60*), *twining* armes (*70*), and *stealing* (*74*). Sensuality of touch is suggested by the hyperbole in line *42*; the hand of Adonis would *dissolve* or *melt* that of Venus. Lines 61–3 depict the coldness of the young hunter in vivid counter-metaphors:

> Fie, *liveless picture*, cold, and *sencelesse stone*,
> *Well painted idoll*, *image dull*, and dead,
> *Statue* contenting but the eye alone.

Changes in the complexion of Venus through mortification and anger are described in lines 75–8: there is *fighting conflict* in her cheek, where 'white and red ech other did *destroy*'; it '*flasht-forth fire*, as lightning from the skie'. Shakespeare and the neo-Platonists believed that love (for which *fancy* was a synonym) was 'engendered in the eyes', and 'with gazing fed'. Eye-play is metaphorically pictured in lines 79–84 as 'a *war of lookes*'. Venus's eyes are *petitioners . . . suing* those of Adonis. *Wooed* (82) and *did rain* (84) are graphic figures of personification and metaphor; and the image-group concludes with *dumbe-play* and *Chorus*, metaphors drawn from the theatre.

So graphic is Shakespeare's account that it has often been supposed that Shakespeare had in mind some painting of Venus wooing Adonis. This possibility was discussed in 'Shakespeare and Italy' (*English Studies in Africa*, Sept. 1961, pp. 117–27), where I conclude that 'the dramatist's genuine eye for a picture with mythological or historical interest is more likely to have been nurtured by the themes of the tapestries than the masterpieces of Italian painting, which were rare in England at the time'.

The procreation plea of Venus was a commonplace among the arguments to love used in the poetry of Renaissance Italy, France and England. Many of the arguments are to be found in Erasmus's *De Conscribendis*, a translated letter which appeared in Thomas Wilson's *Arte of Rhetorique*. T. W. Baldwin in *Literary Genetics of Shakespeare's Songs and Sonnets*, pp. 15–16, points out that the method of argument, *gradatio*, was derived from the Latin poet Terence, who wittily recounted the stages of love. Five steps are enumerated in Rosalind's speech to Orlando in *As You Like It* V. 2.33–45; they resemble those of Horace; seeing, talking, touching, kissing and coition.

The narrative detail of the early stanzas of *Venus and Adonis* is derived from the story of Salmacis and Hermaphroditus in the fourth book of Ovid's *Metamorphoses;* and the reluctance of Adonis to yield to Venus's passion comes from the same source. The account of her pursuit of Adonis in the tenth book is slight; the goddess emulates Diana and joins him in the chase, warning him against dangerous beasts. Ovid's main theme is the killing of Adonis by the boar, the incident that concludes the tenth book. Shakespeare plunges *in medias res*, without explaining the cause of Venus's love; according to Ovid, she had been accidentally wounded by one of Cupid's darts. In Ovid, Adonis is not the immature boy of Shakespeare's poem, but Hermaphroditus is. The 'sweating palm' of Shakespeare's fifth stanza may have been intended as a token of athletic youth, rather than unhealthy amorousness.

The rhetorical diversity of Shakespeare's language differentiates his narrative style from Marlowe's. Shakespeare was interested in figures of repetition as instruments of language patterning, and the schemes of thought are often complex. *Chiasmus* expresses the importance of Adonis's attitude to love throughout the poem; it is combined with alliteration in line 4:

> Hunting he *lov'd*, but *love* he laught to scorne (the alliteration of the lateral consonant *l* gives the line ease of movement).

Another combination of schemes (*antithesis* and *comparatio*) is to be found in line 10:

> More *white* and *red*, than *doves*, or *roses* are (the cross-patterning is semantically effective).

Similarly, *antithesis* and *anadiplosis* occur together in line 22:

> Ten kisses short as *one, one* long as twentie (alliteration and assonance on the numerals at the beginning and end of the line is deliberate).

There is an instance of *amplificatio*, by increment, in line 27:

> Make use of time, let not advantage slip.

Lines 28–30 of the same stanza take the form of *gnomic* utterances; so do lines 47–8, and 52–4. Lines 31–4 combine the figures of *asyndeton* (words or phrases strung together without conjunctions) and *synathroismus* (congeries), in which the words or phrases of similar significance (here 'unattractiveness') are accumulated:

> Were I *hard-favourd, foule*, or *wrinckled old*,
> *Il-nurtur'd, crooked, churlish, harsh in voice*,
> *Ore-worne, despised, reumatique*, and cold,
> *Thick-sighted, barren, leane*, and *lacking iuyce*.

The repetition of *then* at the beginning of two adverbial clauses in line 35 is an example of *epanaphora*; and a similar figure appears in 71. Line 53 combines alliteration, antithesis and *anaphora*:

> *Seeds* spring from *seeds*, and *beauty* breedeth *beauty*.

In the long argument of Venus, there are several examples of *erotema* or rhetorical question (55–6 and 67); and of *ecphonesis* (exclamation) in 61–4, 73–6 and 79. One of the most intricate examples of rhetorical configuration, *ploce*, occurs in the stanza of lines 79–84, with the word play on *eyes* and *wooing*. *Comparatio* in the last line (*Chorus-like*) involves the Renaissance conceit of *raining* tears from the eyes of Venus.

Throughout the poem Shakespeare makes use of metaplasms, such as *aphæresis* in *ginnes* for *beginnes* (6), *syncope* in *tane* (2), *maist* (26) and *Ore* (33), and *parenthesis* (for speaker interpolation), in line 7.

Marlowe's language, to conclude, is analytical, declamatory and vehement; Shakespeare's is flowing, elaborate and passionate. The development of their arguments on sexual unrestraint illustrates the difference. The couplet is well adapted to Marlowe's logical analogies, such as:

> Ah simple Hero, learne thy selfe to cherish
> Lone women like to emptie houses perish.

Leander's pleas in the poem are the rationalizings of a pagan: exquisite things become more precious through use; beauty is such a thing, however divine and chaste; let it then be perpetuated for the benefit of posterity. *Hero and Leander* is closer in detachment of style to the wit and irony of classical poets like Ovid.

In *Venus and Adonis* analogies thinly disguise the impulsive nature of the arguments. Venus unashamedly rationalizes self-indulgence; her attitude to Adonis is one of uninhibited advance. The stanza movement adds seduction to the conceits, and vigour to the controlled imagery.

Sonnets 19, 21, 30, 33, 64, 106, 130

Three notable, but different, exponents of blank verse, Shakespeare, Milton and Wordsworth, were also sonneteers; the reason is that the sonnet form, both Petrarchan and English, has problems of rhythm, pause, linking and closure similar to those of blank verse. Sonneteers differ largely in the arrangement of their matter; for the sonnet must achieve a pattern of thought within strictly formal limits, and demonstrate unity in variety.

Ornamental styles for sonnet themes were almost universal in the English Renaissance, and figures may be used to test the quality of the individual imagination. The Marlovian element in Shakespeare's language was subdued and mastered in the period to which most of the Sonnets have been assigned, 1594–1604. They reflect Shakespeare's growing understanding of the function of imagery in the rhetoric of poetry; what theorists sought to teach by categories and rules, Shakespeare learnt to control by artistic instinct. W. H. Empson, writing of Shakespeare's Sonnets in *Some Versions of Pastoral* (Chatto and Windus, 1935), says:

> Experiences are recorded, and metaphors invented, in the Sonnets, which he went on 'applying' as a dramatist, taking particular cases of them as if they were wide generalisations, for the rest of his life. (p. 90)

Shakespeare chose the four-part sonnet form, improved, if not invented, by Surrey; it suited better the development of antithetical ideas he compressed into the sonnet's fourteen lines. It permitted structures as diverse as the Petrarchan or two-part form, but was more accommodating to the logical thinking in fashion in the later sixteenth century. The pattern has, unfortunately, been sought in the rhyme-scheme, instead of in the semantic relations of the four units, three quatrains and a couplet. Compactness was a *sine qua non* of the total effect. Shakespeare's method of concentrating thought and phrase was not the Petrarchan way, partly because he was trained as a dramatist, practising the discipline of blank verse. In all experiments he showed himself to be a self-perfecting artist.

T. W. Baldwin thinks the argumentation in a Shakespearian Sonnet follows the pattern of the 'Enthymeme', derived by Erasmus from Cicero's *Ad Herennium* (*Literary Genetics*, p. 350). He argues that the first quatrain contains the *propositio*, the second the *ratio*, and the third either *confirmatio, confutatio* or *exornatio* (embellishment by figures and tropes); while the final couplet provides an epigrammatic summing up. Very few of Shakespeare's Sonnets actually conform to Baldwin's pattern.

Of the linking of the quatrains Tucker Brooke wrote (*Sonnets*, 1936):

> A strong pause in sense and rhythm at the close of each quatrain is for Shakespeare the primary law of sonnet harmony . . . in over

two-thirds of Shakespeare's sonnets the chief pause is placed after the twelfth line. . . . Normally, the couplet . . . compacts into itself the true essence of the poem. Less often the couplet introduces a surprise or negation. . . . Climax is seldom its purpose. (p. 6)

The unity of a Shakespearian Sonnet is dependent on the language, design and imagery. The poem often embodies two ideas in antithesis; the ambivalence the reader invariably senses may be emotional as well as rational. Antithesis is often expressed by an elaborate comparison or contrast, from which thoughts and conclusion are deduced. Sometimes the conclusion puts the emotional reactions of the three quatrains in a different and more rational light. In the best Sonnets, structure and syntax are shaped by the intellectual pattern of the argument.

Two aspects of verse technique are immediately observable in Shakespeare's Sonnets: the high proportion of end-stopped lines, compared with those in blank verse; and frequent pentameters composed of monosyllables, especially in penultimate and last lines. The apparent purpose is to retard the movement towards the close. Lines in the body of the poem are often monosyllabic, except for one impressive polysyllable, usually of Latin derivation, or a compound epithet. Sonnet 21 illustrates some technical points here mentioned:

Making a coopelment of proud compare
With Sunne and Moone, with earth and seas rich gems:
With Aprills first borne flowers and all things rare,
That heavens ayre in this huge *rondure* hems

Of the many patterns of harmony in Shakespeare's Sonnets none is more obvious or better adapted to content than alliteration (the Greek figure *parimion*). Shakespeare's reasoning about alliteration is suggested in the words of Holofernes, 'it argues facility' (LLL IV.2). He was particularly partial to *s* and *th* alliteration; and these were also the inflexional endings of verbs in the third person singular present indicative. The frequency of *vowel*-alliteration is apt to be overlooked, except when an observer studies the incidence of principal stresses in the line. Assonance is often cunningly interwoven with alliteration, as in Sonnets I and X. Assonance is used with particular effect by Shakespeare when the modulation involves a spondee, both accents being on monosyllables e.g.

Sonnet XV.8　And were (wear) their *brave state* out of memory.

Claes Schaar in *An Elizabethan Sonnet Problem*, (Lund, 1960), pp. 27–56, shows that the largest group of Shakespeare's Sonnets adopts a 'stair' pattern, in which development in the second and third quatrains *moves away* from the theme stated in the first. Sometimes this pattern takes the form of question and answer; in other Sonnets an initial simile leads to a comparison. The stair structure accorded well with Renaissance ideas on poetics, Italian and English, and with rhetorical figures, such as *prolepsis* (Lat. *propositio*), in which reasoning begins with a general statement.

In a smaller group of Sonnets, all quatrains look forward to the couplet-conclusion, the progression being marked by a series of images, which make vivid the train of thought; repetition may take the place of development.

One of the Sonnets' sources of strength is the interaction of images with the formal structure, and with the ideas the poems contain. The images integrate, rather than elaborate, Shakespeare's experiences and sensations; rhetorical significance is subordinate to aesthetic purpose. For this reason Shakespeare's Sonnets are superior to Sidney's, Spenser's or Daniel's, who all, with a few exceptions, used the English form. Shakespeare alone has the gift of fusing mixed metaphors by associations of feeling.

The principal subjects Shakespeare treats are logically connected and figuratively enriched: they are youth and beauty, and the desire for perpetuation; true love and inconstancy, mutability and the ravages of time; *Carpe Diem* or the hedonist's advice to rid the soul of its frustrations; finally, death and immortality. There are untold resources of visual imagery; as Schaar points out: 'Scenes with birds, flowers, shores, storms, suns and fountains are often detached from the poet's primary, non-tropical themes and presented to us like miniature pictures' (p. 99). The conventional Elizabethan images of the animal, vegetable, mineral and celestial worlds are sometimes treated satirically, as in Sonnets XXI and CXXX.

L. C. Knights, who places the Sonnets between 1592 and 1598, maintains that Shakespeare 'broke away from the formal and incantatory mode' of expression, in order to gain flexibility and transparency of meaning (*Explorations*, Chatto and Windus, 1946). While never abandoning the Petrarchan convention of conceit and hyperbole, Shakespeare invigorated the language by nuances of conversational idiom and by a tone of irony that readers with a biographical bias are apt to miss. The ambiguity of some Sonnets is quite deliberate.

The mature style of the best Sonnets suggests Shakespeare's abandonment of the conventional Platonism of Spenser in favour of realism. The criterion of worth in earlier Elizabethan sonnets had not been sincerity of feeling, so much as the power of words to move the listener or reader. Out of this grew the conviction of decorum. But in Shakespeare there is a selflessness about the attitudes to persons addressed that reveals the character of the poet. The tone of self-criticism is, indeed, the best evidence that Shakespeare did not intend the poems for publication.

Sonnet XIX

Devouring time blunt thou the Lyons pawes,
And make the earth devoure her owne sweet brood,
Plucke the keene teeth from the fierce Tygers yawes,
And burne the long liv'd Phænix in her blood,   4
Make glad and sorry seasons as thou fleet'st,
And do what ere thou wilt swift-footed time
To the wide world and all her fading sweets:
But I forbid thee one most hainous crime,   8
O carve not with thy howers my loves faire brow,
Nor draw noe lines ther with thine antique pen,
Him in thy course untainted doe allow,
For beauties patterne to succeeding men.   12
   Yet doe thy worst ould Time dispight thy wrong,
   My love shall in my verse ever live young.

Technically, the poem belongs to Shakespeare's earliest group of Sonnets, as the conventional compounds *long liv'd* and *swift-footed* show; the only unusual words are *hainous* (wicked) and *antique* (grotesque). Chaucer apparently borrowed *hainous* from French, and it was taken up by Caxton, More and Cheke; Shakespeare employs the word many times in the plays written before 1594, thereafter only in *King Lear* and *Pericles*. *Antique* became an alternative spelling of *antic*, *antick* in the sixteenth century. In the latter form, according to the Oxford Dictionary, it was first used in Hall's *Chronicles* in 1548, with the meaning of 'grotesque', to describe certain uses of decoration in architecture. The source is Italian *antico*, and the word was not differentiated in orthography from *antique* (old), Lat. *antiquus*, until the seventeenth century. Even in this French spelling and significance, the word had the accent on the first syllable until 1700, according to Dr Johnson's *Dictionary*.

The simplicity of the diction in this Sonnet is emphasized by the count of 99 monosyllables, to only 18 words of more than one syllable. In accord with this word choice is the use of adjectives in '*glad* and *sorry* seasons', and '*fading* sweets'. Line 4 is the only one that savours of 'poeticism'.

The movement of the verse is indicated by the minimal punctuation, intended to mark the structural pauses; the principal stops are the colon at the end of line 7 (an unusual position for Shakespeare), and the full-stop at the end of the third quatrain. Internal-pause commas, as might be expected in lines 1, 5, 6 and 13, are dispensed with; the commas at the ends of lines emphasize the end-stopped verse in reading. Words such as *Lyon* (1), *hainous* (8) and *hower* (9) were ambivalent in Elizabethan pronunciation, but the first two are here disyllabic, and the last monosyllabic. *Fleet'st* (5), which is phonetically unmanageable to a reader, was monosyllabic too, to rhyme with *sweets*. In verbs with stem-finals in *-t*, Shakespeare's later plays, such as *Hamlet* and *Antony and Cleopatra*, abandoned the final *-t* of the inflexion in the second-person singular present indicative. The printer probably restored it in this Sonnet for the sake of grammatical propriety. The emphatic position of the adverb *ever* in the final line should be noted. The couplet appears to be an afterthought, and leads cunningly to the 'immortality' vaunt of the last line. The rhyme *wrong/young* was apparently a good one in Shakespeare's day.

The sentence structure is remarkable for its lack of complexity, the only short subordinate clauses appearing in lines 5 and 6. The Sonnet elsewhere consists of a number of co-ordinated imperatives or exhortations to Time. In word order, the only notable line is 11, where *Him* (the admired young man) is in the emphatic first position; *doe* before *allow* is politely persuasive. The use of the emphatic double negative in the preceding line is in accord with contemporary practice.

Time, as depicted in wood-cuts, was one of Shakespeare's commonest emblematic figures, personified here in such phrases as 'swift-footed' (6). The poet maintains in the first quatrain that Time is more devastating than beasts of prey; the latter are supernumerary in a world of universal decay. Earth's *owne sweet brood* (or breed) is mankind. The Phoenix, fabled to feed its young from its own blood and live for six hundred years, was a symbol of longevity. The meaning of the obscure line

And burne the long liv'd Phænix in her blood

seems to be that this bird, in time, will consume itself by dying in its ashes. The *glad and sorry seasons* (5) are summer and winter, and the *fading sweets* of the next line the world's pleasures.

Although Shakespeare sees Time's destruction as an evil (13), he is prepared, in ironic hyperbole of the first two quatrains, to sacrifice all creatures, provided the loved person is spared as 'beauties patterne to succeding men'. If the inevitable happens, this paragon will at least achieve immortality in the verse of the poet. This fantasy, as critics have noted, Shakespeare took from the last book of Ovid's *Metamorphoses* (XV) (cf. the phrase, *Tempus edax rerum*, in line 234). In the last lines of this book, Ovid describes the *Metamorphoses* as 'a work which neither Jove's anger, nor fire nor sword shall destroy, nor yet the gnawing tooth of time'. Then the poet adds; 'With my better part I shall soar, undying, far above the stars, and my name will be imperishable . . . If there be any truth in poets' prophecies, I shall live to eternity, immortalized by fame'. (M. M. Innes's translation, Penguin Classics)

The exhortation in 9 and 10 that the beloved's brow should remain 'untainted' by wrinkles (whether *carved*, *delved* or *furrowed*) was a commonplace of classical poetry; as Leishman points out (*Themes and Variations*, pp. 136–8) it is to be found in *Epode* VIII of Horace, *Aeneid* VII, 417 of Vergil, as well as in Ovid's *Ars Amatoria* II, 117–18, and *Metamorphoses* III, 276.

The metaphors in all three quatrains are logically integrated and hyperbolic in character. In the first the alliterating consonants are harsh plosives, *d*, *b*, *p*, *k* and *t*; in the second they are *s*, *f* and *w*; in the third the voiced consonants *v*, *th*, *l*, *m* and *n*. The Sonnet, as a whole, illustrates the figure of *apostrophe*, which occurs in no less than 134 of Shakespeare's sonnets.

*   *   *

Sonnet XXI

So is it not with me as with that Muse,
Stird by a painted beauty to his verse,
Who heaven it selfe for ornament doth use,
And every faire with his faire doth reherse,   4
Making a coopelment of proud compare
With Sunne and Moone, with earth and seas rich gems:
With Aprills first borne flowers and all things rare,
That heavens ayre in this huge rondure hems,   8
O let me true in love but truly write,
And then beleeve me, my love is as faire,
As any mothers childe, though not so bright
As those gould candells fixt in heavens ayer: 12
  Let them say more that like of heare-say well,
  I will not prayse that purpose not to sell.

While self-contained, this Sonnet follows the preceding one, which begins:

A Womans face with natures owne hand painted,
Haste thou the Master Mistris of my passion

It deplores the use in love poetry of the 'unnatural natural history' of Euphuism, and is generally described as anti-Petrarchan. There seems an intention to deride the figurative language of the rival poet, supposedly Chapman, hinted at by reference to 'selling' his wares in the last line. J. D. Wilson, in his edition of the *Sonnets* (C.U.P., 1966) thinks that number XXI 'is an episode in the war between Poetry and Pedantry' (p. 120).

The diction, characterized by monosyllables (101 out of 119 words), contains a few poeticisms, such as *Muse* (1) for 'poet', *reherse* (4) for 'compare', *cooplement* (5) for 'liaison', *rondure* (8) for 'the enclosing firmament', and *gould candells* (12) for 'stars'. Of the epithets, '*proud* compare' (5) and '*huge* rondure' have a resonant elegance; but '*painted* beauty' (2), '*rich* gems' (6) and '*gould* candells' are conventional. 'Gould candells *fixt in heavens ayer*' is, indeed, a periphrasis which is decorative in the non-functional sense. The phrase 'heavens ayer' is a repetition of one in line 8; and the straining for effect in 12 suggests that Shakespeare is parodying the false diction of his rival. In the three preceding lines of the third quatrain he writes simply and sincerely ('let me but *truly write*') and interpolates *beleeve me* to suggest a conversational and ingenuous tone. His own poetry, he adds in the proverbial last line of the Sonnet, is not 'ornamented' for personal gain.

The movement is similar to that of other Sonnets in this group, most of the lines being end-stopped; the only enjambement is at the end of line 11. The major pauses are at the end of the second and third quatrains; and the printer has therefore wrongly placed the colon at the end of line 6, instead of line 8. The marking of internal pauses is indifferent, those indicated being in lines 6, 10 and 11. Following his usual practice (cf Sonnet XVII.9), the printer should have placed the phrase *true in love* in parentheses (9), thus indicating a further pause.

The Sonnet is an example of Shakespeare's command of complex grammatical structure. In the first two quatrains, participial phrases (past and present) are mingled with relative clauses; and the defining relative *that* is correctly used in 8, 13 and 14. In the last line, *that* should not be taken for a demonstrative pronoun. Equally dexterous is the handling of the concessive clause in lines 11–12, and the use of *will* in the 1st personal singular for the *coloured* future, in the last line. It is probable that the repetition of the periphrastic expletive *doth* in 3 and 4 is Shakespeare's way of parodying the heavy-footed style of his rival. The redundant use of the preposition *of* after *like* (13) is a metrical licence; the phrase *like of* was a colloquialism derived from Cockney.

Du Bellay and Sidney both inveighed against stilted appeals to the Muses for inspiration. The phrase '*painted* beauty' (2) gives point to Shakespeare's dislike of artificiality in diction, as well as in personal adornment. The three references to *heaven* (3, 8, 12) and those to *Sunne* and *Moone* (6) reflect weariness of these sources of simile; but it should be observed that Shakespeare is himself partial to the same comparisons, as well as to 'the seas rich gems' and 'Aprills first borne flowers'. The meaner tone of his style, here and in Sonnet CXXX, is due to deliberate avoidance of hyperbole. But sonnet language was, by convention, hyperbolic, in an exalted sense. Shakespeare, like Sidney, did not *only* 'look in his heart', when he wrote poetry in sonnet form.

Rhetorical devices are not avoided. Shakespeare's love of word play is shown by the use of *ploce* in lines 4 and 9:

And every *faire* with his *faire* doth reherse
O let me *true* in love but *truly* write

The repetition of *with* at the beginning of each phrase in lines 6 and 7 illustrates the partiality of poets for *epanaphora*.

Sonnet XXX

When to the Sessions of sweet silent thought,
I sommon up remembrance of things past,
I sigh the lacke of many a thing I sought,
And with old woes new waile my deare times waste: 4
Then can I drowne an eye (un-us'd to flow)
For precious friends hid in deaths dateles night,
And weepe a fresh loves long since canceld woe,
And mone th'expence of many a vannisht sight.   8
Then can I greeve at greevances fore-gon,
And heavily from woe to woe tell ore
The sad account of fore-bemonéd mone,
which I new pay, as if not payd before.   12
But if the while I thinke on thee (deare friend)
All losses are restored, and sorrowes end.

This Sonnet contains 96 monosyllables, 20 polysyllables. *Sweet* (1) is the most overworked adjective in the sequence (used over 30 times), and since Benson's edition appeared in 1640, may have been responsible for Milton's love of the word. Word choice presents difficulty in only one instance, *sight* at the end of line 8, which reads:

And mone th'expence of many a vannisht *sight*

Tucker Brooke in his edition interpreted this: 'And lament what many an object now lost has cost me'. This seems reasonable; for it accords with the use of the qualifying participle *vannisht*. Although the Oxford Dictionary cites four obsolete examples of the spelling *sight* for 'sigh', (the last in 1584) this use by Shakespeare is not included. The probabilities are against this meaning in context; yet support is found for it in the Variorum Edition of the *Sonnets* by H. E. Rollins (1944). The word *deare* (4) implies 'valuable', *dateless* (6) means 'endless' and *heavily* (10) means 'gloomily'. There is but one grammatical inversion of word order, *greevances fore-gon* (9).

The mellifluous ease of the lines calls for examination of the resources of rhythm. One is the deft alliteration, the initial

recurrence of *s*, *th* and *w*, the medial and final incidence of *l*, *m*,
n and *r*. Assonance is combined with alliteration in lines 4
(*old/woes*, *waile/waste*, *my/times*), 5 (*I/eye*), 6 (*precious/friends*),
13 (*deare/friend*), 14 (*losses/sorrowes*). The principal method of
retarding rhythm (usually in the latter half of the line) is to
group consonants between vowels, especially those bearing
stress. E.g.

1   sweet *s*ilen*t* *th*ought
2   thing*s* *p*ast
4   Añd wi*th*/ old́ woés/ new waíle/ my̌ deáre/ timés wáste
     (This line has a slow reverberation, owing to the spondees)
6   frieńds/ híd iñ/ dea*th*s dáte/ lĕss ní*g*ht (note inversion of stress in
     the third foot, followed by a spondee)
7   ă frés*h*/ loʹves loń*g*/ sińce cán/cel̆d wóe
8   vanni*sh*t s*i*ght
9   greevance*s* *f*ore-gon
11   fore-*b*emonéd *m*one
13   dea*r*e *f*riend
14   all *l*osses

The only enjambed lines are 1 and 10, and the comma after
thought in the first is therefore unfortunate. The rhyme *fore-gon/
mone* (9/11) was once a good one; but *past/waste* (2/4) may
have been acceptable only in dialect. (Wyld on p. 127 of
Studies in English Rhymes, Murray, 1923, explains alleged
identity in the vowel-sound of *past* and *paste;* the analogy can
hardly be extended to *past* and *waste*.)
     The logical structure is of a kind frequently used in the
English sonnet, especially by Shakespeare. Each quatrain
begins with a conjunctival adverb of time, the first with *When*,
the next two with *Then*. The couplet is introduced by the
adversative conjunction *But*. 'Shakespeare's partiality for
polysyllabic concentrations' (F. E. Halliday, *The Poetry of
Shakespeare's Plays*, Duckworth, 1954, p. 85) is well illustrated
in the adverbially-modified participial epithets;

7   loves *long since canceld* woe
11   of *fore-bemonéd* mone

These complex epithets are most effective at the end of lines.
     Metaphor and symbol, from Shakespeare's reflections on
melancholia, law and commerce, are of importance to the
meaning of this Sonnet. In lines 1 and 2 *Sessions* and *sommon*

are symbols of legal procedure, but only the first is a metaphor. In 3 to 9 the transitive use of *sigh* ('lament'), and *mone* ('regret'), together with *waile* and *weepe*, are words associated with melancholy; but, in context, only *sigh* and *mone* are metaphors. Contrasted with the poeticisms are the commercial words in 4 to 14: *deare, expence, tell* ('add up'), *account, pay, losses*. These are ambivalent in meaning (e.g. *tell* and *account* can be used for 'narration'), but only *pay* is metaphorical. The hand of the notary is suggested in terms such as *lacke* (3), *waste* (4) and *canceld* (7). Associated with death by water are the images '*drowne* an eye' and 'un-us'd to *flow*'. 'Hid in *deaths* dateless *night*' (linking *death* with *night*) completes a characteristically Shakespearian pattern.

The rhetorical devices are unobtrusive. Scaliger described as an 'elegant figure' the word play called by Quintilian *contentio*, and by the Greeks *antitheton*, in:

4   And with *old* woes *new* waile my deare times waste

Not only are the juxtaposed epithets contrasted, but the ideas. Each of lines 9 to 12 has a memorable example of *ploce*: '*greeve* at *greevances*', '*woe* to *woe*', 'fore-be*monéd mone*', 'new *pay*, as if not *payd*'. The metaplasms are among the commonest metrical licences of the period: *synalœpha, th*'expence (8), and *syncope, ore* in line 10.

The theme of the Sonnet is 'compensation'.

Sonnet LXIV

When I have seene by times fell hand defaced
The rich proud cost of outworne buried age,
When sometime loftie towers I see downe rased,
And brasse eternall slave to mortall rage.   4
When I have seene the hungry Ocean gaine
Advantage on the Kingdome of the shoare,
And the firme soile win of the watry maine,
Increasing store with losse, and losse with store.   8
When I have seene such interchange of state,
Or state it selfe confounded, to decay,
Ruine hath taught me thus to ruminate
That Time will come and take my love away.   12
     This thought is as a death which cannot choose
     But weepe to have, that which it feares to loose.

Shakespeare's 'mutability' Sonnets expound the transitoriness of existence and the ravages of Time. The idea of the sea's encroachment on the land probably came from Ovid's *Metamorphoses* XV, 288–90.

There are 19 polysyllables to 96 words of one syllable, and deviations from the normal use of words are numerous. The clustered epithets of line 2 have presented difficulties to interpreters since Malone. If *buried age* signifies 'antiquity', the expression is periphrastic, not unlike the latinized phrase *watry maine*, in which Shakespeare anticipates the English Augustans. The dignified tone of the Sonnet suggests the *Odes* of Horace on similar themes.

Fell (1) 'cruel', and *store* (8) 'plenty' are among the commonest Elizabethan poeticisms. *Brass* was, for Shakespeare, a symbol of durability. *Bræs* was used in Old English of the tenth century for the alloy (usually copper and zinc) of which statuary was made by the Greeks. From the eighteenth century this alloy was given the name of *bronze*, from Italian *bronzo;* the word *brass* was then reserved for the new industrial alloy of copper and tin.

The only run-on line is 5; the internal pause in 8 points the antithesis. Metrical structure is orthodox, the decisive pauses coming at the end of each quatrain. Long-vowel modulation is more employed than assonance; the rhythm is bound by alliteration, in which *s* predominates.

The syntactical pattern, with four temporal clauses, follows the logic of the argument explicitly. *Downe rased* (3) and *brasse eternall* (4) are the only grammatical inversions. The 'art' of the language consists partly in choice of epithets and figurative compounding of phrases.

The dominant figures in this Sonnet are metaphor and personification, the latter called by the Greeks *prosopopoeia*, and by Quintilian *conformatio*. Quintilian observed (IX.2): 'We lend a voice to things to which nature has denied it . . . We often personify the abstract, as Vergil does with Fame'. Time is here personified as a cruel destroyer that defaces costly monuments erected by the proud. *Rich* and *proud* (2) are associated with expensive sepulchres; *outworne* links with *defaced* in the previous line, and also with *age*. *Buried* is associated with tombs and the death Time brings, but also with the corrosive effect of earth revealed in excavated statuary.

Shakespeare's mind worked by association in the choice of epithets, not by logical or grammatical connection. *Mortal rage* (4) does not, I think, mean 'deadly fury'. Shakespeare had in mind the figure *contentio* in contrasting *mortall* with *eternall*. *Brass* (bronze), supposed to prolong man's identity, withstands the weathering of Time better than his body does death; but it is *slave* to death (metaphor), because in time, it too is *defaced* beyond identity. *Mortal rage* therefore betokens the 'anger of death'; for *rage* is associated with *fell* in line 1. The first quatrain is thus a coherent unit of images of death's power.

The next quatrain links itself to the first theme ('devouring Time') by the personification *'hungry* Ocean' (5), with its 'corroding' effect upon the shore, metaphorically described as man's *Kingdome* (6). In nature there is action and reaction; sometimes the land gains from the sea; in line 7 *contentio* is thus sustained. The effect of ambivalence is reflected in line 8: what is gained in one aspect of life is nullified by another. Shakespeare here debunks the illusion of man's progress.

The third quatrain continues the ambivalence. In line 9 Shakespeare suggests that the 'little world of man' is subject to fluctuations (*interchange of state*); for 'kingdoms often change hands'. *State* in 9 and 10 has twofold significance: it means the kingdom of individual personality, but also existence itself, which is so *confounded* ('confused') in belief that it is cheated by death. At the beginning of line 11, *Ruine* (a further personification, in that it 'teaches') underlines the idea of *decay* at the end of the preceding line. The reader is back at the tombs of the first quatrain, which caused Shakespeare to *ruminate* upon the nothingness of life. Love, believed to be all in all, is futile, because *Time* (death) will soon deprive the lover of it.

In the final couplet, *death* is an abstraction, meaning 'a sad blow'. It is not Death, but the poet himself, who 'cannot choose/ But weepe to have that which it feares to loose'. The ambivalence of the thinking is clear: 'having' is but a prelude to 'loss'.

The art of the poem lies in finely linked associations; rhetorical devices aid the thinking, yet emphasize the ambiguities. The style Shakespeare evolved, through acquaintance with classical Latin poets and rhetoricians, is universal; not because, as Shaw thought, it is 'vague'. It generates, through word play, the central ideas as well as the diction. The complexity of his mind can be seen in a single line:

8   Increasing store with losse, and losse with store.

This combines four figures: antithesis, alliteration, ploce and chiasmus.

Sonnet CVI

When in the Chronicle of wasted time,
I see discriptions of the fairest wights,
And beautie making beautiful old rime,
In praise of Ladies dead, and lovely Knights,   4
Then in the blazon of sweet beauties best,
Of hand, of foote, of lip, of eye, of brow,
I see their antique Pen would have exprest
Even such a beauty as you maister now.   8
So all their praises are but prophesies
Of this our time, all you prefiguring,
And for they look'd but with devining eyes,
They had not still enough your worth to sing: 12
    For we which now behold these present dayes,
    Have eyes to wonder, but lack toungs to praise.

The use of *blazon* (5), and the parallel in *Twelfth Night* I.5.295, led J. D. Wilson to date this Sonnet as late as 1602 (New Cambridge edition, 1966, pp. 214–15). Despite the *When–Then* sequence for the first two quatrains, the Sonnet is structurally in the Petrarchan mould of octave and sestet. The octave tells what kind of *Chronicle* Shakespeare had read; the resolution begins at 9, because more elbow-room than a couplet is needed to round off the poem. Although addressed to a man, the language of romantic hyperbole is in the tradition of courtly love.

The *Chronicle of wasted time* is the central image, to which others are subordinated; the Sonnet is thus an organic unity. Leishman (op. cit. p. 162) describes it as 'from the Christian and the Platonic point of view far more *idolatrous* than anything Petrarch ever wrote'.

There are 87 monosyllables and 23 polysyllables. The diction is notable for directness, the poeticisms being *wights* (2), *blazon* (5) and *devining eyes* (11). *Wights* is a generic noun, applying to both sexes. In heraldry, *blazon* (verb) meant the painting of coats-of-arms in appropriate colours. Figuratively, the noun came to signify 'praise', as in line 5. *Devining* implies 'foreseeing'; the ghost of a pun is hinted by the adjectival cliché. Shakespeare suggests that descriptions of human beauty by ancient poets were, in reality, inspired guess-work. *Sweet* (5) is the only threadbare epithet.

The smooth end-stopped lines of the first quatrain are modulated in the second by *asyndeton* in line 6, with five pauses. The following line is enjambed with 8, beginning with mono-syllabic *Even* (e'en); there is another run-on sequence at the end of 9. The principal pauses of the poem occur at the end of lines 8 and 12; the medial pause in 14 points the antithesis. The diction is compacted with skill by the use of assonance and alliteration.

The only inversions of word order are *Ladies dead* (4) and *all you prefiguring* (10). The partitive preposition *of*, omitted between *all* and *you*, is a licence of Elizabethan poetry; another is monosyllabic *for* (11), meaning 'because', in subordinate clauses of reason. Relative *which* (13) was permissible for persons until the eighteenth century, when it became rare or dialectal.

The meaning of certain words calls for comment. *Wasted* (1) means 'spent', not 'misspent'. In *antique Pen* (7) the adjective signifies 'old', not 'grotesque', as in Sonnet XIX. *Maister* (8) connotes 'command', 'possess'. *Prefiguring* (10) economically suggests 'describing such a person as you were to become in reality'. *Still* (12) is a contentious word, affecting the meaning of the poem's ending; it has been more often emended than preserved. Tyrwhitt conjectured *skill*, and was followed by Malone, Capell and many editors. But Wyndham in 1898 restored the Quarto reading. The ancient poets (he said)

> *still* . . . lacked something essential, viz. the model which we can behold and wonder at. . . . they had the 'tongues', but lacked the model; we have the model, but not their excellence in the art of description. Tyrwhitt's emendation, by denying the ancients' 'skill', defeats the antithesis of the passage and counters Shakespeare's general view of their excellence in Art. (p. 312)

The symbolism and imagery are the poem. *Chronicle* is a

symbol of the literature of the past, classical and medieval (4 and 5). *Antique Pen* is metaphorical for 'ancient writers', whom the poet admires. *Maister* has metaphorical overtones, and is appropriate to the sex of the person praised. Rhetorical figures are everywhere, e.g.

    3   *beautie* making *beauti*full (*ploce*)
    6   *Of* hand, *of* foote, *of* lip, *of* eye, *of* brow (*asyndeton*, omission of
        conjunctions)
    14 Have *eyes to wonder*, but lack *toungs to praise (antithesis*)

These are diverse devices important to the organic coherence of the Sonnet, and not to be generalized as 'word play'. Love of distinction and likeness should be recognized as a principal source of Shakespeare's imagery.

Sonnet CXXX

My Mistres eyes are nothing like the Sunne,
Currall is farre more red, then her lips red,
If snow be white, why then her brests are dun:
If haires be wiers, black wiers grow on her head: 4
I have seene Roses damaskt, red and white,
But no such Roses see I in her cheekes,
And in some perfumes is there more delight,
Then in the breath that from my Mistres reekes.   8
I love to heare her speake, yet well I know,
That Musicke hath a farre more pleasing sound:
I graunt I never saw a goddesse goe,
My Mistres when shee walkes treads on the ground.   12
    And yet by heaven I thinke my love as rare,
    As any she beli'd with false compare.

This is a parody of the un-Petrarchan, anti-hyperbolic manner, and was not initiated by Shakespeare. Horace and Catullus anticipated it; Chaucer, Lydgate and Dunbar all used unpoetic expressions for the character of a supposed mistress, such as *dun* (dark-complexioned), *wiers* (for hair) and *reekes* (exhales). The tone of the poem, especially in lines 1, 2, 6, 9 and 13, is colloquial, to match the content. But the poem should not be misunderstood, as by G. B. Shaw; Shakespeare is not traducing his mistress, who is *rare* (extraordinary), but explaining a lover's lack of objectivity. He knows her to be an ordinary person who 'treads on the ground', but does not imply that she has no beauty. He attacks the false ideal, which most contemporary poets extravagantly overworked. Burlesque is directed to the meretricious in art, rather than to pardonable defects of a woman. Shakespeare's unconventional taste in feminine beauty appears to have been for dark-complexioned persons – Rosalinde, Cressida or Cleopatra – the antithesis of the man the Sonnets praise.

The diction is, therefore, witty, in the Elizabethan sense of 'clever'. It exploits ambiguity, and finds fun in juggling with words and meanings. Coral is the hackneyed perfection of redness, snow of whiteness, and so on. Shakespeare mocks the comparison of hair with wire; a *damaskt* (or variegated) complexion may, in reality, be blotchy. Perfume may be more delightful than the natural odour of the body, but it is artificial; and speech is demonstrably inferior in sound to music, but it may charm. Shakespeare says no more than this, but subtly suggests that Platonic perfection is hardly desirable in women; a flesh-and-blood mistress is preferable to a goddess, whose grace of movement is a figment of the imagination. Colloquially, disillusionment is emphasized by the intensive *farre more* in 2 and 10, and the oath *by heaven* in 13.

Of the 123 words in the Sonnet, 107 are monosyllabic and 16 polysyllables. Lines 3, 4 (*wiers* is in both cases monosyllabic), 9, 13 (heaven is monosyllabic), consist wholly of words of one syllable; they are deliberate lines on that account, and are modulated by internal pauses.

All the lines in the first quatrain are sharply end-stopped, hence the oracular tone of the pronouncements. The next four lines, still self-contained, move interdependently, because of the linking words *But*, *And* and *Then*. In the third quatrain there is a heavy pause after *found* (10). Not one enjambed line is found in the poem, which consists of 'jerks of invention' to match turns of argument.

The uninflected possessive *Mistres* (1) follows Elizabethan practice in poetry and Scripture, where nouns end in *s*; *lips* (2) is probably a possessive plural. The subjunctive *be* (3 and 4) served a useful purpose in poetry, but was steadily being replaced in prose. *See I* (6), *is there* (7) and the adverbial phrase *from my Mistres* (8) are inversions of word order out of keeping with the colloquial context. Along with poetical *hath*, they were probably used to simulate the diction Shakespeare was travestying.

The Sonnet is nearly bare of metaphor and symbol; *Roses ... in her cheekes* (6) is metaphor declining to cliché. The poem is a sequence of comparisons, yet there is no simile. Shakespeare's crude realism is obviously deliberate. He risks a poeticism in *damaskt*, with meaning similar to its adjectival use in *LLL* V.2.296; OED records only one earlier use of the verb *damask* (1585). It is a precious word like *diapred* in Spenser's *Epithalamion* 51:

> And *diapred* lyke the discolored mead

Alliteration and assonance are ever-present; but there are few examples of other rhetorical devices, except repetition, e.g. *ploce* in 2 and 4:

> Curral is farre more *red*, then her lips *red*,
> If haires be *wiers*, black *wiers* grow on her head

The OED notes that 'from the 13th to the 16th Century golden hair was frequently poetically likened to gold wire', as by Lydgate:

> *Assembly of Gods* 373   Dame Venus . . . Whoos long here shone as
>   *wyre* of goold bryght.

Even when anti-Petrarchan in spirit, the Sonnets examined are poetical. But 'poetic' words, archaisms and inversions of order are not employed on a scale approaching those in Spenser's diction. The vocabulary and grammatical structure of the poems are simple; less than one-fifth of the words have more than one syllable, an unusually low ratio for Shakespeare's time. Frequent end-stopped verses tie the sense to the line. The cohesion of the Sonnet is achieved partly through alliteration and assonance, partly through the word play to which assonance is sometimes a clue.

There is invariably abundance of imagery, especially personification. The underlying ideas are fortified by the pattern of images, which may or may not arise from the word play. The poet's pursuit of semantic association in the complex of meanings, is one of the secrets of his art. Another is the integrating power of rhetorical devices, which he conceals with skill; repetition and antithesis have the greatest structural value. Epithets usually enrich the image; they are not only of the binary type; many are complex phrases, modified or intensified by adverbs. The language gives the impression of naturalness, rather than convention. In view of the sonneteer's delight in hyperbole, this is an achievement.

The ambiguity of Shakespeare's humour often arises from disillusionment with the real, or disappointment in the ideal, in the workings of nature and love. J. B. Broadbent describes the stylistic quality persuasively in *Poetic Love* (Chatto and Windus, 1964):

> The literary characteristics of Shakespeare's sonnets may baffle: the slow weightiness, with sudden acceleration; the abrasion of word on word . . . They are much more impersonal than Metaphysical poems. It is because they have this Eliotic impersonality that they are, paradoxically, so private. (pp. 143–4)

In lyrical composition, Spenser, Marlowe and Shakespeare seem to have respected the ideal of metrical faultlessness. There is little difficulty in scanning their verse or attuning the ear to the beat of their rhythms, once the variations of stress position in polysyllabic words are known. The pronunciation of many Romance loan-words can be inferred from their poetry, especially their rhymes. In the passages analysed, probably written about the same time (1590–1595), the polysyllables of Marlowe and Spenser are in the relation of 1 to 4 monosyllables; but in Shakespeare (*Venus and Adonis* and the *Sonnets*) the ratio is less than 1 to 5.

Josephine Miles in *Major Adjectives in English Poetry* (Univ. of California Press, 1946) showed that the frequency of a poet's vocabulary may be a guide to his literary character. Thus Spenser's commonest words are *see* (verb) and *heart*, Marlowe's *lord* and *king*, Shakespeare's *love* and *good* (adjective), Donne's *love* and *make* (verb), Milton's *heaven* and *God*, Pope's *man* and *see* (verb). On an average, 60 per cent of a poet's adjectives are descriptive, and the remainder either participial or limiting.

In *Renaissance, Eighteenth Century and Modern Language in English Poetry* (1960), the same writer sampled a thousand

lines from each of 200 poets, and found that nouns, adjectives
and verbs account for about one half of a poet's vocabulary; the
nouns are roughly equal in number to the other two parts of
speech. Naturally, there are individual differences: Donne has
fewer nouns than the average, and Milton more adjectives.
Langland is exceptional in using three verbs to one adjective.

There is general consent among Renaissance poets (according
to the investigation) in the use of language that is complex in
clauses and 'highly predicated' (p. 3). But as the concept of
style progresses, modification tends to replace predication, and
participles are substituted for clauses. There is a nice balance
of these grammatical structures in the *Sonnets* of Shakespeare.
Repetition is found to be 'poetry's basic device of form'.

The figures produced for Spenser, Marlowe and Shakespeare's
Sonnets, in this investigation, are instructive; for comparison,
the statistics relating to Donne and Milton are included:

		Nouns	Adjectives	Verbs	Total NAV	Total Words
Spenser	F. Queene and *Amoretti*	1590	1150	1100	3840	8100
Marlowe	Hero and Leander, Ovid *Elegies*	1640	940	1320	3900	7860
Shakespeare	*Sonnets*	1780	1000	1130	3910	8520
Donne	*Songs* and *Sonnets*	1300	660	1230	3190	7100
Milton	*Minor Poems*	1550	1200	770	3520	6720

About one third of the adjectives used by Milton are participial,
nearly double the proportion used by the other four poets.
Spenser, in ten lines, uses 12 adjectives to 16 nouns; Marlowe
in the same space 9 to 16; Shakespeare 10 to 17; Donne 7 to 13;
the proportions for Milton are not given.

Spenser's favourite epithets are *fair*, *great* and *sweet*; his
nouns *eye*, *love*, *heart*, *life* and *man*. Marlowe favours *fair* among
the adjectives, and *love* (70 times) among the nouns. Shake-
speare's commonest adjectival use is *sweet*; among nouns he
chooses *love* (80 times), *beauty* and *time*. The three poets all
employ *make* as their commonest verb; Donne's preference is
for *take*, and Milton's for *come* and *hear*.

Throughout his poems, Shakespeare appears from statistics to be moderate in his taste for epithets; proportionately, only Marlowe and Donne use less than he does. But the group of Renaissance poets discussed is remarkable in another way – for the fluidity of their movement in verse. Phonetically the language has not the facility of French or Italian, because of the ruggedness of most consonants and the predominance of Anglo-Saxon monosyllables. These were difficulties that poets like Spenser, Marlowe and Shakespeare had been able to overcome before 1600.

VI

SHAKESPEARE'S DECLAMATORY AND LYRICAL DRAMAS (To 1600)

One of the most instructive accounts of a Renaissance poet's style is *Shakespeare's Wordplay* (Methuen, 1957), by M. M. Mahood, who writes:

> While the books of rhetoric can show us how the average Elizabethan was taught to embellish his Latin and English verses with tropes and figures, they tell us nothing of the poetic and dramatic function of these ornaments. (p. 19)

Rhetoric was esteemed as an aid to writing partly because of the rudimentary state of grammar, especially in its structural aspect. Writers who desired emphasis were less conscious of the significance of word order than they should have been; they studied appeals to the ear and eye, the repetition of sounds and balance of word against word, as physical means of conveying the importance of ideas or feelings. The disposition of letters, syllables and stresses was planned as a musician or painter plans effects. Through rhetoric, it was possible to demonstrate a cult of writing, aural and visual, leading to self-education. Rhetoric and translation thus became regular activities of an aspiring literate class.

The effect of rhetoric on listeners and readers is mainly psychological; the reader attends to the manner of expression, and unconsciously yields to the power of the language. In an age of baroque the emotional effect of ornament was curiously impressive. Elaborate lists of figures, with illustrations, enabled traditionalists to practise the stylized writing in which much Elizabethan literature abounds. *Arcadia*, *Euphues* and *The Spanish Tragedy* are among the most interesting examples. Amplification, antithesis and repetition, whether of letter, sound or word, were devices of style readily detached from the content of words, and universally regarded as the *dress* of expression. The improvements of Shakespeare and Donne were achieved by transferring the emphasis from decoration to imaginative activity, emotion disciplined by intellect. Though figures of rhetoric were never abandoned, the poet found he could project them less artificially to the surface texture of the poetry. The tools of language were skilfully sharpened.

Sidney spoke of *energeia*, Jonson of *invention;* the difference between these terms may be the measure of departure in their styles. What Aristotle meant by *energeia* was not vigour of expression, but dynamic metaphor. What Jonson meant by *invention* lay somewhere between 'wit' (selection of the best thoughts), and 'a new combination of existing images'; only in the latter sense did *invention* connote 'originality'.

Quintilian was the first to separate tropes from schemes. In rhetoric, figures of thought and word were the more superficial (*figurae* was the Latin equivalent of Greek *schemata*). Some schemes of words, such as metaplasms, found a place in grammar in the eighteenth century. Coleridge recognized that the more important functions in poetry are performed by tropes, 'images of the mind', in such forms as metaphor, simile, personification and hyperbole. Cicero, thinking in prose, regarded them as deviations from the normal manner of speech. Images bring enrichment of the effects of language through surprise; and surprise is accompanied by a heightened perception of relationships, which Lord Kames described in his *Elements of Criticism* (1762) as 'imagination'. A much less precise use of this word had occurred earlier in Hawes's *Pastime of Pleasure* XIV.53 (1509).

The judgement of imagery is subjective, and the criterion is its efficacy in context, assessed by adequacy to the feelings it arouses. The aim is to move and delight, as plain statement rarely does. Poetry moves the listener or reader nearly without his volition. Shakespeare's images seem *true* when they create the impression of sincerity; he must have felt and not feigned the emotions he translated into words. T. S. Eliot speaks of 'a rhetoric of substance . . . which is right because it issues from what it has to express' ('Rhetoric and Poetic Drama', 1919). The advance, as he shows, is 'refinement in the perception of the variations of feeling . . . with a greater command of language, and a greater control of the emotion'.

The Elizabethan dramatist employed tropes consciously for impassioned speech, and the critic needs to be just as sensitive.

Renaissance poets need readers who perceive also the patterns of sound and changes of tempo. The paradox of *decorum* lay in the conception of a poetry designed to be heard to the best advantage, yet free from ostentation.

The paradox of style is tensest in the use of hyperbole, which the Elizabethan poet identified with elevation. Ben Jonson wrote of this in *Discoveries 2002*: 'It may be above faith, but never above a meane'. The convention of hyperbole (it was no more) enabled the speaker to suggest exceptional feeling; and it was often buttressed by other figures, such as alliteration and personification.

Hyperbole is a principal ingredient of 'declamation', a word used by Skelton in his *Goodlie Garlande or Chapelet of Laurell*, 1523; in Senecan tragedy it might be out of character with the functional needs of dialogue. Naturalness, Eliot thought, is determined by the role in which a character sees himself in the play; and irrelevance to verisimilitude of tone is thus a criterion of rhetorical speech. Manner tends to overlay and obscure matter.

A declamatory dramatist consciously uses rhetoric to impress or diffuse the thought. Grandiloquence was, at first, attractive to Shakespeare, because of its success in *Richard II*, *Richard III* and *Romeo and Juliet*. Later, he was able to moderate the fashion for declamation, when he realized that language in drama should make thought and feeling cohere. In Sonnet LXXXII he speaks about the 'strained touches Rhethorick can lend'; and in an earlier Sonnet (LXXVI) he reproaches himself for stereotyping his art:

> Why with the time do I not glance aside
> To new found methods, and to compounds strange?
> Why write I still all one, ever the same,
> And keepe invention in a noted weed (dress),
> That every word doth almost sel (tell) my name

The principal improvement Shakespeare effected after 1600 was the use of image clusters in set speeches; they became nebulae of association, through which he dramatized the whole range of human emotion.

Word play, breaking 'one word into a spectrum of meanings', is likened by Mahood to clustered images, the method of invention being similar. She claims that Shakespeare's imagination worked through puns, though some are so obscure in modernized texts that they escape the reader's notice. Words used in this way are the substance, not the dress, of poetry; 'the best ironic puns are uncomic' (p. 42). The most frequently played-upon words, she finds, are *dear, grace, will, light, lie, crown, hart* (heart), *son* (sun), *colour, use* and *shape* (p. 51). Over 3,000 instances of word play occur in the complete works, an average of 78 in each play, the majority in the first two Acts. In the comedies the punning is preponderantly in the mouths of women and Fools; and Mahood takes this as evidence of superabundant mental energy, rather than resourcefulness of wit. After *Richard II*, Shakespeare's word play showed little development.

Shakespeare's resort to comic touches throughout his serious works, is evidence that he read Thomas Wilson's *Arte of Rhetorique* (1553). This is what Wilson wrote:

> Except men finde delite, they will not long abide: delite them, and winne them: wearie them and you lose them for ever. And that is the reason, that men commonly tarie the ende of a merie Play, and cannot abide the halfe hearing of a sower checking Sermon. . . . The wittie and learned have used delitefull sayings, and quicke sentences, ever among their waightie causes, considering that onely good will is got thereby . . . (pp. 3 and 136)

Blank Verse

Unrhymed iambic-pentameter verse was the creation in England of Henry Howard, Earl of Surrey, who used it in his translation of the Fourth Book of Vergil's *Aeneid*, published in 1554. He followed this with a translation of the Second Book, the two appearing in one volume, published by Tottel in 1557. Blank verse had, however, been employed unconsciously by Chaucer in the prose *Tale of Melibeus;* and something like it (the *versi sciolti* of Luigi Alamanni) had appeared in Italy, from which country most metrical innovations of the sixteenth century had a way of originating. The stiffness of Surrey's versification was due, in part, to the count of stressed syllables in the individual line; but he did permit occasional enjambement.

Surrey worked with two versions of the *Aeneid* before him — the Latin original and a manuscript of Gavin Douglas's earlier

translation, published posthumously in 1553. The new trans-
lation, though indebted to Douglas's, is Surrey's own, and
represents an honest attempt to emulate Vergil's diction in
syntax, figures of speech, and rhetorical patterns. It might have
been better for the worth of Surrey's translation, if he had been
freer in adapting Vergil to the English idiom, and had not been
so close to Douglas, whose dialectal ease, in rhymed pentameter
couplets, displayed a versatile invention.

Blank verse required more than the fluency and syntactical
order that Surrey sought to give it; rhythm and tempo needed
modulation. Syntax conceived in paragraphs of grouped ideas,
rather than metrical units, was an art that took half a century,
or more, to evolve. Dryden was mistaken in suggesting that
Shakespeare adopted blank verse 'to shun the pains of continual
rhyming' (Epistle Dedicatory to *The Rival Ladies*, 1664).

Lines 662–73 of Surrey's second book are a fair sample of
his methods.

> Amid the court under the heven all bare
> A great altar there stood, by which there grew
> An old laurel tree, bowing therunto,
> Which with his shadow did embrace the gods.
> Here Hecuba with her yong daughters all   5
> About the altar swarméd were in vaine,
> Like doves that flock together in the storme;
> The statues of the gods embracing fast.
> But when she saw Priam had taken there
> His armure, like as though he had ben yong,   10
> 'What furious thought, my wretched spouse,' quod she,
> 'Did move thee now such wepons for to weld?'

The first line, a commendable verse with only three primary
stresses, has a pause after the second foot, and the third has
inverted stress. Line 7, which is metrically orthodox, contains a
Vergilian simile. But the other lines are indecisive, especially 2
and 3, where *altar* and *laurel* involve stress inversions in the
second foot, inimical, after a preliminary iamb, to the flow of
blank verse. The colourless adverbial *therunto*, which ends this
line, makes the whole ineffective; but the defect is partly
redeemed by the fine metaphorical use of the verb *embrace* (4).
Both lines 5 and 6 have inelegant inversions of word order (*all*
and *swarméd were in vaine*). *Fast* at the end of 8 illustrates one
of Surrey's weaknesses, the choice and placing of adverbs. Lines

2 and 9 are run-on; and the trochaic inversion *Priam* in the latter is sensitively placed. *Like as though* in 10 is, however, a weak connective in a crucial position. The dialogue of the last two lines is stilted in metrical regularity, and colloquially unnatural.

Saintsbury thought that Seneca's mode of expression had a bad influence on the early tragedians, because his line was too sententious. The woodenness and inflexibility of the blank verse in *Gorboduc* (1561) suggests that Sackville's talent was rather for stanza-patterned lines, linked by rhyme, alliteration and assonance. The enervating effect of the metre is evident in I.1.54–67:

> There resteth all. But, if they faile there-of,
> And if the end bring forth an ill successe,
> On them and theirs the mischiefe shall befall;
> And so I pray the goddes requite it them,
> And so they will, for so is wont to be.   5
> When lordes, and trusted rulers under kinges,
> To please the present fancie of the prince,
> With wrong transpose the course of governance,
> Murders, mischiefe or civill sword at length,
> Or mutuall treason, or a iust revenge   10
> When right-succeding line returnes againe,
> By Ioves iust iudgement and deservéd wrath
> Bringes them to cruell and reprochfull death
> And rootes their names and kindredes from the earth.

The only lines with poetical sensitivity are 8, 9, 12 and 13. The poverty of the words in significant positions is remarkable, especially at the end of lines. *Governance* (8) and *reprocheful death* (13) have some resonance; but *there-of* (1), *to be* (5) and *againe* (11) are debilitating line-endings. The structure has no inherent strength; and this is partly due to the sequence of co-ordinated clauses. No less than four lines begin with *But* or *And*; and two subordinate clauses are introduced by *When*. There is no enjambed line, and this may be why the speech sounds contrived.

Thomas Kyd, a master of Senecan declamation, wrote *The Spanish Tragedie* a generation later (1591); it embodies a long tradition of rhetorical learning. E.g. I.3.330–49:

> Fortune is blinde and sees not my deserts,
> So is she deafe and heares not my laments;

And could she heare, yet is she wilfull mad,
And therefore will not pittie my distresse.
Suppose that she could pittie me, what then?   5
What helpe can be expected at her hands?
Whose foot standing on a rowling stone,
And minde more mutable then fickle windes.
Why waile I then wheres hope of no redresse?
O yes, complaining makes my greefe seeme lesse.   10
My late ambition hath distaind my faith,
My breach of faith occasioned bloudie warres,
Those bloudie warres have spent my treasure,
And with my treasure my peoples blood,
And with their blood, my ioy and best beloved,   15
My best beloved, my sweet and onely Sonne.
O wherefore went I not to warre my selfe?
The cause was mine I might have died for both:
My yeeres were mellow, his but young and greene,
My death were naturall, but his was forced.   20

The first four verses are antithetical in structure, mainly monosyllabic lines with terminal polysyllables. To enforce the antithesis, the first two lines are identical in metrical form. Then follow a series of rhetorical questions (*erotema*) in 6, 9 and 17, partly answered by the speaker, so that he may convey to the audience the state of his mind. This progression gives incisiveness to the argument. The five uses of *And* at the beginning of lines are repetitions of coherence (*epanaphora*). Verisimilitude is given to the dialogue by the colloquialisms *what then?* (5) and *O yes* (10); but these are devices that may be overworked in drama. Lines 7, 13 and 14 are limping ones, each defective in a syllable.

The declamatory nature of the passage is evident from the step-structure of the questions. The first, in line 5, is linked with the preceding line by the repetition of the word *pitie*. The second, in 9, is linked with the climactic second half of the speech by the rhyme *redresse/ lesse* (10), by assonance *then*, *wheres*, *yes*, and by consonance in which *w* and *s* predominate. This consonance (often in alliteration) permeates the structure of the passage, concealing the obvious fact that the lines are all end-stopped, because such is the mould of the rhetorical pattern. *Gradatio* (climax) in 11 to 16 is clinched by the repetitive words *faith* (11/12), *bloudie* (12/13), *treasure* (13/14), *blood* (14/15), *best beloved* (15/16). The final lines (19 and 20) are balanced by antitheses, the punctuational fulcrum being as nearly as manageable in the middle of the line.

The blank verse is contrived, but it sounds and reads better than that of Kyd's predecessors. This is due to the rhetorical pattern, and to internal modulation, line 7 being notable for stress-inversion in the second foot. Most lines have only four primary stresses, and the incidence of these is varied, with the rhythm, by strategic placing of the polysyllables.

The difficulty of early blank-verse experimenters was to combine form, emphasis and rhythm, whether musical or rugged, so as to express the poet's mood. Marlowe limited the number of primary stresses in the line of *Tamburlaine* to four, and thereby introduced some variation into stress positions; his work is conventional metrically. Shakespeare succeeded best in loosening the sinews of blank-verse by introducing feminine endings (*anacrusis*), run-on lines and pause-modulation. The degree of stress on a head-syllable that follows a pause is difficult to determine, except in relation to subsequent phrases; for rhythm is a property, not of the pronunciation of single words, but of verbal groups.

When he had used unrhymed pentameters in dramatic dialogue for some years, Shakespeare recognized its proneness to monotony; his deviations are exercised to the limits permissible to the ear. Robert Graves later enunciated, as a principle, what Shakespeare had established as a practice: 'theme decides what rhythmic variations should be made on metre' ('Harp, Anvil, Oar', *The Crowning Privilege*, Cassell, 1955, p. 101). The right distribution of stresses in Shakespeare's blank verse is not always immediately apparent. According to O. Jespersen in 'Notes on Metre' (*Selected Writings*, Allen and Unwin, 1962) the frequency of stress inversions in his plays is in the following proportion: first foot 90: second foot 1: third foot 15: fourth foot 12. Trochaic inversion is thus six times as numerous in the first foot as in the third, and twelve times as numerous in the fourth foot as in the second, where it occurs, on an average, only once in a play; and this must have been based on Shakespeare's acting experience, to secure a natural delivery. But no rule supersedes the exigencies of the poetic occasion; there are some scenes, such as the storm in *The Tempest*, where the blank verse is barely recognizable.

Not all Shakespeare's speeches above ten lines are intended to be orations; but those that are seem moulded with a dynamic purpose. Even if the mood spells reflection, the words imply action, as in *Julius Caesar* II.1.77–85:

> O Conspiracie,
> Sham'st thou to shew thy dang'rous Brow by Night,
> When evills are most free? O then, by day
> Where wilt thou finde a Caverne darke enough,
> To maske thy monstrous Visage? Seek none Conspiracie,
> Hide it in Smiles, and Affabilitie:
> For if thou path thy native semblance on,
> Not Erebus it selfe were dimme enough,
> To hide thee from prevention.

Speeches in Shakespearian drama, directly or indirectly, induce characters to react in a certain way. Rhetoric had its place, but was not as necessary to Shakespeare as it was to Kyd. He had many other shafts in his armoury. Redundant syllables at the medial pause, as well as at the end of a line, made for naturalness, when the phrases preserved the ordinary rhythms of speech. A redundant syllable often converted an iambic foot to an anapaest, which Shakespeare was bolder to use in blank verse than any of his sixteenth century contemporaries.

The greatest resource in the Shakespearian line was, however, the judicious use of the resonant polysyllable, so placed as to make each a refractive gem of significance; it possesses inevitability for the poetic occasion. There are some speeches in which the splendour of Latin polysyllables is cumulative, as in the *Sermons* of Donne. These orations are weighty discourses, such as Ulysses's eulogy of 'Degree' in *Troilus and Cressida*. Landor described the rhetorical as an *opaque* style; but the qualification is seldom appropriate to Shakespeare. One of the best accounts of his art is the Poet's observation in *Timon of Athens* I.1.22–5:

> the fire i' th' Flint
> Shewes not, till it be strooke: our gentle flame
> Provokes it selfe, and like the currant flyes
> Each bound it *chases*.

(Theobald emended the last word to *chafes*; but *chases* accords better with the simile.)

In *The Poetry of Shakespeare's Plays* F. E. Halliday has this comment on Shakespeare's metrical development:

Imposition of one rhythm, the rhetorical, of which we are fully conscious, on another of which we are only half-consciously aware, is another form of the basic contrapuntal principle in art . . .
(*Footnote:* By rhetoric is meant the consciously constructed speech of the orator, full of devices for attracting attention and emphasizing a point, and addressed to the audience as much as the other characters on the stage.)

Shakespeare transformed the monophonic verse of Marlowe into a new polyphonic or contrapuntal poetry of interwoven rhythms; as a writer of verse his progress is from angularity and regularity to plasticity and variety. (pp. 25–7)

The sense in which *rhetoric* is here used is wider than that attempted in this study; but there may be value in examining the implications of *polyphony* for blank verse. It should not be confined to what Chatman calls 'the English phonological syllable' (*Theory of Meter*, p. 112); for poetry is concerned with sound and silence, in harmony with rhythm, and metre occasionally overrides phonetics. The relations of phonetics, music and rhetoric in dramatic blank verse, if they exist, are not yet understood; and one should recall the *caveat* of Francis Berry: 'when we describe voices, Shakespeare's or anyone's, we must necessarily be subjective and must hence employ metaphor' (*Poetry and the Physical Voice*, p. 124).

In music *polyphony* means 'the harmonizing of several parts, each with a different melody'; the concord is naturally 'note against note'. Analogy with the counterpointed rhythms of blank verse (one of metrical pattern, the other of syntax or rhetoric) is therefore rather tenuous. Egerton Smith in *The Principles of English Metre* (OUP 1923) overcomes this difficulty by maintaining that 'the counterpoint exists mentally . . . the result being a peculiar compromise in the actual or imaginary enunciation' (p. 307).

Leigh Hunt in 'What is Poetry?' (1844) first pointed to analogies that bind poetry, painting and music, and quoted Bacon's view that in these arts we see 'the same feet of Nature, treading in different paths'. Critical appreciation abounds in metaphors of this kind, curious blends of the romantic and analytical. Of the latter kind is Hunt's description of the principles of modulation, on which most theoretical metrists have drawn. His analysis of the poets included in this study produced the following conclusion:

Verse is the final proof to the poet that his mastery over his art is
complete. It is the shutting up of his powers in '*measureful* content';
the answer of form to his spirit; of strength and ease to his guidance ...
I know of no very fine versification unaccompanied with fine poetry;
no poetry of a mean order accompanied with verse of the highest.

Shakespeare, in his practice, must have shared this opinion.
He was helped by daily association with his collaborators, the
actors. From 1594 to 1610 he worked with Burbage, Lowin,
Kempe and Armin, colleagues who stimulated him, not only
with dramatic ideas, but through the individual inflexions and
nuances of their trained voices.

The lyricism of Shakespeare's plays before *Henry IV* often
involves digression from their dramatic purpose, as well as
temptations to imitate the neo-Platonic fancies and conventions
of poets in the school of Spenser. But conventionalism itself can
be attractive in Shakespeare. Fantasies, such as *A Midsummer
Night's Dream*, have more directions of style than many florid
prose romances; in Oberon's line 'Or in the beachéd margent
of the sea' a new dignity links comedy with the courtly language
of *Richard II*. Tragic seriousness in *Romeo and Juliet* unifies the
discrete images and redeems the hyperboles and conceits. In
King John and *Richard II*, the lyricism and rhetoric are
integrated by passionate conviction.

Richard III, I.1.1–40

Now is the winter of our discontent,
Made glorious summer by this sonne of York:
And all the cloudes that lowrd upon our house,
In the deepe bosome of the Ocean buried.
Now are our browes bound with victorious wreathes,   5
Our bruiséd armes hung up for monuments,
Our sterne alarmes changd to merry meetings,
Our dreadfull marches to delightfull measures.
Grim-visagde warre, hath smoothde his wrinkled front,
And now in steed of mounting barbéd steedes,   10
To fright the soules of fearefull adversaries.
He capers nimbly in a Ladies chamber,
To the lascivious pleasing of a love.
But I that am not shapte for sportive trickes,
Nor made to court an amorous looking glasse,   15
I that am rudely stampt and want loves maiesty,

To strut before a wanton ambling Nymph:
I that am curtaild of this faire proportion,
Cheated of feature by dissembling nature,
Deformd, unfinisht, sent before my time   20
Into this breathing world scarce halfe made up,
And that so lamely and unfashionable,
That dogs barke at me as I halt by them:
Why I in this weake piping time of peace
Have no delight to passe away the time,   25
Unlesse to spie my shadow in the sunne,
And descant on mine owne deformity:
And therefore since I cannot proove a lover
To entertaine these faire well spoken daies,
I am determinéd to proove a villaine,   30
And hate the idle pleasures of these daies:
Plots have I laid inductions dangerous
By drunken Prophecies, libels and dreames,
To set my brother Clarence and the King
In deadly hate the one against the other.   35
And if King Edward be as true and iust,
As I am subtile, false and trecherous:
This day should Clarence closely be mewed up,
About a Prophecy which saies that G
Of Edwards heires the murtherers shall be.   40

This soliloquy, early evidence of Shakespeare's unmistakable voice, illustrates the sinewy strength of his developing dramatic technique, in the monologue convention of which he was to become a master. Its primary function is to establish Richard, Duke of Gloucester, as the dominating personality of the play, through the humorous self-revelation of his reflections. Richard appears as a towering, tragi-comic figure, more sinister than Marlowe's *Jew of Malta;* the incarnation of selfish cynicism. Richard is not, like the later cynic, Timon, a disillusioned moralist; he is relentlessly a-moral.

Shakespeare's Richard, based on Sir Thomas More's study of Machiavellian statecraft, was an historical figure only in name; the villainies in the play, including the hypocritical wooing of Anne of Warwick, were largely fictions. Shakespeare chose, therefore, to give Gloucester some redeeming qualities, consonant with his reputed political ability. The planned oratory reveals Richard's will and courage to get what he covets; at the same time, the soliloquy serves as a prologue link with the Gloucester of parts 2 and 3 of *Henry VI.* The physical deformity of Richard is thought to be also unhistorical; for Gairdner's researches showed that Richard's only lack of proportion was his diminutive stature, and slight inequality in height of the shoulders; but deformity adds piquancy to the horror of Shakespeare's portrait. Agile colloquialism characterizes Richard's role in the history; few plays begin with such gusto and irrepressible mockery.

When the scene opens, the Battle of Tewkesbury has been won, mainly through the strategy of Gloucester; the handsome, woman-seeking Edward IV, 'this sonne of Yorke', is securely on his throne. Exulting pride is sounded by such phrases as '*glorious* summer' (2) and '*victorious* wreathes' (5). The adjectives throughout are sonorous and naturalistic; the transferred epithet in '*deepe* bosome' (4) is associated with the fathomless *Ocean*. Then come martial memories in '*bruiséd* armes' (6), '*sterne* alarmes' (7) and '*dreadfull* marches' (8), culminating in '*Grim-visagde* warre' (9) from Sackville's Induction to *The Mirror for Magistrates*, '*barbéd* steedes' (10) and '*fearefull* adversaries' (11); *barbéd* is probably a corruption of *barded*, from French *barde* 'horse-armour'. Contrasts, in the transition to peace, are marked by line to line antitheses: '*merry* meetings', '*delightfull* measures', '*lascivious* pleasing', '*sportive* trickes', '*amorous* looking glasse' and '*wanton ambling* Nymph' (7–17). The last compound is apt, because it is the feminine counterpart to 'capers *nimbly*' in line 12.

Shakespeare is attentive not only to adjectives; the contrast is a chain of matching words and phrases: *lascivious, amorous* and *wanton; nimbly* and *sportive; capers* and *struts; shapte* and *rudely stampt, Cheated* and *dissembling; Deformd, unfinisht* and *halfe made up; weake* and *piping; subtile, false* and *trecherous*. The phrase-making is vividly inventive, mingling the conventional with the startling. The metonymy in *wrinkled front* (9) is a periphrasis for 'frowning forehead'. The emendation *lute* for *love* (13) comes from F_1 and has been universally accepted.

Versification co-operates with the word choice to give the soliloquy impetuous movement. An abundance of liquid, nasal and sibilant consonants, aided by the alliteration and assonance in significant words (e.g. *summer* and *sonne*, *Cheated* and *feature*), contributes to the ease with which phrases roll off the tongue. The emotive words physically advance the meaning, a genuine function of naturalism. Examples are best seen in verb functions: *lowrd* (3), *capers* (12), *piping* (24), *mewed* (38). The lively phrase '*breathing* world' (21) is symbolic of the humanity the words engender.

The technique of the verse resembles that of the Sonnets: end-stopped lines, with figures of repetition and balance to satisfy the ear; only two lines (1 and 34) seem to be run-on. Except in the last 10 lines, internal pauses are rare and of slight weight, because rhythmic projection must not be halted; modulation depends on redundant weak syllables at the end of 12 lines, (4, 7, 8, 11, 12, 16, 18, 19, 22, 28, 30, 35). E. A. Abbott in his *Shakespearian Grammar* (Macmillan, 1869) § 468, says that *maiesty* at the end of 16 is a quasi-dissyllable; but an actor would hardly pronounce it as such. This is probably a twelve-syllable verse, with two terminal unstressed syllables.

Inversions of stress are not numerous; they are mainly in the conventional first or third foot. What Abbott (§ 453) calls pause-accent, (i.e. an initial trochee after an augmented line-ending), occurs only three times, after lines 4, 8 and 18. Shakespeare did not wish to overwork this licence of rhythmic variation. As in all good blank verse, primary stresses, placed emphatically, occur usually in the first, second, third, or fourth foot; e.g. in the opening lines the key words are *Now*, *winter*, *discontent*, *glorious summer* and *sonne*.

In the early blank verse Shakespeare frequently availed himself of the Spenserian convention of a metrical syllable in the *-éd* inflexion of past participles, e.g. *bruiséd* (6), *barbéd* (10), *determinéd* (30). In 29 the sense of the past participle in 'well *spoken* daies' is passive; but Shakespeare may have intended an active sense ('well-speaking'), referring to the Euphuistic revolution through which he was living. In 7, *alarmes* of the Quarto becomes *alarums* in the Folio, to ensure trisyllabic pronunciation; probably Shakespeare exercised another licence, whereby the plural inflexional *-es* could be heard, when metrically necessary. In the early plays poetical *hath* (9) is preferred to prosaic *has*; and Shakespeare usually preserved the correct form *mine* (not *my*) before stressed syllables commencing with a vowel-sound, e.g. *owne* (27). To preserve the vigour of the lines, restraint in using the periphrastic auxiliary *do* is remarkable in the first scene. To the same end, Shakespeare allowed few inversions of the normal order of words; *buried* (5) is placed last for emphasis. The only other syntactical inversions are in 1, 2, 32, 38 and 40.

The imagery is sharp and picturesque, giving perspicuous ease to the monologue. The metaphorical use of *winter, summer, cloudes, lowrd, bosome* and *buried* in the opening lines, for different moods of the royal temperament, is splendid, but conventional. The idea in 3 and 4 is that clouds arising from the ocean sink back into it. *Bruiséd* armes (dented weapons and armour) is ambivalent, since *armes* (6) are also limbs; in the same line *monuments* are also *memorials* (remembrances). In '*sterne* alarmes', which is contrasted with '*merry* meetings' (7), both adjectives are personifications. '*Dreadfull* marches' has two meanings, 'full of fear' and 'abhorrent to the memory'; and '*fearfull* adversaries' (11) may mean, 'awe-inspiring' or 'apprehensive' enemies. The whole of line 9 is an extended personification.

In *lascivious pleasing* (13) the idea of sensual pleasure is transferred from the persons to the instrument (*lute*). *Shapte for sportive trickes* (14) is a metaphor hardly recognized as such; but in the French setting it connotes boudoir habits of a trained poodle. '*Amorous* looking glasse' is an example of transferred epithet. *Rudely stampt*, a metaphor from the mint, and *maiesty* (16) are linked images, since the head of a king is usually on one side of a coin. *Strut* and *ambling* (17) are metaphors of bodily movement, denoting 'affectation' and 'looseness'; *ambling Nymph* is a cynical phrase for a woman who walks with mincing steps. The sportive poodle is recalled in *curtaild* (docked) of line 18, and *dogs barke* of 23; *proportion* (18) is a metaphor for 'handsome figure'. Richard is shown to be envious of the effeminate Edward's attraction for the ladies.

Line 19 returns to personification; *nature* is *dissembling* in *cheating* Richard of *feature* ('good looks'), the last an instance of metonymy. *Unfinished* (to emphasize *Deformd* in 20) is a figure of amplification, linked with *scarce halfe made up* (21) and *lamely* (22).

Richard is said to have been as great a lover of music as Shakespeare, and lines 24 to 27 revert to musical imagery. *Piping* time of peace (the pipe is a pastoral instrument) indicates feebleness of voice, beside *sterne alarmes* and the martial fife of war. The word *descant* (27), (primitive counter-point), was used in the general sense of 'harmonious accompani-ment' by Wyclif, in reference to the organ (c 1380); it was first employed metaphorically as a verb (meaning 'comment') by Sir Thomas More in 1510; and this sense is Richard's, though the musical connotation is present. In 26 the Folio has *see* for *spie* (now a pejorative word); the two words apparently had the same meaning in Elizabethan times. 'Spie *my shadow in the sunne*' looks back to the image of Edward IV in line 2; Richard implies that his destiny is overshadowed by the good-looking and secure King. Throughout the soliloquy the imagery is vitally integrated with the meaning.

In lines 32 to 40 several words call for elucidation. *Inductions*, commonly used by Elizabethan dramatists, were 'preliminaries'. The transferred epithet '*drunken* Prophesies' (33) implies that the prophecy about King Edward's successor was made by a person who pretended to be intoxicated in order to escape arrest. The origin of *libels*, meaning 'little books' or 'pamphlets', is Latin *liber*. *Mew* (38), a late Middle English verb, was borrowed in the fourteenth century from the French noun *mue*, meaning 'a cage for hawks'. *Mews* came to be used for stables only in the reign of Edward VI, when the Royal Stables were erected at Charing Cross.

The rhetorical devices in the soliloquy are diverse, and only a few, such as *epanaphora*, *ploce* and *paronomasia*, need be glanced at. Lines 1 and 5 both begin with the temporal adverb *Now*; lines 6, 7 and 8 begin with *Our* (*epanaphora*). The personal pronoun *I* appears as the antecedent of three co-ordinated relative clauses in 14, 16, and 18. *Ploce* is illustrated by the repetition of *proove* in 28 and 30; less obvious instances are the uses of *hate* (verb and noun) in 31 and 35, and of *Prophecy* (plural and singular) in 33 and 39.

Word play (*paronomasia*) stamps the intellectual wit of Richard. It begins with the quibble *sunne* and *sonne* in line 2, a pun aided by want of distinction in the spelling of most printers (cf the confusion, to modern readers, for which Field was responsible in the 1593 Quarto of *Venus and Adonis*). Ortho-graphy is again the source of the visual pun in 10 (in *steed/steedes*). A related figure *syllepsis* is found in 'half *made up*' (21), the compound verb having a general and a special sense, the latter used by tailors; this gives the word *unfashionable* in the next line an ironic relevance.

'Drum and trumpet histories' implies that plays like *Richard III* are rhetorical in an 'un-poetic' sense. A contrary view would have been held by Elizabethan audiences, who appreciated the speeches as suiting the word to the action; there would have been as much admiration for Shakespeare's *elocutio*, as for the scope of his imagination. However discordant the materials assembled, Shakespeare fused their aural and mental elements. Though audacious in vocabulary, he was seldom bizarre, even in an age intoxicated with words. What is most enduring is expressed in the popular idiom; formalized rhetoric does not destroy his instinct for the fitness of words.

Shakespeare trusted the experience of his eyes and ears, and the language of *Richard III* reveals acute powers of observation. Words that arouse associations have immense potentiality for wit. Despite Dr Johnson, Shakespeare showed that word play in situations of intense passion need not be insincere; tragic moments make quibbles ironical, rather than funny. Catchphrases and proverbs, used with propriety, enabled him to bring a character's reflections into harmony with the thinking of his time.

Richard's personality, in this opening monologue, arouses amused tolerance for his dubious cause. Self-explanation was not intended for the unsophisticated alone; on all audiences its appeal has important psychological effects. Shakespeare's dynamic use of metaphor is *energeia* in the sense of Aristotle's critical usage, rather than of Sidney's. The challenging buoyancy of images, the schematic syntax, gain for Richard's rationalizations a curious attention. This was a monologue for performance, demonstrating the popular conception of a Machiaevellian.

Richard II, Act III, scene 3, lines 62–81, 143–71

The trumpets sound, Richard appeareth on the walls.

Bull. See see King Richard doth himselfe appeare
As doth the blushing discontented Sunne,
From out the fierie portall of the East,
When he perceives the envious cloudes are bent
To dimme his glorie, and to staine the tracke   5

Of his bright passage to the Occident.

    Yorke. Yet lookes he like a King, beholde his eye,
As bright as is the Eagles, lightens forth
Controlling maiestie; alacke alacke for woe,
That any harme should staine so faire a shew.   10

    King. We are amazde, and thus long have we stoode,
To watch the fearefull bending of thy knee,
Because we thought our selfe thy lawful King:
And if wee be, howe dare thy ioynts forget
To pay their awefull duety to our presence?   15
If we be not, shew us the hand of God
That hath dismist us from our Stewardship,
For well we know no hand of bloud and bone
Can gripe the sacred handle of our Scepter,
Unlesse he do prophane, steale, or usurpe   20
. . .

    King. What must the King do now? must he submit?
The King shall do it: must he be deposde?
The king shall be contented: must he loose
The name of King? a Gods name let it go:
Ile give my iewels for a set of Beades: 25
My gorgeous pallace for a hermitage:
My gay apparel for an almesmans gowne:
My figurde goblets for a dish of wood:
My scepter for a Palmers walking staffe:
My subiects for a paire of carvéd Saintes,   30
And my large kingdome for a little grave,
A little little grave, an obscure grave,
Or Ile be buried in the Kings hie way,
Some way of common trade, where subiects feete
May hourely trample on their soveraignes head;   35
For on my heart they treade now whilst I live:
And buried once, why not upon my head?
Aumerle thou weepst (my tender-hearted coosin)
Weele make fowle weather with despised teares;
Our sighs and they shall lodge the summer corne   40
And make a dearth in this revolting land:
Or shall we play the wantons with our woes,
And make some prety match with sheading teares,
As thus to drop them still upon one place,
Till they have fretted us a paire of graves   45
Within the earth, and therein laide; there lies
Two kinsmen digd their graves with weeping eies?
Would not this ill do well? well well I see,
I talke but idely, and you laugh at me.

The great characters of Shakespeare speak verse with
individualized voices; Richard II's is self-pitying, yet lyrical;

Gloucester's was witty, virile and aggressive. The passivity of Richard of Bordeaux in the face of adversity is the pathetic theme of the tragedy. The King, in this scene, is surrounded in Flint Castle (historically it was Conway) by the rebellious arms of Bolingbroke. He realizes that resistance without forces would be vain, and is in the mood to blame all but his own misrule for the state of his fortunes. His proud defiance in the first speech, addressed to Northumberland, is an impotent assertion of the divine right of kings; hysterically he demands the outer forms of reverence.

The second speech of the King is addressed ostensibly to Aumerle, his supporter; but the first part is virtually a monologue, cast in rhetorical mould. The fondness of Richard for the language of the poetical books of the Old Testament is in keeping with the tone of martyrdom.

This is a climactic scene, and the tension is reflected in the emotive adjectives, employed by the King himself, and by the onlookers. The sun image, a symbol of royalty and emblem of Edward IV, is again prominent. The diction is lurid; besides the 'blushing discontented Sunne' (2), there are 'fierie portall' (3), 'envious cloudes' (4), 'bright passage' (6), 'feareful bending' (12) and 'awefull duty' (15). The epithets are, in fact, conventional, but the grouping is evocative. Poetical words, such as portall and Occident (6), are characteristic of Bolingbroke. York uses lightens forth (8) for 'lights up', a nonce phrase in Shakespeare, with transitive meaning. For 'seize' Richard employs the vividly colloquial verb gripe (19). Stewardship (17), used twice in this play, and nowhere else in Shakespeare, has recollections of the New Testament.

In the King's second speech, there is apparent triteness in the choice of adjectives: 'gorgeous pallace' (26), 'gay apparel' (27), 'figurd goblets' (28), 'carved Saintes' (30), 'large kingdome' (31), 'obscure grave' (32), 'tender-hearted coosin' (38), 'fowle weather' (39), 'weeping eies' (47). Familiarity is not really a weakness; Shakespeare is composing within the framework of rhetorical conventions.

The form and spirit of this declamatory verse link the play in time with Love's Labour's Lost, A Midsummer Night's Dream and Romeo and Juliet. The lyricism is partly descriptive, as Spenser's is, and there is a temptation to lapse occasionally into rhyme, as in 4 and 6, 9 and 10, and 46 to 49. These are among the many thought by Dover Wilson to be fossilized rhymes surviving from an earlier version of the play; but they have little structural value, except to underline the self-indulgent passions with which Richard dramatizes himself. This aspect seems to be part of Shakespeare's intention. The advance in versification is the greater use of run-on lines (8 times), despite the occasional use of stops, and less frequent recourse to unstressed syllables at the end of the line (three). Internal pauses are more frequent and varied than in *Richard III*; for the lyrical strain required flexibility of movement.

In general, the accidentals accord with the tone of the language; e.g. *doth* (1 and 2), *hath* (17). Yet the King tends to use the traditional contractions sanctioned for dramatic dialogue: *Ile* (25 and 33), *Weele* (39) and *a* for *on* in the popular oath *a Gods name* (24). There *lies/ Two kinsmen* (46–7) was not regarded as a solecism of concord; for the subject appears after the verb, its normal position being taken by the adverb.

In lines 2 to 6 Shakespeare conveys the image of royalty in an extended simile, using personification, according to the epic-mythological tradition. A red sky heralded a stormy day, and '*blushing* discontent' symbolizes not only the feminine quality of Richard's disposition, but its ready access of feeling. The proud look of the monarch, which York compares with the bright eye of the eagle, symbolizes the awe expected in the kingly presence. The impression created is of dignity in Richard's movements; every line is clothed in ceremonial and suggests the pageantry of the play's presentation. Most significant is the eloquence of Richard in the crises of his fortunes, when action is called for; his lamentations bring home the masochistic failure of his character.

Personification continues in lines 12 to 15: '*fearful* bending of thy knee', 'dare thy *ioynts forget*', '*awefull* duety'. Richard's demand that the disrespectful Northumberland should show 'the hand of God' is characteristic of the 'conceited' strain of his egotism. In line 17 the word *Stewardship* (metonymy) implies his divine right to rule even if he misrules; the epithet *sacred* is transferred from his office to its symbol *the Scepter* (19). The amplification of conceit, to which the King is prone, appears in the hyperbole and metaphor of lines 34 to 37:

> Some way of common trade, where subiects feete
> May hourely trample on their soveraignes head;
> For on my heart they treade now whilst I live:
> And buried once, why not upon my head?

A more self-conscious sequence of conceits is in lines 39–47; the fantasy is so strained that Richard himself offers apology for it. Tears are likened either to pelting rain or to slow drops that *fret* the earth and dig the victim's own grave. *Lodge* (40) in the sense 'beating down' the corn occurs for the first time in this play (see OED); yet it is unlikely Shakespeare himself borrowed it from the French. 'This *revolting* land' (41) has the typical Shakespearian ambiguity, the participle connoting both 'rebellious' and 'personally displeasing'. A similar ambivalence is to be found in *fretted* (45).

The rhetorical patterns, especially the hyperboles, are daring in this scene, but graceful rather than bombastic. Iterations such as *See see* (1), *alacke alacke* (9) and *well well* (48) are characteristic of intense feeling, and were known to the Greeks as *epizeuxis*. It is seen at its most effective, when combined with *antithesis* and *ploce*, in lines 31–2:

> And my *large* kingdom for a *litle* grave,
> A *little little grave*, an *obscure grave*

A favourite device of Greek rhetoricians was *hypophora*, questions asked and answered by the same speaker. In lines 21–4, the figure is perfectly illustrated. This is part of a larger rhetorical scheme (21–32), in which the figures are *epanaphora* (repetition of *my*), *asyndeton* (absence of conjunctions) and *isocolon* (teasing the ear with verses of similar structure). The ascending ladder beginning at line 25, in which Richard plans the dispensation of his symbols of office, is intended to give the actor plenty of rhetorical scope, in tone, pace, gesture and inflexions of the voice. In the final lines *tears*, *woes* and *graves* supply the iterative imagery. Richard is too much the poet-rhetorician to resist the word play on *ill* and *well* in line 48.

The 'golden cadence', as Walter Pater called Shakespeare's lyrical-dramatic strain in *Appreciations*, can be seen early in *Richard II* and *Romeo and Juliet*, as well as in *Love's Labour's Lost*. The power to evoke it never left him. In 'Shakespeare's

F

English Kings', Pater speaks of 'the unity of a choric song', to which 'the perfect drama ever tends to return', and he sees in *Richard II* a classical example. Shakespeare's achievement is not in the spell-binding language alone, but its 'common humanity straight from the heart'. Here is for the English (says Pater) 'the most touching of all examples of the irony of kingship . . . (the) contrast between the pretensions of a king and the actual necessities of his destiny' (pp. 193, 196, 201 and 211).

Tragic heroes, in the Aristotelian sense, are not to be found in Shakespeare's Histories; even Henry V doubts the possibility of understanding between a King and his subjects. *Richard II*, though the finest in tragic dimension, is another of Shakespeare's studies of Machiavellianism; he suggests that the pressures of baronial feudalism require a strong, worldly, even an unprincipled monarch, the type to which Bolingbroke involuntarily conforms. Richard's refinements of eloquence, though the stuff of poetry, are as impotent as his belief in divine privilege. The humanist, Shakespeare, visualizes the ideal monarch, in the Tudor system, as a patriot who can preserve order and ensure social justice.

The sources of Shakespeare's declamatory style have been much studied, and specifically in M. B. Kennedy's *The Oration in Shakespeare* (Chapel Hill, North Carolina U.P., 1942). Believing in the classical origins of Shakespeare's eloquence, he distinguishes in antiquity two divergent rhetorics, that of Gorgias (sophistic rhetoric) and Aristotle (the art of persuasion). Much of this historical and cultural background is irrelevant to Shakespeare, because he was unfamiliar with it. Though he knew of Seneca, who derived his style from the sophistic school of declamation and display, it is possible that Shakespeare did not read Seneca's plays in the original; a complete edition did not appear in print until 1581. It is equally unlikely that he knew the principles of Aristotle's *Poetics*, except at second hand; the Italian translation of Castelvetro was available after 1570, and is the one cited by Sidney and Jonson. Mythology represents Shakespeare's greatest indebtedness to the Classics, and this he derived from Ovid's *Metamorphoses*, probably in Golding's translation.

Kennedy finds that in *Richard II* Shakespeare freed himself of the Senecan-Marlowesque style characteristic of *Henry VI* and *Richard III*, especially in the anathemas of Margaret and Anne. The final rejection of the Senecan style, which was most consistent in *Titus Andronicus*, is to be seen in *Hamlet*. Abandoning schematized eloquence, Shakespeare no longer 'dazzles the eye, strikes the ear, amuses (the) fancy' (p. 147). After *King John*, Shakespeare devotes himself to the Aristotelian and Sophoclean ideal of drama.

Kennedy's account does not, unfortunately, agree with J. A. K. Thomson's in *Shakespeare and the Classics* (Allen and Unwin, 1952); this shows that the influence of Seneca on style was overrated; moreover, that there is little of Shakespeare's classical knowledge that could not have been picked up from Lyly or Spenser (and one may add Sidney, Sackville and Kyd, Thomas Wilson and Puttenham). Ultimately, 'the traditional *ars poetica*' of Elizabethan times derives from the practice, not the theory, of Horace and Ovid, as adapted to the age by the creators of Italian and French models. Thomson writes (p. 224):

> It is in the application of the Shakespearian style to classical dramatic themes that the revolution begun by *Julius Caesar* mainly consists.

What English dramatists got from Seneca was rhetorical abstraction, which was short-lived on the realistic as well as the romantic stage; and what Shakespeare imbibed of the Greek spirit, according to Thomson, was from North's translation of Plutarch, rather than Sophocles. His knowledge of the Greeks shows less sympathy than is evident from his portraits of classical Romans, especially the Stoics. *Richard II* is closer to Aeschylus, whom Shakespeare could not have read, than to Sophocles.

It is probable that Shakespeare's lyrical treatment of *Richard II* arose from his conception of the character, and his experience inside the theatre, as it developed on English soil. It began as the *energeia* of rhetorical virtuosity, concentrating on the individual figure, so as to provide a known actor with the flowing patterns of speech he could make resonant through a trained voice; it developed into a medium of associative imagery, no less favourable to the actor, but of greater integrity to the vision of the dramatist. When in I.3.150–51 the King says to Mowbray:

The slie slow houres shall not determinate
The dateless limite of thy deere exile

we seem to be hearing the language of the *Sonnets*. But the poetry of *Richard II* had not, in general, the stanza rhythm of this collection; and in the later Histories there were many intermediate passages of prose. Within the framework of blank verse, dramatic language therefore assumed a variety of structural guises; the word was chosen to fit, not only the feeling, but the theme's ultimate purpose; and that purpose could be perceived only through the significance of the words themselves.

Among the devices to be jettisoned were long epic similes and showy euphuisms. That improvements were directed to the speaking of verse is shown by the dexterous variation of speed, through spacing the frequency of pauses. This may be illustrated in six of the most dramatic lines in *Richard II* (III.3.178–83), which, however mannered, offered splendid opportunities to an actor like Burbage. Writing on 'Repetition and Pace', J. L. Styan says: 'The reiteration of a word or phrase can be made a simple rhetorical effect, like repeatedly hitting the same note. This may suggest a mind under stress, or remind the audience of a theme playing through a scene, but it always signals the pace and pitch of speech'. (*Shakespeare's Stagecraft*, CUP, 1967, p. 149.) Here are the lines, in which the complex rhetorical schemes (in parentheses) and the varied verse pauses have been indicated:

Downe,/ downe (1) I come,/ like *glistring* (2) *Phaeton* (3)/
   (1. *epizeuxis*, 2. *syncope*, 3. *epenthesis*)
Wanting the manage of unruly Iades.//
In the *base court,/ base court* (4) where Kinges growe *base* (5)/
   (4. *anadiplosis*, 5. *antanaclasis*)
To come at traitors calls,/ and do them grace,/
In the *base court* (6) come *downe:// downe* (7, 8) *court* (6),/
   downe (6) King/   (6. *ploce*, 7. *epizeuxis*, 8. *anadiplosis*)
For *nightowls shreeke/* where mounting *larkes should sing* (9)//
   (9. *antithesis*)

Thought and syntax are no longer confined to the versification of the isolated line. The ultimate gain in dialogue was a natural rhythm, and a more flexible application of language to character, especially to the prosaic character that appears so often in the later history plays.

Beginning with *Richard II*, the thematic substance of a tragedy is located in the poetry spoken by the tragic hero; for most of the images are figments of *his* imagination. They distinguish him from the person of his adversary; they are the instruments of his reflections on life and prime movers of the plot in which he is implicated. The recurring strands of imagery give the play unity. Wit is as much in evidence, but under stricter control, nowhere more so than in *Julius Caesar*.

The Greeks comprehended in the term *icon* much more than metaphor, personification and simile. A vivid, pictorial word is as capable of making an indelible impression; and among such words in *Richard II* are the adjectives *hollow*, *sour* and *sweet*. The images of Richard in the passage analysed depict him as scarcely an heroic figure; compared with Richard III, he is egocentric only in imagination. Nearly all his abstract ideas are expressed in metaphorical language. He describes Bolingbroke, in contrast, as a 'silent king'; and the latter is certainly reticent in exposing the workings of his mind.

At all periods there are traces of mannerisms and formalism in Shakespeare's dramatic poetry; there are more in his prose, which is in the taste of a baroque age. The method of Seneca was high-flown, artificial and extensive; that of the controlled Shakespeare (who stands nearly alone) was of lower tone, naturalistic and intensive. Different styles cannot be isolated or separated by the chronology of Shakespeare's plays; good dramatic poetry, the germ of the mature style, is found in his earliest productions. Shakespeare being a dramatic poet of mixed genre, it is feasible to generalize on the dominant characteristics only, mainly in set speeches. Up to his thirty-fifth year, when the Globe Theatre was opened, it seems clear that language was indulged for its own sake. This freedom gave him a sense of power, which the experimenting poet-dramatist needs.

Romeo and Juliet II.2.1–32

  Ro. He iests at scarres that never felt a wound,
But soft, what light through yonder window breaks?
It is the East, and Iuliet is the Sun.
Arise faire Sun and kill the envious Moone,
Who is alreadie sicke and pale with greefe,   5
That thou her maide art far more faire then shee:

Be not her maide since she is envious,
Her vestall livery is but sicke and greene,
And none but fooles do weare it, cast it off:
It is my Lady, o it is my love, o that she knew she wer,   10
She speakes, yet she saies nothing, what of that?
Her eye discourses, I will answere it:
I am too bold, tis not to me she speakes:
Two of the fairest starres in all the heaven,
Having some busines to entreate her eyes,   15
To twinckle in their spheres till they returne.
What if her eyes were there, they in her head,
The brightnesse of her cheek wold shame those stars,
As day-light doth a lampe, her eye in heaven,
Would through the ayrie region streame so bright,   20
That birds would sing, and thinke it were not night:
See how she leanes her cheeke upon her hand.
O that I were a glove upon that hand,
That I might touch that cheeke.
    Iu. Ay me.
    Ro. She speakes.
Oh speake againe bright Angel, for thou art   25
As glorious to this night being ore my head,
As is a wingéd messenger of heaven
Unto the white upturnéd wondring eyes,
Of mortalls that fall backe to gaze on him,
When he bestrides the lazie puffing Cloudes,   30
And sayles upon the bosome of the ayre.

Shakespeare was thirty-three when a pirated edition of
Romeo and Juliet appeared, testifying to the play's success. The
good second quarto of 1599 apparently represents an approved
version, re-written from a text composed some years earlier.

A wealth of conceit sustains the riotous irrationality of the
language, and it is not confined to the gallantry. The brevity
and reckless despair of love are hinted in the early dialogue
between Romeo and Friar Laurence (II.6.6–10):

    Ro. Do thou but close our hands with holy words,
    Then love-devouring death do what he dare,
    It is inough I may but call her mine.
    Friar. These violent delights have violent endes,
    And in their triumph die like fier and powder:
    Which as they kisse consume.

The 'star-crossed' love of Romeo and Juliet is thus drama-
tically predestined; indeed, the note of fatality is sounded in
the choric Prologue. The Renaissance atmosphere of unrest,

intrigue and disregard for human life; the tempo of the action, the contending imagery of light and darkness, the mercurial and sensuous life, are characteristic of the Italian scene in this period. The excitement is captured by the pulsating rhythm of the verse, and the rapid transition from scenes of passionate love to others of deadly hate. Shakespeare idealizes love, because he passionately believes in its spirituality, although it does not provide a moral solution to the tragedy. He is satirical in handling the folly of the family feud.

Romeo's brief life is like a meteor, full of rash and ill-considered action. All steps are carried forward in haste; and Juliet's 'Gallop apace, you fierie footed steedes' (II.2.1) becomes the central image of a tragedy, whose action Shakespeare skilfully condensed, from several months in Arthur Brooke's version, to a few days. In the final act the tragic irony is worthy of Sophocles or Euripides. Through Romeo, the dramatist lingers morbidly, even sensuously, over the trappings of death.

Shakespeare alone could have written Act IV, scene 5, which defies all classical canons. In this scene musicians had been hired to play at Juliet's wedding; but they were quite unmoved at the report of her death. Their quibbles and unreal lamentations were undoubtedly intended to provide the irony of contrast.

The lovers' misfortunes, which Shakespeare persistently underlines, were partly due to the crude emotions of the bourgeois Capulet family. Perhaps the dramatist intended to represent them as 'the new rich' prematurely risen in the social scale. Domestic episodes and persons, Capulet giving directions to servants in the kitchen, the Nurse, the waiting-men and maids, are English cameos. But for the protagonists Shakespeare has a clearer sense of place, time and period, than is usual in his Italian plays. The bawdy Mercutio, whose death is the turning point in the play, is an individual creation. Coleridge says of Mercutio's wit and fancy that it is 'procreative as an insect'. His name suggests warm blood and the impulsiveness of the temperamental foreigner.

The language of this dramatic poem, indicates that it was written to please a discriminating audience, perhaps aspirant lawyers of the Inns of Court. Students were as unruly in tongue and behaviour as the servants of the two noble houses, who perpetuated the feud. The wit of Mercutio and his companions is that favoured by young law students; and the literary conventions, such as the three sonnets exhibit, were attractive to the poet-scholars among them. Other conventions include an epithalamion (III.2.1–31), in the form of a soliloquy by Juliet; and an aubade, or dawn song (III.5.1–36), in which Romeo and Juliet rhapsodize farewells.

The word choice of the passage shows that Shakespeare, in his greatest moments, found poetry in the diction of the people. Romeo begins with what resembles a proverb; the *wound* is love, and his retort answers Mercutio's overheard mockery about the wooing of Rosaline. For *puffing* (30), Q_1 has *pacing*. In the manuscript of Q_2 was probably written *passing*, which the compositor could mistake for *puffing*; for *bosome* in the next line might induce him to think of swelling cumulus clouds. Most modern editors have, however, retained the reading of the first Quarto, *lasie pacing*, because the 'messenger of heaven' *bestrides* the clouds, thus figuratively riding a horse. Line 10 of the second Quarto has three extra feet; the explanation seems to be that it originally ended at *love*. 'O that she knew she wer' was then added, as an afterthought; but Shakespeare omitted to delete the superfluous words *It is my Lady, o*. The practice of editors is to retain all the exclamations, and give the soliloquy an extra half line. A third compositorial error is *to* for *do* in 16, the preposition at the beginning of the next line having caught the type-setter's eye.

The emotional tension of the passage is heightened by apostrophe, exhortation and hyperbolic description, which in Shakespeare is generally accompanied by classical mythology. The meaning of *soft* (2) is 'wait a minute', rather than 'hush'; Onions in *A Shakespeare Glossary* says it is elliptical for *go soft*. The five run-on lines (15, 19, 26, 28, 29) are in the descriptive verse; but the dominant movement is the self-contained line, with terminal pauses varied in duration. The internal pauses are finely modulated, none being later than the middle of the fourth foot. There is an apparent unstressed syllable in *heaven* at the end of lines 15, 20 and 23; but the word is theoretically monosyllabic; its importance to the tone of Romeo's language should be noted. As Enid Hamer rightly observes (*The Metres of English Poetry*, Methuen, 1930, p. 68) 'the genius is shown in the crossing of the foot-rhythm by the word-rhythm . . . every spondee is plainly intentional, and there is a delicate *shading* in the arrangement of stresses and half-stresses'. In this passage the spondees *faire Sun* (4) and *bright angel* (25), are descriptive of Juliet.

Romeo's apostrophe calls for a number of grammatical conventions, such as poetic *doth* (20), and *thou* for *you* (6 and 25). *Thou* is the affectionate mode of address for lovers, and Juliet continues it in this scene. In line 11, perhaps because it occurs in a casual observation, *saies* is preferred to *saith*, of which there is not a single instance in the play. Periphrastic auxiliary *do* (9 and 15) and disyllabic *wingéd* (28), show Shakespeare's temperate employment of expletive words and syllables.

Meaning and imagery are associated in lines 2 to 9. *Breaks* (2) for 'shines' anticipates the comparison in the next line of Juliet to the sun, rising in the East. The metaphor is continued in the apostrophe which begins in line 4; the Sun is exhorted to *kill* the Moon, who is *sicke and pale* from envy, because Juliet, her maid, excels her in beauty. The mythological names are withheld, because Juliet cannot be identified with Apollo; but *vestal livery* (8) suggests 'chaste Diana' for the *Moon*. The Sun (Juliet) as one of the votaries of the latter is clearly incongruous. The passage, as a whole, illustrates the associative way in which Shakespeare's imagination works; intensity of language forbids that hyperbole should be subjected to close scrutiny. Young girls at puberty were prone to the 'green sickness' (8); Juliet in the next line is urged to relinquish chastity, because only *fools* would prefer not to marry. Court fools in Tudor times wore a livery of green and white (*pale*), and this is the quibble Shakespeare's reference intends. The colour green is traditionally associated with envy. It is difficult to disentangle the parts played by metaphor, hyperbole, personification, apostrophe and folk-lore in language of such imaginative texture.

Lines 11 and 12 use paradox and personification (*eye discourses*). That Shakespeare often chose to strain 'conceit' is demonstrated in 14–21, his play with the concept of Juliet's *eyes* as *stars*. First he imagines two of the brightest stars to be absent on business, and Juliet's eyes taking their place. Then, inconsistently, he pictures an exchange: stars twinkling in

Juliet's head, put to shame by the *brightnesse of her cheek*. Note the simile of the sun and the lamp (19). Finally, Juliet's eye is imagined to be a star so superlatively bright that birds sing, mistaking night for day. The melody of the verse and the romantic associations of the comparison justify the conception, *as poetry*. Coleridge's 'willing suspension of disbelief' implies occasional arrest of the critical conscience.

The word *cheek* (18) now recurs to the poet's mind and invites the tactile image (pictorial only) of the gloved hand touching the cheek (22 to 24). Next, he returns briefly to *speak* in 11, and to an image of sound (24 and 25). But this is short-lived; light prevails in *bright Angel* ('celestial messenger') of lines 25 and 27; the classical figure suggested is the winged god Mercury. Juliet 'shines' above Romeo on the balcony, and the best sight of her is obtained by the viewer prostrated on his back; the *upturned wondring eyes/ Of mortalls* would then be his own, revealing the whites rather than the pupils. The persistent image of light suggests the beauty of Juliet in her white gown, with the light from the window behind her. This light would illuminate the *lazie puffing* (or *passing*) cumulus clouds; on these Mercury is pictured as riding. *Bosome* in the last line is an amorous reminder of Juliet, as well as of the shape of the clouds.

The passage is extravagantly, yet decorously, pictorial. The declamation is lyrical in a different way from *Richard II*, for ecstasy replaces pathos. But the rhetorical means are similar, depending heavily on visual images. Figures are often irrational, but not merely decorative; they arise from the intensity of the passion, which the music of the poetry aids. Perhaps the best description of the style of *Romeo and Juliet* is that of H. Taine in his *Littérature Anglaise*, vol. II, p. 190:

> Objects entered into Shakespeare's mind all complete, they can pass into our minds only disjointed, separated, piecemeal. He thought in blocks, we think in atoms. Hence his style and ours are two opposite languages . . .
>
> Out of his complex conceptions he snatches a fragment, some fibre, all alive and throbbing, and shows it to you; you must divine the rest. Behind the word is a whole picture . . . Forms of speech do more than denote ideas, they all suggest images. Every one of them is the concentration of a complete mimic action . . . Shakespeare is at once strange and powerful, obscure and creative.

The versification of the play shows signs of change in modulation; verse rhythms are adapted to the speech of different characters. The metrical pattern is regular in syllable count and end-pauses, so that the poetry is heard as poetry, and distinct from prose. But there are many verse lines in which syllable number is theoretical rather than actual; weaker stresses are often echoes supplied by the mind. This is specially true of final feet; e.g.

III.1.149–50   There lies the man slaine by young Ro/*meo*/
                                              (disyllable)
                That slew thy kinsman, brave Mercu/*tio*/ (disyllable)
III.3.154   Then thou wentst forth in lamenta/*tion*/ (disyllable)

Elsewhere, the endings of these proper names are monosyllabic:

III.1.189   Not Ro/*meo* Prince,/ he was Mercu/*tios* friend/

A notable modulator of verse rhythms is old Capulet, for instance in II.5.174–80 and IV.5.25–9; the first is here quoted:

Nurse   /Máy nŏt/ ŏne speáke ?//
Father   ×   /Peáce/ yŏu múm/bliñg foóle/
          /Uttĕr/ yoŭr gráv/itie ŏre/ ă Gos/hĭps bowle/ (elision of *i* in
                                                        gravitie)
          /Fŏr here/ wĕ néed/ ĭt nót/
Wife   /Yóu ăre/ tòo hót/
Father /Gods bréad,/ ĭt makes/ mĕ mád/
          /Dáy, níght,/ hoúre, tíde,/ tíme, worke/ pláy,
          /Alóne/ iñ cómp/anĕe, stíll/ m̃y care/ hath beéne/ (elision of *a*
                                                        in *companee*)
          /Tŏ have/ hĕr matcht/

The inversions of stress are unusual in number for the play. The long medial pause in the first line results in the monosyllabic foot (*Peace*), immediately following. Syncope is implied in *gravitie* and *companee*, which are theoretically disyllabic; yet Shakespeare, who makes Capulet speak in character, may have favoured trisyllables. The latter half of 176 *You are too hot* forms what Joseph Mayor (*English Metre*, 1886, Chap. XI and XII) calls a 'common section'; for it also completes line 177; the device is used frequently in the later plays, especially in *Antony and Cleopatra*. Capulet is liberal in the use of spondees; thus line 178, consisting of seven stressed monosyllables, with intermediate pauses, stretches the speaking time beyond that of a normal ten-syllable line.

In the talk of Capulet and Mercutio Shakespeare prepares for greater verse freedoms to come. One evidence of this is the increased use of extra unstressed syllables at the end of the line; another is the frequency of a pyrrhic foot before or after a spondee, devices which are common to all speakers. E.g. III.3.36 (speaker Romeo):

/Ŏn thĕ/ whíte wón/dĕr ŏf/ deáre Iúl/ iĕts hańd/

In the extravagant use of rhyme or word play Shakespeare must have been conscious of artifice and stiffness. For instance, in I.2.93–6 Romeo, whose love images frequently turn to religion, protests eternal devotion to Rosaline:

> When the devout religion of mine eye,
> Maintaines such falshood, then turne teares to fier:
> And these who often drownde, could never die,
> Transparent Heretiques be burnt for liers

The artificial emotion of this quatrain, part of the sestet of a sonnet, reflects the neo-Platonic conception of the character. Banal use of punning is a more serious defect, e.g. III.2.97–8 (Romeo to the Nurse)

> Where is she? and how doth she? and what sayes
> My *conceald* Lady to our *canceld* love?

The strained homophone implied in *conceald* is unjustified at a moment of emotional stress.

In the characters of Mercutio, Capulet and the Nurse (who speaks largely in prose) Shakespeare experimented to secure greater flexibility of movement; e.g. Capulet in III.5.164–5:

/Speáke nót,/ rĕplié/ nót, dŏ̆/ nŏ̆t án/swĕre mĕ/
/Mў̆ fiń/gĕrs itćh,/ wífe, wĕ/ scàrce thóught/ ŭs blést/

The speech of the serving men and Nurse represents the slang and colloquial talk of lower London; Mercutio, however, uses the language of young bloods about town, and occasionally the dialect of provincial courtiers. For this reason, apparently, Shakespeare wrote Act II, scene 4, in prose. Mercutio's *goodden* 'good day' (116), and the Nurse's *quotha* (124, a = you or he), *the properer man* (216) and *the versall world* (218, 'universal') indicate the deliberately lower tone of the language of this scene. In *Romeo and Juliet* Shakespeare extended the use of colloquial contractions, as part of his plan to simulate the natural rhythms of speech.

Mercutio's Queen Mab speech (I.4.53–103) is an exercise in lively descriptive narration; only the first and the last 14 lines, in which Romeo intervenes, are printed as poetry; but there is no difficulty in recognizing the intervening 26 lines of prose as 38 lines of blank verse. One proof is the *-th* ending of the notional verb in this line:

> Sometime she *driveth* ore a souldiers neck (in prose, Shakespeare would undoubtedly have written *drives*).

The speech seems to have been an insertion by Shakespeare to gratify the actor (probably Thomas Pope) who played the part; he must have written the passage straight out, occasionally inserting capitals for new lines.

In his introduction to the Facsimile of the Second Quarto of 1599 (Sidgwick and Jackson, 1949) W. W. Greg wrote: 'it shows textual tangles and duplications that suggest that it was based on Shakespeare's autograph, before this had been everywhere reduced to final shape'. Examples of Shakespeare's orthography shine through in the Queen Mab speech, in Romeo's at V.1.32–86, and in the Friar's at V.3.229–69. Throughout the play there is a worthy attempt to regularize syncope and elision, either by spelling or by punctuation marks. The Shakespearian method of dealing with the endings of weak past participles is indicated in the following interesting lines:

IV.5.55	Beguild, divorc*ed*, wrong*ed*, spight*ed*, slaine (all but the first require *-ed* to be pronounced as an extra syllable)
IV.5.59	Despisde, distress*ed*, hated, martird, kild (here only the second requires an extra syllable)
V.3.227	My selfe condemn*ed*, and my selfe excus*de* (in the ending *de* the final *e* is always silent)

The punctuation of the Second Quarto often goes astray in rhyming groups of lines, where the printer attempted to add to Shakespeare's punctuation. Instances of unnecessary commas are to be seen in Act I, scene 2, for example, in lines 17, 20, 27, 34, 37, 46 and 49; these commas can hardly be Shakespeare's, for they obstruct the rhythm of the verse.

Though the dialogue is dominated by the lyrical strain of the two principal characters, Shakespeare's experiments had the intended effect of restraining the declamation and ornament of future plays. There are very few parentheses in *Romeo and Juliet*, compared with *Richard II*. In the movement of Shakespeare's verse of all periods, the art lies in his intuition for words containing syllables pleasing to the ear, while also suggestive to the mind. The diction is adapted to the nuances and rhythm of a known actor's voice.

In *Romeo and Juliet* the note of exaltation is sustained with most sincerity and poise in the speeches of youthful Juliet, whose mind was not steeped in *Astrophil and Stella*. Act II, scene 2, shows that she was acquainted with the language of the Bible. Her speech is without the alloy of old Capulet's vulgarity, and has less Senecan extravagance than Romeo's utterances. The hero's psychology of passion and death falls an easy prey to the analytical wit of Mercutio, man-of-the-world; for the latter, having read Petrarch, debunks the insincerity of classical and Renaissance love poets, especially in Act II, scene 4. Mercutio's death is cynical, as well as heroic.

The Merchant of Venice, *III.2.41–62 and 73–107*

The play is generally supposed to have followed *Romeo and Juliet*, and takes similar liberties. It is comedy that narrowly averts tragedy. Romance in *The Merchant of Venice* arises from the eccentric will of Portia's father, and adds to the plot the theme of the three caskets, with its coda, the exchange of rings. The ominous plot of Shylock's bond is linked with this through the intervention of lesser characters, Antonio, Jessica and Lorenzo. Shakespeare blends realism in Shylock, with romance in Portia, a Renaissance lady of Venice's affluent period. The trial scene is the confluence and climax of the plots. The language of comedy is paramount, and at its finest in the garden of Belmont, whose unhurried delight Shakespeare contrasts with commercial Venice.

The plot itself turns on antitheses, between love and revenge, between the romance of wealth in generous Antonio, and its misuse by the money-lender, Shylock. The Jewish names are aptly chosen; Shylock (Hebrew *Shalach*) means 'cormorant', in the argot of the Elizabethan underworld a 'usurer'; Jessica signifies 'looker-out'. The casket *motif* occupies five scenes, and is loaded with oratory and sententious matter; the tone of the speeches characterizes the egocentric, the proud and the amiable suitor, in the spirit of a medieval Morality. The contrasted themes are Portia's 'I stand for sacrifice' (II.2.57), and Shylock's 'I stand for iudgement' (IV.1.103). The play seems intended to inculcate the humanist belief in magnanimity, loyalty and tolerance; but there is not a line, even in the speech on mercy, that is didactic.

Shakespeare's art consists in conveying the neo-Platonic philosophy through the *actions* of people in the play. The minor characters serve the purpose of a chorus, giving information necessary to the dramatic role of the major figures; they tell about Venice, its luxury, culture and materialism. The well-known improbabilities of the Romance are made palatable by the poetry, of which the following passages are good examples:

> *Portia.* If you doe love me, you will finde me out.
> Nerryssa and the rest, stand all aloofe,
> Let musique sound while he doth make his choyse,
> Then if he loose he makes a Swan-like end,
> Fading in musique. That the comparison   5
> may stand more proper, my eye shall be the streame
> and watry death-bed for him: he may win,
> And what is musique than? Than musique is
> even as the flourish, when true subiects bowe
> to a new crownéd Monarch: Such it is,   10
> As are those dulcet sounds in breake of day,
> That creepe into the dreaming bride-groomes eare,
> And summon him to marriage. Now he goes
> with no lesse presence, but with much more love
> Then young Alcides, when he did redeeme   15
> The virgine tribute, payed by howling Troy
> To the Sea-monster: I stand for sacrifice,
> The rest aloofe are the Dardanian wives:
> With blearéd visages come forth to view
> The issue of th'exploit: Goe Hercules,   20
> Live thou, I live with much much more dismay,
> I view the fight, then thou that mak'st the fray.

> *Bass.* So may the outward showes be least themselves,
> The world is still deceav'd with ornament
> In Law, what plea so tainted and corrupt,   25
> But being season'd with a gracious voyce,
> Obscures the show of evill. In religion

What damnéd error but some sober brow
will blesse it, and approve it with a text,
Hiding the grosnes with faire ornament: 30
There is no voyce so simple, but assumes
Some marke of vertue on his outward parts;
How many cowards whose harts are all as false
As stayers of sand, weare yet upon their chins
The beards of Hercules and frowning Mars,   35
who inward searcht, have lyvers white as milke,
And these assume but valours excrement
To render them redoubted. Looke on beauty,
And you shall see tis purchast by the weight,
which therein works a miracle in nature,   40
Making them lightest that weare most of it:
So are those crispéd snaky golden locks
which maketh such wanton gambols with the wind
Upon supposéd fairenes, often knowne
To be the dowry of a second head,   45
The scull that bred them in the Sepulcher.
Thus ornament is but the guiléd shore
To a most dangerous sea: the beautious scarfe
vailing an Indian beauty; In a word,
The seeming truth which cunning times put on   50
To intrap the wisest. Therefore then thou gaudy gold,
Hard food for Midas, I will none of thee,
Nor none of thee thou pale and common drudge
tweene man and man: but thou, thou meager lead
which rather threatenst then dost promise ought   55
thy palenes moves me more then eloquence,
and heere choose I, ioy be the consequence.

In this scene, Portia entranced watches Bassanio make the
choice that will determine the success or failure of his suit. She
tells of the power of music to match different emotional
situations, and describes her feelings as a deeply involved
spectator. Bassanio's speech, which follows, is a disquisition on
appearance and reality, a frequent theme of Shakespeare's
Sonnets. In the winning of Portia, Bassanio tempers impulsive-
ness with unusual judgement and reason.

Portia is Shakespeare's apotheosis of cultured womanhood;
her citation of the classics and her handling of the trial scene
confirm her intellectual superiority to Bassanio. She has
delicacy of feeling, good humour, womanly self-surrender, and
yet independence of spirit. The symbolic background of this
episode is music. Shakespeare liked to associate music with the

legends of classical mythology derived from Ovid; and the thought of it inspired him to write Ovidian verse, especially melodious in its movement.

Shakespeare was not, however, a serious classical scholar, as his mythology here reveals. He knew that Roman Hercules had the Greek name, Alcides (whose grandfather was Alcaeus), and tells in lines 15–20 of his rescue of Hesione, sister of Priam, from the sea-monster sent by Poseidon, to whom the Trojans (Dardanians) had to sacrifice a virgin annually. The exploit is described in Ovid's *Metamorphoses*, XI.199, which Shakespeare may have read in Golding's translation. The *Dardanian wives*, who stand aside weeping (18–20), are a picturesque touch of Shakespeare's devising; they do not appear in Ovid's story. But the sorrowing parents of Andromeda are present when Perseus rescues *her* from another sea-monster (*Metamorphoses*, IV.663). Shakespeare appears to have conflated the two stories. Nor did Hercules rescue Hesione for love, as Portia suggests in 14; her father had actually promised him six magnificent horses, and when he failed to keep the promise, Hercules dethroned and killed him, and presented Hesione to his friend Telamon.

The references to Hercules, Mars and Midas in Bassanio's speech (35 and 52) are perfunctory; and the 'crispy snaky golden locks' of line 42 must have been a recollection of the head of Medusa, in the Fourth book of *Metamorphoses*.

The word choice in Portia's speech is a blend of familiar phrases, such as *more proper* (6), with poeticisms, such as *doth* (3), *dulcet* (11) and *visages* (19). *Swan-like end* (4), *watry death-bed* (7) and *new crownéd Monarch* (10) are figurative compounds characteristic of the visual method. The descriptive technique resembles that of translations of Greek and Roman epics in the generation before this play was written; this is to be observed in the poetical use of elaborate similes (9 to 13) and the proper name *Dardanian* for 'Trojan'. The language here has the sublime tone of the grand style. *Dardanian wives* is a suppressed simile, the phrase purporting to describe Nerissa and Portia's maids. The periphrastic auxiliary verb *do* (1, 3, 15), sounded past-participle endings, *crownéd* (10), *blearéd* (19), and conventional epithets *'true* subjects', *'dreaming* bride-groomes', and *'young* Alcides', show that Shakespeare was writing in the tradition of epic translation. '*Howling* Troy' (16) and '*bleared* visages' (19) have more of the genuine Shakespearian touch.

Between this speech and Bassanio's is interposed the song 'Tell me wher is fancie bred', whose words have considerable dramatic significance. 'Fancy' is used in its Elizabethan sense of 'unreality', and this is the cue for Bassanio's disquisition on 'outward showes' of love, which he regards as hypocritical.

Shakespeare records the conclusion of Bassanio's reflections only; hence his beginning with relative adverb *so*. The speaker meditates on the deception of eloquence (56); he argues that smooth words and fanciful appearances may dress lies as pseudo-truths. 'The beards of Hercules and frowning Mars . . . have lyvers white as milk'. Cumulative phrases arraign the part deceit plays in misleading the judgement: *deceav'd, tainted, corrupt, season'd* (i.e. given an unnatural flavour); *show of evill, damnéd error, grosnes, cowards, false, stayers* (i.e. stairs) *of sand, valours excrement, purchast by the weight, snaky, wanton, gambols, guiléd shore, dangerous sea, cunning times, intrap, gaudy gold*. Heaping Pelion upon Ossa is characteristically rhetorical. The 'Quality of Mercy' is a swan-song of ornate declamation. After *Hamlet*, Shakespeare's language becomes a Phoenix that renews itself in each play; compulsive epithets, such as *frowning* Mars, *gaudy* gold, *meager* lead, are rarer, and therefore less obtrusive.

A steady advance in versification is perceptible in *The Merchant of Venice*. There is a proportion of lines, such as 1 and 5, that have only three primary stresses. Lines 5–7 illustrate Shakespeare's resources:

/Fáding/ iñ mú/siq̃ue./ Thàt the/ compá/rišoñ/
/mǎy stánd/ mõre pŕo/pĕr,/ mỹ eýe/ shǎl bĕ/ the streáme/
/añd wá/tŕy deáth-/bèd fòr/ him: hĕ/ mǎy wín/

The first line has trochaic substitution in the first and third feet, a pyrrhic at the line-end, and a feminine caesura (extra unstressed syllable) in the medial position. Feminine caesura is repeated in the second line, and the fourth foot is pyrrhic. The middle foot of the third line is spondaic in tendency, but has secondary stresses relative to the primary ones; the pyrrhic foot following demands stress on the preceding preposition *for*.

Enjambed lines, and the disposition of medial pauses, which are differentiated in duration by the punctuation, are signs of development towards maturity of prosody. The modulation in lines 17 to 22 suggests the tension of Portia, through changes in rhythm. In the 1964 production by Glen Byam Shaw at Stratford upon Avon, Peggy Ashcroft spoke the lines with much feeling for their emotional import.

The movement of Bassanio's speech is more deliberate. The four opening lines are metrically regular and end-stopped. An actor may exploit the feminine caesura in 27, but none will articulate *evill* as though it were monosyllabic. The rhythm thereafter is modulated by internal pauses, by occasional inversion, as at the beginning of 30 and 49, and by feminine caesura, e.g. after the third foot in 48. Action is summoned in line 51, and the rhythm immediately changes:

/Tŏ iñtráp/ thĕ wí/seŝt. Thére/fŏre thèn/ thŏu gaú/dy gold/

The difference of pace springs from a trisyllabic first foot, which the text does not normalize by elision (*T'intrap*); a long caesural pause in the middle of the third foot; and conversion of the pentameter to an Alexandrine; the additional foot is huddled between the third and fourth. *Thee* at the end of 52 is rhetorically stressed. Repetitions of the pronoun *thee, thou* (53), and *thou, thou* (54) are differentiated by emphasis, on the first of the pair in each case. The decisive use of four consecutive heavy stresses in the last line, is dramatic.

57   añd heére/ chóose Í,/ iŏy bĕ/ thĕ cón/sĕquĕñce/

Sounded past-participle inflexions are continued in the speech of Bassanio (*damnéd* 27, *crispéd* 42, *supposéd* 44, *guiléd* 47). In 26 and 36, the participial phrases *being season'd* and *inward searcht*, for adverbial clauses of time, are favourite syntactical compression with Shakespeare. Economy is also secured by the relative use of *but*, with negative function, in line 31. Shakespeare also employs *but* as a down-toner adverb, with the meaning of 'only', in 31, 37 and 47. The unusual past-participle *redoubted* (38) implies the existence of an undiscovered transitive verb *redoubt*. *Maketh* (43) seems a scribal or printer's error for *make*, which is required by both metre and grammar. In 57 the subjunctive, *ioy be the consequence*, is more poetical than *let* or *may*, with the infinitive, which Shakespeare also uses, for instance in line 3.

In line 22, *then thou that mak'st the fray* should precede *I view the fight*, but is given its position for the purpose of rhyme. Inversions of subject and verb occur in 23 and 57; and of object and verb in 51 to 52. The comparative infrequency with which Shakespeare resorts to deviations of order in this play is a mark of progress. He had more resources of verbal syntax than are available to the modern poet, and he made full use of alternative forms of words to suit the needs of his dialogue.

In *The Merchant of Venice* the image patterns suggest, rather than state or describe. The simile *Swan-like* (4), and the metaphor *Fading* (5), referring to flowers and beauty, rather than to sounds, are associated in a state of emotion. The song of the dying swan induces the thought of its death-bed by the river's edge; and this suggests the conceit of Portia's tears, providing the water of the stream (6). If Portia's lover succeeds in his choice, however, the music becomes, in her imagination, a *flourish* that announces the crowning of a king, and a signal for obeisance by his subjects. Coronation suggests a marriage ceremony, when the bridegroom should be awakened at dawn by music; during twilight sleep, the sounds steal gently upon his consciousness. The hackneyed image of *stealth* is, however, abandoned for the suggestive metaphor *creepe* (12). *Presence* (14) suggests comeliness and dignity, of which 'the young Alcides' is the prototype. *Virgin tribute* (16) is a euphemism for 'the sacrifice of an unmarried girl'. '*Howling* Troy' (16) reflects the wailing spectators, as well as anger at her sacrifice, and fear at the monster's appearance (a good example of a portmanteau epithet). Portia sees herself as Hesione, a victim of the crude terms of her father's will; she hopes that Bassanio will be her liberator. *Blearéd* (19) (i.e. dimmed with tears) is more expressive than *blurred*. There may be artifice in this allusive imagery, but as a specimen of Renaissance poetry it is superb.

Key words in Bassanio's speech are *showes* (appearances) and *ornament*. His discourse complements what Morocco and Arragon had said in *their* choices of caskets; the surface appearances of gold and silver served to reveal the character-istics of the men, egotism and vanity. The motto in each casket exposed the fallacies in the reasoning of the suitor. Bassanio had already made up his mind to choose the least attractive leaden casket. He argues that gold is *tainted* (25) and silver *corrupts;* Shakespeare was distressed, as appears in *Timon of Athens,* that men should barter their integrity through greed.

Shakespeare distinguishes the *outward parts* (32) or limbs and features, from the *inward* ones (37) or organs, such as the liver, heart and brain. Medical theory of the Renaissance, following Aristotle's *De Anima,* made the liver the seat of the natural faculties (humours), the heart the seat of the vital faculties (passions), and the brain the seat of the animal faculties (instincts) as well as reason. Sir Thomas Elyot in *The Castel of Helth* (1541) regarded the liver as a hot organ, which (he said) 'is to the stomake, as fyre under a pot'. One of its tasks was to extract blood from the *chyle,* or body's nutriment after digestion, and send it to the heart for distribution through the body. A white-livered man or coward was obviously one whose liver was malfunctioning. The beard of a warrior (35) was a symbol of virility; but this, says Shakespeare, should not be mistaken for true valour; the word *excrement* (37) continues the imagery of the bodily functions. Shakespeare's interest in medical science, seen in the portrayal of Friar Laurence of *Romeo and Juliet,* is maintained in this play. In I.1.81–92 Gratiano, chaffing the melancholy Antonio, says

> And let my liver rather heate with wine
> Then my hart coole with mortifying grones.
> Why should a man whose blood is warme within,
> Sit like his grandsire, cut in Alabaster?
> Sleepe when he wakes? and creepe into the Iaundies
> By beeing peevish? . . .
> There are a sort of men whose visages
> Doe creame and mantle like a standing pond,
> And doe a wilful stilnes entertaine,
> With purpose to be drest in an opinion
> Of wisedome, gravitie, profound conceit

Bassanio's discourse teems with metaphor; *season'd* (26), *stayers of sand* (34), *excrement* (37), *purchast by the weight* (39), *lightest* (41 = most licentious), *snaky* (42), *wanton gambols* (43), *dowry* (45), *Hard food* (52). Personification (or personal metaphor) is seen in *sober brow* (28), *blesse* (29), *voyce* (31), *outward parts* (32), *weare* (34), *redoubted* (38), *fairness* (44), *scull* and *bred* (46), *guiléd* (47), *beauty* (49), *cunning times* (50), *intrap* (51), *pale and common drudge* (53), *threatenst* and *promise* (55), *paleness moves* (56). The only simile is *white as milk* (36). The most deceptive of all appearances, beauty, stirred Shakespeare's fancy to comment in lines 38–51 upon its macabre aspect, 'the dowry of a second head', false hair of one already buried 'in the Sepulcher'. The passage recalls the last Act of *Romeo and Juliet*. A more pleasing image of beauty is the *scarfe* (48), used by an Indian maid to conceal, rather than expose, her charms.

Rhetorical schemes enhance both speeches. *Hypophora* (question answered by the speaker) is combined with simile in 8 to 13; the moment is dramatic, and is clinched by *antithesis*:

14   *with no less* presence, but *with much more* love

Emotive repetition, by the doubling of *much*, is seen in line 21 (*epizeuxis*). The language of statement is varied by rhetorical question in lines 33 to 38 (*erotema* and *ecphonesis*), the purpose of which, like that of *apostrophe* in 51–6, is to rouse emotion by simulating the tone of direct address. *Damnéd* and *sober* are antithetical epithets in 28; *paradox* in 41, and *ploce* (repetition of the word *beauty*) in 48 and 49, belong to the staple of dialectical poetry.

Metaplasms required by versification are usually *syncope*, either explicit in *watry* (7), *mak'st* (22) and *threaten'st* (55), or implied in *even* (9). *Th'exploit* (20) is a metrical use of *apocope*. *Aphæresis* is found in *tweene* (54) and *tis* (89). The increased employment of metaplasms in *The Merchant of Venice* foreshadows contractions on a prodigious scale in the mature plays. Many contractions, such as *Ile* and *tane*, began as conventional licences of versification, the dramatists echoing Elizabethan lyric poets and translators of minor epics.

The comedies and histories of the 1590s were important in the development of Shakespeare's style, as he aimed at relating the language to the conception of new characters; this expressive creativity may be seen in *Love's Labour's Lost*, *A Midsummer Night's Dream*, *Henry IV* (both parts) and *The Merry Wives of*

Windsor. As a man of the theatre, he had probably observed audience reaction, and discovered how spectators are best moved to become participators. Words uttered by real personalities not only induce other characters to respond to the design of the plot, but affect the audience by suggestion; and Shakespeare is more dramatic than his contemporaries because he does not appeal through rhetoric to an anonymous public. Actors are given an opportunity, through their speeches, to establish sympathetic relations with their audience.

Berowne, Shylock, Bottom and Falstaff are dynamic personalities, not types; Shakespeare's style is accommodated to each in an impersonal way. Whether witty, realistic or fanciful, each character has a unique outlook on the world, to which Shakespeare remains faithful throughout the portrayal. The dynamism of the language arises from the tangential mind of the poet, and is reflected in the images. A chain reaction generates, and is generated by, the feelings. Wit does not lie in ambush, but glances from every verbal opportunity; not only the Fool has 'planted in his memory/ An army of good words' (*M of V* III.5.61–2). Shakespeare's love of quibbling may have taken hints from Lyly or from Tarlton; but the method of repartee is his own. What Boyet observed of the sallies of women, is true of Shakespeare:

> their conceites have winges,
> Fleeter then Arrowes, bullets, wind, thought, swifter thinges
> (*LLL*, V.2.260–1)

Love's Labour's Lost is a commentary on linguistic fashions, pedantic and precious, which Shakespeare burlesques, because he had himself discarded them as eccentricities.

Bottom the Weaver, a 'rude mechanical' in a homespun shirt, is for Shakespeare also a romantic. Like most egoists, he is critic and judge as well as performer. His genial enthusiasm for many parts enabled Shakespeare to create an amusing parody of the grand style of acting:

> let the Audience looke to their eyes: I wil moove stormes: I will condole in some measure . . . yet, my chiefe humour is for a tyrant. I could play Ercles rarely, or a part to teare a Cat in.
> (*MND*, I.2.20–3)

Bottom, when 'translated' to the world of Titania, has no

ordinary illusion, but 'a most rare vision'. He is the natural humorist that every member of an audience meets in a lifetime. Gusto and warmth carried off the malapropisms so successfully that the unconscious abuse of words had to be revived, without repetition, in Mistress Quickly and Dogberry.

In *The Merchant of Venice* wit is intellectual; women have the personalities that give wit social status. The play is a comedy of idealized love. *Much Ado about Nothing* is a comedy of sportive love. D. A. Stauffer writes in *Shakespeare's World of Images* (Norton, 1949, p. 66):

> The great argosies of the play are those that venture forth to possess love. The merchant who 'must give and hazard all he hath' is Bassanio . . . Shakespeare . . . has now learned the more specialized art of the poetic dramatist: . . . He knows the secret for making an idea walk like a man.

VII

SHAKESPEARE'S PLAYS
AFTER 1600

Having succeeded in the two parts of *Henry IV* in re-establishing the colloquial tradition of English poetry begun by Chaucer, Shakespeare retreated further from the artificial mode in *Much Ado about Nothing*, *The Merry Wives of Windsor* and *As You Like It*. There is a fair proportion of mannered prose in these comedies, but in a style unlike that of Lyly; it is varied to suit the dramatic situation. Renaissance poetry and prose had common elements of word choice, rhythm and rhetoric. The technique of the ornate style had tended to neglect the activating principles of living speech, which an actor dare not forget. Shakespeare's drama, in poetry or prose, was written with an ear for actors' individual voices, and an eye to performance.

As acting plays, Shakespeare's were progressively adapted to the needs of a company striving for superiority in a competitive market; the dramatist soon had to break with some of the accepted dramatic canons, formal oratory and rhymed couplets. In one aspect, Shakespeare's style after *Hamlet* is a movement to reconcile blank verse with natural rhythms of speech. Ideally, different parts of a play needed verse or prose; but if the aim was dramatic verisimilitude, the two media should not be easily distinguishable. *Hamlet*, a transitional play, shows the diversity of Shakespeare's experiments. The soliloquy in which an actor thinks aloud, the dumb show, the epic sidelights, the classical allusions, are still in evidence; but the prose dialogue of 'What a piece of work is a man' (II.2), Hamlet's advice to the players (III.2), and Ophelia's mad scene (IV.5), are innovations of surprising fertility. The new methods were a challenge to Shakespeare's imagination, and only when invention faltered did he lapse into formalism.

Granville Barker described the art of the stage between 1580 and 1600 as predominantly emotional character-acting, with a flair for orotund delivery and pageantry ('From *Henry V to*

Hamlet', *British Academy Lecture*, Clarendon, 1925). Shakespeare learnt that a player's share in the physical action is less important than the thought and feeling of the character he represents. At first he expressed the new concept naturalistically or ideally. *Hamlet* was, however, the last play in which soliloquy is important to expose the workings of a character's mind.

Heroic verse was too much in Shakespeare's blood to desert him; but he subdued the temptation to rhetoric by resisting conventional patterns of diction. Another character like Hotspur, 'rising to the height of Seneca his style', was unthinkable, except as a parody of rodomontade, to show the new style of acting as superior to the old. The first tragedy in which the new experiment was tried out was *Julius Caesar*. The funeral orations of Brutus and Antony are very different from the speeches of *Richard II*, but as effective in rousing the emotions.

Hamlet was an immediate success in the theatre, but not entirely satisfactory to Shakespeare; he had overdone the exposure of inner conflict through introspection. Less should be said, and more suggested, either by the observations of other characters, or through the hero's own actions, when faced with a difficult decision. There had to be greater concision in the hero's self-revelations – more matter, less art. Shakespeare thought much on contemporary drama, as his criticism in *A Midsummer Night's Dream* and *Hamlet* shows; the censure, in both cases, is aimed at the style of acting, rather than of writing. He knew, instinctively, that drama consists in the illusions of living reality.

The natural speech rhythm Shakespeare sought in the poetry after 1600 is largely psychological. Because it is not mathematically regular, the mind perceives it to the best advantage when an effort is made. Temporal order is satisfied, even if the verse beat is seldom heard in an actor's delivery; for it is the *meaning* that gives the speaker the stress pattern.

Writing of rhythmical irregularities in her dissertation *Shakespeare's Metrics* (Yale Studies in English, 1968), D. L. Sipe says:

> Alleged deviations from an iambic pattern have then been interpreted as signs of Shakespeare's growing impatience with constraint and artifice . . . that he was progressively shifting towards purely accentual verse . . . Shakespeare wrote carefully constructed iambic verse into

which he introduced only those few minor variations considered
permissible in his time. (p. vii) . . .
Meter was the major determinant of word-choice, and probably the
only determinant. . . . Almost all of his neologisms involving form-
shortening were inspired, at least in part, by metrical considerations.
(pp. 179–89)

The issues raised depend on the point of departure of the
researcher. Sipe considers metre in *theory*, as an ideal pattern
that conceals the art of Shakespeare's poetry. What critics like
F. E. Halliday believe more important is the speaking of the
poetry by actors, Shakespeare's immediate problem. Two lines
cited by Sipe on pp. 9–11 will suffice to illustrate this difference:

Tempest I.2.129   /Fátĕd/ tŏ th'púr/pŏse, dĭd/ Añthó/nĭŏ/ ópĕn/
                                (Halliday's scansion)
                  /Fátĕd/ to th'púr/pŏse, díd/ Añthó/niŏ opĕn/
                                (Sipe's scansion)

Halliday reasons that foot substitution is here carried to its
limit; that all the feet are, in fact, irregular (*The Poetry of
Shakespeare's Plays*, p. 30). But the head and front of his offence
is that he reduced the primary stresses to four, and gave
phonemic value to the vowel in *the* and the two vowels in the
ending of Anthon*io*. The particular scansion is of no great
moment; the issue is Shakespeare's intention for the speaking
actor; for the textual evidence of the First Folio is that the
editors planned to regulate the metre to an iambic pattern. The
actor has the option of slurring *io* as one syllable (*yo*); but he
has no wish to pronounce *to th'* as a monosyllable (*tooth*); all
he can do is to speed up the articulation so that two syllables
approximate to the time of one. Prospero's autobiographical
speech is a long one, and Shakespeare converts it to dialogue
by interpolation; he is skilful in modulating the rhythm by
using only four primary stresses in this line.

The other example is from a play written about the time of
Hamlet: *Troilus and Cressida* I.2.5

/Tŏ sée/ thĕ bát/tĕl: Héc/tŏr whŏse/ páciĕnce/ (My scansion)
/Tŏ sée/ thĕ bát/tĕl:/ Hectŏr/ whŏse pá/cĭénce/ (Sipe's scansion)

The choice of metres is contingent on the pronunciation of the
last word; precisely, whether it has two or three syllables. Can
one give the suffix *-ence* a full Chaucerian stress, without

distorting the rhythm and naturalness of the line? No actor (even an imaginary Elizabethan) would attempt this pedantry.

Shakespeare's reforms in blank verse should not, however, be overstated. They were made in the interests of flexibility and ease, and these merits are incompatible with a system of theoretical elisions and syllabic expansions. Shakespeare's advice to the players was 'Speake the speech . . . as I pronounc'd it to you, trippingly on the tongue' (*Hamlet* III.2.1–2). *Trippingly* surely means 'giving its value to each syllable of trisyllabic feet'; the movement implied is of the dactylic or anapaestic kind.

Versification is a means to an end; after 1600 Shakespeare's advances were in character delineation, pictorial vision and narrative skill. He showed men and women to be not wholly noble or debased, but beings with extraordinary truth to the possibilities of their own existence.

Hamlet II.2.473–86, 490–519, 524–41, 585–8

```
The rugged Pirrhus, he whose sable Armes,
Black as his purpose did the night resemble,
When he lay couchéd in th'omynous horse,
Hath now this dread and black complection smeard,
With heraldry more dismall head to foote,                    5
Now is he totall Gules horridly trickt
With blood of fathers, mothers, daughters, sonnes,
Bak'd and empasted with the parching streetes
That lend a tirranous and a damnéd light
To their Lords murther, rosted in wrath and fire,           10
And thus ore-ciséd with coagulate gore,
With eyes like Carbunkles, the hellish Phirrhus
Old gransire Priam seekes . . .
     Play. Anon he finds him,
Striking too short at Greekes, his anticke sword
Rebellious to his arme, lies where it fals,                  15
Repugnant to commaund; unequall matcht,
Pirrhus at Priam drives, in rage strikes wide,
But with the whiffe and winde of his fell sword,
Th'unnervéd father fals:
Seeming to feele this blowe, with flaming top                20
Stoopes to his base; and with a hiddious crash
Takes prisoner Pirrhus eare, for loe his sword
Which was declining on the milkie head
Of reverent Priam, seem'd i'th ayre to stick,
```

So as a painted tirant Pirrhus stood   25
Like a newtrall to his will and matter,
Did nothing:
But as we often see against some storme,
A silence in the heavens, the racke stand still,
The bold winds speechlesse, and the orbe belowe   30
As hush as death, anon the dreadfull thunder
Doth rend the region, so after Pirrhus pause,
A rowséd vengeance sets him new a worke,
And never did the Cyclops hammers fall,
On Marses Armour forg'd for proofe eterne,   35
With lesse remorse then Pirrhus bleeding sword
Now falls on Priam.
Out, out, thou strumpet Fortune, all you gods,
In generall sinod take away her power,
Breake all the spokes, and follies [fellies] from her wheele,   40
And boule the round nave downe the hill of heaven
As lowe as to the fiends. . . .
   Play. But who, a woe, had seene the mobled Queene,
   Ham. The mobled Queene.
   Pol. That's good.
   Play. Runne barefoote up and downe, threatning the flames   45
With Bison rehume [rheume], a clout uppon that head
Where late the Diadem stood, and for a robe,
About her lanck and all ore-teaméd loynes,
A blancket in the alarme of feare caught up,
Who this had seene, with tongue in venom steept,   50
Gainst fortunes state would treason have pronounst;
But if the gods themselves did see her then,
When she saw Pirrhus make malicious sport
In mincing with his sword her husband limmes,
The instant burst of clamor that she made,   55
Unlesse things mortall moove them not at all,
Would have made milch the burning eyes of heaven
And passion in the gods. . . .
   Ham. What's Hecuba to him, or he to her,
That he should weepe for her? what would he doe   60
Had he the motive, and that for passion
That I have.

This 'inset' is one of Shakespeare's most controversial
experiments. It is more realistic than Aeneas's account of the
fall of Troy in *Aeneid* II.469, and closer to the Hecuba passages
in Ovid's *Metamorphoses*, Book XIII. The passage bears little
relation to Thomas Nashe's similar narration in Act II of
Marlowe's unfinished *Dido, Queen of Carthage* (1594), a play
which Nashe completed.

If, as is reasonably certain, Shakespeare's mind was then occupied with *Troilus and Cressida*, the epical style of Chapman's Homer would have been present to him. The bombast in the Prologue and Troilus's speeches in the last Act is not unlike the magniloquence of Chapman. Hamlet's final reference to Hecuba was suggested by a passage from the *Troades* of Euripides, included in Plutarch's 'Life of Pelopides'.

The Player's speech is Shakespeare's attempt to represent the characteristic best of translated classical drama, not a burlesque in 'Cambises vein' of 'English Seneca read by candlelight'. Nor is it likely that the design was to parody the acting methods of the Admiral's Men, who performed *Dido, Queen of Carthage* in 1598. Hamlet's taste for classical tragedy was that of coterie audiences of educated aristocrats, not necessarily Shakespeare's preference. A play 'well digested in the scenes' implies respect for the unities. The play's unpopularity with the 'multitude' perhaps reflects a turn-of-the-century change in the public's reaction to revenge tragedy. The style Hamlet defends in lines 455–65, plain, unsubtle, lacking in salt, yet restrained and dignified, is not confirmed by analysis of the inset. But the heroic manner is clearly differentiated from Shakespeare's own in the rest of the play; the contrast in language is as deliberate as in the feebler *Murder of Gonzago*.

According to Aeneas in Vergil's epic, Pyrrhus, the son of Achilles, was an avenging monster; Shakespeare's exotic diction and polysyllabic phrasing make him equally barbarous. In Chapman and Marston there are few lines as curious as these:

5   Now is he *totall Gules* horridly *trickt*
11   And thus ore-ciséd (sized) with *coagulate gore*
16   *Repugnant* to command; unequall matcht
41   And boule the round nave downe the hill of heaven (one of the three monosyllable lines)
43   But who, a woe, had seene the *mobled* Queene (a Warwickshire dialect word, = 'muffled' or 'veiled'; hence the *clout* or old *mob*-cap on Hecuba's head)
46   With *Bison* rehume (rheum), a clout upon her head (= blinding)
57   Would have made *milch* the burning eyes of heaven

This is an alien and moribund diction; but the epithets often betray Shakespeare's hand. Some are conventional uses in plays before 1595: *rugged* Pirrhus (1), *dread* . . . complexion (4), *tirranous* and *damnéd* light (9), *anticke* sworde (14), *fell* sword (18), *hiddious* crash (21), *reverent* Priam (24), *painted* tirant (25), *dreadfull* thunder (31), *malicious* sport (53), *burning* eyes (57). Others have the genuine Shakespearian touch: *sable* Armes (1), *omynous* horse (3), *unnervéd* father (19), *milkie* head (23), *bold* winds *speechlesse* (30), As *hush* as death (31), proofe *eterne* (35), *bleeding* sword (36), and *ore-teaméd* loynes (48).

The versification is conservative and comparatively regular, for instance lines 45–57. As the verse is narrative, enjambement occurs fairly frequently, e.g. 6, 9, 12, 14, 20, 30, 31, 34, 36, 38, 45, 53 and 57. Trochaic substitution is commonest in the first foot; but is found in the fourth in 6, because *horridly* is a dramatically significant word. Modulation by varying the position of medial pauses is commonest; but there are signs of experimentation, such as the extra unstressed syllables at the end of lines 2, 12, 13 and 31, and of short lines in 19, 27, 37, 44, 57. For some reason the words *Then senselesse Illium* of the first Folio were omitted in printing line 19 of the Quarto; without these words the participial phrase following is anacoluthic. The following lines are of interest:

3 /Whĕn hè/ lày cóu/chĕd ĭn/ th'om̆/y̆noŭs hórse/ (the last foot is theoretically iambic, of *coagulate* in line 11)

10 /Tŏ thĕir/ Lórds múr/thĕr,/ Róstĕd/ ĭn wráth/ ănd fíre/ (feminine caesura)

12 /Wĭth eýes/ lĭke Cár/bŭn̆klĕs,/ thĕ hél/lĭsh Pírr/hŭs/ (only four primary stresses)

24 /Of̆ rév/erĕnt Prí/am̆, seém'd/ ĭ'th aýre/ tŏ stíck/ (*reverent* is disyllabic; *i'th ayre* is theoretically an iambic foot; the double elision of *i'th* marks the advent of Shakespeare's new colloquial contractions in the plays after 1600)

26 /Lĭke/ ă néw/trăll tŏ/ hĭs wíll/ and mát/tĕr/ (F₁ shows that an ampersand was overlooked by the printer before *Like*)

A device that gives the verse formal movement is the use of syllabic *-éd* in the past-participle endings (*couchéd, damnéd, ciséd, unnervéd, rowséd, ore-teaméd*). Alliteration and assonance play a characteristic part; and so do the liquid, nasal, fricative and sibilant consonants, for example in lines 18–19:

But *w*ith the *whiffe* and *win*de of hi*s f*ell *s*word
Th' unnerved *f*ather *f*alls

The onomatopoeic use of the metaphor *whiffe*, for a 'disturbance of the wind', is good. H. Levin in *The Question of Hamlet* (OUP, 1959) says that the metre is stilted, and that this passage 'might be relegated to an earlier period on prosodic grounds' (p. 148); but *metre* becomes stilted only if it is entirely regular, and this is not true of the Player's speech.

Partiality for the periphrastic auxiliary *do* (2, 32, 34, 52), and for *hath* (3) and *doth* (32), do, however, place the grammar in an earlier period. There are numerous changes of tense in the passage, to secure the effect of breathless action. Lines 4–22 are in the graphic present; 23–7 are in the preterite; 28–37 are again in the present; and 45–57 once more in the preterite. Such switches were common in Elizabethan narrative poetry and prose, as the *King James Bible* reveals. The resumptive use of the subject-pronoun *he* in the first line is a licence not often resorted to after 1600. Most frequent of the devices is the inversion of the normal order of the verb, as in 2, 4, 6, 12, 17, 19, 50 and 51.

Placing the verb at the end of line 12, is an imitation of Latin syntax. The initial position of *unequall matcht* (16) simulates the Latin ablative absolute. The long simile beginning with *as we often see* in 28, and ending with *death* in 31, is a further example of Latin order; but it is anacoluthic in English. The phrases *With heraldy more dismall* (5) and *proofe eterne* (35) (noun followed by adjective) might be taken from Vergil or Ovid. The periodic structure of the passage 28–37 is, in manner, reminiscent of Cicero and Vergil; and so is the rhetorical ordering of lines 45–51. The syntax of the Player's speech, more than the word choice and versification, gives this inset its alien flavour; as an imitation of Latin epic narrative, the style is remarkable for its grim impressionism. The parallel between the killing of Priam and the murder of Hamlet's father should not be overlooked.

The language is overloaded with imagery which does not advance meaning in the naturalistic way usual to Shakespeare. The metaphor *couchéd* (3) means 'concealed'. *With heraldy more dismall* anticipates *totall Gules*, the heraldic synonym for 'red', introduced into the vocabulary of heraldry by the Crusaders in the thirteenth century. Another use occurs in *Timon of Athens* IV.3.59. The etymology is disputed; but OED prefers Latin *gula* (throat), representing the open mouth of beasts, depicted in bright red. *Trickt* is the heraldic word for 'sketched', as opposed to *blazoned*, 'described in words'. The image is sustained for several lines; metaphors *bak'd and empasted* (8) refer, not to Pyrrhus or his victims, but to *Gules* and *blood* (7); the streets of Troy were *parching*, because in flames. The participial phrases and epithets (e.g. the metaphor *rosted*) of 10 and 11 refer to Pyrrhus; his *wrath* is identified with the surrounding fire. *Ore-ciséd* (11) means 'covered with glutinous matter', and *coagulate gore* is a periphasis for 'congealed blood'. *Carbunkles* (Latin *carbunculus*) in line 12 was introduced from Norman French in the thirteenth century; Pliny employed the word generally for reddish gems, such as rubies and garnets.

Anticke (14) is a poeticism commonly used by Shakespeare; here it suggests not only 'antiquated', but 'ridiculously small', hence *striking too short*. The imagery in 15 and 16 shifts to personification, in the polysyllables *Rebellious* and *Repugnant* ('resistant'), the latter a nonce use in Shakespeare, but common in this sense in sixteenth century English. The metaphor *Takes prisoner Pirrhus eare* (22) is otiose and confusing, the simple meaning being 'Pyrrhus *hears* the crash'. *Like a newtrall to his will and matter* (26) is a laboured simile for 'undecided'.

The significant words in this part of the scene are *sword* and *falls*. *Sword* in lines 14, 18, 22, 36, is the terminal word; and *falls* in lines 15, 19, 34 and 37, is used three times dramatically at the line-end, and echoed in the quibble '*fell* sword' (18). All uses of the verb prefigure the *fall* of Troy's citadel, described in 20 and 21. The sympathetic collapse of Ilium's walls in *seeming to feele this blowe* (20), is a conceit Shakespeare was unable to resist; it is not in the *Aeneid*. In '*bold* winds *speechlesse*' (30) and '*strumpet* Fortune' (38) there is a return to personal metaphor; while '*bleeding* sword' (36) is a poetic use of transferred epithet. *Boule the round nave* (41) is a metaphor from the game of bowls, *nave* being the hub of a wheel, symbol of Fortune's ruthless progress. The *hill of heaven* (41) is contrasted with the underworld (Hades), implied in the word *fiends* (42).

The picture of Hecuba begins with a strained conceit, typical of Kyd, Marlowe and 'English Seneca':

G

45–6   *threatning the flames*/ With Bison rehume

Rheum, liquid secreted by the eyes, here probably means tears.
Bison is thought to be a corruption of OE *biseonde* (= near-sighted). The conceit is that Hecuba's prodigious weeping
threatens the flames. Greek *Diadem* (47) became a symbol of
royalty, when Alexander the Great adopted the fillet worn by
the Persian kings. *Ore-teaméd loynes* (48), a metaphor for
Hecuba's prolific child-bearing, is a reference to *Aeneid* II.503;
in Elizabethan drama she is the symbol of maternal misfortune.
Traditionally, *fortune* (51) is the personified *foe* of the happy
man, and her often-unmerited workings are inscrutable; lines
50–1 suggest that it is *treason* to speak against her with *tongue
in venom steept* (metaphor). *Mincing* (54) is in keeping with
the barbarous imagery. There are three figures in 57: *milch*
is not only 'milk', but a 'dew exuded', here *tears; burning,*
applied to the bodily functions, was by Shakespeare's time a
dead metaphor; '*eyes* of heaven' is personal metaphor for the
eyes of gods.

The devices of rhetoric, besides sounded past-participle
endings, include various metaplasms:

Apocope: th'omynous (3), Th'unnervéd (19), i'th ayre (24),
a worke (33; *a* being a colloquial contraction of *on*). In *the
alarme* (49) apocope is metrically assumed; the printers were
far from consistent in orthography.

Syncope: The poetical use of *ore* (11 and 48) is a licensed
contraction of *over.* The *a* in *Diadem* is theoretically elided, as
the metre requires a disyllable. In *threatning* (45) elision is
indicated by spelling, not punctuation; this was Shakespeare's
practice.

Aphæresis: Gainst (51). *Passion* (58) was a common
truncation in poetry of 'compassion'.

Schemes of words include repetition for emphasis, as in *black*
(2 and 4), an example of *ploce; Out, out* (38) is a case of
epizeuxis. But schemes of thought are more important. The
apostrophe to Fortune (38 to 42) is the climactic point of the
Player's speech; an actor was expected to make the most of this
Marlovian outburst. *But who, a woe* (43) if intended as a
quibble, is the only visible burlesque in the speech. Tension is
sustained in a long rhetorical question, or exclamation (43–9);
its purpose is emotive. Such a pitiful sight as the half-clad

Hecuba (the speaker claims) would have turned human hearts against the goddess Fortune; and the Queen's *instant burst of clamour* (55) would have moved the gods themselves to compassion.

The technique of the Player's speech is Shakespearian; it is difficult to understand how the inset could have been mistaken by earlier critics for the work of another poet. The figures of Pyrrhus, Priam and Hecuba were chosen as stock classical sources of allusion in Elizabethan tragedy. The purpose of the Hecuba passage was to link the cameo with Hamlet's soliloquy 'O what a rogue and pesant slave am I' a few lines later; it provides the cue for Hamlet's reflections on simulated and genuine emotion, and for his comparisons between the dutiful Trojan queen and the guilty image of Gertrude; between Hyperion (the dead King of Denmark) and a satyr (the usurper Claudius), who is a *painted tirant* like Pyrrhus.

In the 1590s bombastic speeches apparently pleased the multitude. The ranting condemned in Hamlet's advice to the players does not suppose that hyperbole and conceit were contributory factors. The advice speaks of styles of acting, rather than styles of dramatic composition; and the excerpt from 'The Fall of Troy' was presumably interpolated to demonstrate a rival acting method. Hamlet's only comment on writing is to note the playwright's avoidance of affectation in the phrasing, and this kind of artifice would be Lyly's rather than Kyd's. Pope's view that Hamlet's appraisal of the Pyrrhus episode was ironical, to expose the bombast, should not be accepted. No one was a better judge of tumidity than Hamlet himself, as he shows in his struggle with Laertes in V.1.306-7: 'nay and thou'lt mouthe/ Ile rant as well as thou'. For Hamlet, rhetoric implied the insincerity of over-emphasis, a divorce between words and thoughts or feelings:

> What is her whose greefe
> Beares such an emphasis, whose phrase of sorrow
> Coniures the wandring starres, and makes them stand
> Like wonder wounded hearers (V.1.277–80)

The language of the Player's oration is more latinized than usual, because Shakespeare's inset is a pseudo-translation of classical drama; it was deliberately over-written for a wandering group of players with out-of-date portable equipment, as the

Gonzago interlude shows. Hamlet was too sensitive a critic of words not to be aware of the pompousness and guile of Latinisms. In his pointed parody of the speech of Osric, the courtier, the cult is mocked:

> Sir, his *definement suffers* no *perdition* in you, though I know to *devide* him *inventorially*, would dazzle th'*arithmaticke* of *memory*, and yet but raw neither, in *respect* of his quick saile, but in the *veritie* of *extolment*, I take him to be a soule of great *article*, and his *infusion* of such dearth and *rare*nesse, as to make true *dixion* of him, his *semblable* is his *mirrour*, and who els would *trace* him, his *umbrage*. (V.2.117–25)

In the Renaissance concept of poetry, tumidity was a matter of degree; in Shakespeare, the boundary between emotional truth and bombast is rarely crossed. The principal signs of bombast are pretentious diction, unwieldy similes and abnormal syntax.

The diversity of style in *Hamlet* is part of Shakespeare's plan to reform the Ur-Hamlet theme in Kyd's version, written about twelve years earlier. Marston had scoffed at the 'musty fopperies of antiquity' in *The Spanish Tragedy*, and Jonson had been severe in satirizing the same play. Among the important additions Shakespeare made in Kyd's Hamlet must have been the episode with the Players and the great soliloquies, which reflect the hero's changes of mood. The imagery and diction of Hamlet's monologues are unmistakable evidence of an artist's maturity.

Hamlet was undoubtedly an experiment to influence public taste in drama; Shakespeare had sensed a reaction against the Senecan tradition of revenge tragedy. After 1600, he found drama in the presentation of a human problem, to which an audience would not expect or receive a solution. It is no coincidence that the word *question* occurs seventeen times in *Hamlet*. There are no less than 70 marks of interrogation in the graveyard scene. *Hamlet* is a play that asks many questions, but rarely answers them.

Denmark is so corrupt that Hamlet despairs of finding an honest person, except Horatio, in it. The irony of the leading character can be observed in his frequent use of *honest* or *honesty*. In II.2.178 Hamlet reminds Polonius that 'to be honest as this world goes, is to be one man pickt out of tenne thousand'. Later, he reflects upon every man's capacity for self-deception

and admits: 'I am my selfe indifferent honest' (III.1.124).
Words are a surrogate for action; he regards them as devices
for evasion of the truth. 'Appearance and reality' is a dominant
note in the plays of this period; 'Seemes, Maddam . . . I know
not seemes' (I.2.76) is the *leit motif* of this tragedy of irresolu-
tion. As J. C. Ransom remarked:

> The Shakespeare of *Hamlet* is an Existentialist, reacting from un-
> tenable human dignities and pretensions, as set forth in the ideals of
> the Renaissance.
>
> ('On Shakespeare's English', *Sewanee Review*, LV.2, 1947, p. 196)

Othello III.3.451–69; Timon of Athens V.1.213–20

Two passages are linked in this analysis, in order to examine
the subtleties of what G. Wilson Knight called 'The Othello
Music' (*The Wheel of Fire*, Methuen, 1930).

> *Oth*. Now doe I see tis time, looke here Iago,
> All my fond love, thus doe I blow to heaven, – tis gone.
> Arise blacke vengeance, from thy hollow Cell,
> Yeeld up O love thy crowne, and harted Throne,
> To tirranous hate, swell bosome with thy fraught,   5
> For tis of Aspecks tongues.
>   *Iag*. Pray be content.
>   *Oth*. O blood, Iago blood.
>   *Iag*. Patience I say, your mind perhaps may change.
>   *Oth*. Never Iago. Like to the Ponticke Sea,
> Whose Icie Current, and compulsive course,   10
> Nev'r keepes retyring ebbe, but keepes due on
> To the Proponticke, and the Hellespont:
> Even so my bloody thoughts, with violent pace
> Shall nev'r looke backe, nev'r ebbe to humble Love,
> Till that a capeable, and wise Revenge   15
> Swallow them up. Now by yond Marble Heaven,
> In the due reverence of a sacred vow,
> I here ingage my words.

This is a conflation of the Q_1 and F_1 texts, since only the latter
contains lines 7 to 14, which are thought to have been cut in
performance. The difference in orthography of these eight lines
is to be seen in the capitals and colloquial contractions.

The substance of Wilson Knight's assessment of the poetry
in *Othello* is contained in the following extract:

It holds a rich music all its own, and possesses a unique solidity and precision of picturesque phrase or image, a peculiar chastity and serenity of thought. It is, as a rule, barren of direct metaphysical content. Its thought does not mesh with the reader's: rather it is ever outside us, aloof. This aloofness is the resultant of an inward aloofness of image from image, word from word. The dominant quality is separation, not, as is more usual in Shakespeare, cohesion. . . .

The dominant quality in this play is the exquisitely moulded language, the noble cadence and chiselled phrase, of Othello's poetry. . . .

In matters of technique, style, personification – there we see a spirit of negation, colourless, and undefined, attempting to make chaos of a world of stately, architectural, and exquisitely coloured forms. . . . The beauties of the Othello-world are not finally disintegrated: they make 'a swan-like end, fading in music'.

(*The Wheel of Fire*, pp. 97–119)

The passage selected is not cited by Knight, but illustrates the sensuous movement of Othello's rhythm. 'Picturesque phrase' is evident in line 2: 'All my fond love thus do I blowe to heaven'; the supernumerary words *tis gone* Burbage probably spoke with a gesture of finality. 'Aloofness of image' is in *yond Marble Heaven* (16); and there is 'noble cadence' in 13–16, the lines following the 'Pontic sea' description. Shakespeare had obviously read of the impetuous current in Pliny's *Natural History* II.919 (Philemon Holland's translation); the redundancies of Holland's account are *in italics*:

And *the sea* Pontus (Black Sea) evermore *floweth* and *runneth* out into Propontis (Sea of Marmara), but *the sea* never *retireth back againe* within Pontus.

From this ungainly observation, Shakespeare shapes his epic simile. It is more than a sonorous transformation of words; Knight's 'chastity and serenity' of thought are expressed with prosodic virtuosity. Few critics would agree with Pope's opinion that the simile is 'an unnatural excursion in this place'.

The difference in expression between the Vergilian nobility of Othello's sudden agony, and the Homeric grandeur of long-suffering Lear, is palpable. The epithets in Othello's speech are 'proper' in the classical way of the *Aeneid: fond* love, *black* vengeance, *hollow* Cell, *tirranous* hate, *Icie* Current, *retyring* ebbe, *bloody* thoughts, *violent* pace, *humble* Love, *wide* Revenge, *Sacred* vow. *Harted* Throne ('enthroned in the heart') is typical of Shakespeare's syntactical compression; *compulsive* course (10), *capeable* Revenge (15), and *Marble* heaven (16) are vigorous and unorthodox. *Compulsive* appears to have been used for the first time in *Hamlet*, an adjective probably developed from *compulsion*, a noun borrowed from French for legal and ecclesiastical use in the mid-fifteenth century. The OED cites Othello's use of *capeable* ('comprehensive') as figurative and obsolete; Shakespeare's sense seems to be passive ('able to be effected') rather than active. Shakespeare was the first to use *floor* in the figurative sense of 'ceiling', in *The Merchant of Venice* V.1.58–9:

> . . . looke how the floore of heaven
> Is thick inlayed with patterns of bright gold.

This is relevant to *Marble Heaven;* by association with paving, on four occasions he uses *marble*(d) in referring to the sky, the analogy being with certain cloud-effects. *Marble* is appropriate here, because of its coldness and austerity; it suggests an altar, and hence the phrase *sacred vow* in the next line.

In this speech the epic simile is the nucleus; the classical names Pontic, Propontic and Hellespont are echoes of the old poets, and give to the decisive *Never Iago* a note of prophetic doom. The simile of flow without ebb is simulated in the language. Lines 9 to 12 run headlong like an irresistible wave; *ebbe to humble Love* becomes unthinkable. *Bloody thoughts* are like the *violent pace* of the *water* released through the narrow straits. *Wide* Revenge suggests the broad expanse of the Propontic, where Othello's hate is to be swallowed up; it looks back to the monster, *vengeance*, come forth from its *hollow cell* (the mind) in line 3. Throughout the lines, the love-hate alternation is movingly incorporated in the language; *love, crowne* and *throne* (images of controlled rule) in 4 are contrasted with *tirranous hate* (5), *Aspecks tongues* (6) and *blood* in line 7 (images of uncontrollable passion). Othello is remorselessly driven by the *icy* yet *violent,* current of his hatred. Shakespeare's emotive speeches in the great tragedies embody large-scale metaphors.

Emotional tension is raised by the invocations in lines 3–6 and 16–18. Initial plosive consonants *b, t, c* (*k*) of key words are harsh and aggressive; they suggest vindictiveness at the end of words also. But the equable movement of the verse is sustained, in spite of fragmented phrases, inverted stresses, and pyrrhic feet, by Shakespeare's vowel and consonant modulation, and especially the linking of liquid, nasal, trilled and sibilant consonants. The disposition of stresses and pauses in lines 1 to 6, all end-stopped, is subtle; the punctuation indicates the phrasing of the thought for delivery. The headlong movement of the simile is secured by three enjambed lines (11, 13, 15), the only ones in the passage.

In the emotional crises of the great tragedies, phrasal syntax is seldom complex; inversions of word order, as in 1 and 2, are for emphasis. *Tis* is used three times in the passage, but the only other poetical contraction is the triple *nev'r* (11 and 14), shortened by the scribe or printer to normalize the metrical line. This indicates that Shakespeare wrote *never*, not *nere*, the usual poetical orthography of the contraction. In the late plays he introduced many trisyllabic feet and redundant syllables, and there are several in this passage. In *Like to* (9) and *Till that* (15) the preposition and relative pronoun are variants of Elizabethan poetic style.

Coherence of meaning in Shakespeare's dialogue was the product of dramatic abundance and experience. The emotion behind the words is part of the meaning, and the language matches the feelings with an instinctive tact. Devices of rhetoric are never sought, but come through intuitive rightness. Instances are apostrophe, personification and repetition (*nev'r, keepes, ebbe, due*) in Othello's speech. The only poeticisms are *fraught* (5), *Aspecks* (6) and *yond* (16). Shakespeare borrowed *aspic*, a synonym for *asp*, from the sixteenth century French writer Jehan Palsgrave, and repeated the innovation in *Antony and Cleopatra*.

Ate, the goddess of Vengeance, was cast down into Hades by Zeus, and perpetuated evil there by treading lightly on the heads of men. This may account for the reading *the hollow hell* (3) in the First Folio text.

Parts of *Timon of Athens* are in similar vein to the Othello harmony. The following is an instance:

Come not to me againe, but say to Athens,
Timon hath made his everlasting Mansion
Upon the Beachéd Verge of the salt Flood,

Who once a day with his embosséd Froth
The turbulent Surge shall cover; thither come,   5
And let my grave-stone be your Oracle:
Lippes, let foure words go by, and Language end:
What is amisse, Plague and Infection mend.

This speech paraphrases a passage in the 28th story of Paynter's *Palace of Pleasure*. T. S. Eliot named it as an example of the 'fine rhetoric of Shakespeare . . . where a character . . . *sees himself* in a dramatic light' ('Rhetoric and Poetic Drama', *Selected Essays*, p. 39). There is an elegiac note in the music, whose dignity is due to the mingling of Anglo-Saxonisms and Latin polysyllables, as in *everlasting Mansion* (2) and *Beachéd Verge* (3). *Salt Flood* (3), *embosséd Froth* (4) and *turbulent Surge* (5) have a euphemistic manner that is certainly rhetorical. So is the pleonastic personification of the last line.

The prosodic treatment is the master stroke, phonological as well as metrical: the unobtrusive use of alliteration; the cunning thread of liquid, nasal and sibilant consonants; the extra unstressed syllables at the end of lines 1 and 2, and the weak final foot of 6; the enjambement of lines 2 and 4; the effective disposition of medial pauses in 1, 5, 7 and 8. The total effect is that of a speech admirably adapted in phrasing to delivery. Shakespeare avoids periodic structures, and generally prefers the loose, cumulative style. Even when word choice is luxurious, as here, the ordering of the thoughts seems natural. The only subordination in Timon's lines is the relative clause in 4–5. *Who*, for things, was a common relative usage in Elizabethan times, and need not imply personification (*Salt Flood* = Poseidon). The nominative form for accusative function is influenced by the syntactical position of the relative in the clause.

King Lear III.2.4–9, 14–24, 42–60

In *King Lear*, truths are conveyed through images of Nature; the gods themselves are forces of Nature. But natural man is in danger of spiritual blindness, which threatens to curtail his life. The tragedy deals with the abrogation of traditional pieties, religious, political, domestic.

One evil drives out another, and the tempest in *Lear* purges

the King's pride; he recognizes a transformation in IV.6.102–8.
The passage is in prose, which Shakespeare employs to relieve
emotional tension.

> When the raine came to wet me once, and the winde to make me
> chatter: when the Thunder would not peace at my bidding, there I
> found 'em, there I smelt 'em out. Go too, they are not men o' their
> words; they told me I was every thing: 'Tis a Lye, I am not Agu-proofe.

The language of *Lear* is earnest throughout, an amalgam of
courtly writing and innovation; the conventional is seen at its
best in the first scene:

> Of all these bounds even from this Line, to this,
> With shadowie Forrests, and with Champains rich'd
> With plenteous Rivers, and wide-skirted Meades
> We make thee Lady. (F$_1$, I.1.63–6)

The tragedy contains no speech that may be regarded as a
structured oration. Its language is not of equal excellence, but
always indicative of character.

Simplicity of word was never used with greater effect than
in this play; e.g. in IV.3.18–21 (Pied Bull Quarto, 1608)

> . . . patience and sorow *streme*, [strove]
> Who should expresse her goodliest you have seene,
> Sunshine and raine at once, her smiles and teares,
> Were like a better way . . .

Shakespeare's moderate Latinity is to be seen in the low
percentage of Latin polysyllables he employs in *King Lear*.
Invariably they are introduced for a specific purpose; as Ransom
says 'they are in the language but not quite of it' (*Sewanee
Review* IV.2, 1947).

The passages chosen are from the Folio version of *King Lear*;
the Quarto text is guilty of insensitive mislineation:

> *Lear.* You Sulph'rous and Thought-executing Fires,
> Vaunt-curriors of Oake-cleaving Thunder-bolts,
> Sindge my white head. And thou all-shaking Thunder,
> Strike flat the thicke Rotundity o'th'world,
> Cracke Natures moulds, all germaines spill at once
> That makes ingratefull Man.
> . . . spit Fire, spowt Raine
> Nor Raine, Winde, Thunder, Fire are my Daughters;
> I taxe not you, you Elements with unkindnesse.
> I never gave you Kingdome, call'd you Children;

5

You owe me no subscription. Then let fall   10
Your horrible pleasure. Heere I stand your Slave,
A poore, infirme, weake, and dispis'd old man:
But yet I call you Servile Ministers,
That will with two pernicious Daughters ioyne
Your high-engender'd Battailes, 'gainst a head   15
So old, and white as this. O, ho! 'tis foule.
. . .
   Kent. Alas Sir are you here? Things that love night,
Love not such nights as these: the wrathfull Skies
Gallow the very wanderers of the darke
And make them keepe their Caves: Since I was man,   20
Such sheets of Fire, such bursts of horrid Thunder,
Such groanes of roaring Winde, and Raine, I never
Remember to have heard. Mans Nature cannot carry
Th'affliction, nor the feare.
   Lear. Let the great Goddes
That keepe this dreadfull pudder o're our heads,   25
Finde out their enemies now. Tremble thou Wretch,
That hast within thee undivulgéd Crimes
Unwhipt of Iustice. Hide thee, thou Bloudy hand;
Thou Periur'd, and thou Simular of Vertue
 That art Incestuous. Caytiffe, to peeces shake   30
That under covert, and convenient seeming
Ha's practis'd on mans life. Close pent-up guilts,
Rive your concealing Continents, and cry
These dreadfull Summoners grace. I am a man,
More sinn'd against, then sinning.

There are three invocations, and in each the declamation is
loaded with emotion. Simple Anglo-Saxon beginnings work up
to thundering crescendos, in which Latin polysyllables *Vaunt-
couriors* (2) ('advance scouts', Fr. avant-coureur), *Rotundity*
(4), *germaines* (5) (a word Shakespeare apparently invented),
simular (29) and *summoners* (34), are the key words. Imagery
is also implied in epithets, especially compounds, which are
condensed metaphors, such as *Thought-executing* (1), *Oake-
cleaving* (2) and *all-shaking* (3). These are of the same com-
pound type like modern *time-consuming*.

Throughout, the King's imprecations employ harsh aggressive
and vindictive verbs: *execute, cleave, singe, shake, strike, crack,
spill, spit, tax*, let *fall, join battle, gallow* ('frighten'), *roar,
tremble, shake to pieces, rive*. In anthropomorphic terms, these
invoke dislocation or dissolution, and indicate Lear's temporary
mental imbalance.

In the first Quarto *powther* appears for *pudder* in line 25; most modern editors have accepted the dialect word *pudder*. *Powther*, a contemporary spelling for *powder* (dust), is not appropriate to a rain-storm. *Pudder* has a long literary history since the seventeenth century; it is a metaphorical word in the *Lear* context, with powerful emotive force, meaning 'choking atmosphere' (e.g. after gun-fire). The substitution of *Thundring* in Q_2 is weak by comparison. *Simular* (29) for 'simulator' or 'hypocrite' was used by Tyndale; *Caytiffe* (30), through French from Latin *captivus*, means, in context, 'a vagrant imprisoned for plotting against the life of another'. *Close pent-up guilts* (32) is a variant of *undivulged Crimes* (27). *Summoners* were officers of the ecclesiastical courts. In 29–34 Shakespeare reverts to polysyllabic Latinisms, an example being *Rive your concealing Continents* (33), *Rive* being an Old Norse borrowing of the thirteenth century.

The sober language and epithets of Kent in lines 17–24 are intended as a contrast to the tyrannical utterances of Lear; one sign is Shakespeare's use of conventional phrases, such as *wrathfull* skies, *horrid* Thunder and *roaring* Winde.

Chatman says (*A Theory of Meter*, p. 190) that 'the significant urgencies in poetry develop from the meaning, or from meaning expectancy conjoined with metrical expectancy'. In this scene the vehemence of the language often breaks the metrical bounds, as in line 23, an Alexandrine; from this springs the mislineation of the Q_1 text. Shakespeare would not have included the many elisions that appear in the Folio text; they were probably the work of a syllable-counting editor; and he is at a loss to show that *horrible* (11) should be a disyllable.

Prominence is secured for the semantically important compound epithets in lines 1–6 by the spondaic slowing of the rhythm. The fragmentation of the verse (Lear is still defiant, still giving orders) accounts for the irregularity of the ictus within the lines; the medial pauses are particularly well placed. The pedantic use of commas by the editor, as in 24 and 34–5, indicates a rhetorical use of punctuation. The movement of the verse shows Shakespeare's declamatory skill at its most resourceful. G. W. Williams observes of the first of these declamations ('The Poetry of the Storm in *King Lear*', *Shakespeare Quarterly* II.1, 1951):

Most notable is the frequency of fricatives and stops in clusters of onomatopoeic vernacular words chosen to suggest the roughness and harshness of the weather. (p. 60)

Shakespeare felt the inadequacy of sound effects on the stage, and suggested the effects of the storm through the language of Lear.

Syntax has a small part in the effect of Lear's imprecations; inversions of word order occur in lines 5 and 30 only. But in Kent's speech (21–3) inversion has a deliberate rhetorical effect. The unstudied sentences of Lear are reflected in the solecisms of grammar, e.g. the singular verb *makes* (6), and the plural *are* (7); this latter is due to regarding the four elements as a plural subject. The present singular *Ha's*, instead of Shakespeare's usual verse form *hath*, is in the orthography of Jonson, and may be the work of the Folio editor.

In Celtic mythology the king's actions were believed to cause dispensations of weather and production of crops. He was thought to have direct power over the elements, and Lear invoked each of them in turn. But powers were inverted to curse universal ingratitude. The tempest came without his bidding; he believed that the elements were no longer 'Servile Ministers' (13), but had taken arms with his daughters to destroy him. Allegories of Noah's flood, and the Last Judgement were much in Lear's mind. He called for the total destruction of a universe conceived in Platonic terms: 'Cracke Natures moulds' (5). The form of the earth, which he believed to be round, he commanded to be flattened.

Lear, comparing the remorseless weather to his disloyal daughters, welcomes inclemency, because the elements owe him nothing. Metaphors are integrated with the mode of thinking: *taxe* (8) and *subscription* (10), revenues of a king, are functional, as is the oxymoron *horrible pleasure* (11).

In his third outburst Lear calls on the gods to punish enemies of the moral order; he demands retribution of the Natural Law. The image-language belongs to the law-courts, as *Unwhipt of Iustice* (28) reveals. When language is charged with emotion, metaphors are apt to go unnoticed; for instance, *pudder*, *practis'd on*, *guilts* and *grace* (mercy).

Lear's declamations are not rhetorical in the Isocratic sense of words used for effect. *Ecphonesis* (exclamatory expressions revealing the passions of the mind) and personal metaphor characterize the eloquence of an exasperated spirit. The pathos of line 12 is due, in part, to verbal simplicity. When Shakespeare simulates the thunder, he avoids vociferation, and skilfully alliterates plosive and sibilant consonants (27 to 35). Devices such as *ploce* are reserved for the speech of Kent:

17–18   Things that *love night*/ *Love* not such *nights* as these.

The whole of the Kent passage is marked by an intricate use of alliteration.

The imagery of the storm scene, fraught with bodily anguish, shows Lear's petulant egotism beginning to crumble. The commentary of the Fool (omitted here) is a bitter purgative in Lear's transformation; it is pathetic rather than tragic. The Fool's choric function is to hold the mirror, so that Lear may perceive the distorted image of his tyrannical nature. As the garments of pomp are shed, pride is humbled. The symbolic language of *King Lear* is complex, yet strong with a simple compression and intensity.

The cosmic unity of the play is to be seen in the homogeneity of the natural imagery. Here, as in *Othello*, Shakespeare made plentiful use of Pliny's *Natural History*, translated by Philemon Holland; he embodied tragic significance in an holistic metaphorical plan. The shared experience lies not so much in the physical tensions of the passions at war as in the moral allegory they symbolize.

Macbeth II.1.33–64

Is this a Dagger, which I see before me,
The Handle toward my Hand? Come, let me clutch thee:
I have thee not, and yet I see thee still.
Art thou not fatall Vision, sensible
To feeling, as to sight? or art thou but   5
A Dagger of the Minde, a false Creation,
Proceeding from the heat-opresséd Braine?
I see thee yet, in forme as palpable,
As this which now I draw.
Thou marshall'st me the way that I was going,   10
And such an Instrument I was to use.
Mine Eyes are made the fooles o'th'other Sences,
Or else worth all the rest: I see thee still;

And on thy Blade, and Dudgeon, Gouts of Blood,
Which was not so before. There's no such thing: 15
It is the bloody Businesse, which informes
Thus to mine Eyes. Now o're the one halfe World
Nature seemes dead, and wicked Dreames abuse
The Curtain'd sleepe: Witchcraft celebrates
Pale Heccats Offrings: and wither'd Murther,   20
Alarum'd by his Centinell, the Wolfe,
Whose howle's his Watch, thus with his stealthy pace,
With Tarquins ravishing *sides*, towards his designe [strides]
Moves like a Ghost. Thou *sowre* and firme-set Earth [sure]
Heare not my steps, which *they may* walke, for feare [way they]   25
Thy very stones prate of my where-about,
And take the present horror from the time,
Which now sutes with it. Whiles I threat, he lives:
Words to the heat of deedes too cold breath gives.
I goe, and it is done: the Bell invites me.   30
Heare it not, Duncan, for it is a Knell,
That summons thee to Heaven, or to Hell.

The speech is a tour-de-force in conveying the atmosphere of foreboding through a chain of images. It may have been suggested to Shakespeare by a reading of Seneca's *Hercules Furens* and Montaigne's essay on 'The Power of the Imagination'. Great actors have played this scene in many ways (see the footnotes in the Variorum edition), because technical difficulties are involved. The suspended dagger and other supernatural incidents in *Macbeth* must have taxed the ingenuity of Shakespeare's company, and aroused public interest.

Macbeth is remarkable for the combination of sublime language with classical condensation. If the extant text is a pruned one, no cutting appears in the powerful dramatic scenes; they gave the poet's invention full scope. Filled with the horrid project of regicide, Macbeth's mind was in a turmoil of apprehension. He moved inexorably to the act, fully conscious of its enormity.

Shakespeare's purpose was to reveal a man of nervous temperament, abetted by his wife's ambition, whose conscience never became altogether hardened; yet a mind susceptible to supernatural suggestion. He particularly interested himself in the torment of an over-wrought mind, knowing that a lurid imagination gives objective reality to hallucinations.

The passage chosen contains one of the cathartic moments of the play; it is imaginative and dignified. Evil is shown as an active force in the universe, hatched in darkness; and darkness lends itself to the vague and impalpable. The picture conjured up in this soliloquy is that of an imaginative man premeditating the horror of his criminal plan. The function of the imagery is to intensify and vivify. The pattern guides the choice of words, and supplies the dominant motives.

When Shakespeare uses words from source-books, they are given a special power in their new contexts, and often different rhythmical functions. The sources are important, because many of Shakespeare's images result from reflection upon operative words in his reading. His memory was associative, and acted as a transformer; the emotive phrasing helped to implant the dramatic situation in the mind.

There are no set orations in the play; but universal reflections in soliloquy raise the tone of the language and move the passions of the mind. In the first 14 lines Macbeth addresses the imaginary dagger that seems to tempt him. Shakespeare alternates apostrophe with graphic description and pictorial images, followed by an apostrophe to the earth.

There are three Latinisms at the end of line 4. *Sensible* means 'perceptible to touch'; *Vision* implies that Macbeth was aware that the dagger was a delusion, a 'false Creation,/ Proceeding from the heat-oppressed Braine' (6–7). Other Latinisms are *palpable* and *Instrument*. Lines 10 to 14 contain three words of French origin: *marshall'st* (summonest), *Dudgeon* (box-wood handle) and *Gouts* (drops). *Informes* (16) is used with its original sense of 'takes shape'. *The one halfe World* (17) refers to the northern hemisphere. Lines 19 to 24 contain nine Latinisms. *Alarum* (21) came into the language as a noun in the fourteenth century, until Marlowe used it as a verb in *Tamburlaine*.

The balance of indigenous and foreign words is a feature of Shakespeare's mature style. Epithets in descriptive lines are forward-looking and vital: *fatal* Vision (4), *wicked* Dreames (18), *Curtain'd* sleepe (19), *wither'd* Murther (20), *stealthy* pace (22), Tarquin's *ravishing* strides (24), *firme-set* Earth (25), *cold* breath (29).

The sense of the words accords with the tempo of the situation. In lines 1–12 terse phrasing falls naturally into the rhythms of common speech. Modulation of stresses is helped by

weak final syllables (1, 2, 6, 10 and 12), by a pyrrhic fifth foot
in *sensible* and *palpable* (4 and 8), and by the short line (9). In
his later verse Shakespeare admits prepositional phrases, such
as *but/ A Dagger*, (5–6), in which a preposition is separated
from the governing noun by line-division. Line 12 probably
contained 12 syllables, but *of the* has been reduced by the Folio
editor to *o'th'* for the sake of metrical conformity. That
Shakespeare was not averse to trisyllabic feet can be seen by
the use of *ravishing* in 23. The descriptive passage (14–28) is
daring in modulation, secured by inversion of stresses, as in the
nine-syllable line (19), where the deficient syllable is com-
pensated for by the long pause after *sleepe:*

/Thĕ Cúr/taĭn'd sléepe:/ Wĭtchcràft/ célĕ/bŕates.

The use of *thou, thee* and *thy* in the invocation (2–14) has
emotive force. The phonetically correct use of *Mine* before *Eyes*
(12) is observed by Shakespeare, to avoid hiatus between the
diphthongs. The profuse capitals in the passage are unlikely to
be Shakespeare's, for they have no rhetorical significance. But
the punctuation (perhaps the Folio editor's) carefully marks the
phrases for delivery, the function of the colons being to
demarcate manageable speech units. Though the accidentals are
of small poetical significance, the variant prepositions *toward*
(2) and *towards* (23) are in accordance with Elizabethan
practice (cf. the noun *where-about* (26), and the conjunctive
adverb *whiles* (28)). The solecism *gives* (singular for plural)
is apparently due to the juxtaposition of *breath*.

Imagery is important for the emotive meaning of words.
Metonymy in *Vision* associates evil with the delusion of the
dagger; Shakespeare amplifies the effect by the appositional
metaphors *Dagger of the Minde* and *false Creation* (6). *Mar-
shall'st* (metaphor) emphasizes the compulsive nature of
Macbeth's yielding. *Instrument* is an evasive euphemism
suggesting that the crime was predestined (cf *Business* in 16).
The unreliability of the senses implied in the ambivalent
personification of lines 12 and 13 expresses the dubiety in
Macbeth's mind.

Personification and metaphor are continued in the phrase-
making lines 18 to 24. '*Curtain'd* sleepe' (transferred epithet)
suggests 'the quietness of seclusion', abused by '*wicked*

Dreames'. 'Witchcraft *celebrates*/ Pale Heccats *Offrings*' (19–20) conveys ritualistic inevitability. *Wither'd Murther* calls up the image of Death. The ravenous *Wolfe* accords with the predatory spirit of the passage. The most convenient interpretation of *Whose howl's his watch* is to assume that the last word is a shortening of *watch-word*. The 'ravishing *strides*' of Tarquin look back to Lucrece 162–8 (transferred epithet). Portents of doom and unnatural secrecy are suggested by *stealthy pace* (22) and *Moves like a Ghost* (24). In the crucial lines there are, unfortunately, three misreadings in the Folio text: *sides* for *strides* (23), *sowre* for *sure* (24), and *they* for *way* (25).

Though rhetorical devices are of secondary importance in Shakespeare, they contribute here to the atmosphere of tension. E.g.

Erotema (rhetorical question): lines 1 to 7.

Hypophora (supplying one's own answer): lines 8 to 17.

Ploce: 2   *Handle* toward my *Hand*.

　　　14, 16   *Blood . . . bloody*

Sense antithesis: 28–9   whiles I *threat*, he *lives:*
Words to the *heat* of *deedes* too *cold* breath gives.

Comparatio: 24   *Moves like a Ghost.*

Onomatopoeia: 30–2   *Bell . . . Knell . . . Hell.*

Hyperbaton (dislocation of normal order):

25   Heare not my *steps, which way they walke*

29   Words to the heat of deedes too cold breath *gives*

　Anticlimax: 32   . . . to Heaven, *or to Hell* (the comma is important to the actor).

These are a few of the rhetorical figures that Shakespeare conceals by his art; most would have been identified by educated Renaissance audiences.

Antony and Cleopatra I.3.66–104

Coleridge thought that the 'happy valiancy' of *Antony and Cleopatra* (a translation of Horace's *feliciter audax*) distinguished Shakespeare from all other poets. The style is not classic, but neo-Platonic, glorifying wonder; the art depends on the bold juxtaposition of words. Passionate utterance fuses fragmented images in the manner of Byzantine mosaic. The largesse of phrase is romantic, as the language of love tragedy should be.

The play seems to have been worked on in desultory fashion; there are no act or scene divisions in the First Folio text. The Brechtian scope, the paradoxes, the kaleidoscopic pageant of two worlds (Egypt and Rome), represent irreconcilable ways of life. The death of Antony is enacted earlier, and in a lower key, than that of Cleopatra. Shakespeare transformed the protagonists of Plutarch by his graphic imagery.

Antony, as presented in the first two Acts, and again in the last, is Hercules *redivivus:* 'demi-Atlas . . . the Arme/ And Burganet of men'. He is the universal man of the Renaissance, described by Cleopatra as the 'Crowne o'th' earth'. In the last Act, when the fever of war and politics is over, it is Cleopatra who becomes the Colossus of sublime poetry. The idealized style of this Act recalls the vastness of Michelangelo. The deaths of Antony and Cleopatra are conceived in the noble Roman tradition – Cleopatra's sole concession to the Roman way of life. Her willingness to match Antony in the stoic style is shown in V.2.237–40:

> My Resolution's plac'd, and I have nothing
> Of woman in me: Now from head to foote
> I am Marble constant: now the fleeting Moone
> No Planet is of mine.

This is not as exotic and Alexandrian as her sensual interest, nor does it resemble Lady Macbeth's abrogation of her sex.

The final scenes afford Shakespeare the opportunity of returning to the love-death imagery of the ending in *Romeo and Juliet*. The paradox of pagan mysticism mingled with Christian theology is shown by no less than eleven references to the Book of Revelation in the last Act (see W. Blissett, *Shakespeare Quarterly*, XVIII.2, 1967, p. 165).

With all his frailty of flesh, Antony is magnanimous, whereas Cleopatra is the embodiment of sensual, possessive and personal love. The very names of characters from Plutarch (Eros, Thidias, Mardian, Alexas, Charmian and Iras) are woven by Shakespeare into the tapestry of the verse. *Thidias* for Plutarch's *Thyreus* can only be explained as a lapse of memory.

Shakespeare's eloquence surpasses in taste and variety the language of Marlowe in *Tamburlaine*. Analysis of *Antony and*

Cleopatra's cleverly alternated scenes shows that the grandi-loquence of passion is moderate. Cleopatra and Antony seldom appear together in the first two Acts. Enobarbus, a choric figure, is a plain-spoken, cynical commentator, who only once lets himself go. His account of Cleopatra's first meeting with Antony ('The barge she sat in') is an inset to keep her theatrical image before the audience. The steely austerity of Octavius is antipathetic, but true to the Roman character; he is a foil in the play to the vacillating voluptuary, Antony; Shakespeare depicts the lover as a world-figure relentlessly crushed by Roman imperialism.

State business, warfare and comic interludes are conducted mainly in prose, but so flexible is the blank verse that the two media are difficult to distinguish. A natural rhythm was undoubtedly part of Shakespeare's design and severe com-pression sometimes leads to syntactical obscurity. For Shake-speare hurriedly converts Plutarch's narrative into dialogue, and his art in doing this is his own secret.

Granville Barker remarks that, in this play, description is 'as nothing compared with suggestion' (*Prefaces to Shakespeare*, Batsford, Vol. III, p. 23); and the language of suggestion is often in the mouths of minor characters. Pompey, for instance, alludes to the sottishness of Antony's 'lascivious Wassailes' in seven lines (II.1.21–7):

> Salt Cleopatra soften thy wand lip,
> Let Witchcraft ioyne with Beauty, Lust with both,
> Tye up the Libertine in a field of Feasts,
> Keepe his Braine fuming. Epicurean Cookes,
> Sharpen with cloylesse sawce his Appetite,
> That sleepe and feeding may prorogue his Honour,
> Even till a Lethied dulnesse.

Variety of diction is procured by alternations of realism and romance, and large-scale experiments with words in vicarious functions. There seems to be a plan to give words new senses through symbolic associations. The image clusters are vivid in emotive dialogue; the tone of the poetry in the last two acts is often elegiac, as in IV.14.50–4, where images have been italicized:

> Stay for me,
> Where *Soules do couch on Flowers*, wee'l hand in hand,

And *with our sprightly Port make the Ghostes gaze:*
Dido and her Aeneas shall want Troopes,
And all the *haunt* be ours. Come Eros, Eros.

A tragedy that is episodic and wanting in structural unity
compelled Shakespeare to sustain the heroic interest by the
technical mastery of the verse. The selection for analysis is
from the first Act; it illustrates the clash of wills and wits that
makes dialogue between the protagonists vital. Antony had no
illusions about Cleopatra; she was always his 'Serpent of old
Nile'; he confessed to Enobarbus: 'She is cunning past mans
thought'. Yet every mood becomes her; it is by her personality,
rather than her beauty, that Antony is captivated.

Ant. Quarrell no more, but bee prepar'd to know
The purposes I beare: which are, or cease,
As you shall give th'advice. By the fire
That quickens Nylus slime, I go from hence
Thy Souldier, Servant, making Peace or Warre,   5
As thou affects.
    Cleo. Cut my Lace, Charmian come,
But let it be, I am quickly ill, and well,
So Anthony loves.
    Ant. My precious Queene forbeare,
And give true evidence to his Love, which stands
An honourable Triall.
    Cleo. So Fulvia told me.   10
I prythee turne aside, and weepe for her,
Then bid adiew to me, and say the teares
Belong to Egypt. Good now, play one Scene
Of excellent dissembling, and let it looke
Like perfect Honor.
    Ant. You'l heat my blood no more?   15
    Cleo. You can do better yet: but this is meetly.
    Ant. Now by [my] Sword.
    Cleo. And Target. Still he mends.
But this is not the best. Looke prythee Charmian,
How this Herculean Roman do's become
The carriage of his chafe.
    Ant. Ile leave you Lady.   20
    Cleo. Courteous Lord, one word:
Sir, you and I must part, but that's not it:
Sir, you and I have lov'd, but there's not it:
That you know well, something it is I would:
Oh, my Oblivion is a very Anthony,   25
And I am all forgotten.
    Ant. But that your Royalty

Holds Idlenesse your subiect, I should take you
For Idlenesse it selfe.
   Cleo. 'Tis sweating Labour,
To beare such Idlenesse so neere the heart
As Cleopatra this. But Sir, forgive me,   30
Since my becommings kill me, when they do not
Eye well to you. Your Honor calles you hence,
Therefore be deafe to my unpittied Folly,
And all the Gods go with you. Upon your Sword
Sit Lawrell victory, and smooth successe   35
Be strew'd before your feete.
   Ant. Let us go.
Come: Our separation so abides and flies,
That thou reciding heere, goes yet with mee;
And I hence fleeting, heere remaine with thee.

In few scenes presenting the protagonists is word choice so
sparing in Latin polysyllables. Yet the syntax and the sense
are occasionally incongruous; interpretation of many lines calls
for conjecture. The gibes of Cleopatra are taunting, sarcastic,
ironical. She mocks Antony in the presence of Charmian by
speaking of him in the third person (lines 17–20). Individually,
the words need no gloss, but their intent is as ambiguous as
the lovers' feelings. Simplicity of vocabulary in Shakespeare
may often be deceptive.

Subtlety is inherent in the semantic difficulties, such as these:
line 2, *purposes I beare* = 'plans I have in mind'; *are, or cease* =
   'come or go'.
lines 3 and 6, *you, thou.* The change of address probably indicates
   a change to affection in Antony. When he swears, by the
   Nile, devotion to Cleopatra, he ceases to be irritated. A
   similar change of emotional attitude can be observed in the
   pronouns of lines 27 and 38/39. *Thou* and *you* throughout this
   scene reflect the fluctuating feelings of the characters.
line 3, *fire*, a metaphor for the sun.
line 6, *affects* = 'prefer'. *Cut my Lace* was a common colloquial
   expression, when a woman became upset or hysterical.
   Immediate relief was expected by snipping the lace of the
   stomacher.
line 8, *So* = 'as', not 'provided that'.
lines 9–10, *give true evidence to his Love, which stands* etc. = 'give
   honest testimony concerning the love of him who stands on
   trial'.

lines 11–12, *say the tears/ Belong to Egypt* = 'pretend the tears are shed for Cleopatra'. Note the frequent metonymical use of *Egypt*.

lines 12–14. The tongue-in-cheek suggestion is that Antony is play-acting and insincere.

line 15, *heat my blood* = 'anger me'.

line 16, *meetly* = 'passably good'.

line 17, *Target* = 'shield'. Cleopatra completes the common-place oath of the swashbuckler, 'By my sword and buckler (target)'. The effect is to demean the soldierly Antony to a mountebank.

line 19, *Herculean Roman*. According to Plutarch, Antony resembled and dressed like Hercules, supposing himself to be descended from the worthy's son, Anton.

line 20, *chafe*. The verb was borrowed from French *chaufer* in the fourteenth century. According to OED the noun, meaning 'anger', first occurred in Ascham in the mid-sixteenth century.

line 21, *Courteous*. The epithet is derived from Plutarch's account. Hence Antony's modes of address: *precious Queene* (8) and *your Royalty* (26).

line 24, *would* = 'wish for'.

lines 25–6, *Oh, my Oblivion is a very Antony,/ And I am all forgotten. My* is here an objective genitive. The meaning is 'forgetting me is typical of Antony, and I shall be completely unremembered'. The ambiguity of these lines is due partly to misunderstanding of Elizabethan grammatical practice.

lines 27–8, *Idlenesse*. The ambiguity in the two uses of this word is known as *antanaclasis*. The first has the sense of 'sportiveness' or 'coquetry', the second means 'childishness', 'irresponsibility' or 'want of feeling'. There is a semantic antithesis between *Royalty* (26) and *subiect* (27). Antony implies that the queenly Cleopatra abuses her privilege with unfeeling jests at the expense of her subject. According to Plutarch, Fulvia behaved as a shrew to Antony, and his passivity towards Cleopatra was the result of his first wife's railing.

lines 28–9, *'Tis sweating Labour/ To beare such Idlenesse so neere the heart*. The image of childbirth excuses Cleopatra's frivolity as a disguise for her pain.

line 31, *becommings* = 'that which befits or graces a person'. The paradox is Cleopatra's realization of her failings (hence *unpittied Folly, 33*). According to OED the use of this verbal noun in the early seventeenth century was peculiar to Shakespeare.

line 32, *Eye* (verb) = 'appear in your eyes'. The number of nouns used as verbs in this play is legion, and evidence of Shakespeare's desire to avoid clichés.

line 35, *smooth* = 'unruffled'. The metaphor is that of an easy path.

The metaphorical and metonymic language in *Antony and Cleopatra* is apt to pass unnoticed, for instance in lines 4, 6, 9, 10, 13, 15, 17, 20, 25, 28, 31, 32, 36, 37. Invariably it accompanies personification, which is the mark of Shakespeare's humanism. Rhetorical figures of repetition are not numerous, but *epanaphora* occurs in lines 22 and 23, only three words being changed in the second line. The paradox of the exchanges is summed up in the last three lines of the passage; 38 and 39 are pointedly antithetical:

> Our separation so *abides* and *flies*,
> That thou *reciding heere, goes* yet with mee;
> And I *hence fleeting,* heere *remaine* with thee.

Antony here speaks of spiritual presence and absence in the metaphysical terms of Donne. Shakespeare had been moving in this direction since *Hamlet.*

Grammatical features are by no means negligible. The compulsive effect of Cleopatra's whims is suggested in the use of *shall* in line 3. The *-s* inflexion, for *-st*, of *affects* (6), was a licensed phonetic facility in verbs whose stems ended in *-t* or *-st;* ease of an actor's delivery was more important to Shakespeare than the technical requirements of verse. The indicative *loves* (8) is the clue to the meaning of the conjunction *so;* had the sense been 'provided that' the subjunctive would have been used. *His* (9) is one of many uses of the objective genitive, avoided in modern English because of its syntactical obscurity. Shakespeare's use of pronouns is not always meticulous; for instance, *it* in line 14 must refer to *dissembling* not *scene*, but neither antecedent is comparable with *perfect Honor* (15). Shakespeare is, however, more concerned with dramatic effect.

Meetly (16) (*meet* would have sufficed) supplies evidence that the *-ly* suffix was not confined to adverbs; survivals of this freedom are *comely* and *lovely*. *Do's* (19) was unusual in Shakespeare's verse until the later plays, when colloquial forms (and orthography) came under the influence of Ben Jonson. The tone of Cleopatra's frivolity explains the usage here. *Goes*, for *goest* (38), resembles *affects* above; the balanced line requires a monosyllable for smooth effect; the elision of *e* in *go'st yet* would have produced an awkward juxtaposition of *t-* sounds.

The flexibility of the verse in this dialogue is important to the dramatic impact, and reveals Shakespeare's craftsmanship at its maturest. Inversions of stress and enjambement have an emphatic and rhythmic purpose. The occasional stiffness and artificiality of the early plays is relaxed; when matter and manner are ideally matched, the listener's attention is not strained. Notice, for example, the deft use of alliterating *p* and *s* in lines 1 to 6. The Greek figure of *parimion* is extended by Shakespeare to word-juncture (linking sounds), an example being *quickens Nylus slime* (4). The movement of the verse is helped by the brevity of the sentences, especially the rare subordinate clauses. There is a knack of fragmentation, and a skilful handling of pauses; naturalism does not destroy the poetic quality of the blank verse.

Dover Wilson claimed that the text of the play is only one remove from Shakespeare's manuscript. Whoever the stage-reviser or editor was, his conception of the versification seems to have been different from Shakespeare's; and this accounts for the large-scale elisions and poetical contractions. As they stand in the Folio text, many lines tend to obscure Shakespeare's purpose, e.g.

3 /Ăs yóu/ shăll gíve/ th'advíce/. Bў thĕ/ fírĕ/

The line can only be normalized syllabically by making *fire* a disyllable; the situation is not helped by asserting that Shakespeare did not himself require elision in the third foot. What one needs to know is whether the actor observed the elision in the actual speaking of the verse. M. A. Bayfield in *Shakespeare's Versification* (CUP, 1920) distinguished between necessary abbreviations, which have remained in English verse, and extraordinary licences, such as *th'head, doo't, i'th'right, to'th'*

Court, in't. The latter class abound in *Antony and Cleopatra*, and
are not demanded by metrical requirements. Shakespeare, as in
other plays, would have used expanded forms, naturally, as
modifications in the shape of hypermetrical syllables, feminine
endings, pyrrhic or trisyllabic feet. The motivation behind the
Folio's intention to reduce blank verse to ten-syllable lines
cannot have been Shakespeare's; and the execution is painfully
inconsistent; e.g.

9 . /Aňd gíve/ trúe é/vidĕncĕ/ tǒ hǐs Lóve,/ whǐch stánds/

There is no elision here, because the 'reviser' did not know
where to put it – in *evidence*, *to* or *his* – and so left the position
of a lightly slurred syllable to the judgement of the actor.

A fragmentary-line speech, between others of greater length,
often completes a broken line of verse that precedes or succeeds
it. This was called a 'common section' by J. B. Mayor in *English
Metre* (CUP, 1886, p. 146). The phenomenon was first noticed
by Abbott (*Shakespearian Grammar* § 513), who named it an
'amphibious section'; he found examples in *Richard III*, *Julius
Caesar* and *Measure for Measure*, though the device was used
with much more freedom after *Hamlet*. One purpose was to
sustain the rhythm of dialogue within a scene, as though the
speeches were return strokes in a rally at tennis. *Antony and
Cleopatra* makes the freest use of common sections, as in the
following interchange:

18–21   *Cleo.* Looke prythee Charmian,
            How this Herculean Roman do's become
         // Thĕ cár/riăge ŏf/ hǐs cháfe./
            Ant. /Ilĕ leáve/ yǒu Lá/dў//.
            Cleo. //Cóur/teǒus Lórd/, one wórd.//

Antony's five syllables metrically complete both fragmentary
speeches of Cleopatra; but they better amplify the second,
because the last syllable of *Lady* makes up an iambic foot with
the first syllable of *Courteous* in the next line.

The play abounds in what rhetoricians used to call 'loose'
structures. Shakespeare's blank verse lays stroke on stroke,
avoiding the periodic structure of Milton, with its planned
subordination. Granville Barker describes Shakespeare's method
acutely in *Prefaces to Shakespeare*, Vol. II:

Dramatic emphasis is the thing, first and last; to get that right he will sacrifice strict metre – yet never music. (p. 55)

James Sutherland amplified this in 'The Language of the Last Plays':

He brushes past the syntactical obstacle, and the meaning comes through by reason of its force and with the help of the speech rhythms.
(*More Talking of Shakespeare*, Longmans, 1959, p. 146)

Sutherland thinks Shakespeare's style, in his last period, is a kind of 'rough impressionism . . . straining after the maximum of intensity', a statement truer of *The Winter's Tale* than *Antony and Cleopatra*.

Antony and Cleopatra represents a conflict of personalities. As Cleopatra is a witty extrovert, she is given no soliloquy. Her language is invariably sensuous; in the trappings of her death there are symbols of sexual fertility (the basket of figs, the asp as a baby at the breast, the assumption of the role of the generative goddess Isis). Her fatal ascendancy over Antony, whom she recognizes as the greatest of her lovers, is symbolized by the donning of his sword, and by dressing him in her own garments – a clever twist to the fable of Hercules and Omphale. At the crisis of his fortunes Hercules is invoked by Antony under the Greek name Alcides (IV.12.43–7):

The shirt of Nessus is upon me, teach me
Alcides, thou mine Ancestor, thy rage.
Let me lodge Licas on the hornes o'th'Moone,
And with those hands that graspt the heaviest Club,
Subdue my worthiest selfe.

Images of vastness are not confined to the principal characters. Throughout the tragedy they symbolize the clash of *amor* and *imperium*, the 'immortal longings' of Cleopatra and the 'realms and islands' dropped, like plates, from Antony's pocket. Not only Cleopatra, but her maids, especially Charmian, embody the luxury and exotic attraction of Egypt. Antony's choice of Egypt, in preference to Rome, symbolizes, as S. L. Bethell points out, 'the life of the spontaneous affections' (*Shakespeare and the Popular Dramatic Tradition*, Staples Press, N.Y., 1944, p. 128). The lovers are 'star-crossed', not, as in *Romeo and Juliet*, by a chain of misfortune, but by the egotism of their passion. Shakespeare's portrait of Cleopatra makes little of

Plutarch's statement that she was unpopular with the Egyptians. Antony's preoccupation with power, and Cleopatra's suspicion of his uneasy fidelity, suggest that Shakespeare's theme is a paradox of misunderstanding, to which the ambiguity of the language contributes magnificently.

The Tempest I.2.377–83 and 390–422

Enter Ferdinand and Ariel, invisible playing and singing.
Ariel Song. Come unto these yellow sands,
   and then take hands:
   Curtsied when you have, and kist
   the wilde waves whist:
Foote it featly heere, and there, and sweete Sprights beare 5
   the burthen   *Burthen dispersedly.*
Harke, harke . . .
Fer. Where shold this Musick be? I'th aire, or th'earth?
It sounds no more: and sure it waytes upon
Some God 'oth'Iland, sitting on a banke,   10
Weeping againe the King my Fathers wracke.
This Musicke crept by me upon the waters,
Allaying both their fury, and my passion
With it's sweet ayre: thence I have follow'd it
(Or it hath drawne me rather) but 'tis gone.   15
No, it begins againe.
 Ariel Song. Full fadom five thy Father lies,
   Of his bones are Corrall made;
   Those are pearles that were his eies,
   Nothing of him that doth fade,   20
   But doth suffer a Sea-change
   Into something rich and strange:
   Sea-Nimphs hourly ring his knell.
       Burthen: ding dong.
Harke now I heare them, ding-dong bell.
Fer. The Ditty do's remember my crown'd father, 25
This is no mortall business, nor no sound
That the earth owes: I heare it now above me.
 Pro. The fringéd Curtaines of thine eye advance,
And say what thou see'st yond.
 Mira. What is't a Spirit?   30
Lord, how it lookes about: Beleeve me sir,
It carries a brave forme. But 'tis a spirit.
 Pro. No wench, it eats, and sleeps, and hath such senses
As we have: such. This Gallant which thou seest
Was in the wracke: and but hee's something stain'd 35
With greefe (that's beauties canker) thou might'st call him

A goodly person: he hath lost his fellowes,
And strayes about to finde 'em.
   Mir. I might call him
A thing divine, for nothing naturall
I ever saw so Noble.

            40

The Tempest, last written of Shakespeare's comedies, was the first printed in the First Folio. Sir Walter Greg advanced as the reason that the manuscript, with elaborate stage directions resembling those of court masques, was prepared by the Company's scrivener, Ralph Crane, to serve as a model for subsequent texts, especially in orthography and punctuation. The relevance of this to the versification will appear later.

The Tempest is one of the plays of reconciliation, written by Shakespeare between 1609 and 1611. Classical discipline consists in the static and retrospective treatment of character, and the unities of time and place. The action covers only about three hours, insufficient time for the characters to develop.

The spirits of Shakespeare's island were the demons that shipwrecked colonists on the island of Bermuda expected to find in the New World. In Jewish demonology, names ending in *-el* (the suffix meant 'God') were given to angels such as Ariel. He represents the spirit of air and freedom, such freedom as the tired Shakespeare would willingly have exchanged for the superior magic of Prospero.

The uncouthness of Caliban is his intractability to the 'great chain of being'. He is insensitive to human feeling, because his elements are earth and water. Just before the scene chosen, Caliban, whose name is an anagram of *cannibal*, is addressed by Miranda:

>   thou didst not (Savage)
> Know thine owne meaning; but wouldst gabble, like
> A thing most brutish. I endow'd thy purposes
> with words.

His reply is

> You taught me Language, and my profit on't
> Is, I know how to curse.

Critics have interpreted the allegorical theme of *The Tempest* as a clash between Prospero's acquired art and Caliban's earthy nature. Caliban is a figure that makes an instant appeal to other poets; indeed, Browning, Auden and Graves have shown that the play is the most seminal of Shakespeare's myths in inspiring further reflections. Not what the play says, but what it suggests about the 'brave new world', makes it a superb finale to the dramatist's achievement.

There are a number of subsidiary themes: the place of chastity in love (anticipating Milton's *Comus*), the need for forgiveness to triumph over revenge, and the Arcadian simplicity of the fertile Golden Age (suggested by Vergil, Ovid and Spenser's *Faerie Queene*). The father of Renaissance pastoral romance was the Italian poet-playwright, Guarini, whose *Pastor Fido* was translated by Richard Fanshawe; but the ultimate source of the genre was Longus's *Daphnis and Chloe*.

Prospero, the controlling genius of the action, is a prince turned mage or wise man using the arts of white magic. He is the exemplar of *melior natura*, restraining animal appetite through learning and art. As magician he is secretive, and the motivation of many speeches and actions is obscure. As practical philosopher (the complete man of the Renaissance), he derives principally from Plato; but he owes much to Boethius's *Consolations of Philosophy* and something to the humanism of Montaigne. The long account of his past life to Miranda shows that there is a lack of communication between himself and his daughter. Being innocent of Court intrigue, Miranda does not understand Prospero's resentment. The characters are finely shaded in the language of the first Act. Shakespeare proposed in *The Tempest* also to contrast the contemplative with the active life, for those born to rule. The plotting courtiers brought to the island by Prospero's magic are self-seekers, upon whose barren ground the 'good seed' of education and gentility has produced no crop of moral values. The compassionate Gonzalo is their foil.

The narrative functions of the play are discharged mainly by Prospero, the descriptive by Caliban. The latter's images are of the simple sensuous pleasures of the island; though his reactions are primitive, they have a visual quality which is Shakespeare's:

> I 'prethee let me bring thee where Crabs grow;/ and I with my long nayles will digge thee pig-nuts;/ show thee a Iayes nest, and instruct thee how/ to snare the nimble Marmazet. (II.2.167–70)

This is wrongly printed in the Folio as prose, for no other reason than that it is embedded in the prose of Trinculo and Stephano; but Caliban's first speech in this scene was a long one in verse.

The comedies beginning with *As You Like It* and *Twelfth Night* use music increasingly to symbolize the power of harmony. Whenever Prospero controls the action in *The Tempest*, music and song are his allies. They have a supernatural effect upon Ferdinand; and Ariel is Prospero's instrument of change. It is to music alone that Caliban responds with a spark of humanity. The play integrates music and morals as metaphysical power, the identification made by Plato. Plato owed it to Pythagoras, and Ficino was responsible for transmitting the idea to England. In the last Act of *Pericles*, Shakespeare revived the belief that the music of the spheres is inaudible to human ears; Ferdinand imagines that the sweet sounds he hears in this scene are in the air or underground; the audience is cognizant of their real cause.

The songs in *The Tempest* are not interludes for atmosphere, but part of the play's purpose, aptly described by W. H. Auden ('Music in Shakespeare', *Encounter*, Dec. 1957):

> Ariel *is* song; when he is truly himself, he sings. The effect when he speaks is similar to that of *recitativo secco* in opera, which we listen to because we have to understand the action . . . Yet Ariel is not an alien visitor from the world of opera who has wandered into a spoken drama by mistake. He cannot express any human feelings because he has none. . . .
>
> The effect on Ferdinand of *Come unto these yellow sands* and *Full fathom five*, is more like the effect of instrumental music on Thaisa: direct, positive, magical. . . . The song comes to him as an utter surprise, and its effect is not to feed or please his grief, not to encourage him to sit brooding, but to allay his passion so that he gets to his feet and follows the music. . . . Ferdinand is able to accept the past, symbolized by his father, as past, and at once there stands before him his future, Miranda.

Ship-wrecked strangers on an unknown island would naturally be attentive to unfamiliar noises. Sound provides the pervasive images, and none so numerous as the voices of the sea. The storm-scene, with which the play opens, is graphic in a different way from the tempest in *King Lear*. As the storm abates, the panic subsides into a serene melody. From this point the poetry is lyrical rather than dramatic. *The Tempest*, like *Pericles*, is a tale of survival from the terrors of the sea, and brings with it the mystery of moral regeneration; hence phrases such as *sea-sorrow* and *sea-change*. T. S. Eliot's allusion to this scene in *The Waste Land* is in the same spirit as his *Marina*, significantly included among the 'Ariel' poems. *Miranda* (wonder) and *Marina* (daughter of the sea) are figures closely associated in Shakespeare's mind.

Emile Montegut thought that *The Tempest* is 'of all poetic generalizations . . . the most refined and the clearest' (*Revue des Deux Mondes*, LVIII, 1865). Few scenes confirm this observation better than the one chosen; lines 30–41 are among the most pellucid Prospero and Miranda utter. Yet the first song of Ariel is not without ambiguity. *Curtsied when you have, and kist* (3) is a reference to formal court dances, to which a *kiss* was the finale. *The wild waves whist* (4) is an absolute construction, in which *whist* means 'being hushed'. *Foote it featly* Shakespeare seems to have borrowed from Lodge's *Glaucus and Scilla* (1589). *Burthen* (6) means 'refrain' (the animal noises have been omitted). Ariel, who plays on a tabor (small drum) and a pipe, is responsible, as Ferdinand tells us (12–13), for the quelling of the storm. The curtsey that began the dance was known as a 'reverence'; hence the suggestion of Ferdinand that the *music waytes upon/ Some God o'th' Iland* (9–10). He is aware of the supernatural purpose of Ariel's second song, for he says *This is no mortall business* (26).

The poetry of *The Tempest* tends to compress the dialogue, and to practise unusual syntactical dislocation, such as one finds in the earlier speeches of Leontes in *The Winter's Tale*. Using compound epithets instead of qualifying phrases and clauses, Shakespeare uniquely transmutes the meaning of both components. *Sea-change* (21) is the only example in this passage, but the play abounds in original doublets, such as *hag-seed*, the phrase with which Prospero dismissed Caliban a little earlier. The technique gives a coarse finish to the texture of the verse, resembling the surface of Michelangelo's last sculptures.

Inversions of word order are fairly common in song, owing to exigencies of rhythm and rhyme; but the placing of the participle *Curtsied* before the conjunction of the adverbial clause (3) is unusual in Shakespeare. The second song has less startling dislocations in lines 17 to 19.

Each character is mirrored in the language of the dialogue. Ferdinand is courtly yet direct in speech, revealing an unsophisticated and uncomplex nature. Prospero is a prince of an earlier generation; his speech has an old-world ostentation of image and phrase, contrasted with his daughter's simplicity. *The fringéd Curtaines of thine eye advance* (29) has an artificial Latinity about it; the periphrasis is a frigid way of saying 'Look!' Only a bookish man would speak to his self-tutored child of 'the dark-backward and Abisme of Time'. Whenever Prospero embarks on a long narration, his syntax becomes contorted. Shakespeare's method of composing possibly shows that obscurity was the outcome of complex exposition.

The contrasted language of Ferdinand and Prospero reveals itself in the imagery. Ferdinand's reference to music that *'waytes upon/ Some God 'oth'Iland'* (9–10) and *'crept . . . upon the waters'* (12) takes the natural form of personification. In 29 Prospero's *fringéd Curtaines* (a metaphor for 'eye-lids') reminds us that Miranda had just woken from sleep, suddenly to be confronted with the apparition (as she thought) of Ferdinand. *Advance* (29) was several times used by Shakespeare meaning 'to direct the attention of the eye'; this verb gives the image its precious quaintness. *Stain'd/ With greefe* (that's *beauties canker*) (35–6) contains a twinned metaphor, the implication being that grief is both a disfigurement and a consuming disease. The image is conventional, rather than outlandish.

Apparent grammatical laxity is a symptom of Shakespeare's late libertarianism. The only actual solecism is one of concord in line 18: 'Of his bones *are* Corrall made'; here the plural *bones* usurped the position of the subject, and misled Shakespeare. *Spright* (5) and *Spirit* (30, 32) in the same passage are not inconsistencies, since the first was employed in poetry as a monosyllabic variant of the second. Typical Elizabethanisms are *shold* for *may* (8); *againe* for *against* (i.e. 'opposite') in 11; the uninflected plural *fadom* (fathom) in 17; and the double negative *nor no* (26). *It's* (14), the neuter possessive for *his*, was a Jacobean innovation still unusual, and may have been Crane's, the scrivener's. Poetical *hath* and *doth* are used throughout the passage, with one exception *do's* (25). In plays after 1600 Shakespeare rarely accepted this colloquial form of Jonson

H

and Fletcher in poetry; the *s* inflexion appears mainly in First Folio texts, editorial interference being a possible explanation. *Do* as a periphrastic auxiliary verb occurs three times in this excerpt, twice in Ariel's dirge, where it adds a touch of archaic solemnity.

An orthographical feature of the text is the frequent use of brackets to mark parentheses. In Shakespeare's last plays there were many such breaks in the thought, to secure the naturalness of ordinary talk. Stage convention employed parentheses as a sign to the actor to drop his voice, indicating an interpolation. The brackets must have been supplied by Ralph Crane; they seldom appear in the good Quartos of the earlier Shakespeare, but frequently in the transcripts of Fletcher's plays made by Crane. He seems to have treated the text of *The Tempest* with special care, as a guide to the First Folio editors. Among the devices of rhetoric, *ploce* is found in 30 and 32, and in the repetition of *such* (33–4).

Shakespeare's versification had been steadily growing in freedom and resource, as F. Kermode observed in the New Arden edition of *The Tempest* (Methuen, 1954):

> Shakespeare grew increasingly fond of the pentameter which spreads itself over two half-lines, and the heavy pause in the middle of the 'straddled' line tends to remove emphasis from the true sense-ending. (Introduction, p. xvii)

This movement was an assault on the techniques of blank-verse declamation. The reform was hardly to secure a more relaxed style; but the results appeared natural to audiences of tragi-comedy, and added to the resources of modulation. The employment of extra unstressed syllables at the end of the blank-verse line is a feature of *The Tempest*; of the 22 such lines in this passage, 11 have the redundant syllable.

More ubiquitous in the text of Crane are the metaplasms, especially *aphæresis*, *syncope*, *apocope* and *synalœpha*, which appear in lines 8, 10, 15, 30, 32, 35, 36 and 39. The last of these contractions, *'em* for *them*, was adopted from Fletcher in the course of Crane's transcriptions of his plays. Most of the contractions, except the poetical conventions *'tis* and *see'st*, nullify Shakespeare's new-found freedom, and must be Crane's attempt to normalize the blank verse on Italian prosodic lines. They do not occur, it should be noted, in the songs, for Crane knew that Elizabethan musicians and composers gave a note to every syllable. What procures for the lyrics in this passage their rhythmical delight is the cunning use of trisyllabic feet, trochaic substitution, alliteration and vowel play.

Prospero used his magic powers to ensure the meeting of the lovers, but could not control their passions. Their love is spontaneous and immediate. Although Prospero's presence throughout the play has the authority of an all-seeing power, he himself experiences a change of heart; he becomes less tyrannical, moving from vengeance to a greater serenity of mind. With this change, the tempo and tone of the verse change.

The masquers in Act IV speak with the accents of aristocratic pageantry used in the Jacobean court masques. The language is not dramatic, but stately, measured and formal, in the Spenserian manner. Shakespeare's sympathetic handling in *The Tempest* illustrates his versatility:

> Ceres, most bounteous Lady, thy rich Leas
> Of Wheate, Rye, Barley, Fetches, Oates and Pease;
> Thy Turphie-Mountaines, where live nibling Sheepe,
> And flat Medes thetchd with Stover, them to keepe:
>
> You Sun-burn'd Sicklemen of August weary,
> Come hether from the furrow, and be merry,
> Make holly day: your Rye-straw hats put on,
> And these fresh Nimphes encounter every one. (IV.1.60–4, 134–7)

The stylized movement and choice of epithets are here deliberately cultivated.

The last Act conveys, in pagan as well as Christian terms, Prospero's transformation. If Shakespeare, like the abdicating mage, was spiritually resigned at the end of the play, this is the resignation of pessimism, not optimism. The note of human intransigence, like the doctrine of Original Sin, was characteristic of Renaissance thinking.

Shakespeare was a theatre poet, writing for known voices and trained capacities; his gifts were seemingly inexhaustible, but recognizable by certain hallmarks. As a dramatic poet, he worked to no set plan, but gave every play an individual character. The language needs to be heard and characterization visualized in actual performance, for Shakespeare conceived every character in terms of dialogue. He experimented in transforming the rhetoric of Kyd and Marlowe by the free association of ideas and feelings into speech that would be psychologically moving.

Important as image clusters are, the mature plays are not metaphoric poems, but studies in motives and passions, which actors can understand and interpret. The vestigial rhetoric in plays after 1600 was unconscious; but an actor of Shakespeare can always make significant points, because phrases have the force of gestures. Experience in the theatre taught Shakespeare what kinds of self-revelation, and what forms of expression, were dramatically effective. There must have been adjustments, excisions and additions in the playhouse; the final test was the attention-holding and activating power of the speeches.

The ideal critic of Shakespeare's diction should therefore be a sensitive listener and educated beholder, theatre-trained, and using his analytical powers. Such critics have been William Poel, Granville Barker, Wilson Knight, John Gielgud and Michael Redgrave. The plays should not be studied simply as dramatic poems. As formal works of literary art, they have deficiencies that were not important to thinkers of the High Renaissance. The plot of an Elizabethan playwright, whether historical or fictional, moves to a designed end; and speeches were intended to produce effects on characters represented by living actors, who were expected to respond in a natural way.

The revealing power of imagery was not Shakespeare's discovery; his associative use of it nevertheless had important effects on the future of English poetry. Intuition helped him to understand the subconscious mind, from which the most telling images arise. Other images came from the language of his sources, such as Holinshed and Plutarch. Imagery in Shakespeare conceals art and makes the dialogue appear natural. In most plays recurrent images sustain the *motif*, as Caroline Spurgeon and Wilson Knight discovered. They are pervasive, not always functional for the immediate context, as topical images are. A third variety of image suggests a speaker's mood, or it creates emotional climate at a critical situation. Shakespeare regarded these purposes of imagery as poetic. Brian Vickers in *The Artistry of Shakespeare's Prose* (Methuen, 1968) points out that 'we seldom if ever find prose images which enoble their object or subject, or present it in any positive or admirable way' (p. 22). The use of metaphor in poetry extends the consciousness by multiplying resources of language. Borrowing terms from an imaginary related object, the poet resists the temptation to take words from a worn or debased coinage.

Shakespeare understood the three 'voices' of poetry named by T. S. Eliot, which were operative in his time. Some effects are best displayed in the Poems and Sonnets. But whatever the voice, the language is not manipulated; diversity seldom depends on external ornament. The plays before 1600 were in the conventional rhetorical tradition, but were saved by their Shakespearian vitality, and because the later artistry was there in embryo. Blank verse was being moulded by nuances and intonations characteristically English, not Senecan or Ovidian. Spenser and Shakespeare appreciated that vernaculars had capacities of their own, according to lexical range, pronunciation and grammar. The older native words have more accretions of meaning, gathered with use. Shakespeare admired the diction of the common man, as the sensitive recorder of social change; he had enough Latin to borrow and coin from it judiciously. Latin was precise, and its polysyllables were resonant in the rhythm of blank verse; they offered subtle modulations of stress. Naturalized Latin words suggested cadences for a speech dignified in articulation. But Shakespeare saw that Latinisms must be used with sensitivity and restraint.

Grammar may not have been a major consideration for Shakespeare, but word formation and derivation were. A noun or adjective used as a verb could have metaphorical force, especially when the range of appropriate verbs was limited. The practice was not confined to participles, such as *candied*, *sicklied*, *beggar'd*, *muddied*; it is vivid in Cleopatra's '*boy* my greatness' and 'he *words* me'. This subject was ably discussed by Bernard Groom in *The Diction of Poetry from Spenser to Bridges* (Toronto U.P., 1955, pp. 43–6). The critic points to Shakespeare's lexical additions by the use of prefixes and suffixes, which account for many firsts in the OED, verbs such as *unhand* and *dislimn*. As the language was establishing its literary values, Shakespeare had virtually a free hand. His invention of picturesque verbs accords with Quiller-Couch's conviction: 'the verb is the very nerve of the sentence . . . in matters of intellectual or emotional persuasion the verb takes charge'. ('On Basic English', *Times Literary Supplement* 30/9/1944.)

Shakespeare hardly ever sacrifices the human to the aesthetic, yet he satisfies most canons of taste. He exemplifies the fundamental aspects of style variation: fragmentation, deviation and elaboration. In his plays the 'misshapen chaos' of naturalistic utterance is reduced to 'well-seeming forms' by a sense of rhythm. He gives the surface of his poetry variety by his deviate use of words, yet he seldom appears bizarre or eccentric. Elaborations are expansions of the sense, so that a listener or reader may linger on the relevance of words and phrases; these are echoed or balanced one against another, so that the dramatic effect is memorable.

Shaw and William Archer, who were obsessed with the musical virtuosity of Shakespeare's blank verse, cannot be ignored; for some things were artfully said. For instance, this from *Our Theatre in the Nineties*, 1895:

> The Shakespearean 'delineation of character' owes all its magic to the turn of the line, which lets you into the secret of its utterer's mood and temperament, not by its commonplace meaning, but by some subtle exaltation, or stultification, or slyness, or delicacy, or hesitancy, or what not in the sound of it. (I. 24)

Shaw repeated that Shakespeare's durability was due to his word music. But Archer had a further bias:

> What is not song is oratory – rhythmic oratory, always with a lyric thrill in it . . . It is true of a very large part of his work that it consists, like Greek tragedy and Italian opera, of an alternation between recitative and aria.
>
> (*The Old Drama and the New*, Heinemann, 1923, p. 10)

Shaw unjustly blamed Shakespeare for the exhaustion of the blank verse technique, in his Preface to *Three Plays for Puritans*; but was sound in comparing Shakespeare with Michelangelo, and affirming that technical skill, alone, does not make a great artist. Archer wrote of blank verse that it 'was a facility not a difficulty; it aided the actor's memory and dispensed the poet from a *nice observance of nature*' (ibid p. 49, my italics). In this, he was not thinking of the blank verse of Shakespeare, but of the realistic prose drama of his time.

VIII

DONNE

The scope of Donne's poetry is narrower than Shakespeare's, but his scholarly interests seem to have been wider. Donne first wrote of love in all its aspects. When his wife died, her place in his poetry was taken by religion. The *Songes*, which are predominantly irregular in form, seem more daring, passionate and impetuous than the *Elegies*; it is easier in them to appreciate the cynical, assumed indifference, that is refreshing after the complaints of Wyatt and Raleigh.

The early poetry is most memorable in form and expression, but Donne's work is all of a piece. As a skilled dialectician, he contrived harmony out of difference, arguing, like the neo-Platonists, for the indivisibility of the soul and the body:

> Loves mysteries in soules doe grow
> But yet the body is his booke

> (*The Exstasie*, 71-2)

There is a connection between the theology of Donne's *Sermons* and the speculations of his *Holy Sonnets*. Despite the naturalism of expression, the mystical side of Donne's nature is near the surface, and revealed in his belief that knowledge of God cannot be attained through the intellect. R. C. Bald has played down the Catholic mysticism in Donne's thinking, but the evidence can be recognized in the *Hymn to Christ* and *Holy Sonnets* IV, V, IX and XII.

Donne's poetry is dramatic in sense perception and presentation. In both periods of development, the imagery is arresting and revealing. The Italian influences on the style, notably Marino's, were not those that attracted Spenser. Donne's poetry of 1593–1600 proved to be imaginative in an unusual way – the images fused physical, emotional and intellectual experience. His synthesis of simile and metaphor often involves contrariety; but Donne was satisfied that contrarieties actually exist in nature.

An example of Donne's method may be seen in lines 21–8 of
Loves Growth:

> If, as in water stir'd more circles bee
> Produc'd by one, love such additions take,
> Those like so many spheares, but one heaven make,
> For, they are all concentrique unto thee;
> And though each spring doe adde to love new heate,
> As princes doe in times of action get
> New taxes, and remit them not in peace,
> No winter shall abate the springs encrease.

The stanza-simile is realistic and surprising, yet elaborate.
Identifying love's increase with the advent of Spring is con-
ventional; but relating it to converging circles in pond water,
and to a prince's powers of taxation, implies novelty of conceit
that is extraordinary.

Donne's evocative, subjective imagery is accompanied by
abrupt rhythms and colloquial use of words, the principal
sources of his sensuous, cerebral vigour. The fragmented
utterance is partly caused by deviation from the normal order
of words, either for rhyme or for rhetorical emphasis. He stated
more than once in his poetry that the Spenserian tradition of
fluidity was an artistic seduction. In the fragmentation of
rhythm, Donne's technique differs also from the early style of
Shakespeare, who was the older man. Shakespeare's constant
recourse to mythological allusions, Donne rejected. In *Aire and
Angels* he described romantic love as 'some lovely glorious
nothing'.

But in the dialogue of *Hamlet* a different relationship
emerges. Some of the soliloquies use a technique of feeling and
association similar to that in Donne's *Elegies,* which Helen
Gardner ascribed to dates before 1596. But the *Elegies* are in
epigrammatic couplets, and the versification is therefore
different from Shakespeare's. The metaphysical element in
Shakespeare began with the logic in some of the Sonnets; and
in the 1590s Shakespeare and Donne became the inscrutable
purveyors of ambiguity in poetry. Ambiguity arose through the
associative employment of imagery, which greatly extended
the ordinary meanings of words.

The posthumous publication of Donne's poems in 1633
delayed their impact to the second quarter of the seventeenth

century, when Ben Jonson predicted that Donne would perish
for want of understanding. His 'conceited' style did not, in fact,
survive the age of the Caroline Court poets. Conceit, compres-
sion and contorted syntax are the causes of Donne's occasional
obscurity.

The origin of conceit in metaphysical poetry is cognitive: it
is of the mind, rather than of the senses. This turn of expression
can seldom be used as ornament, for it is not simply figurative.
Conceits are devices of rhetoric, dependent on the principle of
analogy. Donne's analogies are mainly satirical: a few are
evocative. All illuminate some significant point, and are
functional, even when far-fetched. A conceit is strained when
the comparison is either too complex, or too contrived. The
balance between image and reality needs to be poised, and this
is unusual if the conceit involves hyperbole.

Thomas Carew, in his Elegy on the death of Donne, called
his wit a 'rich and pregnant fancy', and praised the poet for his
'masculine expression'. But no critic until Dr Johnson under-
stood the reasons for Donne's inimitability. His method
involved the sacrifice of melody to meaning, through compres-
sion. In his second *Sermon* (49–50), he said of the biblical
Psalms: 'where all the words are numbered, and measured, and
weighed, the whole work is the lesse subject to falsification'.
There is an example of Donne's compression in line 11 of *Holy
Sonnet* XIII:

> No, no, but as in my idolatrie
> I said to all my profane mistresses,
> *Beauty, of pitty, foulnesse onely is*
> A signe of rigour: so I say to thee,
> To wicked spirits are horrid shapes assign'd,
> This beauteous forme assures a pitious minde.   (lines 9–14)

Donne's meaning is: 'Beauty is a sign of pity, but foulness is
only a sign of rigour'. The clarity of the final couplet gives a
clue to the sense of the compressed line.

A style so 'poetical' could not be acclaimed, because it was
too excogitated. Donne's liberties with the accentuation of
syllables, of which Ben Jonson complained, were largely due to
the same compression. Dryden's conviction that Donne's poetry
was crude in versification and imperfect in rhythm and cadence,
does not bear examination. The doctrinaire system of elision

imposed on the verse by syllable-counting editors, often obscures his conversational ease. H. J. C. Grierson says little about Donne's practice of elision, but observes that he did not prepare his poems for the press:

> (he) was exceptionally fastidious about punctuation and such typographical details as capital letters, italics, brackets . . . Punctuation is that of the manuscript from which they (the poems) were taken, revised by the editor or printer . . . (who) had prejudices of his own.
> (*Poems*, Vol. 2, p. cxxii)

Donne is most difficult when metaphysical conceits are couched in terms of scholastic philosophy. The logic is not a confinement of liberty; he sports it in paradoxes and disciplines exuberance of feeling by his good sense and earnestness, as in *Holy Sonnet* XIV, addressed to God:

> Yet dearely 'I love you, and would be lov'd faine,
> But am betroth'd unto your enemie,
> Divorce mee, 'untie, or breake that knot againe,
> Take mee to you, imprison mee, for I
> Except you 'enthrall mee, never shall be free,
> Nor ever chast, except you ravish mee.

The modulations of rhythm in the first, third and fifth lines depend on internal sense-pauses and trisyllabic feet. The marks of elision are theoretical, and possibly intended to suggest the pace in reading. The rhythm reflects the spiritual struggle of the religious seeker.

A similar discipline prevents Donne's personal feelings from becoming theatrical. The baroque is wittily treated in lines with which he is supposed to have introduced his book:

> Goe, and catche a falling starre,
> Get with child a mandrake roote,
> Tell me, where all past yeares are,
> Or who cleft the Divel's foot,
> Teach me to heare Mermaides singing

Such poetical *adunata* (impossible feats), said to be derived from Ovid's *Tristia*, were among the absurdities of love poetry Donne disdainfully satirized.

No idea from philosophy, theology or science was intractable for Donne's use as a poetic image or conceit; eighteenth century critics therefore charged him with extravagance. His

Influence on religious poetry was more lasting than that on the cavalier lyrics. For half a century there were poets who treated themes similar to his.

The tone of Donne is confidentially discursive, in some of the *Holy Sonnets* occasionally sublime. He was studious to avoid 'poeticisms' in his diction, and words charged with already-felt emotion. His phrasing is original, but not recondite; rhetorical devices that 'pattern' structure are fairly numerous. *Ploce* or repetition in the following lines illustrates the devious and indirect approach to the summit of Truth:

> On a hill
> Cragged, and steep, Truth stands, and hee that will
> Reach her, *about must,* and *about must* goe;
> And what the hills suddennes resists, winne so.   (3rd *Satire*)

On metrical deviation and natural-speech rhythms, Donne founded the principles of his art. Anisometric patterns and intricate stanza forms were a challenge to him, and he needed no dithyrambic fervour to surmount it. He argued with great agility, and plentiful logical connectives held his thoughts together. He is not an esoteric poet whose imagination is canalized. His best work, as he maintained in his letters, was the fruit of imagination, not of realistic experience.

Donne begins with an arresting and germinal line, and leaves the reader with a feeling of consummation. The poems in small compass are satisfying in completeness and integrity, like the classical best of Jonson. The control of thought is collateral with the form of expression; the sense determines metre and rhythm. He does not succeed equally on all occasions, but when he does there is finality both in the economy and simplicity. He does not depend on the expectancy of tunes in the verse; a harsh, refracting exterior, is like veined ore whose diversity of texture is homogeneous throughout.

Donne was a Renaissance poet of transition, whose 'America', whose 'new-found-land', was the discovery of techniques for keeping poetry in contact with new ideas and vital rhythms of expression. His correspondence shows that he valued his *Sermons* and religious prose more highly than his secular poetry, which he did not wish to see in print. The rhetorical language in which the *Sermons* were conceived was itself revolutionary. He sifted from poetry the dross of Ovid and

Petrarch; and his love-themes bore no resemblance to the enervated tradition of Provence. To the idealization of love he reacted with clinical efficiency, for the reasons given by Grierson:

> The fundamental weakness of the mediaeval doctrine of love, despite its refining influence and its exaltation of woman, was that it proved unable to justify love ethically against the claims of the counter-ideal of asceticism.
>
> (*Poems of John Donne*, Vol. II, p. xxxv)

There were large areas of experience which Donne excluded from his consciousness. He is the least descriptive of poets. Though Shakespeare spent most of his working life in London, the inspirations of nature never left him; but Donne resembled the urban poets Jonson and Pope, who were classical intellectuals, reared on Horace, Juvenal and Martial. Donne, like T. S. Eliot, reacted scathingly to his town environment ('Cities are Sepulchres; they who dwell there/ Are carcases', he wrote to Sir Henry Wotton); but he had sensitive Anglo-Catholic roots, deeply embedded in scholastic philosophy and Christian Platonism.

Helen Gardner's grouping, dating and improving the text of Donne's poems have proved a valuable supplement to Grierson's pioneering edition of 1912. In studying development, I have accepted her chronological order, which shows that the *Satires* and *Elegies* were the earliest of Donne's works (1593–5). The latter resemble the poems in Ovid's *Amores*. Donne had the distinction of being the first writer of classical elegies in English. In a poet so personal and complex as Donne, the circumstances of the poems, and the range and occasion of his reading, are of particular importance, even though few poems can be precisely dated.

Letter to Sir Henry Wotton, lines 1–8, 47–58, 63–70

Sir, more then kisses, letters mingle Soules;
For thus friends absent speake. This ease controules
The tediousnesse of my life: But for these
I could ideate nothing, which could please,
But I should wither in one day, and passe   5
To'a bottle'of Hay, that am a locke of Grasse.

Life is a voyage, and in our lifes wayes
Countries, Courts, Towns are Rockes, or Remoraes;
   . . . . .

Be thou thine owne home, and in thy selfe dwell;
Inne any where, continuance maketh hell.   10
And seeing the snaile, which every where doth rome,
Carrying his owne house still, still is at home,
Follow (for he is easie pac'd) this snaile,
Bee thine owne Palace, or the world's thy gaile.
And in the worlds sea, do not like corke sleepe   15
Upon the waters face; nor in the deepe
Sink like a lead without a line: but as
Fishes glide, leaving no print where they passe,
Nor making sound; so closely thy course goe,
Let men dispute, whether thou breathe, or no.   20
   . . . . .

But, Sir, I advise not you, I rather doe
Say o'er those lessons, which I learn'd of you:
Whom, free from German schismes, and lightnesse
Of France, and faire Italies faithlesnesse,
Having from these suck'd all they had of worth,   25
And brought home that faith, which you carried forth
I throughly love. But if my selfe, I'have wonne
To know my rules, I have, and you have
                 DONNE:

Nearly all the verse epistles of the sixteenth and seventeenth
centuries, which were modelled on those of Horace, were
written in iambic pentameter couplets; they contain social and
moral sentiments, and personal observations. Wotton was him-
self an exemplar of Latin *urbanitas* in this form; consequently
this early letter is in Donne's best colloquial style. It seems to
have been written in 1597 or early in 1598, and resembles the
epigrammatic epistles of Ben Jonson – the figures fit and gentle,
yet strong, 'to show the composition manly' (*Discoveries*, LXV).

The couplet epigram of English was adapted from the style
of melic or personal poetry, found at its best in *The Greek
Anthology*, imitated and improved in Latin by Horace and
Catullus. Grierson explains that Donne's epistle to Wotton
arose from a debate in the Earl of Essex's literary circle, to
which Bacon and Wotton also contributed. The subject: 'Which
kind of life is best, that of Court, Country or City?' was taken
from two epigrams in *The Greek Anthology*, translated by
Nicholas Grimald and George Puttenham.

In the 28 lines chosen from this 70-line epistle, there are few
words that require glossing. According to the OED, Donne
was the first to use *ideate* ('think', 'conceive'), and he may have
coined the verb to explain Plato's theory of ideas; the early
uses of the word by different writers are all Platonic. *Bottle*
and *locke* (6), as employed by Donne, were similar in meaning
('bundle', 'tuft'), and continued to be used in the same sense
by Thomas Hood and Thomas Hardy in the nineteenth century.
In line 8 *Remora* (a sucking-fish described in Pliny's *Natural
History* XXXII.1) was considered a marine creature so powerful
that it could attach itself to a ship and restrain it. The adverb
where (meaning 'place') in line 10, is characteristic of Donne's
manner.

While the movement of the verse in 3 is unorthodox, the
rhythm is resilient in naturalness, and anticipates many of
Donne's later verses:

2–3   /Fŏr, thùs/ fríends àb/seńt speáke./ Thĭs eáse/ coñtroúles/
       /Thĕ té/diŏusnesse/ ŏf my/ lĭfe: Bùt/ fŏr thése/

The hall-marks of these lines are subtlety of pause-modulations
(especially in 3), grammatical enjambement, and varied dis-
position of primary stresses (four in the first and three in the
second). Donne's movement has the realism of ordinary speech,
for instance, in the use of the spondee in line 2, and two
juxtaposed pyrrhic feet in 3.

The elisions in 6 and 27 (*To'a bottle'of Hay* and *I'have wonne*)
raise an important issue. They may be Donne's; but note that
the use of the apostrophes involves no loss of one of the
contiguous vowels. This implies a reading of lightly enunciated
syllables in trisyllabic feet; in other words, the apostrophe is
a signal to the reader that no syllables should actually be
suppressed. The use of trisyllabic feet in an iambic base,
combined with extreme variation of pause, is one of Donne's
means of changing the pace of his lines. There is no mark of
elision in line 21.

Lines 7 and 8 secure their effect by stress inversion and
alliteration; the latter line is one of the few that have five
primary stresses. In 9 the ictus is forced on to *thy* in the fourth
foot; thus *thou* and *thy* become emphatic words, and provide the
correct reading of the line:

/Bĕ *thóu*/ thíne oẃne/ home, aňd/ iň *thý* selfe/dwéll/

The heavy emphasis on the spondees *worlds sea* and *corke sleep* in 15 exemplifies the matching of sense and rhythm. A group of iambic lines that run smoothly is soon followed by an abrupt stress modulation:

18 /Físhĕs/ glíde, léa/viňg nŏ/ prínt whére/ thĕy passe/

This is Donne at his most inventive – two trochees, a spondee and a pyrrhic in a line of five feet, where only the last is iambic. Compare the following:

26 /Aňd broúght/ hóme thăt/ faíth, whĭch/ yŏu cár/riĕd fórth/

Here only the first and fourth feet are in step with the pattern; scansion is only a theoretical base, for the line is deliberately contrapuntal. The only line deficient in a syllable is 23.

Even in the epistles, Donne of the first period (1593–8) takes every opportunity to roughen the surface-texture of his poetry by prosaic rhythms. One method is the near subversion of the iambic pattern of stresses in about one line in four. As he employs a colloquial language, Donne does not invert the normal order of words, except for a specific need of this kind; for instance, *friends absent* (2) brings two principle stresses together in an emphatic position. Another syntactical characteristic is to delay the relative clause qualifying the subject, until the predication is complete, e.g.

5–6 But *I* should wither in one day, and passe
To'a Bottle'of Hay, *that am a locke of Grasse.*

The effect of this is to avoid the uncolloquial periodic structure of the sentence. In lines 23–7 the object relative *whom* is separated from its governing verb *love* by four lines.

The colloquial tendency in Donne is aided by the *I–thou* relationship in most of his poems; he is usually speaking to a lover, a friend, a respected patroness, or the Deity. The pronoun of address is generally *thou*; and Francis Berry has remarked on this in *Poets' Grammar* (Routledge and Kegan Paul, 1958, pp. 86–92):

Is the stress on 'thou' one of specifically poetic intention rather than of grammatical reason? For certainly the word is extraordinarily stressed – by its rhythmic positioning, by the weight of meaning it bears, and by the sheer frequency in the *Songs and Sonnets* . . .

There is, in Donne, none of that humility we find in the earlier and middle sonnets of Shakespeare . . . Donne assumes that he is on the same plane as his mistress, though he has the initiative on that plane through belonging to the superior (as the Schoolmen would have taught him) sex . . .

He uses 'thou', not only in consequence of pious custom and literal rendering of Number as observed in the Latin of the Catholic liturgy to which he had been bred, but also because in the passion of his devotion to God he was still exploring a singular 'thou'-ness with as much fervour as when a mistress had been the object of his devotion . . .

The one section of his verse where Donne might seem most regardless of whether he uses 'thou' or 'you' is in his *Verse Letters*. But compare the forms he uses there with those in the Prose Letters, and it is evident that they are indices of the degree of acquaintance he owed to his correspondents. To his familiar friends he uses 'thou'; to those above him in station (or to those he knows less well) he uses 'you'.

Almost throughout the letter to Wotton, *thou* is used as the pronoun of address to a personal friend (see 9–20), but in the ending (21–8) *you* is employed because Donne's mood has changed from familiarity to deference, as shown by the courtesy word *Sir* (21) with which the letter began. *You* is, of course, also a rhyme word (22), and as such has positional emphasis, but this was not a compelling reason for the poet's change from *thou*. Sense emphasis is very important in Donne's poetry; hence the inverted order *not you* in 21.

Donne's reading in liturgical and medieval literature may explain his preference for the subjunctive, e.g. *breathe* (20), and for *-th* endings in the 3rd person singular present indicative of verbs, e.g. *maketh* (10), *doth* (11). The latter word also illustrates his frequent employment of *do* as a periphrastic auxiliary. There is an emphatic example, at the end of line 21, where *doe* is a rhyme word. In the negative combination *do not* (15) *do* is unemphatic, and therefore spelt without a final *-e*. This distinction in spelling is also made between emphatic and unemphatic pronouns *he* and *we*, and common notional verbs, e.g. *goe* (19).

The seeming distortions that Donne practises to secure his rhetorical emphases, especially with personal pronouns, are significant for meaning, as lines 10, 15, 21 and 28 show. But equally important is the twist of meaning the poet gives to words through the individuality of his private experience. The comparison between *letters* and *kisses* in the first line is an instance. The phrase *mingle Soules* ('communicate spirits'), like *ideate nothing* (4), is characteristic of Donne's diction. He owes the first to a speech of Bembo in Castiglione's *The Courtier*. The verb *controules* (2) is a poetic economy with a special sense, as is *passe* (change) in 5. *Wither* (5), *voyage* (7), *Rockes* and *Remoraes* (8) are metaphors of singular fitness in context; the implication is that whether one spends one's life in country, court or town, the dangers incident to life are everywhere present.

In lines 9–14 the analogy, rather than simile, exemplifies Donne's subtle intellectualism. The wise man, like the snail, should take refuge in himself, for living physically in any one place is to endure spiritual ennui. *Inne any where, continuance maketh hell* (10) is the kind of line only Donne could have written; and how fine a specimen of *anadiplosis* is *still, still* of line 12! He anticipates Pope in the antithetical balance of the metaphors in line 14:

Bee thine own *Palace*, or the worlds thy *gaile*

The capitalization of *Palace* marks it as the emphatic word in this line; the spelling of *gaile* is a compromise between *gaol* and *jail*.

Lines 15–20 contain three vivid similes, of the drifting cork, dull sinking lead, and impressionless gliding fish. These suggest undesirable mental attitudes induced by life, respectively, in the country, in town, and at court. They are taken up again (23–4) in *German schismes* (lead), *lightnesse of France* (cork) and *Italies faithlesnesse* (silent fish). The Donne-ish line

20 Let men dispute, whether thou breathe, or no

is a good example of metaphysical wit.

In lines 21–8 Donne assumes the role of a disciple: Wotton is a man whose ship of life has escaped the *Rockes and Remoraes* of spiritual disaster. The metaphor *suck'd* (25) happily fits the sense of 'imbibed'. Wotton, in his European travels, took what was best from Germany, France, and Italy, and returned intact with the faith of his inheritance. The last couplet is ambiguous; Donne suggests, however, that whatever self-knowledge he finally achieved he owed to Wotton.

Elegie X – The Dreame

Image of her whom I love, more then she,
  Whose faire impression in my faithfull heart,
Makes mee her *Medall,* and makes her love mee,
  As Kings do coynes, to which their stamps impart
The value: goe, and take my heart from hence   5
  Which now is growne too great and good for me:
Honours oppresse weake spirits, and our sense
  Strong objects dull; the more, the lesse wee see.
When you are gone, and *Reason* gone with you,
  Then *Fantasie* is Queene and Soule, and all;   10
She can present joyes meaner then you do;
  Convenient, and more proportionall.
So, if I dreame I have you, I have you,
  For, all our joyes are but fantasticall.
And so I scape the paine, for paine is true;   15
  And sleepe which locks up sense, doth lock out all.
After a such fruition I shall wake,
  And, but the waking, nothing shall repent;
And shall to love more thankfull Sonnets make,
  Then if more *honour, teares,* and *paines* were spent.   20
But dearest heart, and dearer image stay;
  Alas, true joyes at best are *dreame* enough;
Though you stay here you passe too fast away:
  For even at first lifes *Taper* is a snuffe.
Fill'd with her love, may I be rather grown   25
Mad with much *heart,* then *ideott* with none.

This, the tenth Elegy in Grierson's *Poems of Donne*, was
excluded by Helen Gardner from the classification found in the
1635 edition, because it is not elegiac in 'theme, mood, and
style'. The 26 lines consist of six quatrains and a couplet; the
Elegies proper are entirely in epigrammatic couplets. The poem
is neo-Platonist in idea, rather than classical.

Not until 1614 did Donne realize that his poems would be
collected and published, and he then found it necessary to
borrow copies from his friends. In the Gardner edition (Claren-
don, 1965) its title is *Image and Dream*, to distinguish it from
Donne's lyric *The Dreame*, which it resembles, except in
versification. The poem has the title 'Elegy' in all manuscripts
but one, where it is headed *Picture*. The stanzas are unseparated
in the manuscript, and yet they are self-contained, except at the
end of the first.

Contrast between 'image' and 'reality' is one of Donne's

frequently used ideas, because of his fondness for paradox. According to Ficino and Castiglione, the imagination may conjure up a vision of beauty that exceeds the evidence of the senses. Helen Gardner finds the source of the argument in Leone Ebreo's *Dialoghi d'amore* (1535).

Literally, the language is extremely simple. A few words, *Medall* (3), *Taper* (24) and *ideott* (26), have symbolic meanings, but these are readily gleaned from the context. A *medal* was a circular disc with a figure impressed upon it, usually to commemorate some past event; and lovers wore them as gift-tokens. *Taper* signifies 'light' or the 'energy of life'. *Ideott* (originally an eccentric) is contrasted by Donne with *Mad* in the same line. The Elizabethans used *mad* for 'a person permanently defective in intellect', to be distinguished from one who is temporarily 'out of his wits'.

For Donne, the verse is comparatively regular, with stress inversions principally in the first foot, and occasional spondees in emphatic positions, e.g. *weak spirits* (7). The abruptness usually associated with Donne is absent. Arresting lines are the first three:

/Imáge/ öf hér/ whöm Í/ lóve, móre/ thën shé,/
/Whôse fáire/ imprés/sión iñ/ my faíth/ füll héart,/
/Mäkes mée/ hèr Mé/dåll, añd/ makes hér/ lo̊ve mée/

The tendency to take the first line as a series of dactyls in falling rhythm is resisted only when the pattern of the iambic line is sensed in the second. In the third, emphasis on the personal pronouns retards the pace of the line, so that distinctions may be perceived. In line 13 the rhetorical figure *epizeuxis* has a peculiar stress interest:

/Só, if/ Ï dreáme/ Ï háve/ yoü, Í/ håve yoü/

Here the repeated clauses are differently stressed, the first on the notional verb, the second on the subject and object pronouns. The logically stressed connective *So* is also significant.

The first two stanzas are syntactically connected. The subject of the imperative *goe*, in the first line of stanza 2, is *Image*, first word of the initial stanza. The object of the last verb in the first stanza, *impart* (4), is *value* (5), in the beginning of stanza 2. Donne is punctilious about the relative accusative *whom* (1), but writes *she* instead of *her* at the end of the line, to rhyme with *mee* (3). Argument hinges firmly on the use of logical connectives *As* (4), *When* (9), *So* (13), *For* (14), *And* (16, 18 and 19), *But* (21), *Though* (23), *For* (24). The periphrastic auxiliary *doth* (16) is mildly emphatic; and the unusual order of *such* in *a such fruition* (17) is heavily so. Infrequent inversions, e.g. at the ends of 18 and 19 (object before verb), are designed for sense emphasis. Short clauses, studied punctuation and an emphatic order commonly set the pattern of Donne's argumentative manner.

The manner in this argument is paradoxical, since the poem is similar in complexity to *The Legacie*, where two lovers become one by exchange of hearts. Compression in paradox is illustrated in the half-line *the more, the lesse wee see* (8).

The sense is briefly this: The poet addresses a likeness of his lady, which he says he loves more than the woman herself. He is her medal, in the sense that *her* image is impressed on *his* heart; *her* love for *him* simply results from his doting, and resembles the regard kings have for coins that bear *their* image. Such is the devotion that it has become insupportable and he begs the lady to relieve him. The honour the image bestows weighs upon his spirit, inasmuch as man's senses are dulled by overpowering impressions. The greater the object, the less sight can assimilate. If the beloved were not there, Reason (whose domain is the heart) would go with her, and Fancy, child of sensual desire, would prevail. The joys of Fancy are less demanding, more moderate and tolerable. Thus, if he merely *dreamed* he possessed the lady, virtually he would enjoy her; for what are joys but fabrications? One advantage of dreaming is the absence of pain, an undeniable fact of love. Sleep suspends the senses, and excludes impressions. When a lover wakes from a dream relationship, there is nothing to regret, except the awakening. The gratitude of a lover can be expressed in poetry, without love's inevitable burden of honour, tears and pain. Finally, the heartless poet relents and begs his lady to stay. Real joys are, after all, insubstantial, life is short and birth brings with it the promise of death. Consumed with love, he would rather dote with the heart's surfeit, than live without reason and be thought a fool.

Modern psychology makes Donne's thinking on the functions

of reason and fantasy difficult to follow. One would expect the
reverse of what the poem argues. The Elizabethans, however,
regarded the soul as the sum of mental and spiritual activities
and they located understanding in the brain, reason in the heart
and the senses in the liver. Understanding is shared with the
Angels, and is the source of will. The heart (reason) mediates
between understanding and the sensual faculties. The senses
(shared with animals) store images in the memory. Fancy, one
of the lower faculties, often sports with images of a sensual
kind, but these need not tax the understanding.

The poem is a sustained metaphor, of which the key words
are printed in italics, beginning with *Medall*. Important images
also bear capitals. *Honour* (7), *Reason* (9) and *Fantasie* (10)
are abstract nouns personified. Thus Reason is *King*, and
Fantasie Queen, in the realm of *Soule* (10). *Even at first life's
Taper is a snuffe* (24) is an impressive figure. Like the later
Shakespeare's, Donne's rhetoric is suited to the matter, and so
deeply involved in style that it is hardly perceived as devices.

The Dreame (from *Songs and Sonnets*)

Deare love, for nothing lesse then thee
Would I have broke this happy dreame,
    It was a theame
For reason, much too strong for phantasie,
Therefore thou wakd'st me wisely; yet   5
My Dreame thou brok'st not, but continued'st it,
Thou art so truth, that thoughts of thee suffice,
To make dreames truths; and fables histories;
Enter these armes, for since thou thoughtst it best,
Not to dreame all my dreame, let's act the rest.   10

As lightning, or a Tapers light,
Thine eyes, and not thy noise wak'd mee;
    Yet I thought thee
(For thou lovest truth) an Angell, at first sight,
But when I saw thou sawest my heart,   15
And knew'st my thoughts, beyond an Angels art,
When thou knew'st what I dreamt, when thou knew'st when
Excesse of joy would wake me, and cam'st then,
I must confesse, it could not chuse but bee
Prophane, to thinke thee any thing but thee.   20

Comming and staying show'd thee, thee,

But rising makes me doubt, that now,
    Thou art not thou.
That love is weake, where feare's as strong as hee;
'Tis not all spirit, pure, and brave,   25
If mixture it of *Feare, Shame, Honor,* have.
Perchance as torches which must ready bee,
Men light and put out, so thou deal'st with mee,
Thou cam'st to kindle, goest to come; Then I
Will dreame that hope againe, but else would die.   30

Helen Gardner prefers the following readings: 7, *true* for *truth*; 19, *doe* for *must*.

The ten-line stanza of this poem of 30 lines is in the pattern a(4), b(4), b(2), a(5), c(4), c(5), d(5), d(5), e(5), e(5) — the figures represent the feet in the lines. This is an unusual combination, six of the lines being in iambic pentameters, the last four in pentameter couplets.

The beloved person is now, whimsically, deified in terms of scholastic philosophy; the passage Donne had in mind was Aquinas, *Summa Theologica* I.6.5. According to this philosophy, God and the Angels (spiritual messengers) can understand a man's thoughts, but God alone has power over man's will.

The latter part of the poem is crowded with paradox, in which repetitions of the pronoun *thou, thee* are in rhetorical figures, such as *epizeuxis* or *ploce. I saw thou sawest* (15), and play with *knew* and *when* in 16 and 17, are further instances of *ploce. Epanilepsis* (a line beginning and ending with the same word) is used in line 17.

The language contains a few Latinisms, less than one in ten words. Like Shakespeare, Donne employs Latin polysyllables for rhythmical nuance, and he is more remarkable for the complex development of arguments than range of vocabulary. The only difficult inversions are in lines 26–8. The punctuation is elaborate, to secure the reading required. Grierson, whose version is followed, preserved the stopping intact in the first stanza.

The first quatrain of each stanza has lines of variable length, skilfully modulated by the positions of internal pauses. The pause before *yet* (5) is in the middle of the last foot – an unusual position. The double elision in *wakd'st* (5) (only the second signalled) is not euphonious, unless *d* is unarticulated;

but for the editor's eye it was metrically correct. There is similar harshness in the preterite inflexions -st of brok'st and continued'st in 6, and cam'st 29.

The poem's significance is its problem. In the first stanza, the lover is wakened by his lady in the midst of a dream about her, and the poem tells the aftermath of the interruption. Anything but her presence, he says, would have made him unhappy. The content of the dream did not suggest fancy (desire), but reason (the heart), because it was so powerful. His lady's intervention was timely, because the vision was not really broken, but continued. She (standing before him) so resembled truth (God's reality) that thinking of her made the dream-fiction a verity. Since she saw fit to arrest his bliss, they should embrace, and enact in their persons the conclusion of the dream.

The remaining stanzas give a detailed account of the awakened lover's reactions and thoughts. He was not disturbed by noise (he says), but by lightning, the brightness of his lady's eyes. At first, like truth, she appeared to him as a perfect spiritual form (an Angel); but soon he perceived that she possessed more than an Angel's capacity; for she, by waking him at a propitious moment, when excessive joy should have done it, gave proof of premonition. He then saw her as anything but herself, to be profane, as an indescribable deity.

However, present and abiding, she must indeed be a real woman. Risen from his arms, she can but be what he believed she was. Love is frail, if timidity is a match for Cupid's strength. Love will not be pure and courageous, as long as fear, shame and honour prompt misgivings. Perhaps she regarded him as a flaming torch that could suddenly be extinguished, and kept ready for next use. She had come to kindle his desire, and departed tantalizingly. The lover is left hopefully to dream again, or die.

This 'Dreame' poem uses many of the words in the former, such as reason, phantasie, truth, honor, joy, love, heart and taper, and it embodies a similar philosophy. But there is a note of frustration, whereas Elegy X is playful and teasing. When Donne dramatized thoughts, conceits were often sources of rhetoric, and the improbable situation gave rise to ingenious hyperboles; cf. lines 7–8 and 13–20. J. B. Leishman in The

Monarch of Wit (Hutchinson, 1951) treats this poem as a work
of pure imagination:

> I think it is more likely to have been all dream than, as it professes
> to be, half dream and half fact. (p. 183)

Twicknam Garden

Blasted with sighs, and surrounded with teares,
   Hither I come to seeke the spring,
   And at mine eyes, and at mine eares,
Receive such balmes, as else cure every thing;
   But O, selfe traytor, I do bring   5
The spider love, which transubstantiates all,
   And can convert Manna to gall,
And that this place may thoroughly be thought
True Paradise, I have the serpent brought.

'Twere wholsomer for mee, that winter did   10
   Benight the glory of this place,
   And that a grave frost did forbid
These trees to laugh, and mocke mee to my face;
   But that I may not this disgrace
Indure, nor *leave this garden* Love let mee [Gr. yet leave loving] 15
   Some senslesse peece of this place bee;
Make me a mandrake, so I may *grow* here, [Gr. groane]
Or a stone fountaine weeping out my yeare.

Hither with christall vyals, lovers come,
   And take my teares, which are loves wine,   20
   And try your mistresse Teares at home,
For all are false, that tast not just like mine;
   Alas, hearts do not in eyes shine,
Nor can you more judge womans thoughts by teares,
   Then by her shadow, what she weares.   25
O perverse sexe, where none is true but shee,
Who's therefore true, because her truth kills mee.

The text is from Helen Gardner's edition; it differs from
Grierson's in lines 15 and 17, as shown. The date suggested is
after 1609. Donne's patroness, the Duchess of Bedford, who
lived at Twickenham, may have been the recipient of this poem;
but it does not reflect a close relationship. There is a lyrical
quality in the despair of this monologue that Donne did not
often indulge; *balmes* (4) and *christall vyals* (19) are poeticisms.
The contrast between the joy of spring and a lover's misery is

commonplace. Grierson traced the analogy with the 'stone fountain' to Petrarch's *Canzone* XXIII and Habington's *Castara*.

Lines 6–7 and 17 are characteristic of Donne's metaphysical manner and cynical disillusionment. The religious symbol *transubstantiates* refers to the Communion service, but in reverse – love is rejected, the sweet becomes bitter. According to *Exodus* XVI, *Manna* when baked resembled a small wafer made of honey. The *serpent* (9) probably refers to the deadly sin of envy. The *mandrake*, a narcotic plant, was fabled to cry out when it was plucked; hence Grierson's preference for the reading *groane* in 17.

The stanza of 9 lines is another tribute to Donne's inventiveness. It has the following rhyme-scheme: a(5 feet), b(4), a(4), b(5), b(4), c(5), c(4), d(5), d(5). Donne begins arrestingly; the inversions of stress in the first line suggest a trisyllabic falling rhythm, which Helen Gardner describes as 'a lack of metrical tact'; for the versification thereafter disappoints expectation. Donne tried to secure the right emphasis in colloquial rhetoric, for example, *asyndeton* in line 3. Emphatic inversion of stress is used in *Manna* (7). He never hesitates to force the stress on to an unemphatic word, for rhyme, as in the enjambed line 10:

/Twere whóle/ sŏmĕr/ fŏr mée,/ thăt wín/tĕr dìd/
/Bĕnigĥt/ thĕ gló/rў of/ this plaće/

Juxtaposition of primary stresses is common, not only at the beginning of the line (9 *True Paradise*), but in the middle (5 *selfe traytor*, 12 *grave frost*), or at the end (16 *place bee*, 17 *grow here*, 20 *loves wine*, 23 *eyes shine*, 27 *kills mee*).

There are inversions of word order in lines 2, 3, 9, 14, 19, 23 and 25, and three uses of the periphrastic auxiliary *do*, *did* in 5, 10 and 12. A poetical licence is the uninflected possessive *mistresse* in 21.

Feeling and tone in *Twicknam Garden* are suggested by the metaphors and they are more numerous than a first reading suggests: *Blasted* with sighs, and *surrounded* with teares (1), *balmes* and *cure* (4), *traytor* (5), *spider* love and *transubstantiates* (6), *convert Manna to gall* (7), *Paradise* (9), *Benight the glory* (11), *disgrace*/ Indure (14), *senslesse peece* (16), *mandrake* (17), *loves wine* (20), hearts do not in eyes *shine* (23). There are several personifications, for instance 12–13: a *grave* frost did *forbid/* These trees to *laugh*, and *mocke* mee (a characteristic conceit); try (test) your mistresse *Teares* (21); *tast* (22); her truth *kills* mee (27).

Meaning becomes difficult when the thoughts are esoteric, as in:

> 6–7   The *spider* love, which *transubstantiates* all,
>   And can convert Manna to Gall

Donne here suggests that the lover who bemoans his fate brings bitterness to fair surroundings: the symbols are the *spider* and the *serpent* (9). The spider poisons the bliss of the garden, and the serpent introduces untruth.

J. B. Douds in 'Donne's Technique of Dissonance' (*PMLA*, LII, 4, 1937) uses line 6 of *Twicknam Garden* to illustrate an aspect of the poet's imagery worth remembering:

> The dissonant effect of Donne's imagery depends sometimes upon the undecorative quality of the minor term . . . We may ask two questions about a given image: (1) Is the minor term undecorative (or of no 'imaginative value')? (2) Is there only one point of contact (i.e. likeness) between the two terms? . . . Donne's most typical image is both, but the two characteristics do not necessarily or invariably occur together, and the poetic functions they perform are not identical . . . 'The spider love' from the stanza already quoted is a condensed and startling example . . . There is one point of likeness between the terms – the power of 'transubstantiate' . . . Further, there is a clash *within* the area of likeness. 'Transubstantiation' is a purely physical process with the spider [the minor term], a psychological process with love . . . Donne is very fond of this particular type of dissonance – between the abstract and concrete, the physical and spiritual planes of imagination. (pp. 1053–4)

Douds says of the word *transubstantiates* that 'its very length makes a savage thrust among the dominant monosyllables'. (p. 1056).

In lines 19–22 the figures are drawn from alchemy and from medieval tests for chastity; lovers should take samples of the poet's tears to test those of their mistress; the tears will be artificial, unless they are bitter as the poet's. The final couplet is paradoxical in syntax:

> none is true but shee,
> Who's therefore true, because her truth kills mee.

The distressed lover appears to be rejected because the lady is

loyal to someone else. The proposition 'none is true but shee'
has a sting-in-the-tail corollary: 'her fidelity to truth means
death to the poet'.

The argument illustrates how intense and self-centred
Donne's poetry can be. His personality disarms because, while
stunning, it is candid. His language excites because, like Sir
Thomas Browne's, it is full of curious learning. The poems are
arcana of mental process, not activity; he is a poet who
soliloquizes without inhibitions. The reader witnesses the
struggle and shares the feelings, but no outcome relieves the
poet's frustration.

A Litanie (Stanzas I, III, VI, VIII, XV)

I
The Father

Father of Heaven, and him, by whom
It, and us for it, and all else, for us
   Thou madest, and govern'st ever, come
And re-create mee, now growne ruinous:
     My heart is by dejection, clay,
     And by selfe-murder, red.   5
From this red earth, O Father, purge away
All vicious tinctures, that new fashionéd
I may rise up from death, before I'am dead.

III
The Holy Ghost

 O Holy Ghost, whose temple I   10
Am, but of mudde walls, and condenséd dust,
   And being sacrilegiously
Halfe wasted with youths fires, of pride and lust,
     Must with new stormes be weatherbeat;
     Double in my heart thy flame,   15
Which let devout sad teares intend; and let
(Though this glasse lanthorne, flesh, do suffer maime)
Fire, Sacrifice, Priest, Altar be the same.

VI
The Angels

  And since this life our nonage is,
And wee in Wardship to thine Angels be,   20
   Native in heavens faire Palaces
Where we shall be but denizen'd by thee,
     As th'earth conceiving by the Sunne,
     Yeelds faire diversitie,

Yet never knowes which course that light doth run,   25
So let mee study, that mine actions bee
Worthy their sight, though blinde in how they see.

VIII
The Prophets
Thy Eagle-sighted Prophets too,
Which were thy Churches Organs, and did sound
That harmony, which made of two   30
One law, and did unite, but not confound;
Those heavenly Poëts which did see
Thy will, and it expresse
In rythmique feet, in common pray for mee,
That I by them excuse not my excesse   35
In seeking secrets, or Poëtiquenesse.

XV
From being anxious, or secure,
Dead clods of sadnesse, or light squibs of mirth,
From thinking, that great courts immure
All, or no happinesse, or that this earth   40
Is only for our prison fram'd,
Or that thou art covetous
To them whom thou lov'st, or that they are maim'd
From reaching this worlds sweet, who seek thee thus,
With all their might, Good Lord deliver us.   45

A few of Donne's *Divine Poems* were written before his
ordination in 1615, and most of the *Holy Sonnets* were begun
only after the death of his wife in 1617. *A Litanie* belongs to the
middle years; Helen Gardner suggests late 1608, Grierson
1609–10. In a letter to Goodyere, Donne describes the petitions
in 28 stanzas as 'a meditation in verse', or supplication written
during one of many illnesses, while he lived at Mitcham. His
spells in bed induced a 'low devout melancholie'. Disappointed
with the world of affairs, and left in poverty with a young
family, he penned *A Litanie* in a mood of resignation rather
than despair. The style is as personal as in the secular poems;
but Donne writes as a man whose temperament is now under
control, in a language influenced by his devotional reading,
Thomas à Kempis's *Imitation of Christ*, as well as the Bible.

The biblical simplicity of *A Litanie* admits of few poeticisms.
Tincture (8) 'colouring matter' came into the language at the
beginning of the fifteenth century, but was little used before
the seventeenth. Tinctures were used for dyeing; hence
Donne's metaphorical sense of 'stain' or 'blemish'. The reference

is to 'selfe-murder, *red*' and 'this *red* earthe' in 5 and 6. The loan-word *sacrilege*, meaning 'theft of objects dedicated to religious service', was in use by the early fourteenth century, but *sacrilegious* did not appear until the *Rheims Bible* of 1582. Donne's adverb *sacrilegiously* (12) is one of the earliest uses. He suggests his dedication to religion in the word *temple* (10), but admits that his earlier life was a defilement of it. *Denizen'd* (22), meaning 'naturalized', is found also in Donne's *Sermons;* the verb was employed from the late sixteenth century only, though the noun was in use a century earlier. *Poetiquenesse* (36) is a nonce-word presumably coined by Donne. The first instance of *immure* (39), in the sense of 'enclose', was in Stubbes's *Anatomy of Abuses* (1583); the OED shows that it was more often used by Shakespeare than by Donne.

A Litanie has nine-line stanzas, the scheme of which is: a(4 feet), b(5), d(4), b(5), c(4), d(3), c(5), d(5), d(5). In each of the two opening stanzas, invocation is not well distinguished from self-evaluation. Jonson said that 'Donne, for not keeping of accent, deserved hanging'. The accusation would be difficult to sustain in this poem, though line 43 is an example. Line 2, entirely composed of particles and unemphatic words, is almost invertebrate, and the syntax is too involved to afford accentual clues. Presumably the scansion is

/Ĭt, ănd/ us fòr/ ĭt, ănd/ all ĕlse,/ fŏr ús/

Govern'st in line 3 is an awkward elision; cf. the anomaly of *I'am* (9), in which the apostrophe probably indicates avoidance of elision. The pronunciation of the normally suppressed past-participle inflexion in *fashionéd* (8) serves the purpose of rhyme, but is metrically strained.

The enjambement of I/*A*m in lines 10–11 is an unwarranted licence in serious verse. The copula is normally reduced in colloquial pronunciation, but Donne's line division forces the stress on to *Am*, thus:

/Am, bŭt/ ŏf múdde/ wálls, ănd/ cŏnden/sĕd dúst/ (two substitutions)

Line 12, a tetrameter, has only one primary stress. Donne's juxtaposition of stressed syllables in spondaic feet is well illustrated in 18:

/Fíre, Sác/rĭfĭ̆ce,/ Príest, Ál/tă̆r bĕ/ thĕ̆ same/.

Donne did not reduce his recourse to the periphrastic auxiliary *do* (see lines 17, 31, 25, 29 and 32), or to the subjunctive alongside of the indicative (see lines 19 and 20). Like most Elizabethans, he is fond of modulation by clausal parenthesis, as in line 17. The stanza in which Donne apologizes for poetic excesses contains two uses of the archaic relative *which* for persons (29 and 32). Rhetorically, the last stanza, in periodic structure, is the most effective. It consists of a lengthy series of objects, all governed by the principal clause *Good Lord deliver us*, which comes last.

Donne seems to have enjoyed working in complex stanza forms, which enabled him to elaborate his syntax. The structure has to be grasped to arrive at the meaning. In line 1 *him* refers to Christ, the Son; the double use of *it* (2) stands for *Heaven*. Line 2 must thus be regarded as a multiple inverted object, governed by *Thou madest* in 3. *Ruinous* (4) describes the petitioner's sick state, physical and moral, and gives significance to *re-create*. Earth's 'dry humour' is responsible for melancholy, whose usual colour is red, linking it with the metaphors *clay* and *selfe-murder* (5, 6). *Re-create* leads to the idea of spiritual restoration, before resurrection (9).

In lines 10–14 the sick poet sees himself as a dedicated *temple*, the walls built of mud compounded with dust. He has *sacrilegiously* (12) wasted his life in sensual pleasure (cf *selfe-murder* in 6), and is unable to weather the *stormes* (14) of disease. Tears are the earnest of his penitential fervour, and the *flame* (15) is perilously housed in the frail *glasse lanthorne* (17) of the flesh. At one and the same time, he is the fire, the sacrifice, the officiating priest and the altar. The stanza employs religious symbolism of the Old and the New Testaments.

The key to the next stanza (19–27) is *nonage* (spiritual immaturity). In the span of life, we, the children, are wards of the guardian Angels of God in Heaven. We become *denizens* (naturalized citizens) only by God's redemption. The symbolism then turns to a pagan simile of the Father-*Sunne* (note the word play on *Son*), engendering *faire diversitie* (24) in Mother-Earth. The meaning of lines 25–7 seems to be: 'As the faithful mother awaits the outcome of her conception, let me, in blindness, learn to perform deeds acceptable to God, through the light of his faith'. The analogy is obscure, because Donne is intent on the final paradox of sight and blindness.

In 28–36 the Prophets are *Eagle sighted* (far-seeing). Donne
compares them to church organs that sound the harmony and
so unite the spirits of the two Christian laws, of the Old
Testament (works) and the New Testament (faith). Having
in mind books like *Isaiah*, he sees the prophets as true poets,
interpreting the will of God, and he begs them to pray sympa-
thetically for him lest he use their authority to excuse his own
poetical excesses.

The last stanza, with its fine use of antithetical metaphors in

38   *Dead clods* of sadnesse, or *light squibs* of mirth

chooses a middle-way of thinking and feeling. God's aid is
sought to assure us that the world is no prison; that the Almighty
is not jealous of those he loves, nor does he punish those who
zealously seek salvation through life's joys. Donne here denies
the necessity for mortification of the flesh, the ascetic way to
God. As a convert to Anglicanism, he seems to have kept an
open mind on the Catholic doctrine of Purgatory.

A Hymne to Christ, at the Authors last going into Germany

In what torne ship soever I embarke,
That ship shall be my embleme of thy Arke;
What sea soever swallow mee, that flood
Shall be to mee an embleme of thy blood;
Though thou with clouds of anger do disguise   5
Thy face; yet through that maske I know those eyes,
    Which, though they turne away sometimes,
        They never will despise.

I sacrifice this Iland unto thee,
And all whom I lov'd there, and who lov'd mee;   10
When I have put our seas twixt them and mee,
Put thou thy sea betwixt my sinnes and thee.
As the trees sap doth seeke the root below
In winter, in my winter now I goe,
    Where none but thee, th'Eternall root   15
        Of true Love I may know.

Nor thou nor thy religion dost controule,
The amorousnesse of an harmonious Soule,
But thou would'st have that love thy selfe: As thou
Art jealous, Lord, so I am jealous now,   20

Thou lov'st not, till from loving more, thou free
My soule: Who ever gives, takes libertie:
  O, if thou car'st not whom I love
    Alas, thou lov'st not mee.

Seale then this bill of my Divorce to All,   25
On whom those fainter beames of love did fall;
Marry those loves, which in youth scattered bee
On Fame, Wit, Hopes (false mistresses) to thee.
Churches are best for Prayer, that have least light:
To see God only, I goe out of sight: 30
  And to scape stormy dayes, I chuse
    An Everlasting night.

On 12 May 1619 Donne accompanied Viscount Doncaster to Germany on a mission of mediation to the Princes. His visit lasted seven months and took him as far as Vienna. The poem, which is formally one of Donne's most perfect, was anticipated by his Sermon of Valediction, delivered on 18 April of the same year.

The hymn is a renunciation of the world and prayer for union with God through death. The feelings are consecrated in the final stanza, but in lines 21–4 the characteristic twists of Donne's paradox are found. In the third stanza, where freedom and restraint are bandied, Latin polysyllables abound (*religion, controule, amorousnesse, harmonious, jealous, libertie*). *Ploce* is the principal scheme of rhetoric, in lines 13–15 (*root* and *winter*), and in lines 19–24, where *love* occurs five times, *jealous* twice. The language is lucid, dignified, reverential, and the thoughts are centripetal. Poeticisms such as *twixt* (11) are rare.

The metrical form is an eight-line stanza, consisting of three iambic pentameter couplets, followed by an unrhymed four-foot line, and a trimeter which matches the rhyme of the third couplet. Donne uses minimal modulation of stress, consisting of occasional trochaic substitution in the first foot, and spondees and pyrrhics within the line. A good example is

29 /Chúrchĕs/ ăr̆e beśt/ fŏr Práyer,/ thăt hăve/ leást líght/

Spondees in the final foot are rarer than in Donne's secular poetry. Metrical use of the periphrastic auxiliary *do* occurs once in each stanza, and syntactical enjambement twice as frequently.

Donne's repeated use of *embleme* (2 and 4) in the first stanza is significant. *Emblems*, accompanied by mottoes, appeared as book-illustrations and were the source of much symbolism, as well as Elizabethan and Jacobean images and conceits. E. N. S. Thompson in *Literary Bypaths of the Renaissance* (New Haven, 1924, p. 32) says that over seven hundred emblem books had appeared by the second decade of the seventeenth century, when this *Hymne* was written. Donne, like the Italian scholar-poets, seems to have used them freely. Some were the source of his abstruseness and pseudo-scientific imagery, as Mario Praz has shown (*Studies in Seventeenth Century Imagery*, London, 1939).

Secular love-emblems were converted by Catholic theologians and apologists to the uses of religious mysticism, as Donne employs them in this poem. The body-soul dichotomy of Donne's pleading was probably of this origin. The *Hymne to Christ* shows that there was no cleavage, in his mind, between sacred and profane love. In the preceding poem, *A Litanie*, he used the symbol of the church-organ as the emblem of harmony. In the *Hymne* the emblems are the *Arke* (2), the *blood* of Christ (4), the *Iland* (9) or corporeal man, the *Soule* (16) and *Everlasting night* (32) or eternity.

It is on these symbols that the metaphorical structure of the poem hinges. It begins with *torn* (i.e. unseaworthy) ship, which recalls Noah's *Ark*. This carries images of the *flood*, which he envisages as the emblem of Christ's blood of sacrifice. The Flood of Noah brings memories of God's anger with men, in the storm-clouds which hide His face.

The *Iland* of stanza 2 is Donne himself. Though he says in his 17th Meditation 'No man is an Iland, intire of it selfe; every man is a peece of the Continent, a part of the maine', a voyager on a ship surrounded by sea knows himself to be isolated. The sea is the symbol of separateness. As the poet renounces those who love him and are loved, he asks that his sins be not only washed away, but excluded. The emblem of a tree in winter (the time of Donne's departure) provides the next image. As the sap returns to the base, so he, in the winter of life, seeks the 'Eternall' tap-root of Christ's love.

This theme of the Saviour as the root of love leads, in stanza 3, to a comparison of Christ with a lover who is jealous. Though love, the harmony of the Soul, is not restrained by religion, no lover brooks a rival. God cannot love us fully, until he is assured that no greater love than His is sought by

I

us. The freedom of the Soul is a paradox: it receives abundantly the more it gives. God loves us only when He *cares* about the nature of *our* love.

This image of the jealous lover leads Donne naturally to the 'bill of my Divorce to All' in stanza 4. He relinquishes *all* worldly love, because it is love of an inferior kind. (Note the metaphor *fainter beames* (26)). The true marriage is one that sublimes all the former hopes and ambitions of youth (*false mistresses* (28)); it calls for complete dedication to God. The final antithesis of light and darkness has major force, beginning with the proverbial utterance:

29   Churches are best for Prayer, that have least light.

Donne implies that, in the gloom of isolation, we see God truly. So, to escape the *stormy days* (sorrows of life), we await death without apprehension.

The key to Donne's poetic reason is the chain of symbols and metaphors he worked upon, with all the logic of *conceit*. The Italians called these emblems *impresa* and they are the basis of 'metaphysical' poetry. Each poem is an entity, built round a group of related images. Between two poems, however, there may be philosophical inconsistency. In *A Litanie*, for instance, the Almighty is benign, as in the New Testament: in the *Hymne to Christ*, He is a jealous God, as in the Old.

J. B. Douds claimed that 'the creation of a technique for rendering the complex moment of feeling was probably Donne's greatest contribution to English poetry' (*PMLA*, LII.4, 1937). A new medium had been found for the personal element in poetic style, an amalgam of wit and fantasy, in Donne's sense of 'curious thinking', contrasting the grave with the playful. Donne's best images were capable of great delicacy of insight. Extremes of contrast were seldom forced, except in the *Satires*. Straining after metaphysical effects led ultimately to Cleveland-ism, and its absurdities brought that kind of poetry into disrepute. The wit of Donne is masculine and intellectual, and there is, as yet, no sign of upper-class decadence.

The principal ingredients of style in Donne are paradox,

conceits, syntactical fragmentation, and metrical originalit
sometimes so daring that the pattern is in danger of annihilatioи.
Rhetoric is not a series of skilfully disposed niches to be filled
with *objets d'art*; tropes, images and symbols soon ousted
shallower devices. Donne was fond of analogies between the
known functions of the body and the unknown workings of the
mind. In isolated metaphors there may be dissonance between
major and minor terms, the thing described and the likeness
implied. But Donne's temperate, classical logicality finally
harmonizes disparate elements; image clusters are the blood
and sinews of his new poetry. Ideas are usually dramatic in
presentation, pleading or paradoxical, and the best poems are
skilful in the balance of antithesis and hyperbole, meiosis and
irony.

The classical poet Donne most resembles is Catullus. Lexis,
rhythm, syntax, meaning and rhetoric co-operate in the poetry
of both with a sincerity that is holistic. The images cohere and
the argument concentrates, and therefore the better poems tend
to be short. Discourse in Donne cannot be prolonged beyond
the limits of a poem like *The Exstasie*, which consists of 76 lines.

Donne's style is thus the antithesis of Spenser's expansive
method. Elizabethan poets abound in personal metaphors, but
Donne's are more subjective than the figures of the descriptive
school. His feelings are less objectified; he is perplexed by, and
seeks to account for, his own reactions; a love affair is ego-
tistically focused on his own behaviour, rather than the moods
of the other person. Nature animates the physical phenomena
of this individual psychology. The method is vivid, but not with
Shakespeare's impartial observation. C. S. Lewis likened Donne
to a 'burning-glass' that concentrates the light at a single point.
His metaphors are a means to thought condensation.

Donne's originality lies largely in his introspective and
analytical power; poems are logical patterns of association. For
instance, Elizabeth Drury in *The Second Anniversary* is thus
idealized:

> She of whose soule, if wee may say, 'twas *Gold*,
> Her body was th'*Electrum*, and did hold
> Many degrees of that, wee understood
> Her by her *sight;* her pure and *eloquent* blood
> *Spoke* in her cheekes, and so distinctly *wrought*,

That one might almost say, her body *thought;*
Shee, shee, thus *richly* and largely *hous'd*, is gone   (lines 241–7)

A rational connection can be seen in the image sequence. The ancients used an alloy of silver and gold, whose brightness depended on the right addition of the first element (not less than one fifth part); this they called the *Electrum*. The meaning of *sight* in 244 is 'appearance', and *hous'd* (247) refers to the Platonic belief that the soul is 'lodged' in the body. Fine speech is proverbially *silver*-tongued, and high *thoughts* are associated with a heart of *gold*. *Rich* metals are *wrought* by the goldsmith, and words are shaped into sentences by the rhetorician. More is revealed in these seven lines than Donne's interest in alchemy, rhetoric and the craftsman's handiwork.

Although Donne's feelings may not have been deeply affected by the death of the youthful Elizabeth Drury, there is a felt intensity in his figurative expressions. He is not describing, but evaluating. The enjambed movement of lines 2 to 4 fits the sequential nature of his exposition, for Donne strives to make the sense articulate through metaphor.

The classical strain in Donne's language, which makes it difficult to distinguish some of his epigrammatic verse from Jonson's, arises from the tendency to rational emphasis. Though Donne is never simply exclamatory, his method of argument and address employs many predications and vocatives. He depends heavily on particles, connectives and clausal development. Personal pronouns and monosyllabic active verbs have considerable semantic significance. He is not a phrase-maker, and his vocabulary is as parsimonious as Jonson's in the use of adjectives. His language belongs to the Renaissance in a different way from Spenser's; it expands the speculative imagination. He was not, even in the estimation of his time, a philosophic poet, whose arguments embody the values of preceding ages. In his cosmology he uses both the Ptolemaic and Copernican theories. The appeal of his meditations depends less on the truth or falsity of his psychology or his natural science than on the percipience of his poetic personality.

IX

MILTON

Milton was the last and greatest Renaissance humanist writing in English. Despite admiration for the classical poets and dramatists, Homer, Vergil, Sophocles and Euripides, he chose Italian models for most of his important poems; yet, in a special way, he became an original poet, excelling in nearly all the forms he borrowed. Milton acknowledged a debt to Spenser; but, except in the epithets and musical delight of his diction, his obligation was slight. In the early poem, *At a Solemn Music*, he apostrophized 'Voice and Verse' as 'Sphere-born harmonious sisters', and never lost sight of the relationship.

No English poet but Coleridge was more studious of literary theory than Milton. In *Church-Government*, Bk 2, he spoke of the need for 'industrious and select reading', as well as 'steady observation'; and in the tractate *Of Education* he described rhetoric as one of the organic arts. The theorists who influenced him most were Aristotle, Horace and Castelvetro (for the dramatic works), Minturno (for prosody), Mazzoni (for allegory and imagery), Longinus and Tasso (especially *Discorsi del Poema Eroico*) for the grand style.

Allegory and didacticism were essential to narrative poetry of the Renaissance in Italy and England. Mazzoni, in particular, was responsible for the theory that allegory and personification enhanced the wonder of epic poetry, and gave it instructive credibility. Moral truth, not history, was the germinal 'matter' of Milton's major poems. He was a poet with a mission, 'soaring in the high region of his fancies, with his garland and singing robes about him' (*Church-Government*, Bk 2). Good poetry, he said, is 'simple, sensuous and passionate'; but the maker must contemplate, be patient for inspiration, which was an article of faith to Milton. He made a fetish of the 'fit audience though few', ignoring the tastes and judgements of unscholarly readers.

Because he was the greatest of England's poets in the Latin

idiom, it is generally assumed that Milton's English style was latinized. Upon inspection, however, it turns out to be characteristically English, though not always idiomatic English. Believing with Jonson and Dryden in the need to refine the English language and perpetuate it in the purest state, Milton identified the prosperity of a nation with the respect it accords to the status of its speech. *At a Vacation Exercise*, written in Milton's nineteenth year, shows his earliest care for the disciplining of his thoughts in English. The 'late fantastics' were undoubtedly the 'metaphysical' poets.

> Hail native Language, that by sinews weak
> Didst move my first endeavouring tongue to speak,
> And mad'st imperfect words with childish tripps,
> Half unpronounc't, slide through my infant-lipps,
> . . . . . .
> Here I salute thee and thy pardon ask   5
> That now I use thee in my latter task:
> Small loss it is that thence can come unto thee,
> I know my tongue but little Grace can do thee:
> . . . . . .
> But haste thee strait to do me once a Pleasure,
> And from thy wardrope bring thy chiefest treasure;   10
> Not those new fangled toys, and triming slight
> Which takes our late fantasticks with delight,
> But cull those richest Robes, and gay'st attire
> Which deepest Spirits, and choicest Wits desire:
> I have some naked thoughts that rove about   15
> And loudly knock to have their passage out;
> And wearie of their place do only stay
> Till thou has deck't them in thy best aray;
> . . . . . .
> Yet I had rather if I were to chuse,
> Thy service in some graver subject use,   20
> Such as may make thee search thy coffers round,
> Before thou cloath my fancy in fit sound.

For Milton the art of writing was 'to pick and order a set of words judiciously' (*An Apology*, III.256). He was a practising advocate of retrenchment of all that (to use his own words) is superfluous, useless and foreign. Yet there were unclassical exuberances he was never able to resist. The conventional use of epithets, and generalized imagery were present in *L'Allegro* and *Il Penseroso*; the magniloquent phrases and odd syntactical order of the blank verse were in embryo in *Comus*. *At a Vacation Exercise* has such idiosyncrasies as these:

1. Ten inversions of word order, of which *sinews weak* (1), *pardon ask* (5), *triming slight* (11), *subject use* (20), and *coffers round* (21) are in the last two feet, and have the same rhythmical cadence, (′ x ′).

2. Compounding of a distinct Miltonic type, with or without hyphens; e.g. my *first endeavouring* tongue (2), *Half unpronounc't* (4), *infant-lipps* (4), *new fangled* toys (11). These poeticisms do not resemble some of Milton's later compound epithets, which Bernard Groom attributes to biblical paraphrase, medieval allegory and Spenser (*SPE Tract* XLIX, 1937). Milton reacted to the far-fetched conceits of the metaphysicals, and common speech accounts for the triteness of many adjectives.

3. Considerable liberties with the kind and positioning of adverbs and adverbial phrases; e.g. *Half unpronounc't* (4), *now* (6), *thence* (6), *strait* and *once* (9), *out* (16), *only* (17), *round* (21). Milton was fond of what R. D. Emma called 'flat' adverbs, those in which the *-ly* suffix is omitted (*Milton's Grammar,* Mouton, The Hague, 1964).

4. Poetical use of archaic words, nearly as common as Spenser's, e.g. *Hail* (1). Conjunctions, in particular, are preserved in archaic forms, such as *ere, whenas, whereat*. But archaisms tend to disappear after the composition of *Comus*.

5. Retention of the fast-declining subjunctive, e.g. *use* (6 and 20), *cloath* (22).

6. Invocations, involving the second personal pronoun *thou* and verbal inflexions *'st* (with elision). These were more commonly used by Milton than by other poets.

The extent of Milton's violence to English grammar has been exaggerated by nearly all critics, except C. S. Lewis and E. M. W. Tillyard. Usually, he is judged by modern and not Elizabethan or Jacobean standards, to which he clung. The principal cause of deviation is similar to Donne's – poetic compression. Other influences were Cicero's periodic structure of sentence for rhetorical emphasis, and the style of Italian poets or critics he had been perusing, especially Bembo, Tasso and della Casa. (See F. T. Prince, *The Italian Element in Milton's Verse*, Clarendon, 1954.) The ultimate source of Milton's sentence emphasis was undoubtedly Latin. But Latin systems of ranking and subordination were not possible to Milton, because of the different character of Latin and English as inflected and uninflected languages. It should never be overlooked that Milton in his poetry favours co-ordinated sentences, rather than subordinated ones. Emma has shown that, in the poems, nearly 47 per cent of the sentences are loose, 10 per cent periodic, and 40 per cent agglomerations in which one or other of these structures predominates (op. cit. p. 152). The same critic finds that 83 per cent of Milton's verse sentences preserve the normal English order.

The Latin element in Milton's style, predominantly techniques of Vergil and Horace, is not to be found in the syntax, so much as in the tone, the epithets, and the natural imagery. In these respects he attempts to marry the classical to the English style of writing. In epic poetry he is statuesque in line and relations of mass, but the minor poems have fewer arresting pictorial images, because less precise in detail. The conventional descriptions of the minor poems can be observed in the choice of epithets:

> *Russet* Lawns, and Fallows *gray,*
> Where the *nibling* flocks do stray,
> Mountains on whose *barren* brest
> The *labouring* clouds do often rest,
> Meadows *trim,* with Daisies *pide,*
> *Shallow* brooks, and Rivers *wide.*

(L'Allegro, 71–6)

The classical ideal is inevitably for harmony of impression and a sedate emotional key. As Walter Raleigh observed in his pioneering study, *Milton* (Arnold, 1900):

> The strongest words in the language lose their vital force because they are set fluttering hither and thither in multitudes, with no substantial hold on reality. There is nothing that dies sooner than an emotion when it is cut off from the stock on which it grows.

Raleigh quotes a song from *Comus,* which may contain 'a certain Dorique delicacy', but better illustrates the unreality of Milton's imagery:

> Sabrina fair
> Listen where thou art sitting
> Under the *glassie,* cool, *translucent waves,*
> In twisted braids of Lillies knitting
> The loose train of thy *amber-dropping hair*   (lines 859–63)

Not only are the epithets *glassie* and *translucent* pleonastic, but they imply a smoothness on the river Severn's surface that is incompatible with the word *wave*. *Amber-dropping hair* is an unusual conceit. The poet apparently had in mind 'liquid amber', originally the sperm of a whale. When Milton used *translucent*, he invariably associated it with *amber*, in its second meaning, 'a luminous fossil resin of yellow colour'.

Milton was a learned poet, and rarely finds the reader who has the patience and industry to match his scholarship. A few critics, such as Alan Tate (*The New Republic*, 21 October, 1931), have noticed the importance of myth and fable in Milton's work. Tate said 'it is the myth ingrained in his very being, that makes the style'. In Plato, and among classical poets, mythology provided not only analogues, images and ethical themes, but living examples of the creative imagination at work – how man, for instance, personifies the forces of nature. Milton used classical mythology as an integral part of figurative language (1) in similes; (2) in adaptations to his own major fables, three of which were Hebraic in origin; (3) for humanizing descriptions of nature; and (4) as pyramids of allusion:

> Not that fair field
> Of Enna, where Proserpin gathering flours
> Her self a fairer Floure by gloomie Dis
> Was gatherd, which cost Ceres all that pain
> To seek her through the world; nor that sweet Grove
> Of Daphne by Orontes, and th'inspir'd
> Castalian Spring, might with this Paradise
> Of Eden strive   (*P.L.* IV, 268–75)

Milton's ideal of Paradise is here a field of flowers, based on a picturesque incident in the fable of another poet. This was no casual tangent of classical allusions. In his younger days at Horton, Milton used the same analogy, in a letter to Diodati:

> Ceres never sought her daughter Proserpine (as the legend tells) with greater ardour than I do this Idea of Beauty, like some image of loveliness; ever pursuing it, by day and by night, in every shape and form.

Ovid's *Metamorphoses* was as important a source-book for Milton as for Shakespeare. He used it expansively, as though its allusions were a legitimate elaboration. Shakespeare

employed Ovid only incidentally, for illumination or evocation.
Both methods had poetic advantages.

On Shakespeare 1630

What needs my Shakespear for his honour'd Bones,
The labour of an age in piled Stones,
Or that his hallow'd reliques should be hid
Under a star-ypointing Pyramid?
Dear son of memory, great heir of Fame,   5
What need'st thou such weak witnes of thy name?
Thou in our wonder and astonishment
Hast built thy self a live-long Monument.
For whilst to th'shame of slow-endeavouring art,
Thy easie numbers flow, and that each heart   10
Hath from the leaves of thy unvalu'd Book,
Those Delphick lines with deep impression took,
Then thou our fancy of it self bereaving,
Dost make us Marble with too much conceaving;
And so Sepulcher'd in such pomp dost lie,   15
That Kings for such a Tomb would wish to die.

This is one of four epitaphs written by Milton in the classical
style of epigram. The models were brief Latin or Greek poems,
suggested by inscriptions on tombs of the famous dead. Milton
emulates the dignity and sincerity of Horace, in an English
form perfected by Ben Jonson – iambic pentameter couplets.
The sixteen lines appeared anonymously in the Second Folio
Shakespeare of 1632; in the 1645 edition of Milton's Poems,
heart was substituted for *part* at the end of line 10. The tone of
the epitaph recalls Shakespeare's Sonnets.

The language is characteristic of Milton's early style,
especially the condensed syntax, Greek allusions and compound
epithets, rhetorical and descriptive. As Milton developed, he
simplified his vocabulary. Here there are 24 words of Greek or
Latin origin, which give weight and cadence to the lines,
especially in the phrases *hallow'd reliques* (3), *star-ypointing
Pyramid* (4) and *Sepulcher'd in such pomp* (15). The *y*- prefix
in *ypointing*, borrowed from Spenser, was an archaism retained
by Milton for metrical reasons. *Name* (6) and *unvalu'd* (11)
mean 'reputation' and 'invaluable', respectively; and *Delphick*
(12) probably implies 'oracular'.

The sense-grouping in epigrammatic couplets makes run-on lines superfluous; there is one true metrical enjambement, however, terminating line 10. At the end of 3 and 7 there are slight metrical pauses, but they do not require punctuation. The movement is poised and regular, the principal modulation occurring in lines 5, 6, 9 and 14, the last having double rhyme with extra unstressed syllable:

5 /Deár són/ ŏf mé/mŏrў̆,/ greát heír/ ŏf Faḿe/
6 /Whăt néed'st/ thŏu sùch/ weák wĭt/nĕs ŏf/ thў̆ naḿe/
9 /Fŏr whĭlst/ tŏ th'sháme/ ŏf slów/-ĕndéa/voúring árt/
14 `/Dŏst máke/ ŭs Már/blĕ wĭth/ toó mùch/ coñcea/vĭng/

Milton is careful in marking elisions, especially in verb-inflexions, cf. *honour'd* (1) and *piléd* (2). *To th'shame* (9) is a Jonsonian elision; in the same line he does not think it desirable to elide *ou* between the consonants *v* and *r* of *endeavouring*.

The syntax of 10–14 illustrates the impressionism of Milton's thinking, for the sense is hard to unravel. The difficulty lies in the connectives *For* (9), *and that* (10), *Then* (13), and the anacoluthic temporal clause beginning with *whilst* (9). *For* seems to be understood before *that* in line 10, *for that* having the meaning of 'because'.

The epitaph begins with a double rhetorical question. Milton associates his tribute with the pyramids, tombs and monuments of the Egyptian dynasties. Shakespeare needs no memorial, for in his works he created his own. *Honour'd Bones* of the first question is repeated as *hallow'd reliques* in the second. In the poetical invocation that follows, Shakespeare is 'son of memory', i.e. of Mnemosyne, mother of the Muses. The real monument of Shakespeare is our wonder at his achievement. Milton admits that the spontaneous art of Shakespeare puts his own pains-taking verses to shame. Shakespeare's flashes of phrase have left unforgettable impressions. Wealth of imagination impoverished the efforts of his successors. In the last three lines hyperbolic conceits are in the Renaissance fashion. Younger poets are as cold as marble through intellectual commitment to Shakespeare's complex creations; yet such poets are the substance of his memorial, since his work lives in them. It is we who are dead, and Shakespeare that is immortal.

In the first seven lines personification is the dominant figure.

Hallow'd reliques suggests that Shakespeare is a saint; his tomb points heavenwards; he is eternally (*live-long*) consecrated to Fame. In the last four lines the images are metaphors, emotive, traditional, conceptual, not strictly visual. For aural appeal, prosodic harmony, archaic associations, determine Milton's choice of images.

Sonnet VII

How soon hath Time the suttle theef of youth,
  Stoln on his wing my three and twentith yeer!
  My hasting dayes flie on with full career
  But my late spring no bud or blossom shew'th.
Perhaps my semblance might deceive the truth,   5
  That I to manhood am arriv'd so near,
  And inward ripenes doth much less appear,
  That som more timely-happy spirits indu'th.
Yet be it less or more, or soon or slow,
  It shall be still in strictest measure eev'n   10
  To that same lot, however mean, or high,
Toward which Time leads me, and the will of Heav'n;
  All is, if I have grace to use it so,
  As ever in my great task Masters eye.

Of Milton's 23 sonnets, the first ten were published in the 1645 collection of the *Poems*, one half being in Italian. Another nine were published in *Poems upon Several Occasions* in 1673, and four, dealing with Cromwellian figures, remained in manuscript until 1694. Milton was born on 9 December 1608 and it has been assumed that this sonnet was written on his birthday (or soon after) in 1631; but W. R. Parker and A. S. P. Woodhouse argued, from line 2, that 'Stoln . . . my three and twentieth yeer' implies the poet's twenty-fourth birthday (1632).

Milton was the first English poet to return to the Petrarchan form of the sonnet, after the early experiments of Wyatt, Sidney and Constable had given way to the Shakespearian form. English practitioners of Italian models deviated principally in the rhyme-schemes of the tercets. Milton's scheme in Sonnet VII is abba, abba, cde, dce; enclosed rhyme in the quatrains, and a variation in the three-rhyme order of the second tercet that had been anticipated by Petrarch. The sonnet is disciplined

and classical in form, whereas most Elizabethan sonneteers had
favoured the medieval-romance style of sweetness, (cf. 'Shake-
speare's *sugred* Sonnets') smoothness and melody. Classical
turns of phrase characterize the group of Milton's sonnets
addressed to distinguished friends, Lawes, Lawrence and
Skinner, and these resemble epistles or gratulatory odes of
Horace.

Sonnet VII confines the clausal sense within each of the
quatrain-groupings of which Italian sonnets were composed.
As J. S. Smart showed in the *Sonnets of Milton* (OUP, 1921,
Introd. p. 32–3), there is no ground in Italian sonnet theory
for insisting on the *volta* or 'turn' after the eighth line of the
quatrains, though Milton demonstrates its use admirably in
this sonnet. The tercets are syntactically connected by the
subordinate relative clause in line 12.

The choice of words shows how Milton was affected by the
idiom of Spenser and Shakespeare. The preference for archaic
poetical forms *hath* (1) and *doth* (7) is a gesture to literary
elegance; so is *indu'th* (8). *Suttle* (1) implies 'secret' or
'clever'; *deceive* (5) means 'conceal'. *Timely-happy* (8) and
eev'n (10), presumably meaning 'equitable', have the ambiguity
of some of Shakespeare's Sonnets; *timely* implies 'compatible
with age', and *happy* signifies 'fortunate'. The *spirits* (literary
persons) in line 8 have been identified with several of Milton's
contemporaries, Charles Diodati, Thomas Randolph and
Abraham Cowley.

The Spenserian technique is evident in the alliteration and
vowel-play of the first two lines. The intricate weaving of
sibilant and fricative consonants *s* and *th*, with liquids and
nasals *l*, *m*, and *n*, continues throughout the sonnet. The verses
in the quatrains are usually end-stopped: internal pauses seem
reserved for the balanced structure of the tercets. There is some
freedom in the matching of the rhyme words, though much
depends on the London pronunciation of the relevant vowels and
diphthongs. The use of elision in the rhymes is daring.

The first quatrain has three lines of sequential imagery. In
the first two *Time* is likened to a harpy that stealthily robs the
young of their years. *Time*, the thief, was a conventional
Elizabethan metaphor. In 4 the image shifts to Time, not as
despoiler, but as a tree that promises fulfilment. Milton, a

poet younger in looks than his years, was then in the late
spring-time of his career, yet no *bud or blossom* had rewarded
his aspirations. The only figure in the second quatrain is
ripeness (7), a continuation of the *Spring* metaphor. Milton
complains of delayed maturity: other poets ripen earlier. *It* in
9 and 10 refers to *inward ripeness* (7). The paradox contained
in the sestet is reflected in the antitheses, e.g. *less or more, soon
or slow* (9), *mean or high* (11). Milton in 12 personifies *Time*
as the *will of Heav'n*. Finally, Calvinist predestination induces
him to see God as a just Taskmaster, in whom he is content to
repose his trust. In the years at Horton, immediately after
Cambridge, Milton was anxious, like Keats, to let his develop-
ing mind lie fallow, until ripe for greater achievement.

The pattern of Miltonic sonnets is Petrarch's, but he wrote
three hundred years later than his predecessor. The internal
structure of the lines more resembles sixteenth-century Italian,
Milton's model being Giovanni della Casa (1503–56), whose
Sonnets he began to study in 1629. This poet taught Milton the
art of French enjambement, of discontinuity of the syntax with
the metrical units, which made for flexibility in the movement
of the sonnet as a whole. A fine example is the maturer Sonnet
XV *On the Late Massacher in Piedmont*. This freer movement,
deplored by some of Milton's nineteenth-century critics, did
not become a regular practice until after the poet's return from
Italy in 1639. The late sonnets on distinguished Parliamentarians
carried the enjambed syntax a stage further, and they were
probably suggested to Milton by Tasso's prolific *Heroic
Sonnets* which numbered 486.

The formal language of Sonnet VII indicates Milton's
confidence in adapting Elizabethan English to Italian elabora-
tion. The thoughts were to be few, but apt and well balanced.
The words might outnumber the ideas, but rhythmical ease and
dignity should conceal their art. The controlled power of Milton
holds the reader and creates the illusion of terse directness,
even when amplification is present. The complexity of the later
sonnets prepared the ground for the two epics and *Samson
Agonistes*, and their diction was the logical fulfilment of the
blending of English and Italian syntax, for which Milton was
preparing himself.

*   *   *

Comus (lines 520–60)

This piece had no other title than *A Mask* in Milton's collected works. John Dalton's production of 1738 was the first to give it the name *Comus*. The Masque was originally performed before the Earl of Bridgewater, at Ludlow Castle, in September 1634, and published in 1637. The entertainment was commissioned by Henry Lawes of the Chapel Royal, one of the King's principal musicians, who provided the musical setting, and himself played the part of the Attendant Spirit, dressed as the shepherd Thyrsis. Five songs were provided, three for the Spirit to sing.

Masques had been popular since the reign of Henry VIII, both as a primitive dumb-show and a stately costume-dance, in which courtiers participated. The entertainments became more sophisticated and dramatic when words were added in the late sixteenth century. They were always performed by amateurs of the gentleman class. The language was formal, often stilted. The pastoral convention, favoured by poets who were lovers of the Classics, was chosen by Milton for *Arcades* and *Comus*. The theme of the latter, chastity tempted, was designed for three young performers, who were adolescent children of the Earl, and who came from Middlesex to Ludlow in Shropshire, supposedly in search of their parents. The Attendant Spirit was their guardian and spiritual guide.

The plot of *Comus* is in the form of a Spenserian allegory, in which elements of 'faery', enchantment and chivalry condition the tone. The language is full of artifice, without being quite artificial. The indirect sources of the masque were the *Faerie Queene*, Bks I–III and VI, Peele's *Old Wives Tale* (1595), Fletcher's *Faithful Shepherdess* (1610), *The Tempest* (1612), William Browne's *Inner Temple Masque* (1614), Homer's *Odyssey* X and XII (Comus is actually the son of Circe), the *Hippolytus* of Euripides, Plato's *Phaedo*, Ariosto's *Orlando Furioso* (1516), Tasso's *Aminta* (1581) and Guarini's *Pastor Fido* (1585). The genius of the river Severn, Sabrina, comes from Geoffrey of Monmouth's *History of the British Kings*. This river flows in the neighbourhood of Ludlow Castle, on the Welsh border, where the scene of *Comus* is laid. The range of Milton's influences indicates his powers of assimilation and transformation.

Dr Johnson, thinking in terms of theatrical performance, complained that the speeches of *Comus* were long declamations 'deliberately composed, and formally repeated, on a moral question'. Masques were, however, cultivated abstractions, in which virtues and vices were personified, and gods and goddesses intervened. In such compositions poeticism prevails, speeches tend to be studies in rhetoric, and conceits and repetitions abound. Relief takes the form of pastoral lyricism, usually in short lilting measures.

Of its 1023 lines 774 (more than two thirds) are in blank verse. The style of Shakespeare is to be seen everywhere; but Milton has more sonorous flights, greater volubility of argument, bookishness of phrase, and wealth of allusions. The partiality for long verse debates never left him.

As the following speech of the Attending Spirit reveals, Milton writes with the classical and Renaissance tradition of art and learning in his blood:

> Within the navil of this hideous Wood,
> Immur'd in cypress shades a Sorcerer dwels
> Of Bacchus, and of Circe born, great Comus,
> Deep skill'd in all his mothers witcheries,
> And here to every thirsty wanderer,   5
> By sly enticement gives his banefull cup,
> With many murmurs mixt, whose pleasing poison
> The visage quite transforms of him that drinks,
> And the inglorious likenes of a beast
> Fixes instead, unmoulding reasons mintage   10
> Character'd in the face; this have I learn't
> Tending my flocks hard by i'th hilly crofts,
> That brow this bottom glade, whence night by night
> He and his monstrous rout are heard to howl
> Like stabl'd wolves, or tigers at their prey,   15
> Doing abhorréd rites to Hecate
> In their obscuréd haunts of inmost bowres.
> Yet have they many baits, and guilefull spells
> To inveigle and invite th'unwary sense
> Of them that pass unweeting by the way.   20
> This evening late by then the chewing flocks
> Had ta'n their supper on the savoury Herb
> Of Knot-grass dew-besprent, and were in fold,
> I sate me down to watch upon a bank
> With Ivy canopied, and interwove   25
> With flaunting Hony-suckle, and began
> Wrapt in a pleasing fit of melancholy

To meditate my rural minstrelsie,
Till fancy had her fill, but ere a close
The wonted roar was up amidst the Woods,   30
And fill'd the Air with barbarous dissonance,
At which I ceas't, and listen'd them a while,
Till an unusuall stop of sudden silence
Gave respit to the drowsie frighted steeds
That draw the litter of close-curtain'd sleep.   35
At last a soft and solemn breathing sound
Rose like a steam of rich distill'd Perfumes,
And stole upon the Air, that even Silence
Was took e're she was ware, and wish't she might
Deny her nature, and be never more   40
Still to be so displac't.

The immediate response to this dignified vocabulary is its indebtedness to Spenser. Few words are certain archaisms, but the number of poetic words is high: *Immur'd* (2), *banefull* (6), *visage* (8), *mintage* (10), *whence* (13), *abhorréd* (16), *guilefull* (18), *inveigle* (19), *unweeting* (20), *ta'n* (22), *besprent* (23), *sate me* (24), *canopied* (25), *minstrelsie* (28 'music'), *wonted* (30), *respit* (34). These, with the compound epithets *Deep skilled* (4), *dew-besprent* (23), *drowsie frighted* (34), *close-curtain'd* (35) and *rich distill'd* (37), recall the leisurely pictorial method of Spenser. Many adjectival choices have the Spenserian conventionality: *obscuréd* haunts and *inmost* bowers (17), th'*unwary* sense (19), *savoury* Herb (22), *flaunting* Hony-suckle (26), *rural* minstrelsie (28), *barbarous* dissonance (31).

Emma (op. cit. p. 112) has shown that the ratio of adjectives to other words, such as nouns and verbs, is higher (26.3 per cent) in *Comus* than in any other of Milton's poems; but the poem has the lowest proportion of adverbs (5 per cent).

The movement of the blank verse, on the other hand, suggests the narrative-descriptive style of Oberon in *A Midsummer Night's Dream*, sometimes (as in lines 10–17 and 30–35) of Prospero in *The Tempest*. Especially Shakespearian is the use of nouns as verbs: *Character'd* (11), *brow* (13), *canopied* (25), *curtain'd* (35). The verse is painstakingly correct in its preference for a four-beat line; the elisions are carefully marked; the enjambement is sparing, and feminine endings are scarcely used as a means of modulation. The rhythm is skilfully controlled by the varied disposition of internal pauses, but most delicate in its smoothening effect is the use of vowel-change and alliteration, e.g.

> 7   With many murmurs mixt, whose pleasing poison
> 33   Till an unusuall stop of sudden silence
> 35   At last a soft and solemn breathing sound

Milton's syntax in *Comus* is prone to the usual Spenserian inversions:

> Of Bacchus, and of Circe *born* (3)
> With many murmurs *mixt* (17)
> The visage quite transforms *of him that drinks* (8)
> *This have* I learnt (11)
> *Yet have they* many baits (18)
> Of Knot-grass *dew-besprent* (23)
> With Ivy *canopied* (25)

An archaic effect seems to be deliberately sought, in imitation of Spenser, in reflexive constructions, (24 I *sate me* down), and in prepositionless pronouns, used to simulate the old dative case (32 and listen'd *them* a while).

Though nature plays an un-Wordsworthian part in Milton's philosophy, harmony with natural forces was a conviction amounting nearly to a faith. The pastoral setting and pageantry of this masque demanded imagery of a visual kind. The use of *navil*, rather than 'heart', in line 1 is an example of Milton's naturalism. The early Greeks described Delphi as the 'navel' of the earth (*omphalos*). *Immur'd in cypress shades* (2) implies that the Sorcerer is imprisomed in the darkness of his own evil. Light is the symbol of liberation and free will.

Circe (3) is a central figure in the allegory, the child of Sol and Persis (daughter of Oceanus) and therefore herself a goddess as well as an enchantress. Being the symbolic offspring of the physical elements, heat and water, she engendered intemperate appetite, and her charms could only be withstood by the white-flowering plant Moly (bringer of wisdom and courage), the gift of Mercury, by which Odysseus was preserved (*Metamorphoses*, Bk XIV). *Haemony* is the medicinal herb preferred by Milton in *Comus*, Medea's charm to renew the youth of Jason (*Metamorphoses*, Bk VII), and it is intended in this masque to stand for divine grace, which Milton was careful to distinguish from human nature. *Baneful cup* (6), *murmurs*

(7, 'incantations'), *pleasing poison* (7) all describe, in meta-
phorical terms, the potion mixed by Circe, in Ovid's account,
which is continued in lines 7–17. By the same means Comus,
the tempter, transforms humans to beasts: chiefly the count-
enance, in which reason (the soul) is mirrored. *Unmoulding
reasons mintage/ Character'd in the face* (10 and 11) is a typical
Miltonic periphrasis, a series of metaphors derived from the
plastic arts. *Stabl'd wolves* (15) is a recollection of Vergil,
Eclogues, III.80. *Hecate* (16), originally a moon deity, became
the goddess of sorcery and the Underworld, and the reference
here is to Ovid, *Metamorphoses* XIV, 405. Milton used many
past participles in their Latin sense, e.g. *abhorréd* (16) for
'malignant', 'wicked', and *obscuréd* (17) for 'unseen', 'secret'.

In lines 18–20 Milton pleonastically insists on the relation
of lust with deception, cf. *baits, guilefull, inveigle, unwary,
unweeting*. In this kind of rhetorical emphasis he is most skilful.
The metaphors inspired by Nature, *bank/ With Ivy canopied*
(25) and *flaunting Hony-suckle* (26), are personal rather than
visual. So is the oxymoron *'Wrapt in a pleasing fit of melancholy'*
(meaning 'reverie' rather than 'sadness'). *By then* (21) is a
poetical compression of 'by the time when'; *meditate* (28)
means 'practise', a verb borrowed from Vergil, *Eclogues* I.2;
and *close* (29) signifies 'musical cadence'.

The complex conceit in lines 34–5 contains two references to
Shakespeare: *2 Henry VI*, IV.1.3–6 and *Macbeth* II.1.51. All
printed versions of *Comus* have *drowsie frighted*, which is
preferred in the Darbishire edition of Milton; but the Bridge-
water MS has *flighted*. Shakespeare's lines are

> And now loud houling Wolves arouse the Iades
> That dragge the Tragicke melancholy night:
> Who with their drowsie, slow, and flagging wings
> Cleape dead-mens graves.

Curtain'd sleep (35) is an image in *Romeo and Juliet* as well as
Macbeth. The artifice is carried further: a solemn *sound* (the
lady's song) is likened to *'a steam of rich distill'd Perfumes'*.
Silence (personified) is ravished by it, and wishes never to be
her self again, so seductive is the sound's pleasure. The train
of conceits is characteristic, not only of Milton's allusive
image-making, but of his delight in the natural passions. He

tends to personify, rather than to keep his eye on the objects of nature.

As the passage is narrative and descriptive, very little use is made of rhetorical effects, even repetition (e.g. 13, *night* by *night*). Metaplasms in Milton's blank verse are prominent devices in guiding versification, e.g.

12   *i'th* hilly crofts
19   To inveigle and invite *th'*unwary sense (N.B. elision is unmarked in *To*)
22   Had *ta'n* their supper

Of no allegory can it be said with greater truth than of *Comus* that the poem is an extended metaphor. The figurative language has certain features peculiar to the masque. In such pictorial imagery as one finds, there is little concreteness, because the theme represents a conflict, as well as a contrast, between abstract virtues and vices. This is a reason why the characters in a masque are static.

Light and *water*, symbols of spiritual illumination and purification, are motivating forces in *Comus*. Because of traditional association, symbolism clarifies, but ambiguity obscures. Ambiguity in Milton is like that of his forebears: it sometimes arises from grafting Christian ideals upon pagan, mythological concepts.

Comus was described by Charles Williams as 'a kind of philosophical ballet' (Introd. to *English Poems of John Milton*, OUP, 1940); it was also a rudimentary form of opera. The Attendant Spirit has more of Prospero than Ariel in his disposition, and he has the magician's love of pageantry and fantasy. Because of the adolescence of the performers, doctrinal morality could not be stressed. The Elder Brother's disquisition on virtue speaks directly from Plato's *Phaedo*; but there is more of mythological naturalism than allegory in the characters. The Puritan in Milton made this inevitable.

Lycidas

The publication in 1638 of *Obsequies to the Memory of Mr Edward King*, in which *Lycidas* first appeared, was occasioned by the untimely drowning of King off the coast of North Wales in August 1637. King was a young Fellow of Christ's College, Cambridge; but there is no evidence that he was as close a friend of Milton as was Diodati, for whom he wrote the *Epitaphium Damonis* (1638). The invitation to contribute was honoured by Milton in November 1637 and a few improvements were added when the elegy was reprinted in 1645. The poem was correctly described as a Monody, or personal lyric; its irregular pattern of rhymed and unrhymed pentameters, with occasional trimeters, owes most to Italian *canzoni*. The only English funeral ode like it was the November Eclogue of Spenser's *Shepheardes Calender*.

In Greek, the elegiac poems of the Ionians were in dactylic couplets consisting of an hexameter, followed by a pentameter, and they were accompanied by the music of a flute, in keeping with their pastoral setting, the grazing hills of Lydia. But the original elegies were not confined to dirges. Milton's convention is in line with the idylls of Theocritus, Bion and Moschus, especially their funeral poems over Daphnis, Adonis and Bion. These elegists used the patterns of the later Alexandrian school, tastefully adapted in Latin by Tibullus, Ovid and Vergil of the Eclogues, whose diction Milton emulates. The doyen of the artificial school of lyrists in Alexandria (founded 332 B.C.) was a librarian, Callimachus, whose poetry was literary, affected and bookish. Theocritus (born 315 B.C.), though of Dorian origin, was a native of Syracuse living amid the scenes and sounds of nature. He used the Doric dialect of Greek (see *Lycidas* line 189) and he sang of Sicilian shepherds and goat-herds on the slopes of Mt Etna, among them Thyrsis, Corydon, and Lycidas, who figures in his seventh Idyll as the chief of flute-players. The name appears again in the second Idyll of Bion and the ninth Eclogue of Vergil.

Theocritus and Vergil were an inspiration rather than a model for Milton, who was a poet of independence and originality. Like Vergil, he graduated through the pastoral convention to a sensibility for epic diction. *Lycidas* was a new conception, an advance in craftsmanship, and a step in the evolution of the Miltonic pentameter line. The craft lies in the integration of linear structure with verse paragraphs. There are eleven paragraphs in the 193 lines of the elegy, of which the shortest is the last of 8 lines, in formal *ottava rima*. In all, there are ten unrhymed lines, and a further 13 that contain only six syllables. The sporadic rhyme marks a determination to break with stanzaic forms. Milton's ambition was to extend the classical tradition, not to imitate it. The verse of *Lycidas* anticipates the choric odes of *Samson Agonistes*.

The title of the poem was probably suggested by a passage in the seventh Idyll of Theocritus, the scene of which is laid in the island of Cos, which the poet had visited. In this poem Lycidas opens his song to Simichidas (Theocritus himself) with a petition for a fair voyage for Ageanax to Mytilene:

> The south wind chases the *wet waves*, when Orion held his feet above the Ocean. . . . The halcyons will lull the waves, and the south wind and east, that stirs the sea-weed on the farthest *shores*, they that are dearest to the *green-haired mermaids*, of all the *birds that take their prey* from the *salt sea*.

This mythological language has the spirit of make-believe of Milton's elegy, which dwells much upon death by water and images of the sea:

> He must not flote upon his *watry* bear
> Unwept, and welter to the *parching wind* . . .
> Where were ye *Nymphs* when the *remorseless deep*
> Clos'd o're the head of your lov'd Lycidas? . . .
> His goary visage down the *stream* was sent,
> Down the swift Hebrus to the Lesbian shore . . .
> But now my Oate proceeds,
> And listens to the *Herald of the Sea*
> That came in *Neptune's plea*,
> He ask'd the *Waves*, and ask'd the *Fellon winds*,
> What hard mishap hath doom'd this gentle swain?
> And question'd every *gust of rugged wings*
> That blows from off each beaked Promontory . . .

Milton is richer, fuller and poetically more passionate than Theocritus, though he clings to the traditional epithets and images: *watry bear*, *parching wind*, *remorseless deep*, *goary visage*, *gentle swain*. Milton's periphrases for the destroying sea are brilliantly resourceful, and so are the resonant words and phrases *welter*, *Fellon winds*, *rugged wings* and *beakèd Promontory*. Milton was moved by the musical associations and sympathetic spirit of nature in the pastoral originals, and turned their artifice into a climactic diction. As Rosamund Tuve has said, *Lycidas* is also 'a lament for the death of Poetry'

(*Images and Themes in Five Poems by Milton*, Harvard UP, 1967, p. 93).

It is essential to an understanding of *Lycidas* to be acquainted with its literary background. The pastoral machinery is a key to the poem's emotional impact; and some hold the elegy to be the greatest of its kind, enshrining what is best in a long tradition. The style, not the depth of Milton's personal feelings, gives the poem unity. The tripartite division of the poem is worth noting:

Lines 1–84. Lycidas, the poet-shepherd, is dead before his prime. There is universal lament, in which pastoral nature joins. The linking passage (70–84) is a disquisition of Fame, which shows the futility of earthly ambition.

Lines 85–131. Lycidas is also a priest-shepherd, the servant of the Church. All the guardian spirits of the waters are questioned about his death. Peter comes last and laments the loss of so promising a priest. He then denounces, in simple colloquial language, the corrupt Church of the time (113–31), and speaks of divine retribution. This passage links the second to the third part.

Lines 132–85. The pastoral deities are recalled. The death-bed of Lycidas is to be decked with flowers of the valleys, and the poet pictures him floating on the waves beyond the coasts of Britain. In 165–85 Lycidas is in Heaven with the Saints and angelic choirs, redeemed by the blood of the Lamb, as in the Book of Revelation.

Nature symbolism, especially the pathetic response of flowers, trees and plants, is significant throughout the poem for the poet's moods of grief and re-assurance. Each section begins with an invocation in the manner of Theocritus or Vergil. The first is to the Laurels and Myrtles of a poet's crown; the second and third to deities of fountains or rivers in Sicily, Italy and Greece (Arethusa, Mincius and Alpheus). Arethusa, a nymph of Elis and attendant on Artemis (Diana), bathed in the river Alpheus, and the fable tells how the god of the stream fell in love with her. With the aid of Artemis, she was conveyed under the sea to the island of Ortygia, off Syracuse, and there became a fountain. It was on the banks of the Mincius, near Mantua, that Vergil was born.

A convention of the classical elegy holds that the premature

death of an honoured human must be unnatural. By line 165, if
not before, it is clear that the meaning of *Lycidas* is not to be
sought in the death of King, but in the faith Milton shared
with Orpheus in the power of his art. He had come to believe
in the capacity of poetry to transform an unhappy world into
a stoical retreat for the inconsolable. A strain of saintliness in
suffering runs through all the later heroic poems of Milton.
Poetry confers on the Christian humanist a freedom that no
earthly recompense can equal, and this triumph is celebrated in
the rhythmic virtuosity of *Lycidas*. Willingness to digress into
moral or denunciatory prophecy is a sign of maturity demon-
strated in the work of Theocritus, Ovid and Vergil. The right
to protest arises from a sense of 'bitter constraint'.

Lycidas is the culmination of a kind of artifice, which the
Renaissance encouraged. 'The true meaning is so uncertain and
remote', said Johnson, 'that it is never sought'; but Walter
Raleigh's *Milton* (Arnold, 1900), and numerous studies since,
have cleared up most of Johnson's semantic uncertainties.

The distinction between Milton's language and style is
stated by Emma (*Milton's Grammar*, pp. 20 and 67–8):

> My investigation finds Milton surprisingly 'modern' in his language
> at the same time that he prolongs in it, as in his intellectual assurance,
> the capacious, many-detailed 'basic simplicity and strength' of the
> Elizabethans . . . Milton's extensive use of descriptive adjectives may
> be said to mark him as a poet of qualification more than of predication:
> one who prefers words that qualify and describe to those that express
> action. Comparative studies show that Milton is, in fact, more
> concerned with qualification by adjectives than any major NE poet
> who precedes him except Spenser; but the observation is perhaps
> oversimple. Milton's resemblance to Spenser in the extent to which he
> uses adjectives should not be allowed to conceal fundamental differences
> in the manner in which the two men use them. Milton's practice . . . is
> less baroque, his manner more functional and economical . . . Unlike
> Spenser, he seldom piles up adjectives in a single line . . .

Lycidas 132–85

Return Alpheus, the dread voice is past,
That shrunk thy streams; Return Sicilian Muse,
And call the Vales, and bid them hither cast
Their Bels, and Flourets of a thousand hues.
Ye valleys low where the milde whispers use,   5
Of shades and wanton winds, and gushing brooks,

On whose fresh lap the swart Star sparely looks,
Throw hither all you quaint enameld eyes,
That on the green terf suck the honied showres,
And purple all the ground with vernal flowres.   10
Bring the rathe Primrose that forsaken dies.
The tufted Crow-toe, and pale Gessamine,
The white Pink, and the Pansie freakt with jeat,
The glowing Violet.
The Musk-rose, and the well attir'd Woodbine,   15
With Cowslips wan that hang the pensive hed,
And every flower that sad embroidery wears:
Bid Amaranthus all his beauty shed,
And Daffadillies fill their cups with tears,
To strew the Laureat Herse where Lycid lies.   20
For so to interpose a little ease,
Let our frail thoughts dally with false surmise.
Ay me! Whilst thee the shores, and sounding Seas
Wash far away, where ere thy bones are hurld,
Whether beyond the stormy Hebrides,   25
Where thou perhaps under the whelming tide
Visit'st the bottom of the monstrous world;
Or whether thou to our moist vows deny'd,
Sleep'st by the fable of Bellerus old,
Where the great vision of the guarded Mount   30
Looks toward Namancos and Bayona's hold:
Look homeward Angel now, and melt with ruth.
And, O ye Dolphins, waft the haples youth.
    Weep no more, woful Shepherds weep no more,
For Lycidas your sorrow is not dead,   35
Sunk though he be beneath the watry floar,
So sinks the day-star in the Ocean bed,
And yet anon repairs his drooping head,
And tricks his beams, and with new spangled Ore,
Flames in the forehead of the morning sky: 40
So Lycidas sunk low, but mounted high,
Through the dear might of him that walk'd the waves
Where other groves, and other streams along,
With Nectar pure his oozy Lock's he laves,
And hears the unexpressive nuptiall Song,   45
In the blest Kingdoms meek of joy and love.
There entertain him all the Saints above,
In solemn troops, and sweet Societies
That sing, and singing in their glory move,
And wipe the tears for ever from his eyes.   50
Now Lycidas the Shepherds weep no more;
Hence forth thou art the Genius of the shore,
In thy large recompense, and shalt be good
To all that wander in that perilous flood.

This is from the last section of *Lycidas*, and has three different themes: the pastoral, the fabulous and the religious. Resounding proper names help to make musical the roving imagination: *Alpheus*, *Amaranthus* (a flower of the Greek classics symbolizing immortality), *Hebrides*, *Bellerus* (a name Milton invented, from Bellerium, an old name for Land's End), *Namancos*, *Bayona*.

Milton's use of the multiple qualifier is not distinguished from compound epithets, and there is uncertainty (perhaps the printer's) in the use of hyphens, as in *well attir'd Woodbine* (15) and *new spangled Ore* (39).

Word choice aims at idealization and decorum. As Bernard Groom observes:

> The words are subordinate to the melodious surge of the great paragraphs ... Milton does not describe, but name. In description, language should appear fresh and new, in naming, it should appear old and mellow.
>
> (*The Diction of Poetry*, pp. 78–9)

Milton's epithets comprise more than 17 per cent of his vocabulary. Their use therefore calls for closer scrutiny:

Swart Star: Sirius, the Dog-Star, brightest in the heavens, so-called because it is in the constellation *Canis Major*. The rural year of Egypt was calculated by the rising of Sirius, as it emerged from the sun's rays and became visible before sunrise. In the Mediterranean this usually coincided with a period of oppressive heat, and consequent tanning of the human skin. *Swart* here means 'blackening'; the word became archaic and poetical in the seventeenth century, when the adjective *black* replaced it in common use. For Milton the adjective *swart* had overtones and associations.

Enameld eyes: This poeticism, made current by Marlowe in *Hero and Leander* (see Chap. V) and Milton in *Arcades*, lasted until the nineteenth century. Originally a prosaic French borrowing, it was employed also by Shakespeare. Purchas used it in the Miltonic sense in his *Pilgrimage* (1621). *Honied showres:* The conceit is in the pair of lines 9–10:

> Throw hither all your quaint enameld *eyes*,
> That on the green terf *suck* the *honied showres*

Brooks and Hardy in *Poems of Mr John Milton* (Harcourt Brace, 1957, p. 181) make the interesting suggestion that 'eyes that suck' balances the earlier 'blind mouthes'. *Honied* is associated with the bee; the anomaly of the conceit is that the flowers are fed rather than feeding.

Vernal flowers: The word *vernal* ('of the spring') was borrowed from Latin by Sir Thomas More in reference to the Equinox. Most uses in the OED are scientific; as a poetic word it is rarely found after the eighteenth century. It was first used by Beaumont and Fletcher in *The Maid's Tragedy* (1611); then by Crashaw, Milton, Prior and Gray. There are further examples in *An Epitaph* and *Samson Agonistes*.

Rathe Primrose: Rathe, from OE *hræd* 'quick', was uncommon before 1400. Meaning 'early', it was used by Drayton in *The Tragical Legend of Robert Duke of Normandy* (1596). Referring to premature flowers and fruits, it appeared in *England's Helicon* (1600), but the poeticism was undoubtedly popularized by Milton's use in *Lycidas*. The word was unknown to Shakespeare, but it is still heard in dialect.

Pansie freakt with jeat: The verb *freak* 'capriciously variegated' was coined by Milton, perpetuated by Thomson in *The Seasons* and repeated by Swinburne.

Sad embroidery: C. S. Lewis in *Studies in Words* (CUP, 1960, pp. 75–85) has shown that *sad* from O.Norse *saddr* originally meant 'gorged', 'sated'; it is related to Latin *satur*. The word assimilated a number of other meanings from Latin words, for which the English equivalents are *grave, composed, pensive,* etc. *Sad embroidery* is an instance of Ruskin's 'pathetic fallacy' (Vol. III, part 4, *Modern Painters*). Flowers are pictured by Milton as wearing mourning colours in sympathy with Lycidas; cf. *sad habiliments* in Spenser, *Faerie Queene* I.12.5.

Laureat Herse: The epithet means 'crowned with laurel', the emblem of distinction among the Greeks and Romans. Milton dallies 'with false surmise' in this flower passage, as well as in the next paragraph, since the drowned poet could have no 'hearse'. The poet probably had in mind Spenser's November Eclogue, where the word, a symbol of death, is used in the refrain of each stanza. *Laureat* is an epithet appropriate to the melody, secured by alliteration and assonance in *Lycid lies* (20).

Whelming tide: The present participle is from OE *hwelman* 'to overturn'. In the sense of 'destroy by drowning' the word was not much employed in poetry until the sixteenth century. It became overworked as a poeticism by Milton, Dryden and the Augustans.

Moist vows: W. P. Ker points out (*Form and Style in Poetry*, pp. 163–4) that *vows* is used by Milton as the equivalent of Latin *vota* (prayers). *Moist* is another example of the pathetic fallacy, signifying 'tears of lamentation'. Ker continues: 'The art of poetic music is such that the artifice in no way hinders the pure lyric effect. What one gets from it . . . is the mood of sorrow.'

New spangled Ore: Apollo being the god of poetry, Lycidas is compared to the setting sun (called by Joshua Sylvester the '*day*-star'), which rises again with renewed brightness. *Spangles* were small discs of metal used to decorate textiles; the noun was first used by Lydgate in his *Assembly of Gods*, and the verb (from German *spangeln*) by Hall in his *Chronicles*. In both forms the word was used by Sylvester in his translation of Du Bartas's *Divine Weeks and Works*, by Drummond, Shakespeare and other late sixteenth century poets. The image in *Lycidas* pictures the sun-god as deflecting beams from his forehead, adorned with precious metal.

Unexpressive nuptiall song: The nuptiall song was the hymn sung at the marriage supper of the Lamb, in Revelation XXI.4, where the promise is given that there will be no more death or sorrow. The *lamb* was the symbol used by John the Baptist for Christ, this animal being the commonest sacrifice of the Jews to God. In Revelation, Christ is represented as the bridegroom and the Church as the bride. *Unexpressive*, in Milton's phrase, means 'inexpressible'; joy will be infinite, and therefore indescribable in human terms.

The decorous use of poeticisms is nowhere better illustrated than in *Lycidas*, e.g. *Muse* (1), *Flourets* (3), *purple* (10, verb), *Daffadillies* (19), *ruth* (32), *waft* (33), *tricks* (39, verb), *groves* (43), *Nectar* (44), *laves* (44). The phrase *melt with ruth* is found both in Chaucer's *Troilus and Criseyde* and Spenser's *Faerie Queene*. The adjectives are of the conventional classical type made current by imitators of the sixteenth century, beginning with Surrey: *dread* voice (Lat. *dirus*), *milde* whispers (*lenis*), *wanton* winds (lascivus), *gushing* brooks (*effundens*), *quaint* . . . eyes (*lepidus*), *green* terf (*viridis*), *pale* Gessamine (*pallidus*), *glowing* Violet (*fervens*), Cowslips *wan* (*pallidus*),

pensive hed (*pendulus*), *false* surmise (*falsus*), *stormy* Hebrides
(*iratus*), *monstrous* world (probably from *monstra natanta*,
Horace, *Odes* I.3.18), Bellerus *old* (*antiquus*), *great* vision
(*magnus*), *woful* Shepherds (*tristis*), *watry* floar (*aquosus*),
drooping head (*languens*), *dear* might (*carus*), Nectar *pure*
(*purus*), *blest* Kingdoms (*beatus*), *solemn* troops (*sanctus*), *sweet*
Societies (*jocundus*), *large* recompense (*largus*), *perilous* flood
(*periculosus*).

Milton has often been blamed for trite classical names and
qualifiers, which were novel when he first used them, but
became commonplace in the hands of his neo-classical imitators
of the eighteenth century. He was never a close observer of
nature, and personified impressions to create a mood. Theo-
critus, Ovid, Horace and Vergil offered him adjectives long
associated with the myths that he loved to allegorize.

The versification of *Lycidas*, by standards other than John-
son's Augustan ones, was a triumph of deftness and harmony.
The freedom of unpremeditated rhyme, the clever use of short
lines (suggested by the Greek choric odes) agreed with the
musical intention of the Italian canzone, adapted to English by
Spenser. The rhymes, not usually separated by more than two
lines, have the impact of figures of rhetoric. The paragraph is
full of surprises, yet the movement has decorum, for Milton
paid most attention to the development of sense within the line.
There are only four enjambed lines 2, 26, 30 and 53.

Milton's metrical resources in *Lycidas* include the disposition
and diversification of internal pauses, and the delicate, restrained
insinuation of trisyllabic feet, as in 20 and 54. He is as sensitive
as Shakespeare in modulating the stresses by the use of spondees
and pyrrhic feet, e.g.

1 /Retúrn/ Alphé/us, the/ dréad voíce/ is pást/ (pause in middle of
                                                    third foot)
11 /Bríng the/ ráthe Prím/róse that/ forsá/ken diés/
15 /The Músk/-róse, and/ the wéll/ attír'd/ Woódbíne/ (pause in
                                                    middle of second foot)
22 /Let our/ fráil thoúghts/ dálly/ with false/ súrmíse/

Milton's syntax reveals a fondness for variation in the
position of qualifiers. The example of Latin verse led him to
favour the adjective in post-position, e.g. valleys *low* (5),
Cowslips *wan* (16), Bellerus *old* (29), Nectar *pure* (44). When

there are two qualifiers, he sometimes places one before and one after the noun, e.g. *blest* Kingdoms *meek* (46). Where possible, the relationship is marked by an opposed weighting of syllables: for instance, a monosyllabic adjective and disyllabic noun, or *vice versa*; e.g. *milde* whispers (5), *wanton* winds (6), *false* surmise (22), *sounding* Seas (23). Attributive participles are a feature of his style. There are 19 in this passage, and the weak past participles are preferred, because of the syllabic ambivalence of the *-ed* inflexion.

Inversions, known to rhetoric as *hyperbaton*, are frequent in Milton, as in most Renaissance poets well read in Latin verse; there are examples in lines 3, 7, 9, 17, 18, 23, 26, 28, 37, 39, 43, 44, 47 and 49. Deviations from normal syntax occur in nearly half the lines in *Lycidas*, an unusually high percentage. Often Milton employs defining relative clauses as larger qualifying groups, e.g. in 2, 9, 11, 16, 17, 42, 49. There are six *where*-clauses, some adjectival, others adverbial. Emma is thus justified in describing Milton as a poet of qualification, rather than of action or predication.

Despite his limited poetic vocabulary, Milton's sense compression makes him occasionally difficult:

> 5 Ye valleys low where the milde whispers *use* (= are wont to be found).

Sparely (7) means 'very seldom'; *purple* (10) suggests 'enrich with gay colour', for instance, that of the *Crow-toe* (wild hyacinth). *Fable* in 29 is a good example of thought condensation; 'Sleep'st by the *fable* of Bellerus old' suggests that the body of Lycidas may have come to rest near the shore of legendary Bellerium (Land's End). In the line

> For Lycidas your *sorrow* is not dead

sorrow means 'the one for whom you sorrow'.

Milton's choice of imagery, as a rule, is more homogeneous than Shakespeare's. Personification is the main source of visual imagery throughout the passage; the mythological subject matter lends itself to the scheme of thought, *prosopopoeia*. *Vision* (30) and *Angel* (32) refer to St Michael, said to have appeared to monks in their cells on the Mount. The tidal island was named after the Saint, and stood opposite Bayona, a Spanish fortress near Cape Finisterre, in the district of Namancos. St Michael became the guardian of Protestant England against Catholic Spain. In '*tricks* his beams' (an expressive phrase) the verb signifies 'to dress with a touch of artifice'; it was borrowed from French in the sixteenth century, and used by Milton in *Il Penseroso* (123).

Milton had an extensive, if not exact, knowledge of geography. The '*monstrous* world' (27) probably refers to sea-monsters that decorated seventeenth century maps, as in the atlases of Ortelius and Mercator. The bookishness of his images often comes from works on astronomy, alchemy, history and theology, especially Old Testament commentaries. Before blindness afflicted him, Milton read, and often translated from Hebrew, Aramaic and Syriac texts; his translations from the *Psalms* are thought to have had some influence on the freer verse of *Lycidas*.

Improvements in the text of *Lycidas* are important as evidence of Milton s self-criticism. Lines 11–19 were not in the original of the Trinity College manuscript; but on a separate sheet are penned two different insertions after 'vernal showres'. The first reads:

> Bring the rathe Primrose that *unwedded* dies,
> *Colouring the pale cheeke of uninjoyéd love,*
> *And that sad flower that strove*
> *To write his own woes on the vermeil grain;*
> *Next add Narcissus that still weeps in vain,*
> The woodbine and ye pancie freakt with jeat,
> The glowing Violet,
> The *cowslip* wan that *hangs his* pensive head;
> And every *bud* that *sorrows livery* wears,
> *Let* daffadillies fill their cups with tears.
> Bid Amaranthus all his *beauty* shed

The second series of corrections follows the text of 1645, adopted by Helen Darbishire, except for the following:

   (a) 15   *garish Columbine* for well *attir'd Woodbine*
         17   *escutcheon* for *embroidery*
         18   *beauties* for *beauty*
   (b) lines 18 and 19 are inverted.

There are improvements of equal significance in later lines. For '*frail* thoughts' (22) Milton's first choice was *sad*; for '*whelming* tide' (26) the original epithet was *humming*; and for *Bellerus* (29) the Trinity MS favoured *Corineus*, a legendary figure that was to re-appear in Milton's prose *History of Britain* (published 1670, but probably written by 1655).

All the changes must have been made for aesthetic reasons. The flower passage was an afterthought, and a worthy example of Miltonic ornament, in the spirit of Aristotle's *Poetics* and Alessandro Lionardi's *Dialogi della Inventione Poetica* (1554). Both critics condoned elaboration as a colourful means of enhancing the poet's design. The objection to Milton's original words (italicized) is mythological vagueness; no reference has been found for the fable that the primrose died *unwedded* or *forsaken*. Why should 'every bud' be dressed in the robes of *sorrow*, or the Columbine be 'garish' (an overworked poeticism)? J. C. Ransom's justification of Milton's procedure in *Lycidas* is interesting:

> *Lycidas* is a literary exercise; and so is almost any other poem earlier than the eighteenth century; the craftsmanship, the formal quality which is written on it, is meant to have high visibility. . . . For Lycidas he [Milton] mourns with a very technical piety.
> ('A Poem nearly Anonymous', *The American Review* I, 1933)

But for 'technical piety' *Lycidas* would not have become the poem Milton finally left. Yet Charles Lamb reacted typically to workshop evidence (*Life and Works*, ed. Ainger, New York, 1899, Vol. II, p. 300):

> I had thought of the Lycidas as of a full-grown beauty – as springing up with all its parts absolute – till, in an evil hour, I was shown the original copy of it . . . in the library of Trinity . . . How it staggered me to see the fine things in their ore! interlined, corrected! as if their words were mortal, alterable, displaceable at pleasure! . . . as if inspiration were made up of parts, and these fluctuating, successive, indifferent! I will never go into the workshop of any great artist again.

Schemes of words play a part in Milton's contractions and amplifications. Among the metaplasms, *Visit'st* (27) and *Sleep'st* (29) are examples of metrical *syncope*; *Lycid* (20) for *Lycidas* is an instance of *apocope*. The repetitive device *Weep no more* in 34 and 51 is known as *epimone*; poets used it with emotive effect in odes and elegies. In 36, 37 and 41 the verb *sink*, repeated in different grammatical forms, exemplifies *polyptoton*, while *sing, and singing* (49) is a use of *ploce*.

In schemes of thought Milton excels. *Ecphonesis* (exclamation expressing passions of the mind) is employed throughout the

poem, e.g. *Ay me!* (23), *O ye Dolphins* (33). The flower
passage (11–19) involves *merismos* (Lat. *distributio*), the listing
of kinds, with specific details. The colourful enumeration of
place-names 25–31 was known to classical rhetoricians as
topographia. The long simile in 37–40 is an instance of *chrono-
graphia*, delight in celebrating a fugitive period of time. Milton
was as meticulous as a painter in the particulars of his descrip-
tions: the figure *pragmatographia* emulates Spenser in lines
2–10 and 38–50.

Figures of rhetoric are not now regarded as significant for
Milton's art, but they reflected the Renaissance poet's respect
for formal structures, and they gave writers a sense of style.
Some figures were tonal, others syntactic: all were seen as
handmaids of decorum. In weaker hands, rhetorical patterning
often neglected the primacy of meaning, but in *Lycidas* the
figures were a source of strength. Among the English classical
poets, Milton, Dryden and Pope were the last to use rhetoric,
with varying success, to give tensile power to their versification.
Language of an intellectual cast calls for classical discipline,
and this Milton partly acquired through experimental composi-
tions in Latin and Italian.

The paradox of *Lycidas* is that originality is born of
eclecticism; emulation is transformed by passion into a work of
art. In spite of pastoral conventions, from Theocritus to
Spenser, the poem has individuality, visible in the care devoted
to the structure and diction of each line. The lines on ambition
are significant, as expressing Milton's aim to excel the work of
predecessors, even Vergil. Milton's designation of *Lycidas* as a
monody is just, for it has both the rapture of an ode and the
vehement voice of a Puritan revolutionary. The different strains
are unified by a sustained lyricism that controverts the charge
of pedantry. The poem accommodates itself, with ease, to the
narrative, dramatic and reflective moods.

K

X

PARADISE LOST AND SAMSON AGONISTES

Milton began to think of the theme of *Paradise Lost* as early as 1641, and sketched the plot of a tragedy 'Adam Unparadized'. The decision to produce the work as an epic was not reached until 1658. In the earlier books the design and arguments were cast in the dramatic mould, then transposed to narrative-heroic dialogue. Twenty-one years had elapsed since the writing of *Lycidas* before the work was ready for publication in 1667. During the Commonwealth he was occupied mainly with controversial prose.

Modern studies of Milton have concentrated on *Paradise Lost* for a good reason: it is the only English epic coherent, methodically planned, and meticulously finished. Milton was the Palladian architect of English poetry, the master of spatial magnificence. In *Paradise Lost* a universal mind, after long and dedicated reflection, realizes a national ambition, to give to English prestige through its poetry, to plan 'things unattempted yet in Prose or Rhime'. The measure of Milton's achievement is the matching of an austere, grand style with transcendent subject matter. It is a style charged with simile rather than metaphor, conceived for the myth of Creation, and unadaptable to works of punier imagination.

Milton's universe is a composite of Plato's *Timaeus*, Ovid's *Metamorphoses*, and the Book of Genesis. Man is endowed with the 'Sanctitie of Reason' (*P.L.* VII.508). The primacy of reason was the burden of most of Milton's pamphlets, in which he sharpened powers of forensic and persuasive eloquence. The finest of the debates are to be found in the first two books of *Paradise Lost*. Understanding of the Scriptures had deepened with experience, and Milton no longer saw the Fall of Man as a tragedy. The promise of redemption made it preferable to depict a moral struggle, rather than a catastrophe.

The *raison d'etre* of the epic, as Milton finally saw it, had to be a triumph of faith, even though it was at the expense of Platonic reason. Obedience is the core of faith, and forbidden knowledge the heresy that undermines it. Milton was not now motivated by personal feelings, as in *Lycidas*, but by symbolic events on a cosmic scale. The epic would fail, however, unless he could sustain its sublimity by 'adventurous song'. He framed the twenty-six-line invocation of the first book for 'the upright heart and pure', and to 'justify the ways of God to men'. The style was kept at that high level until the temptation scene in Book IX, when Adam and Eve sacrificed innocence for self-knowledge.

For Milton, as for most seventeenth century believers, literal truth of the Bible was final, and evidence of the senses suspect. The irony of Milton's situation was his theological individualism. Heretical convictions took shape in *De Doctrina Christiana*, which was completed about 1661, though it remained unpublished until 1825. Milton was not the man to shrink from upsetting a conscientious believer; but he was aware of his own doctrinal uncertainty. He tried to live down his early Christian Platonism, for Puritan intellectuals were on the side of scientific rationalism, and disbelieved in emblems, images and allegories. The theological inconsistencies of *Paradise Lost* were perceived by Richard Bentley, who drew attention to vagueness in certain parts of Milton's language. Critical misunderstandings arose from the inconvenience of treating a contentious biblical theme within the framework of the humanist tradition of epic.

Though Bentley was a classical scholar, he did not understand the style in which Milton wrote *Paradise Lost*. This is shown by unhappy attempts to improve the text, which he believed had been corrupted by the blind poet's amanuensis. The gravamen of his complaint was that Milton's syntax was disorderly in an indefensible way; that elements of long similes were irrelevant; and that the rhythm *sounded* imperfect on classical principles, especially those of Milton's master in epic, Vergil.

Milton's developed prose style was of great advantage to the structure of his blank verse. Emma, in *Milton's Grammar* (p. 140 et seq), shows that, in both verse and prose, Milton's sentence patterns are mainly paratactic and colloquial. Some notions are subservient to others, but the sense relationship favours the use of co-ordinating conjunctions, participles, infinitives, rather than finite verbs and subordinate clauses. Two of Emma's examples must suffice to illustrate this:

Comus 442–4:	she tam'd the *brinded* lioness/ *And spotted* mountain pard, *but* set at naught/ The frivolous bolt of Cupid
Par. Lost I. 50–6:	Nine times the Space that measures Day and Night/ To mortal men, he with his horrid crew/ Lay *vanquisht, rowling* in the fiery Gulfe/ *Confounded* though immortal: *But* his doom/ Reserv'd him to more wrath; *for* now the thought/ Both of *lost* happiness *and lasting* pain/ Torments him

The fluid, cumulative effect of the verse recalls Vergil's *Aeneid*, but the syntax, except in the placing of adjectives after substantives, and the emphatic location of verbs, is unlike that of Latin.

In the blank verse of *Paradise Lost*, the line to line development is adapted to the larger structure of the verse paragraph. Milton describes the method as 'the sense variously drawn out from one verse into another', but enjambement is not the only factor to consider. The progress of Miltonic lines is by 'feeling sensed', rather than by logical communication. As sentences are long (an average of 31 words, says Emma), the phrasing has to diffuse and continue the sense, while finding sounds that satisfy the ear. The surface texture is rugged, yet the style is elaborate, the adjectives outnumbering the verbs. In England the experiment met with a mixed reception, but the results were far-reaching in France, Italy and Germany. Critics in Europe recognized a poet of greater universality than the metaphysicals, and of the same lineage as Homer and Vergil. (See J. G. Robertson's 'Milton's Fame on the Continent', *Proceedings of the British Academy*, VIII, 1908).

As the actor-critic is the most reliable interpreter of Shakespeare, the receptive critic has the most sensitive taste for Milton. *Paradise Lost* should be read *in extenso*, with a trained ear for cumulative rhythm. Milton of the epics relies less than Spenser on the illuminating metaphor. His skill lies in expansive, homely and re-assuring similes, the most evocative of which occur in the narrative parts, not the dramatic, and they are indispensable to the Miltonic technique.

'To write poetry . . . with nothing poetic about it, poetry

standing naked in its bare bones' was T. S. Eliot's ambition, but not Milton's. The later books of *Paradise Lost* are reflective and Hebraic in temper, and they called for serener treatment. Several strata of diction are discernible in the epic, as will appear from different extracts. The first is from Book I, where Milton describes Mammon and the smelting of ore from the Earth; gold, the 'precious bane', was mined in Milton's Hell. What follows is an architect's dream of an Olympian temple:

> As in an Organ from one blast of wind
> To many a row of Pipes the sound-board breaths.
> Anon out of the earth a Fabrick huge
> Rose like an Exhalation, with the sound
> Of Dulcet Symphonies and voices sweet,   5
> Built like a Temple, where Pilasters round
> Were set, and Doric pillars overlaid
> With Golden Architrave; nor did there want
> Cornice or Freeze, with bossy Sculptures grav'n,
> The Roof was fretted Gold. Not Babilon,   10
> Nor great Alcairo such magnificence
> Equal'd in all their glories, to inshrine
> Belus or Serapis thir Gods, or seat
> Thir Kings, when Aegypt with Assyria strove
> In wealth and luxurie.   15
>
> (lines 708–22)

As Arnold Stein points out, Milton 'is under no more compulsion to try to get beyond poetry than Bach to get beyond music'. (*Answerable Style*, Washington U.P., 1953, p. 139). At this stage the highest art for Milton was to fit the word and the rhythm to the sensuous impression.

In mythology, not only this temple, Pandaemonium, but cities such as Thebes and Troy, were created to the harmony of music. Milton had in mind Ovid's accounts of palaces of the gods in *Metamorphoses*, I, 171–2 and IV, 762–4 – that figure of allusion which rhetoric classified as *topothesia*. What more sublime for such a creation than the voice of the organ? His father, an accomplished musician and composer, had taught him to play this instrument. 'The sound-board breath's' (2) is a personal metaphor that enhances the simile of the opening lines; it links up with *Exhalations* (4) ('vapour') a word used by Gower in *Confessio Amantis*. *Fabrick* (3) for 'building' (a product of skill) was a French borrowing of Caxton, but the word did not come into use for textiles until the eighteenth

century; *symphony* meant simply 'a concord of sweet sounds'.
Dulcet ('pleasant sounding'), a French loan-word of the
fifteenth century, became a poeticism only in the seventeenth.
Pilasters (6), a loan-word from Italian architecture, were
square, built-in pillars, but the word was loosely used also for
round ones. Other architectural terms, *Doric pillars* (7),
Architrave (8), *Cornice* and *Freeze* (9), the last two probably
borrowed from Sylvester's *Eden* (518–19), have no descriptive
precision; they are words of sonantal value, paralleled by the
place-names *Babilon*, *Alcairo*, *Aegypt* and *Assyria* (10–14), and
the gods *Belus* (Baal) (whose temple in Babylon was described
by Herodotus) and *Serapis*, the name of Osiris when King of
the nether regions. The effect of the catalogue is *wealth and
luxurie* (15). The architect mentioned is Mulciber, the Roman
name for Hephaestus, legendary builder of the temples of
Olympus. Milton's interest in the baroque may derive from his
appreciative viewing of Bernini's work in St Peter's, Rome.

The purpose of blank-verse syntax may be usefully explored
in a paragraph that would have been described by Bentley as
'disorderly': —

Book IV, 393–410

So spake the Fiend, and with necessitie,
The Tyrants plea, excus'd his devilish deeds.
Then from his loftie stand on that high Tree
Down he alights among the sportful Herd
Of those fourfooted kindes, himself now one,   5
Now other, as thir shape servd best his end
Neerer to view his prey, and unespi'd
To mark what of thir state he more might learn
By word or action markt: about them round
A Lion now he stalkes with fierie glare,   10
Then as a Tyger, who by chance hath spi'd
In some Purlieu two gentle Fawnes at play,
Strait couches close, then rising changes oft
His couchant watch, as one who chose his ground
Whence rushing he might surest seize them both   15
Grip't in each paw: When Adam first of men
To first of women Eve thus moving speech,
Turnd him all eare to hear new utterance flow.

Had Milton lived a hundred years later, he could hardly have written in this style, but normality appears in historical perspective. The order of words might not have seemed libertine to a Jacobean poet, but to an Augustan like Dr Johnson, the expression is 'so far removed from common use, that an unlearned reader ... finds himself surprised by a new language'. Here is Milton's paragraph in normalized syntax:

> The fiend spoke thus, excusing devilish deeds
> With false necessity, the tyrant's plea.
> Then from his lofty place on that high tree
> He swiftly drops among the sportive herd
> Of four-limbed beasts, which he by choice resembled,
> Taking each shape as best might serve his end.
> Watching his prey with stealth, all unsuspected,
> He studies natures that he seeks to know
> Either through word or action. Round he stalks,
> First as a lion with glaring fiery gaze,
> Then as a tiger, that by chance has spied
> Two gentle fawns at play in some close glade;
> At once he'll crouch low down, then rise again
> And eye them keenly, like one who chooses ground
> From which to pounce and seize them unperceived,
> One in each paw. In such a way the fiend
> Turned his sharp ear to hear our father Adam
> Discourse with Eve, the first made of earth's women.

The paraphrase may be clearly perceived, but it does not achieve the poetic momentum of Milton's verse paragraph. Grasping Milton's intentions means understanding the function of prosody in his rhetoric, and so sensing the tempo of the modulations. The punctuation of the second edition of *Paradise Lost*, based on Milton s instructions, is of the first importance, as Helen Darbishire has shown (*The Poetical Works of John Milton*, Clarendon, 1952, Vol. I, pp. ix–xxi):

> Edward Phillips writes that during the composition of *Paradise Lost* Milton submitted to him from time to time 'a parcel of ten, twenty or thirty lines which ... *might want correction as to orthography or pointing*'.... No one who has studied the first or second edition of *Paradise Lost* can doubt that punctuation was important to Milton. The music and meaning of his long metrical paragraphs depended on a close interlocking of grammatical construction with metre. A delicate adjustment of stops was needed, to mark at once the right articulation of his sentence and the due degrees of metrical pause. ...
> The semicolon is a somewhat lighter stop and seems in Milton's use to mark steps in a process, successive events, or to separate items in a

catalogue, or groups arranged in sequence. The functions of colon and semicolon are closely allied; the main difference seems to be that the semicolon implies continuity of movement, the colon an arrest, a stepping aside, something staccato. . . . The comma is used in the modern way; but it is generally omitted before a relative clause with restrictive or defining function.

In a modernized version, such as the above paraphrase, the stops have to be more frequent and of longer value. There are three full-stops and a semicolon, where Milton had one full stop and two colons. Milton's ten inversions of word order, involving the subject-predicate-object relationship, as well as the place of adverbs and adverbial phrases, were designed to make the sense flow unimpeded, until the final periphrasis, *utterance flow*, is reached. Critics have found that one source of Milton's ambiguity is his double syntax, the use of a word or phrase with alternative functions, citing line 18 as an instance:

> Turned *him* all eare to hear new utterance flow

In the modernization, I have taken *fiend* in line 1 as the subject of *Turnd*, and *him* (referring to Adam) as an ethic dative, not as a personal pronoun used reflexively. Darbishire seems mistaken in her note (p. 296), when she says 'it is Eve who is all ear'.

When Satan assumes the shape of a lion (9–10), the rhetorical figure is *comparatio;* but in the tiger image (11–16) the force is that of *simile*, the 'gentle Fawnes' being Adam and Eve. Johnson's complaint that Milton 'expands the adventitious image beyond the dimensions which the occasion required', is understandable.

The later books of *Paradise Lost* are less spectacular; the passage for analysis shows Milton in a mood less opulent, but still individual in his syntactical arrangements. But for 22 inversions of word order, the blank verse would approach that of Wordsworth's *Prelude:*

Book *VIII*, 249–99

So spake the Godlike Power, and thus our Sire.
For Man to tell how human Life began
Is hard; for who himself beginning knew?

Desire with thee still longer to converse
Induc'd me. As new wak't from soundest sleep   5
Soft on the flourie herb I found me laid
In Balmie Sweat, which with his Beames the Sun
Soon dri'd, and on the reaking moisture fed.
Strait toward Heav'n my wondring Eyes I turnd,
And gaz'd a while the ample Skie, till rais'd   10
By quick instinctive motion up I sprung,
As thitherward endevoring, and upright
Stood on my feet; about me round I saw
Hill, Dale, and shadie Woods, and sunnie Plaines,
And liquid Lapse of murmuring Streams; by these,   15
Creatures that livd, and movd, and walk'd, or flew,
Birds on the branches warbling; all things smil'd,
With fragrance and with joy my heart oreflow'd.
My self I then perus'd, and Limb by Limb
Survey'd, and sometimes went, and sometimes ran   20
With supple joints, as lively vigour led:
But who I was, or where, or from what cause,
Knew not; to speak I tri'd, and forthwith spake,
My Tongue obey'd and readily could name
What e're I saw. Thou Sun, said I, faire Light,   25
And thou enlight'nd Earth, so fresh and gay,
Ye Hills and Dales, ye Rivers, Woods, and Plaines,
And ye that live and move, faire Creatures, tell,
Tell, if ye saw, how came I thus, how here?
Not of my self; by some great Maker then,   30
In goodness and in power præeminent;
Tell me, how may I know him, how adore,
From whom I have that thus I move and live,
And feel that I am happier then I know.
While thus I call'd, and stray'd I knew not whither,   35
From where I first drew Aire, and first beheld
This happie Light, when answer none return'd,
On a green shadie Bank profuse of Flours
Pensive I sate me down; there gentle sleep
First found me, and with soft oppression seis'd   40
My droused sense, untroubl'd, though I thought
I then was passing to my former state
Insensible, and forthwith to dissolve:
When suddenly stood at my Head a dream,
Whose inward apparition gently mov'd   45
My fancy to believe I yet had being,
And livd: One came, methought, of shape Divine,
And said, thy Mansion wants thee, Adam, rise,
First Man, of Men innumerable ordain'd
First Father, call'd by thee I come thy Guide   50
To the Garden of bliss, thy seat prepar'd.

The *Godlike Power* (1) is Raphael, 'the sociable Spirit', whom God had sent to be Adam's guide, interpreter and adviser, a role important enough to occupy four books (V to VIII). (It should be remembered that the first edition of *Paradise Lost* contained only ten books, which Milton expanded to twelve in the second edition of 1674). A baroque work is many-sided, and in the later books Milton speaks with the voices of both Raphael and Adam. Adam is curious to know God's reasons. In this scene he explains to Raphael his first sensations and experiences on Earth.

The decorative use of compound epithets and mythological allusion is less noticeable in this passage. Wordsworth pleaded for the language of ordinary men in poetry, and Milton uses it sporadically in the latter part of *Paradise Lost*. The authentic vocabulary is, however, noted in such phrases as *flourie herb* (6), *Balmie sweat* (7), *gaz'd* (10 – the verb used transitively), *thitherward* (12), *liquid Lapse* (15), *warbling* (17) and *methought* (47). Vigour of phrase is at its best in *reaking* moisture (8), for the sun's evaporation, *enlight'nd* Earth (26, an epithet Empsonian in its ambiguity), and power *præeminent* (31). Generalized epithets, however, outnumber these: *wondring* Eyes (9), *ample* Skie (10), *instinctive* motion (11), *shadie* woods and *sunnie* Plaines (14), *murmuring* Streams (15), *supple* joints and *lively* vigour (21), *faire* Light (25), Earth so *freshe* and *gay* (26, reminiscent of Chaucer), *happie* Light (37), *green*, *shadie* Bank *profuse* (38), *gentle* sleep (39), *soft* oppression (40, a Miltonic oxymoron), *droused* sense (41), state *Insensible* (43), shape *Divine* (47), Men *innumerable* (49). Vergil, the universal, is in these qualifiers, which were classically congenial to epic poetry. For Milton they carried associations of Italian Renaissance art, in the spirit of which Milton's Eden was written. The aim was not surprise, but decorous colour and sensuous profusion.

Milton s paragraph, of which this is less than half, has the usual enjambement; but there are only 18 run-on lines, slightly higher than a third, in the passage selected. This is less than the average for *Paradise Lost*, and considerably lower than the enjambement rate in Shakespeare's last plays. The punctuation seems to have been influenced by Milton's compositional design, since it aids the rhythm rather than the line of thought.

The forward-looking rhythmical phrasing is dynamic, without obscuring the pentameter structure of the individual line, e.g.

/Desire/ with thee/ still long/er to/ converse/	5 stresses
/Induc'd/ me. As/ new wak't/ from soun/dest sleep/	5 ,,
/Soft on/ the flou/rie herb/ I found/ me laid/	5 ,,
/In Bal/mie Sweat,/ which with/ his Beames/ the Sun/	4 ,,
/Soon dri'd,/ and on/ the rea/king mois/ture fed/ . . .	5 ,,
/And said,/ thy Man/sion wants/ thee, A/dam, rise,/	5 ,,
/First Man,/ of Men/ innu/merable/ ordain'd/	5 ,,
/First Fa/ther, call'd/ by thee/ I come/ to Guide	6 ,,
/To thee/ Garden/ of bliss,/ thy seat/ prepar'd/	4 ,,

Modulation is through the disposition of primary stresses, unusual lines being the last two. The disjunctive tendency in the rhythm is produced mainly by medial pauses; but when this takes place, the line following is invariably orthodox, with the pentameter emphasized by monosyllabic terminals.

Milton used few of the feminine endings common in Shakespeare's last plays, and their effect is to impede a continuous rhythm. Four of the above nine lines begin with stressed syllables. The metrical pattern is thus firmly established.

It is not often that the flowing rhythm exceeds ten stresses without punctuational pause. The length of the rhythmic units is seemingly irregular, but it is controlled by the rhetorical structure of the verse; the method is apparently contrapuntal. Occasionally lyrical variation is secured by a change of pace, but the general tenor of the movement is serene and dignified. Milton always endeavoured to match the rhythmic pattern to the ideas, situations or images. For instance, lines 19–23 admirably suggest joy in Adam s discovery of his mobility, and uncertainty about the purpose of his existence:

My selfe I then perus'd,/ and Limb/ by Limb/
Survey'd,/ and sometimes went,/ and some/times ran/
With sup/ple joints,/ as lively vigour led:
But who I was, or where, or from what cause,
Knew not

Enjambement in pentameters 1 and 2 involves an overlap of one foot in the first case, and two feet in the second, producing rhythmic units of three feet and four feet, respectively. When

the overlap runs to five feet, as occasionally happens, e.g.
IV.919–21, the paragraph structure is even more successfully
tightened.

A departure from *Comus* in the metrics of *Paradise Lost* is
the rejection of extra-metrical weak syllables after a medial
pause. Redundant syllables do occur, but are expendable by
Italian principles of verse elision, well known to English poets;
for instance in line 1:

> So spake the Godlike Pow*er*, and thus our Sire

In the verse of *Paradise Lost* syllabic structure is precise and
mathematically elaborate. Elision is of such importance that the
rhythmical movement of the paragraph is dependent on its
metrical observance, without prejudice to flexible interpretation
in reading.

Jonathan Richardson in *Explanatory Notes and Remarks on
Paradise Lost* (1734) recorded that Milton dictated his epic
piecemeal in batches of some forty lines 'at a breath'. After-
wards he reduced the number of lines to about half. This may
account for the compression of syntax. Unlike Ben Jonson,
Milton did not think or draft his lines in prose. In the composi-
tion of *Paradise Lost*, blindness compelled him to visualize and
hear his batch of verses as a whole. He makes minimal use of the
copula, and there is a much lower percentage of verbs in his
vocabulary than in Shakespeare's. Preferably, the verbs he
employs are monosyllabic and forceful. Twenty-nine of the 51
lines in the selected passage end in verbs of this kind. To get
them in this rhythmically important position (a device noticed
by Matthew Arnold), involved frequent inversion, as in lines
3, 8, 9, 11, 13, 18, 32, 37, 40, 49.

Subordination is usually avoided in *Paradise Lost* by employ-
ing participles for finite verbs. Ten past participles and six
present participles occur in the passage. C. S. Lewis in the
seventh chapter of his *Preface to Paradise Lost* (pp. 45–6), cites
an example of what he claims to be Miltonic ambiguity:

> Milton's Latin constructions in one way tighten up our language, in
> another way they make it more fluid. A fixed order of words is the
> price – an all but ruinous price – which English pays for being
> uninflected. The Miltonic constructions enable the poet to depart, in
> some degree, from this fixed order and thus to drop the ideas into his
> sentence in any order he chooses. Thus, for example,

> soft oppression seis'd
> My droused sense, untroubl'd, though I thought
> I then was passing to my former state
> Insensible, and forthwith to dissolve. (VIII, 288–91)

| The syntax is so artificial that it is ambiguous. I do not know whether *untroubled* qualifies *me* understood, or *sense*, and similar doubts arise about *insensible* and the construction of *to dissolve*. But then I don't need to know. The sequence *drowsed – untroubled – my former state – insensible – dissolve* is exactly right; the very crumbling of consciousness is before us and the fringe of syntactical mystery helps rather than hinders the effect.

There is more perversity than ambiguity in this. *Untroubl'd* is a second participial qualifier of *sense*, and *Insensible* an adjective qualifying *state*, in post-position. *To dissolve* is a present infinitive with future meaning. A slight adjustment of the word order, and the sense is immediately clarified, thus:

> Soft oppression seized my drowsed, untroubled sense, though I thought I was passing to my former insensible state, and forthwith about to dissolve.

Milton's account of Adam's self-discovery requires glossing, for though it is his interpretation of the Creation in Genesis, it is illuminated from readings in Homer, Plato and Ovid's *Metamorphoses*. Adam's instinctive assumption of an upright posture (11–13) finds fuller rationalization in Book VII, 506–11:

> A Creature who not prone
> And Brute as other Creatures, but endu'd
> With Sanctitie of Reason, might erect
> His Stature, and upright with Front serene
> Govern the rest, self-knowing, and from thence
> Magnanimous to correspond with heav'n

This is an elaboration of the situation described in *Metamorphoses* I, 76–86; but Milton had read learned discussions in Plato's *Timaeus* 90 A and Cicero's *De natura deorum* II.56.

Another classical retrospect is Adam's address to the *Sun* in 25–6, which recalls Book V, 171–4, where the Sun is venerated as an Orphic deity; this was a mystic symbolism of Plato's *Republic*. Lines 44–7 recall the misleading dream of Agamemnon at the beginning of the second book of the *Iliad*. Homer there personifies the 'dream' as a messenger or apparition sent by

Zeus, and the personification is retained in Milton's allusion. Lines 48–51 look back to Genesis II, 8 and 15; *Adam* (whose name means 'red earth') was not born in Paradise, but introduced into it by God. Hence the sentence 'Thy Mansion wants thee, Adam' in 48. Without knowledge of these allusions, the significance of Milton's wording cannot be fully appreciated.

In line 15 *liquid Lapse* ('falling water') has been condemned as a latinized periphrasis. The word *Lapse* (Lat. *lapsus*) was undoubtedly a debt to his classical reading, and it may also be a pun on the transgression of Adam.

Milton was partial to *antonomasia* for the sake of variety, as in *Godlike Power* (for Raphael) in the first line; but *hyperbaton* (which includes most of the 22 inversions of word order) and *alliteration* are the predominant figures. Throughout *Paradise Lost*, *prosopopoeia*, as in *all things smil'd* (17), is commoner than other kinds of metaphor. There is a much criticized use of *zeugma* (syntactical incongruity) in lines 17–18:

> all things smil'd,
> *With fragrance* and with joy *my heart oreflow'd*

The verb *oreflow'd* has two modifiers, one of which is incompatible: the figure was commoner in analytical languages, such as Greek and Latin.

Lines 22–9 abound in rhetorical figures, such as

22–3   *Eclipsis* (syntactical economy, by omission of words proper to a prose construction): *But who I was, or where, or from what cause/ Knew not* (cf 29 *how here*, 32 *how adore* and 49 *thy seat prepar'd*)

23   *Polyptoton:* to *speak* I tried, and forwith *spake* (cf 49 *Man . . . Men*)

25   *Ecphonesis: Thou Sun*, said I

25–6   *Ploce:* faire *Light*,/ And thou en*light*'nd Earth (cf use of *first* in 36)

28–9   *Anadiplosis:* faire Creatures, *tell*/ *Tell*, if ye saw

George Santayana wrote in *Reason in Art* (Scribner, 1926): 'Rhetoric and utility keep language going, as centrifugal and centripetal forces keep a planet in its course' (p. 81). No Renaissance poet demonstrates this truth better than Milton in *Paradise Lost*. Personification, simile and epithet were the expressive instruments of his design, used as a painter would

colour; but he never lost sight of the biblical fable, or the
tradition of his form. His aim was to balance grandeur with
grave lucidity.

Most remarkable, in view of Milton's Arianism, was the
dramatic and narrative objectivity of the epic. Jonathan
Richardson said justly: 'All his images are pure antique, so that
we read Homer and Virgil in reading him'. This love of
antiquity, aided by the genuinely metaphysical nature of the
theme, gave to the diction of *Paradise Lost* an erroneous
impression of vagueness. To a humanist of the Greek, Latin and
neo-Platonic tradition, the language was allusive and dignified.

Samson Agonistes (lines 1721–58)

Milton's last major work, published with *Paradise Regained* in
1671, resembled *Comus* in versification and command of
rhetoric. This led a few critics to place the composition as early
as 1653; but the only support for this date is the lament on
blindness (67–100), which suggests a recent affliction. (Milton
went completely blind in 1652.) The obliquity of the rugged
language and the hardened puritanism of Samson's outlook,
argue for a much later date of composition.

Except in the episode with Dalila, Milton avoided the
embellishments of Elizabethan imagery. Nearly ten per cent of
the lines in *Samson Agonistes* make use of rhyme, in spite of
Milton's objections to it; and the rhyme occurs not only in the
lyrical choruses, in which Milton looks back to the *Prometheus
Bound* of Aeschylus. Milton's favourite Greek tragedian was
Euripides, and there are traces of his realistic phrasing in the
dialogue.

The dramatic conception of *Samson Agonistes* is, however, in
the spirit of Sophocles. Scholars have compared the tragedy
with the *Trachiniae*, in which Heracles resembles Samson, and
with *Oedipus Coloneus*. Classical influence from three sources is
thus undoubted; and the Hebraic origin of the theme (Judges
XIII to XVI), and Christian morality, add to the complexity of
the final product. The anguish of Samson has recollections of
the passion of Christ, and this may explain the word *Agonistes*
in the title. Milton's epistolary preface stated that the play was

not intended for the theatre: it was entirely out of sympathy with the spirit of the Restoration.

There are usually good reasons why a work written in dramatic form is unsuitable for the stage. *Samson Agonistes* is unactable because there is no dramatic crisis. Many speeches are long, and questions are asked to which the speaker is compelled to give his own answer. Despite past exploits, Samson of the plot is an unheroic figure; and there is a want of humanism in his conception. A tragedy, Greek in design, is incompatible with the Hebraic spirit; and *Samson Agonistes* exalts passivity when the playgoer expects action.

Samson Agonistes is modelled on the theory of Aristotle in the *Poetics*. The plot is simple, and the development retrospective. Characters are introduced as visitors to Samson in captivity, and discuss his past life. The hero is depicted as a man chosen by God to deliver his people from the Philistines; but he is not immune to temptation. With the pride of Job and the spiritual blindness of Gloucester in *King Lear*, Samson is redeemed in his repentance and stoical refusal to evade fate by surrender of his principles. The hero's fall is not autobiographical, but there are constant reminders of the bitterness of Milton's personal experience. Allusions are made to the failure of Cromwell and the Commonwealth to save England from the libertine Royalists.

The choruses of *Samson Agonistes* are prosodic triumphs of Milton's maturity. Whether in sympathetic lamentation or moral censure, they recall the book of Job. The *Parode* of 61 lines that responds to the *Prologue* of Samson's soliloquy (114 lines) leads to the first *Episode*, in the form of a dialogue between the Chorus and Samson. There are four other episodes, with Samson's father Manoa, with his concubine Dalila, with the giant Harapha, and with the Officer of the Lords of Philistia, and all episodes end with a *Stasimon* or commentary from the Chorus. A Chorus serves also to introduce each interlocutor. The play ends in the formal manner of the Greek dramatists, with the *Exode*, a dialogue between the Chorus and Manoa, interrupted by a Messenger, who reports, in graphic detail, the *Catastrophe* (64 lines). Action and reaction are the themes of the semi-choruses; then the *Kommos*, or finale, is taken up by Manoa. The concluding Ode of 14 lines (like an octosyllabic

sonnet) simulates Euripides; but the verse pattern, according
to F. T. Prince, is to be found in the rhymed choruses of
Guarini's *Pastor Fido*. The *Stasimon* at the end of each episode
provides Milton with opportunities for dramatic irony, especially
after the first harangue of Manoa.

Only in the finale does *Samson Agonistes* achieve Hellenic
perfection: the language has the statuesque dignity of Milton's
epic poetry. The passage chosen depicts the last scene of the play:

Nothing is here for tears, nothing to wail
Or knock the breast, no weakness, no contempt,
Dispraise, or blame, nothing but well and fair,
And what may quiet us in a death so noble.
Let us go find the body where it lies   5
Sok't in his enemies blood, and from the stream
With lavers pure and cleansing herbs wash off
The clotted gore. I with what speed the while
(Gaza is not in plight to say us nay)
Will send for all my kindred, all my friends   10
To fetch him hence and solemnly attend
With silent obsequie and funeral train
Home to his Fathers house: there will I build him
A Monument, and plant it round with shade
Of Laurel ever green, and branching Palm,   15
With all his Trophies hung, and Acts enroll'd
In copious Legend, or sweet Lyric Song.
Thither shall all the valiant youth resort,
And from his memory inflame thir breasts
To matchless valour, and adventures high: 20
The Virgins also shall on feastful days
Visit his Tomb with flowers, only bewailing
His lot unfortunate in nuptial choice,
From whence captivity and loss of eyes.
   Chor. All is best, though we oft doubt,   25
What th' unsearchable dispose
Of highest wisdom brings about,
And ever best found in the close.
Oft he seems to hide his face,
But unexpectedly returns   30
And to his faithful Champion hath in place
Bore witness gloriously; whence Gaza mourns
And all that band them to resist
His uncontroulable intent,
His servants he with new acquist   35
Of true experience from this great event
With peace and consolation hath dismist,
And calm of mind all passion spent.

The first five lines are simply worded. The Elizabethan realism of *Sok't in his enemies blood* (6) leads to *lavers pure* (7) and *clotted gore* (8), the assonance being reminiscent of early Shakespeare. After three lines of pure English come the periphrastic elaborations *silent obsequie* and *funeral train* (12). These introduce a succession of Miltonisms, beginning with poetic inversions: *Laurel ever green* (15, a recollection of *Lycidas*), *Trophies hung* and *acts enroll'd* (16). The adjectives *copious* and *sweet* (17) are not felicitous.

The choice of words should not be separated from Milton's prosody. Enjambed lines (15 of the 38) represent a high proportion. The incidence of weak or feminine endings in the blank verse (4 in 24 lines) is less impressive. Most are the terminals of run-on lines, since the licence has uses in dramatic poetry that epical blank verse can do without. Dignity arises from the total movement, and is partly due to the distribution of internal pauses. No lines present difficulties to the scanner or reader. The choric verses are notable for the dexterity with which Milton employs trochaic modulation, as in 29, which reduces the line of eight syllables to seven. Of the 14 choric lines, only four (31, 32, 36 and 37) are iambic pentameters.

At a time when neo-classical metres were being trimmed and balanced in self-contained couplets, Milton gave poetry a freedom of movement that anticipated the later experiments of Gerard Manly Hopkins and T. S. Eliot. Innovations of prosody were accompanied by a sensitive blending of Latin and Anglo-Saxon words; the placing of monosyllables, as well as poly-syllables, in effective positions is masterly. Referring to the intervention of Providence through Samson, God's instrument, Milton writes (32–8):

> whence Gaza mourns
> And all that band them to resist
> His *uncontroulable intent*
> His servants he with new *acquist*
> Of true experience from this great event
> With *peace* and *consolation* hath dismist,
> And *calm* of mind all *passion* spent.

The use of Latinisms (*acquist* is a rarity) was not the simplest way of expressing the poet's meaning; but disposed as they are, the words have prophetic grandeur, completely in accord with

Aristotle's belief in *catharsis*. Robert Bridges observed a significant effect of Milton's versification:

> The relation of the form of the verse to the sense is not intended to be taken exactly; it is a matter of feeling between the two . . . Matter and form should be in live harmonious relation.
>
> (*Milton's Prosody*, p. 63)

Nuances of style can best be appreciated, if one accepts Milton's syntactical individualisms as indispensable. Three lines in the passage are characteristically Miltonic:

20	To matchless valour, and adventures high
23–4	His lot unfortunate in nuptial choice
	From whence captivity and loss of eyes.

The antithesis of the first involves counterpoised phrases, in which the substantive is a Romance word and the qualifier an Anglo-Saxon one; the variation is in the disposition of accented syllables and the inverted order of the second phrase. Both phrases have medieval chivalry as their background. The placing of *high* after the noun it qualifies would be arbitrary in prose, but here it is enjoined by rhythmical emphasis. Ending on a significant monosyllable, the line gains in strength and meaning; for the line suggests that the example of Samson may inspire other crusaders to high ideals.

The second example resembles the first in the use of abstract nouns. *Nuptial choice* is a periphrasis for 'marriage'. In both of his euphemistic marriages, Samson *chose* the woman from an alien people, and the choice was an entanglement of convenience and desire. The lines of Manoa's speech are mellifluous, and Milton therefore selected words with liquid, nasal and sibilant consonants; but this was not the sole reason for *nuptial choice*.

Milton, like Shakespeare, freely adapts parts of speech to his requirements; the rhetorical device is *enallage*. The verb *dispose* is used as a noun in 26, and the past participle *aquist* in the same function in 35. Grammatical transference sometimes enjoys great latitude; for instance, *Bore* (32) is a preterite used for a past participle. Adverbs and participial phrases repeatedly link rhythms to avoid subordination. As in Latin, non-significant words, such as articles and prepositions, are omitted to achieve condensation. The singular, *Obsequie* (12) seems to have been derived from Spenser's *Faerie Queene* II.1.60.

In a century of shifting meanings, semantic precision was difficult. Milton must have known that a palm tree has no branches (see *branching* 15); the alternative, *fronds*, did not, however, come into use until the eighteenth century. *Legend* (17, 'reading matter') was already archaic, and *Lyric Song* (same line) is a redundancy. Honouring a hero's memory at his monument, where youths engage in athletic exploits, and maidens scatter flowers (14–22), was proper to Greek ceremonies, but inappropriate to Hebrew ones.

Milton in this tragedy avoids one danger of artifice; the rhetorical figures are mostly functional. Tropes and images, rhyme, assonance, alliteration, hyperbaton and metaplasms excluded, the range of rhetorical figures in *Samson Agonistes* is nevertheless large. *Asyndeton*, the omission of conjunctions, is perhaps the commonest (e.g. lines 1–3); the iterative figure *epanaphora* accompanies it, the negative *no* being repeated five times. The same combination of schemes occurs again with *all* in line 10; and there is a further example of *epanaphora* at the beginning of 34 and 35. In *plant it round with shade/ Of Laurel* (14–15) there is a fine Miltonic instance of *hendiadys;* two nouns functionally related by a preposition take the place of an adjective (*shady*) + noun. There are several uses in the passage of *eclipsis*, the sacrifice of one or more words needed to complete the sense, e.g.

8   I with what speed‸the while/. . ./ Will send for all my kindred (*I can* omitted)
11   To fetch him hence and solemnly attend‸/ . . ./ Home to his Fathers house (*him* omitted)
28   and‸ever best found in the close (*it is* omitted)
31   And to his faithful Champion hath in‸place/ Bore witness gloriously (*this* omitted)

Rhetoric may be used to depersonalize, or exert a rational control over, the power of emotive language; or it may restrain poeticism. Curbs on figurative language were being recommended by the Royal Society, about the time Milton was composing his greatest poetry. He never forsook the erudition that was second nature to him; scholarship and a good memory tempted him to fulsome enumeration of allusions, whenever the occasion arose.

*   *   *

The twentieth-century reaction against Milton's style seems to have been initiated by J. Middleton Murry's *The Problem of Style* (1922). Murry spoke of it as 'a superficial idiosyncrasy' (p. 106) and borrowed from Keats the phrase 'verse of art' to describe the diction of *Paradise Lost*. In *Revaluation* (Chatto and Windus, 1936), this idea was taken up by F. R. Leavis, who complained of 'the routine gesture, the heavy fall, of the verse'. The grand manner, which he described as 'impressive stylization', was condemned for its monotony of 'heavy stresses' and familiar cadences; they have only rarely 'a peculiar expressive felicity'. Milton's verse, Leavis concluded, 'functions by rote, of its own momentum, in the manner of a ritual . . . The mind that invented Milton's Grand Style had renounced the English Language' (pp. 45–52).

When Leavis deplored Milton's anarchies of syntax, his criticism was generalized. 'Pressure of speech' and 'mechanical externality' were phrases he neither explained nor illustrated by examples.

T. S. Eliot's first criticism of Milton (*Essays and Studies* of the English Association, 1936), placed the emphasis in another quarter; but he, too, wrote of 'the peculiar kind of deterioration' to which Milton subjected English in using it as though it were a dead language. Eliot maintained that Milton's 'sensuousness . . . had been withered early by book-learning', and that his 'gifts were naturally aural'. The imagery of his poetry is artificial, in the sense that it was impoverished by sensory limitations, and aggravated by blindness; the syntax is determined by 'musical significance', rather than 'actual speech or thought'; and it is therefore *rhetorical*.

It would be difficult to justify *rhetorical* in the sense Eliot used it, although Milton did employ rhetoric of another kind. J. B. Broadbent has shown ('Milton's Rhetoric', *Milton*, ed. A. Rudrum, Macmillan, 1968) that the poet preferred the iterative and schematic figures used so effectively in the theological discourses of *Paradise Lost*. In lyrical and non-dramatic verse, the tropes of Milton are seldom true images. Care in the patterning of words does sometimes obscure the communication of sense. But this is hardly what Eliot's criticism implies. Rhetoric is not undisciplined in Milton; he seldom employs it as a prop, except to underpin the sense and strengthen the metre. The evidence does not support Eliot's contention that Milton's rhetoric caused a 'dislocation' between the sound and the sense.

Eliot's lecture on Milton to the British Academy in 1947 was an exercise in semi-retraction; it amounted to saying: 'The ban is ended; time and circumstance have made it safe for poets to study Milton, provided they do not imitate him'. But, in the event, the critic withdrew as much as he conceded:

> His style is not a *classic* style, in that it is not the elevation of a *common* style, by the final touch of genius, to greatness. It is, from the foundation, and in every particular, a personal style, not based upon common speech, or common prose, or direct communication of meaning. . . . Every idiosyncrasy is a particular act of violence which Milton has been the first to commit. There is no cliché, no poetic diction in the derogatory sense, but a perpetual sequence of original acts of lawlessness. His work illustrates no general principles of good writing.

Milton's poems were the experiments of an individualist who was ambitious to do something different, within the framework of established classical forms. The biblical themes he chose for the major works in blank verse were difficult to reconcile with the humanist tradition. The artistic toughness of Milton's innovations was overlooked by Eliot, not because he found Milton 'antipathetic' as a man (as well as a theologian), but because his critique was not based on the analysis of copious samples of Milton's verse.

One adverse textual comment that Eliot did venture in his British Academy Lecture of 1947 concerned a passage from *Paradise Lost:*

> Contrive who need, or when they need, not now.
> For while they sit contriving, shall the rest,
> Millions that stand in Arms, and longing wait
> The Signal to ascend, sit lingring here (I.53–6)

Christopher Ricks commented in *Milton's Grand Style* (pp. 11–13):

> Mr Eliot's slip (and Dr Leavis's) is in objecting that 'millions that stand in arms could not *at the same time* sit lingring'. They could not, but Milton doesn't say they could. He has a future and a present tense:
>
> > *shall* the rest,
> > Millions that stand in Arms, and longing wait
> > The Signal to ascend, sit lingring here . . .

> There is no inconsistency here, there is a deliberate clash . . . Men who stand will be made to sit. Men who long will be made to linger, as the echo from the previous line (longing/ lingring) reminds us.

Ricks is at fault in describing *shall* (line 2) as a future; it is in the present tense, meaning 'must'; but the force of his argument is not invalidated.

Having in mind Eliot's criticism that Milton is deficient in visual images, T. H. Banks in *Milton's Imagery* (Columbia U.P., 1950) examined closely the whole body of the poetry, and found that 'even after his blindness, his images remained prevailingly visual' (p. 124).

T. S. Eliot in defining a *classic* style as 'common speech' elevated by a touch of genius and achieving 'direct communication of meaning', could not have thought of any extensive or diverse body of ancient literature, which covers such individualists as Pindar and Plato, Lucretius and Vergil. There is no order of words in Milton that cannot be paralleled in poets of the previous century; the alleged 'lawlessness' of his syntax was designed, and became habitual.

Milton added a new dimension to poetry by writing musically sustained and subtly modulated verse; resonance is not sporadic, but radiated throughout the poem. The circumstances of his work were unique, and are ably described in Francis Berry's *Poetry and the Physical Voice*, pp. 101–12:

> Milton conceived his poems as objects for performance, and for performance by his own physical voice. . . .
> Milton cannot be read aloud at the pace at which we have become accustomed to read silently; and to read him silently at the pace at which we normally read silently is to destroy him. To say the lines of Milton more rapidly than the pace he heard and designed them is to raise the pitch – and the pitch of *Paradise Lost* is part of the meaning. It is also to reduce the silences during which so much happens, or ought to happen. For it must be admitted that when language is spoken above a certain rate individual words can lose semantic richness; they are not allowed time for the release of their various levels of meaning or of their associations on one level. The tempo of *Paradise Lost* is slower than that of the early poems, and is a property of Milton's later voice. The pace is not solely regulated by the pauses // or / any more than it is solely by the length of the vowels or consonantal combinations. The one requires, and is dependent on, the other, and both are consequent on acoustics and on Milton's conviction that an epic ought to be sublime. . . .

The 'meaning' can only appear meagre or inadequate when the text is read by the eye alone and at the rapid pace to which the eye is now accustomed. When that happens the meaning is weighed by the intellect in disengagement from the act of hearing. . . . Read aloud in Milton's voice, the meaning has an encasing grandeur of sound. That encasement does not inflate the meaning, rather it produces the meaning intended. . . .

What happens in the dialogue of Milton is that the characters inflect the voice of the narrator with tones agreeable to the moods and roles the Fable obliges them to adopt. . . .

Since *Paradise Lost* and its successors were dictated (they are the only considerable poems we know of to have been dictated), they are exceptionally good examples to adduce in support of the theory that a poet's physical voice conditions his work . . .

Milton's supreme accomplishment was the use he made of his ear for rhythm. There is a difference between his harmonic structure and the word melody of poets like Spenser. The latter compose for linear euphony, but the architectonics of Milton's verse embraces larger units. His memory enabled him to dispose stresses, pauses, vowels and consonants in massive waves; the syntactical habits had a conscious musical purpose.

Milton's emulation of Spenser was not confined to word choice; it involved careful attention to the terminal words of lines, and to the tempo resulting from open vowels and diphthongs, combined with the disposition of consonant clusters. His indebtedness to Italian poets and prosodists, in this art, is well documented; as a consequence of this study, Milton outdistanced all predecessors in phonetic sensibility.

Milton presents a unified aspect through his work, in spite of the duality of his style, which is sometimes elevated and sometimes barren ('stripped of ornament'). It is a just criticism, if not used as a generalization, that the language sounds literary, rather than natural. But he was neither an 'eccentric' (Eliot's phrase) nor a bigot; the ideals of his poetry were achieved in isolation. Though out of touch with his age, he remained, to the end, loyal to his ideals. The integrity and self-discipline of his poetry are no less than T. S. Eliot's, but Milton's has greater range and flexibility; not a line but reflects the *energeia* of creation that Sir Philip Sidney thought necessary to Renaissance art.

XI

CONCLUSIONS

1

In the century commencing with the publication of *The Shepheardes Calender* England produced poets of excellence in Spenser, Shakespeare, Donne and Milton, whose diversity argues little benefit to their work from the educational system. The writers discussed determined the course of poetry for the next 250 years, and provided endless themes for debate on the nature and value of poetic ideas. What characteristics do artists so different in outlook share, to be representative of the English Renaissance? Literary historians offer no explanations comparable to the less systematic criticism of George Rylands, T. S. Eliot, C. S. Lewis and W. H. Empson.

In *Words and Poetry* G. H. W. Rylands provided valuable insights into the roots of Renaissance sensibility. Poetry in the period 1575 to 1675 arose from certain Platonic ideas, beginning with the naming of natural objects, and with the emotions of wonder that words can arouse. It was felt that a precise area of meaning for words of creative intensity would curtail their evocative power. A poetic idea lives through its appeal to the senses; abstract qualities gather associations of meaning by repeated use. Epithets enrich names through experiences of sensory perception, and ideas are thus enlarged and clarified. Fundamentally, the feelings evoked by words do not require artifice. But the qualification of names by means of adjectives provides a demonstrable source of decoration.

In European vernacular poetry the exigencies of metre, rhyme and rhythm added vastly to the use of ornament, and other figures arose through the desire for comparison. A poet's technical skill depended on his range and handling of words. Image and symbol enabled him to clothe ideas in a novel dress, provided he managed the ornament with discrimination. Thus diction (choice of words) in the Renaissance writer came to include all the resources of style at his command. Though poetry was metaphorically a 'language of the heart', its diction, patiently acquired, was in reality a code of symbols and verbal patterns.

Mallarmé held that poetry is not written with ideas, but with words; but the Renaissance poets endeavoured to enjoy the best of both worlds. Being venturesome, they experimented in a variety of techniques and they had the example of classical antecedents to discipline their exuberance. Ben Jonson's *Timber* or *Discoveries* was nothing but an anthology of critical *sententiae*, from Greek and Latin authorities, to remind writers of *decorum*, the accepted canons of taste. Artificiality was not, in itself, an impropriety; only excess led to what Shakespeare called 'maggot ostentation', that might destroy the fruit of an artist's labours.

Amplification was part of a Renaissance poet's training: another was contrast, especially the verbal variety. For example, the disposition of monosyllabic and polysyllabic words, the balance of homely and exotic ones, was practised by every poet that mattered. Poets often went to extremes; and modern critics, such as Rylands, rightly described Milton's '*tame, villatic* fowl' in *Samson Agonistes* as 'pompous and absurd' (p. 46). Epithets are an instructive study, for Renaissance poets were aware that the suggestive word is better than much pictorial detail; above all, they understood the meaning of 'enchantment'. This depends, in some measure, on the emotive use of adjectives, whose appeal is to the senses. All the great Renaissance poets were masters of the colloquial as well as the ornate. They established what were to become the 'consecrated images' of poetry.

2

The refinement of the language, to which Ben Jonson, Dryden and other critics repeatedly refer, was a movement initiated by a handful of vernacular-loving dons at Cambridge. Its object was not only to screen the literary language from unwanted foreign importations, but to standardize orthography and grammar, and to exclude competing dialect forms. The use of regional dialects on the stage was channelled into conventional

patterns styled Northern, Midland and Southern speech. Only
the academic poets of Elizabeth's age, such as Jonson, were
directly interested in this movement; but indirectly all writers
in English exerted an influence. The leading seventeenth
century crusaders for reform were Bacon, Hobbes and Dryden.

In the first book of *The Advancement of Learning* (1605),
Bacon described one aim of the renascence of ancient learning
as a desire to emulate the cogent, lucid and orderly style of
classical writers. Bacon saw in pulpit oratory, and other kinds
of rhetoric, designs of the medieval Schoolmen to impose upon
the credulity of 'the vulgar sort'; he argued that such training
led to the elevation of words above content. As a philosopher,
Bacon wanted the seductions of phrase-making, clausal cadences,
tropes and figures removed from expository utterance; he
opposed to the persuasion of rhetoric the intellectual aims of
seriousness, reason, and judgement; but he acknowledged,
inadequately, the value of imagination in poetry.

Hobbes, in his Answer to Davenant's Preface to *Gondibert*
(1650), took the cause of Bacon much further:

> The subject of a Poem is the manners of men, not natural causes;
> manners presented, not dictated; and manners feigned, as the name of
> Poesy imports, not found in men.

The advice was borrowed from Horace, but given a different
slant. Hobbes understood English poetic diction better than
Bacon, but disliked the excesses of Elizabethan poetry; for
example, words of 'magnifique sound' that 'have no sense at
all', writing that conceals meaning by awkwardness of syntax.
Hobbes ascribed the prevalence of metaphor and simile to
book-learning; the object was novelty and the avoidance of
hackneyed turns of speech.

In the Preface to his translation of the *Odyssey*, Hobbes, an
admirer of Homer, valued the perspicuity and structure of
heroic poetry; he understood the vigour of an epic style. The
function of the poet, he says, is to conceal his technique and
reveal his natural ability. By attention to the order of words a
reader 'may foresee the length of his period, as a torch in the
night shews . . . the stops and unevenness in his way'. If the
rules of verse 'put great constraint upon the natural course of
Language', the poet's duty is to choose alternative modes of

expression, which do not yield the primacy to metre or rhyme. Fancy, discreetly handled, is a source of sublimity and wit; it offers more delight to the reader than imagination and judgement. A poet is, in sum, an attractive painter who employs words instead of colours.

When Dryden wrote his later critical essays, he was in a position to see refinement of the language in perspective. Neo-classical and Gallic predilections led him mistakenly to assess the *furor poeticus* of the Elizabethans as a malady of adolescent society. In *The Dramatic Poetry of the Last Age* (1672) he wrote:

> Let any man who understands English, read diligently the works of Shakespeare and Fletcher, and I dare undertake that he will find in every page either some solecism of speech, or some notorious flaw in sense . . . But the times were ignorant in which they lived. Poetry was then, if not in its infancy among us, at least not arrived to its vigour and maturity.

Dryden's targets in Shakespeare, and even Jonson, were bombast (which he cited from *Macbeth*), grammatical laxity, such as the use of prepositions at the end of sentences, ill-placing of words with resulting confusion of sense, and the favouring of Latinisms to the loss of English idiom. New words might enrich the language, especially of the courtly class, and give subtlety and variety to ornament; but the sophistication of English by French borrowing was being carried to the limits of snobbery and jargon.

Dryden's arguments overlooked the truth that grammatical form is no guarantee of sense. As a practitioner of heroic drama he could not see that the tumidity of Elizabethan tragic speeches was often superseded by the anachronism of the heroic vaunt. In the language of plays, utterances are tied to the nature of the action; unreality is suspect whether the situations are historical or fictional.

3

Most of the later seventeenth-century critics found Elizabethan poetry unsatisfactory in several aspects, and they were not impressed by claims of spontaneity. They did not find fault with its 'rhetoric', the pejorative sense of which arose when the system no longer comprehended all techniques of composition; by the eighteenth century rhetoric was saddled with schematic manipulations that seemed reprehensible. Rhetoric in the sixteenth-century universities could not have been merely classificatory and without value judgements: Sidney, Puttenham, Daniel and Jonson disabuse our minds of this prejudice. Despite inadequate analysis of the images and tropes, the system made poets phrase-conscious; writers were praised or blamed for individual taste and execution. As grammar was unteachable, rhetoric provided an alternative discipline; in method, it was comparable to modern critical analysis. Rhetoric as a 'box of tricks' is a misunderstanding of its purpose; it was not taught as a surrogate for sensibility. The individuality of Spenser, Shakespeare, Donne and Milton, began with their different personalities, but was complemented by divergent means of integrating schemes and tropes in their thinking.

It is impossible to imagine what blank verse would have been like by 1580, if rhetoric had not given it shape and vigour. Complex forms of lyrical poetry, the sonnet, ode and elegy, were equally in need of discipline. Elizabethan narrative and descriptive poetry, Spenser's, Marlowe's and Shakespeare's, is most readable because rhetoric and translation gave it relevance, cohesion and variety.

Poets believed that, without pattern, style could hardly exist. Elizabethan poetry demonstrated conclusively that the syntax of English was flexible enough for manifold kinds of emphasis and rhythm. By 1600, rhetoric had advanced from elementary principles of order to aesthetic control of words. Poets exercised control in three ways:

(a) by associating ideas and feelings; (memory and perception were the agents);
(b) by word play, in forms of balance and repetition;
(c) by intelligent gradation of groups of words (schematization).

The best example of this organization was the quality of the blank verse; *Paradise Lost* was the culmination of development in that form. The virtuosity of Shakespeare's great tragedies at the beginning of the seventeenth century, and of *Samson Agonistes* near its end, made further advance in the rhythmical structure of iambic pentameters an impossibility. The blank verse of Wordsworth, Keats, Tennyson, Browning and Arnold is of different movement and emphasis, stripping itself of formal rhetoric, to its own loss; it is mostly blank verse without spinal anatomy. In 1921 T. S. Eliot diagnosed the malaise as a 'dissociation of sensibility', but his own tactic was to tauten the sinews of verse by studying the technique of seventeenth-century poetry, including the choruses of *Samson Agonistes*. No modern poet better illustrates the resurgence of rhetoric, and its relevance to modern free verse.

Renaissance poetry was an harmonious organization of language within the humanist tradition. However elaborate the imagery, or intricate the thinking and arrangement, the reader arrives at an individual interpretation by the light of good sense and mature taste.

Modern poetry places the emphasis on symbolic suggestion, on the relation of image, feeling and tone. Unity is the cumulative effect of figures and phrases, which must be relevant to the emotive idea. A poem may communicate its fugitive life by analogy with a number of arts, music, painting, sculpture and cinematography, and readers interpret by personal identification.

At the time T. S. Eliot was experimenting with new ideas, Guillaume Apollinaire, who died in November 1918, was writing of 'The New Spirit and the Poets':

> In keeping with the very order of nature, the poet puts aside any high-flown purpose. There is no longer any Wagnerianism in us . . . However far one advances on the path of new freedoms, they will only reinforce most of the ancient disciplines and bring out new ones which will not be less demanding than the old. . . .
>
> *Surprise is the greatest source of what is new*. It is by surprise, by the important position that has been given to surprise, that the new spirit distinguishes itself from all the literary and artistic movements which have preceded it. . . . The poet is he who discovers new joys, even if they are hard to bear. . . .
>
> The new spirit is above all the enemy of estheticism, of formulae, and of cultism. It attacks no school whatever, for it does not wish to be a school, but rather one of the great currents of literature encompassing all schools since symbolism and naturalism. . . . The poets wish to master prophecy, that spirited mare that has never been tamed.

4

A difference of approach has been responsible for misunder-

standing the nature of Renaissance poetry. The explanatory
treatises that recommended Classical, Italian or French models
to Elizabethan poets, invariably prescribed the theme and
treatment proper to the technical forms of poetry. Ornament
was the special privilege of a poet, and the success of a
Renaissance poem depended on its reception by a particular
audience.

Ben Jonson was taught at school by his Master, William
Camden, to cast his verses first in prose. Throughout the
seventeenth century, imagination was not welcomed as the
mainspring of poetry. Dryden wrote in the Epistle Dedicatory
to *The Rival Ladies* (1664):

> Imagination in a poet is a faculty so wild and lawless, that like a
> high-ranging spaniel, it must have clogs tied to it, lest it outrun the
> judgement.

Coleridge's theory of imagination was able to distinguish
between the inherently figurative and the adherently ornamental
style. Of the latter kind are some of Spenser's similes and most
of Milton's mythological allusions; but both were the venial
sins of learned poets. Poets of the Renaissance repeated
technical forms known to have proved successful, and the style
sometimes lapsed into mannerism. Kenneth Burke might have
been thinking of the Renaissance when he spoke of the two
extremes to which poetry is liable (*Counterstatement*, Hermes
Publications, California, 1931, pp. 55–6),

> the extreme of utterance, which makes for the ideal of spontaneity and
> 'pure' emotion, and leads to barbarism in art; and the extreme of pure
> beauty, or means conceived exclusively as an end, which leads to
> virtuosity, or decoration.

The structural linguist, G. N. Leech, informs us that a
writer's objects 'transcend the limits of ordinary language';
that the emotional and perceptual relations of metaphor lie
outside language and belong ideally to psychology (*Essays on
Style and Language*, pp. 154–6). If we hold this scientific view,
there is reason to understand the reaction of critics to Shakes-
peare and Milton after the Restoration. Bacon, Hobbes and the
New Science had, by 1660, transformed the atmosphere breathed
by intellectuals; ever since they have been sceptical of the role
of rhetoric in poetry.

BIBLIOGRAPHY

A. Texts

Geoffrey Chaucer, *Complete Works*, ed. F. N. Robinson, Oxford, 1957.

Gest Hystoriale of the Destruction of Troy, ed. G. A. Panton and D. Donaldson, EETS, 1869, 1874.

Morte Arthure, ed. E. Brock, EETS, 1871.

Sir Thomas Wyatt, *Collected Poems*, ed. K. Muir, Routledge and Kegan Paul, 1949.

Tottels Miscellany, ed. H. E. Rollins, 2 vols, Harvard U.P., 1928–9.

Henry Howard, Earl of Surrey, *Poems*, ed. E. Jones, Clarendon, 1964.

The Mirror for Magistrates, ed. L. B. Campbell, Cambridge, 1938.

Thomas Sackville, Lord Buckhurst, *The Complaint of Henry Duke of Buckingham*, Yale U.P., 1936.

Sir Philip Sidney, *Poems*, ed. W. A. Ringler, Clarendon, 1962.

Edmund Spenser, *Works* (Variorum), ed. E. Greenlaw, H. G. Lotspeich, C. G. Osgood, F. M. Padelford, Johns Hopkins, Baltimore, 1943.

Edmund Spenser, *Works*, ed. J. C. Smith and E. de Selincourt, Clarendon, 1909–12.

Thomas Kyd, *The Spanish Tragedy 1592*, ed. W. W. Greg and D. N. Smith, Malone Soc., 1948.

Christopher Marlowe, *Works*, 6 vols, ed. R. H. Case et al. Methuen, 1930–33.

William Shakespeare, *First Folio, 1623*, Facsimile, ed. Sidney Lee, Clarendon, 1902.

Poems, Facsimile Quartos 1593–1609, Sidney Lee, Clarendon, 1905.

Works, Facsimile Quartos, ed. P. A. Daniel and others, 42 vols, C. Praetorius and W. Griggs, from 1885.

Plays, Facsimile Quartos, ed. W. W. Greg, Sidgwick and Jackson, 1939–52.

Plays, Facsimile Quartos ed. W. W. Greg and C. Hinman, Clarendon, from 1957.

Works, New Cambridge Edition, ed. J. D. Wilson, G. I. Duthie, A. Walker and J. C. Maxwell, Cambridge, 1921–66.

Works, New Arden Edition, various editors, Methuen, from 1951.

Works, Variorum Edition, ed. H. H. Furness, H. E. Rollins and others, Lippincott, from 1871.

Poems, ed. G. Wyndham, Methuen, 1898.

Sonnets, ed. C. Knox Pooler, Arden, Methuen, 1918.

Richard II, A New Quarto, ed. A. W. Pollard, Quaritch, 1916.

Antony and Cleopatra, Facsimile, ed. J. D. Wilson, Faber and Gwyer, N. D.

The Tempest, ed. A. Righter, Penguin, 1968.

John Donne, *Poems*, ed. H. J. C. Grierson, 2 vols, Oxford, 1912.

Divine Poems, ed. H. Gardner, Clarendon, 1952.

Elegies and Songs and Sonnets, ed. H. Gardner, Clarendon, 1965.

Sermons on the Psalms and Gospels, ed. E. M. Simpson, California U.P., 1963.

John Milton, *Poetical Works*, ed. H. Darbishire, 2 vols, Clarendon, 1952–5.

Poems, ed. J. Carey and A. Fowler, Longmans, 1968.

Poems 1645, Type facsimile, Clarendon, 1924.

Poems 1645, ed. C. Brooks and J. E. Hardy, Harcourt-Brace, 1951.

Dramatic Poems, ed. G. and M. Bullough, Athlone Press, 1958.

Sonnets, ed. J. S. Smart, 1921, Clarendon reprint, 1966.

Sonnets, ed. E. A. J. Honigmann, Macmillan, 1966.

Paradise Lost, ed. A. W. Verity, Cambridge, 1910.

Paradise Lost, Books I and II, ed. F. T. Prince, Oxford, 1962.

B. Other Sources

J. M. Manly, *Specimens of the Pre-Shakespearian Drama*, Ginn, Boston, 1897.

Thomas de Quincey, 'Style', *Works*, ed. D. Masson, Black, 1897.

L

Elizabethan Critical Essays, ed. C. Gregory Smith, 2 vols, Oxford, 1904.

Critical Essays of the Seventeenth Century, ed. J. E. Spingarn, 3 vols, Oxford, 1907.

J. M. Berdan, *Early Tudor Poetry*, Macmillan, New York, 1931.

E. M. W. Tillyard, *Sir Thomas Wyatt, A Selection and a Study*, Chatto and Windus, 1949.

Aspects of Shakespeare, ed. J. W. Mackail, Clarendon, 1933.

H. G. Barker and G. B. Harrison, *A Companion to Shakespeare Studies*, Cambridge, 1949.

H. G. Barker, *Prefaces to Shakespeare*, 4 vols, Batsford, 1963.

More Talking of Shakespeare, ed. J. Garrett, Longmans, 1959.

Shakespeare's Plutarch, ed. T. J. B. Spencer, Penguin, 1964.

Early Shakespeare, ed. J. R. Brown and B. Harris, Arnold, 1961.

Later Shakespeare, ed. J. R. Brown and B. Harris, Arnold, 1966.

Spenser's Critics, ed. W. T. Mueller, Syracuse U.P., 1959.

Form and Convention in the Poetry of Edmund Spenser, ed. W. Nelson, Columbia U.P., 1961.

E. S. Donno, *Elizabethan Minor Epics*, Routledge and Kegan Paul, 1963.

Elizabethan Poetry, ed. P. J. Alpers, Oxford, 1967.

Milton Criticism, ed. J. Thorpe, Routledge and Kegan Paul, 1951.

Milton's Epic Poetry, ed. C. A. Patrides, Penguin, 1967.

Approaches to Paradise Lost, ed. C. A. Patrides, Arnold, 1968.

Milton, ed. A. Rudrum, Macmillan, 1968.

Ovid, *Metamorphoses*, trans. M. M. Innes, Penguin, 1955.

C. Rhetoric

Thomas Wilson, *The Arte of Rhetorique* (1560), ed. G. H. Mair, Oxford, 1909.

T. S. Eliot, 'Rhetoric and Poetic Drama', *The Sacred Wood*, Methuen, 1920.

H. D. Rix, *Rhetoric in Spenser's Poetry*, Pennsylvania State College, 1940.

M. B. Kennedy, *The Oration in Shakespeare*, Chapel Hill, 1942.

M. Joseph, *Shakespeare's Use of the Arts of Language*, Columbia U.P., 1947.

L. A. Sonnino, *A Handbook to Sixteenth Century Rhetoric*, Routledge and Kegan Paul, 1968.

D. Prosody

J. B. Mayor, *English Metre*, Cambridge, 1886.

G. Saintsbury, *A History of English Prosody*, 2 vols, Russell, New York, 1961 (reprint).

B. Ten Brink and F. Kluge, *The Language and Metre of Chaucer*, Macmillan, 1901.

J. G. Southworth, *Verses of Cadence*, Blackwell, 1954.

J. E. Bernard, *Prosody of the Tudor Interlude*, Yale U.P., 1939.

M. A. Bayfield, *A Study of Shakespeare's Versification*, Cambridge, 1920.

D. L. Sipe, *Shakespeare's Metrics*, Yale U.P., 1968.

H. C. Wyld, *Studies in English Rhymes from Surrey to Pope*, Murray, 1923.

P. F. Baum, *The Principles of English Versification*, Harvard U.P., 1922.

Egerton Smith, *The Principles of English Metre*, Oxford, 1923.

E. Hamer, *The Metres of English Poetry*, Methuen, 1930.

L. Abercrombie, *Principles of English Prosody*, Secker, 1923.

L. Abercrombie, *Poetry: Its Music and Meaning*, Oxford, 1932.

R. Bridges, *Milton's Prosody*, Oxford, 1921.

S. E. Sprott, *Milton's Art of Prosody*, Blackwell, 1953.

J. Thompson, *The Founding of English Metre*, Routledge and Kegan Paul, 1961.

S. Chatman, *A Theory of Meter*, Mouton, The Hague, 1965.

K. Shapiro and R. Beum, *A Prosody Handbook*, Harper and Row, 1965.

The Structure of Verse, ed. H. Gross, Fawcett Publications, 1966.

E. Diction and Style

O. Barfield, *Poetic Diction*, Faber and Faber, 1928.

W. P. Ker, *Form and Style in Poetry*, Macmillan, 1928.

G. H. W. Rylands, *Words and Poetry*, Payson and Clarke, New York, 1928.

H. C. Wyld, *Some Aspects of the Diction of English Poetry*, Blackwell, 1933.

B. Groom, *Formation and Use of Compound Epithets in English Poetry*, SPE Tract XLIX, Clarendon, 1937.

V. L. Rubel, *Poetic Diction in the English Renaissance*, Oxford, 1941.

J. Miles, *Major Adjectives in English Poetry*, California U.P., 1946.

J. Miles, *Renaissance, Eighteenth Century and Modern Language in English Poetry*, California U.P., 1960.

G. Rostrevor Hamilton, *The Tell-Tale Article*, Heinemann, 1949.

D. Davie, *Articulate Energy*, Routledge and Kegan Paul, 1955.

B. Groom, *The Diction of Poetry from Spenser to Bridges*, Toronto U.P., 1955.

Style in Language, ed. T. A. Sebeok, M.I.T. Press, Cambridge, Mass., 1960.

Essays on the Language of Literature, ed. S. Chatman and S. R. Levin, Houghton Mifflin, 1967.

F. W. Bateson, *English Poetry and the English Language*, Russell and Russell, N. York, 1961.

G. Hough, *Style and Stylistics*, Routledge and Kegan Paul, 1969.

E. Ekwall, *Shakespeare's Vocabulary*, Uppsala, 1903.

F. P. Wilson, 'Shakespeare and the Diction of Common Life', British Academy XXVII, 1941.

B. I. Evans, *The Language of Shakespeare's Plays*, Methuen, 1952.

F. E. Halliday, *The Poetry of Shakespeare's Plays*, Duckworth, 1954.

M. M. Mahood, *Shakespeare's Wordplay*, Methuen, 1957.

H. M. Hulme, *Explorations in Shakespeare's Language*, Longmans, 1962.

R. A. Fraser, *Shakespeare's Poetics in Relation to King Lear*, Routledge and Kegan Paul, 1962.

S. Burckhardt, *Shakespearean Meanings*, Princeton U.P., 1968.

B. Vickers, *The Artistry of Shakespeare's Prose*, Methuen, 1968.

R. D. Havens, *The Influence of Milton on English Poetry*, Harvard U.P., 1922.

W. B. C. Watkins, *An Anatomy of Milton's Verse*, Louisiana State U.P., 1955.

C. Ricks, *Milton's Grand Style*, Oxford, 1963.

M. W. Croll, *Style, Rhetoric and Rhythm* (ed. J. M. Patrick), Princeton U.P., 1966.

A. D. Ferry, *Milton's Epic Voice*, Harvard U.P., 1967.

F. Linguistics

G. J. Tamson, *Word-Stress in English*, Halle, 1898.

L. Spitzer, *Linguistics and Literary History*, Princeton U.P., 1948.

G. Grammars

E. A. Abbott, *A Shakespearian Grammar*, Macmillan, 1869.

H. W. Sugden, *The Grammar of Spenser's Faerie Queene*, Linguistic Soc. of America, Pennsylvania, 1936.

F. Berry, *Poet's Grammar*, Routledge and Kegan Paul, 1958.

O. Jespersen, *Selected Writings*, Allen and Unwin, 1962.

R. D. Emma, *Milton's Grammar*, Mouton, The Hague, 1964.

H. Dictionaries

A. Schmidt, *Shakespeare Lexicon*, Williams and Norgate, 1874.

C. T. Onions, *Shakespeare Glossary* (2nd ed.), Clarendon, 1919.

Oxford New English Dictionary, 13 vols, Clarendon, 1933.

J. T. Shipley, *Dictionary of World Literary Terms*, Allen and Unwin, 1955.

B. Deutsch, *Poetry Handbook*, Jonathan Cape, 1958.

I. Imagery

R. Tuve, *Elizabethan and Metaphysical Imagery*, Chicago U.P., 1947.

C. Brooke-Rose, *A Grammar of Metaphor*, Secker and Warburg, 1958.

H. W. Wells, *Poetic Imagery*, Russell and Russell, New York, 1961.

C. F. E. Spurgeon, *Shakespeare Imagery*, Cambridge, 1935.

W. H. Clemen, *The Development of Shakespeare's Imagery*, Methuen, 1951.

J. E. Haskins, *Shakespeare's Derived Imagery*, Kansas U.P., 1953.

D. A. Stauffer, *Shakespeare's World of Images*, Indiana U.P., 1966.

C. S. Lewis, *Spenser's Images of Life*, Cambridge, 1967.

K. Matsuura, *A Study of Donne's Imagery*, Tokyo, 1953.

T. H. Banks, *Milton's Imagery*, Columbia U.P., 1950.

J. Monographs and Special Studies

T. Rich, *Harrington and Ariosto*, Yale U.P., 1940.

J. Swart, *Thomas Sackville*, Groningen, 1948.

J. Buxton, *Sir Philip Sidney and the English Renaissance*, Macmillan, 1954.

W. F. Schirmer, *John Lydgate*, Methuen, 1961.

M. Pollet, *John Skelton*, Didier, Paris, 1962.

W. L. Renwick, *Edmund Spenser*, Arnold, 1925.

B. E. C. Davis, *Edmund Spenser*, Russell and Russell, New York, 1962.

H. G. Lotspeich, *Classical Mythology in the Poetry of Edmund Spenser*, Princeton U.P., 1965.

P. J. Alpers, *The Poetry of the Faerie Queene*, Princeton U.P., 1967.

R. K. Root, *Classical Mythology in Shakespeare*, Yale Studies in English, 1903.

J. A. K. Thomson, *Shakespeare and the Classics*, Allen and Unwin, 1952.

C. Schaar, *An Elizabethan Sonnet Problem*, Lund Studies in English, 1960.

T. W. Baldwin, *On the Literary Genetics of Shakespeare's Poems and Sonnets*, Illinois U.P., Urbana, 1950.

J. B. Leishman, *Themes and Variations in Shakespeare's Sonnets*, Hutchinson, 1961.

H. Landry, *Interpretation in Shakespeare's Sonnets*, California U.P., 1963.

A Case Book on Shakespeare's Sonnets, ed. G. Willen and V. B. Reed, Crowell, N. York, 1964.

T. W. Baldwin, *The Organization and Personnel of the Shakespearian Company*, Princeton U.P., 1927.

F. Berry, *The Shakespeare Inset*, Routledge and Kegan Paul, 1965.

J. L. Styan, *Shakespeare's Stagecraft*, Cambridge, 1967.

A. C. Bradley, *Shakespearian Tragedy*, Macmillan, 1904.

G. Gordon, *Shakespearian Comedy*, Oxford, 1944.

A. Quiller Couch, *Shakespeare's Workmanship*, Cambridge, 1931.

S. L. Bethell, *Shakespeare and the Popular Dramatic Tradition*, Staples Press, N. York, 1944.

H. Krabbe, *Bernard Shaw on Shakespeare*, Aarhus, 1955.

G. H. W. Rylands, 'Shakespeare's Poetic Energy', British Academy XXXVII, 1957.

U. Ellis Fermor, *Shakespeare the Dramatist*, Methuen, 1961.

N. Coghill, *Shakespeare's Professional Skills*, Cambridge, 1964.

M. R. Ridley, *Shakespeare's Plays: A Commentary*, Dent, 1937.

H. Levin, *The Question of Hamlet*, Oxford, 1959.

R. B. Heilman, *The Great Stage*, Washington U.P., 1963.

E. M. W. Tillyard, *Shakespeare's Last Plays*, Chatto and Windus, 1938.

D. Traversi, *Shakespeare: The Last Phase*, Hollis and Carter, 1954.

D. Traversi, *Shakespeare: The Roman Plays*, Hollis and Carter, 1963.

D. G. James, *The Dream of Prospero*, Clarendon, 1967.

F. Berry, *Poetry and the Physical Voice*, Routledge and Kegan Paul, 1962.

G. Williamson, *The Donne Tradition*, Harvard U.P., 1930.

R. C. Bald, *Donne's Influence in English Literature*, St John's College Press, 1932.

J. B. Leishman, *The Monarch of Wit*, Hutchinson's University Library, 1951.

D. Hunt, *Donne's Poetry*, Yale U.P., 1954.

A. Alvarez, *The School of Donne*, Chatto and Windus, 1962.

A. Stein, *John Donne's Lyrics*, Minnesota U.P., 1962.

J. Webber, *Contrary Music*, Wisconsin U.P., 1963.

M. F. Maloney, *John Donne, his Flight from Medievalism*, Russell and Russell, New York, 1965.

C. G. Osgood, *The Classical Mythology of Milton's English Poems*, Gordian Press, N. York, 1900.

W. Raleigh, *Milton*, Arnold, 1900.

J. G. Robertson, 'Milton's Fame on the Continent', British Academy VIII, 1908.

C. S. Lewis, *A Preface to Paradise Lost*, Oxford, 1942.

D. Saurat, *Milton, Man and Thinker*, Dent, 1944.

D. Bush, *Paradise Lost in our Time*, Cornell U.P., 1945.

A. H. Gilbert, *The Composition of Paradise Lost*, North Carolina U.P., 1947.

T. S. Eliot, 'Milton', British Academy, XXXIII, 1947.

E. M. W. Tillyard, *Studies in Milton*, Chatto and Windus, 1951.

E. M. W. Tillyard, *The Metaphysicals and Milton*, Chatto and Windus, 1956.

J. Whaler, *Counterpoint and Symbol*, Anglistica VI, Copenhagen, 1956.

R. Tuve, *Images and Themes in Five Poems by Milton*, Harvard U.P., 1957.

B. Rajan, *Paradise Lost and the Seventeenth Century Reader*, Chatto and Windus, 1962.

J. I. Cope, *The Metaphoric Structure of Paradise Lost*, Johns Hopkins Press, 1962.

J. Arthos, *Dante, Michelangelo and Milton*, Routledge and Kegan Paul, 1963.

I. Langdon, *Milton's Theory of Poetry and Fine Art*, Russell and Russell, New York, 1965.

H. Gardner, *A Reading of Paradise Lost*, Clarendon, 1965.

N. Frye, *Five Essays on Milton's Epics*, Routledge and Kegan Paul, 1966.

K. Burke, *Counterstatement*, Hermes Publications, California, 1931.

K. Miscellaneous

S. T. Coleridge, *Biographia Literaria*, ed. J. Shawcross, Oxford, 1907.

J. H. Leigh Hunt, 'An Answer to the Question: What is Poetry', *English Critical Essays* (Nineteenth Century), Oxford, 1916.

W. Archer, *The Old Drama and the New*, Heinemann, 1923.

G. Saintsbury, *The Earlier Renaissance*, Blackwood, 1923.

I. A. Richards, *Principles of Literary Criticism*, Routledge and Kegan Paul, 1924.

G. Murray, *The Classical Tradition in Poetry*, C. E. Norton Lectures, 1925.

E. E. Stoll, *Poets and Playwrights*, Minnesota U.P., 1930.

H. S. V. Jones, *A Spenser Handbook*, Appleton-Century-Crofts, New York, 1930.

A. E. Housman, *The Name and Nature of Poetry*, Cambridge, 1933.

G. B. Shaw, *Prefaces*, Constable, 1934.

W. H. Empson, *Some Versions of Pastoral*, Chatto and Windus, 1935.

F. R. Leavis, *Revaluation*, Chatto and Windus, 1936.

L. C. Knights, *Explorations*, Chatto and Windus, 1946.

L. C. Knights, *Further Explorations*, Chatto and Windus, 1965.

Itrat-Hussain, *The Mystical Element in the Metaphysical Poets*, Oliver and Boyd, 1948.

English Institute Essays, 1948, ed. D. A. Robertson, Columbia U.P., 1949.

M. Mahood, *Poetry and Humanism*, Jonathan Cape, 1950.

W. B. C. Watkins, *Shakespeare and Spenser*, Princeton U.P., 1950.

C. Ing, *Elizabethan Lyrics*, Chatto and Windus, 1951.

J. Danby, *Elizabethan and Jacobean Poets*, Faber, 1952.

T. S. Eliot, *Selected Prose*, ed. J. Hayward, Penguin, 1953.

J. H. Hanford, *A Milton Handbook*, Appleton-Century-Crofts, 1954.

L. L. Martz, *The Poetry of Meditation*, Yale U.P., 1954.

C. S. Lewis, *English Literature in the Sixteenth Century* (OHEL), Clarendon, 1954.

D. C. Allen, *The Harmonious Vision*, Johns Hopkins Press, 1954.

G. Wilson Knight, *The Wheel of Fire*, Methuen, 1930.

G. Wilson Knight, *The Mutual Flame*, Methuen, 1955.

Interpretations, ed. J. Wain, Routledge and Kegan Paul, 1955.

J. Miles, *Eras and Modes in English Poetry*, California U.P., 1957.

R. L. Brett, *Reason and Imagination*, Hull U.P., 1960.

M. C. Bradbrook, *Shakespeare and Elizabethan Poetry*, Chatto and Windus, 1961.

Theodore Spencer, *Shakespeare and the Nature of Man*, Macmillan, 1961.

K. G. Hamilton, *The Two Harmonies*, Clarendon, 1963.

L*

M. Krieger, *A Window to Criticism*, Princeton U.P., 1964.

J. B. Broadbent, *Poetic Love*, Chatto and Windus, 1964.

L. Journals

J. H. Hanford, 'The Pastoral Elegy and Milton's Lycidas', *PMLA* XXV, 1910, pp. 403–47.

J. B. Douds, 'Donne's Technique of Dissonance', *PMLA* LII, 1937, pp. 1051–61.

B. Groom, 'The Varieties of Style in Hamlet', *Essays and Studies*, XXIV, 1938, pp. 42–63.

C. S. Lewis, 'The Fifteenth-Century Heroic Line', *Essays and Studies*, XXIV, 1938, pp. 28–41.

C. L. Wrenn, 'On Re-Reading Spenser's Shepheardes Calender', *Essays and Studies* XXIX, 1943, pp. 30–49.

G. D. Wilcock, 'Shakespeare and Rhetoric', *Essays and Studies* XXIX, 1943, pp. 50–61.

Theodore Spencer, 'The Poetry of Sir Philip Sidney', *English Literary History* XII, Dec. 1945, pp. 251–78.

J. Lederer, 'John Donne and the Emblematic Practice', *Review of English Studies* XXII, 1946, pp. 182–200.

J. M. Nosworthy, 'The Structural Experiment in Hamlet', *Review of English Studies* XXII, 1946, pp. 282–8.

J. C. Ransom, 'On Shakespeare's Language', *Sewanee Review* LV.2, 1947, pp. 181–98.

R. D. Altrick, 'Symphonic Imagery in Richard II', *PMLA* LXII.1, 1950, pp. 339–65.

U. K. Goldsmith, 'Words out of a Hat? Alliteration and Assonance in Shakespeare's Sonnets', *Journal of English and Germanic Philology* XLIX, 1950, pp. 33–48.

J. Paterson, 'The Word in Hamlet', *Shakespeare Quarterly* III.1, 1951, pp. 47–55.

G. W. Williams, 'The Poetry of the Storm in King Lear', *Shakespeare Quarterly* II.1, 1951, pp. 57–71.

W. S. Johnson, 'The Genesis of Ariel', *Shakespeare Quarterly* II.3, 1951, pp. 205–10.

W. M. T. Nowottny, 'Formal Elements in Shakespeare's Sonnets 1–6', *Essays in Criticism* II.1, Jan. 1952, pp. 76–84.

A. Adler, 'In What Sense can Poetic Meaning be Verified', *Essays in Criticism* II.2, Apr. 1952, pp. 197–206.

L. D. Lerner, 'The Miltonic Simile', *Essays in Criticism* IV, 1954, pp. 297–308.

D. Davie, J. B. Broadbent, F. W. Bateson, 'Sixteenth-Century Poetry and the Common Reader', *Essays in Criticism* IV, 1954, pp. 421–30.

D. G. Cunningham, 'The Characterization of Shakespeare's Cleopatra', *Shakespeare Quarterly* VI.1, 1955.

F. D. Hoeniger, 'Prospero's Storm and Miracle', *Shakespeare Quarterly* VII.1, 1956, pp. 33–8.

E. S. Donno, 'Cleopatra Again', *Shakespeare Quarterly* VII.2, 1956, pp. 225–33.

W. H. Auden, 'Music in Shakespeare', *Encounter*, Dec. 1957, pp. 31–44.

S. Barnet, 'Recognition and Reversal in Antony and Cleopatra', *Shakespeare Quarterly* VIII.3, 1957, pp. 331–4.

R. F. Hill, 'Shakespeare's Early Tragic Mode', *Shakespeare Quarterly* IX.4, 1958, pp. 455–69.

A. M. Z. Norman, 'Daniel's The Tragedie of Cleopatra and Antony and Cleopatra', *Shakespeare Quarterly* IX.1, 1958, p. 11–18.

B. T. Spencer, 'Antony and Cleopatra and the Paradoxical Metaphor', *Shakespeare Quarterly* IX.3, 1958, pp. 373–8.

C. Gesner, 'The Tempest as Pastoral Drama', *Shakespeare Quarterly* X.4, 1959, pp. 531–9.

J. M. Nosworthy, 'Music and its Function in the Romances of Shakespeare', *Shakespeare Survey* 11, 1958, pp. 60–9.

M. Lloyd, 'Cleopatra as Isis', *Shakespeare Survey* 12, 1959, pp. 88–94.

W. M. T. Nowottny, 'Some Aspects of the Style of King Lear', *Shakespeare Survey* 13, 1960, pp. 49–57.

L. J. Mills, 'Cleopatra's Tragedy', *Shakespeare Quarterly* XI.2, 1960, pp. 147–62.

R. R. Reed, 'The Probable Origin of Ariel', *Shakespeare Quarterly* XI.1, 1960, pp. 61–5.

A. C. Partridge, 'Shakespeare and Italy', *English Studies in Africa*, Sept. 1961, pp. 117–27.

R. C. Harrier, 'Cleopatra's End', *Shakespeare Quarterly* XIII.1, 1962, pp. 63–5.

D. Daiches, 'Imagery and Meaning in Antony and Cleopatra', *English Studies* XLIII, 1962, pp. 343–58.

K. V. MacMullan, 'Death Imagery in Antony and Cleopatra', *Shakespeare Quarterly* XIV.4, 1963, pp. 399–410.

M. St. Clare Byrne, 'Foundations of Elizabethan Language', *Shakespeare Survey* 17, 1964, pp. 223–39.

W. Blissett, 'Dramatic Irony in Antony and Cleopatra', *Shakespeare Quarterly* XVIII.2, 1967, pp. 151–66.

R. Hapgood, 'Shakespeare's Thematic Modes of Speech: Richard II to Henry V', *Shakespeare Survey* 20, 1967, pp. 41–9.

R. E. Fitch, 'No Greater Crack?', *Shakespeare Quarterly* XIX.1, 1968, pp. 3–17.

J. Smith, 'The Language of Leontes', *Shakespeare Quarterly* XIX.4, 1968, pp. 317–27.

J. T. Fair, 'Some Notes on Ariel's Song', *Shakespeare Quarterly* XIX.4, 1968, pp. 329–32.

INDEX

One hundred and nine rhetorical terms, marked (rhet.), are in roman type if naturalized in English; in italic, if Greek or Latin technical borrowings.
Words that appear, *passim*, in this study, e.g. *imagery, meaning, metre, movement, rhetoric, rhyme, rhythm, syntax, tempo*, are not included, except in special applications.